Knowledge Discovery Process and Methods

to Enhance
Organizational Performance

T0300380

Knowledge Discovery Process and Methods

to Enhance Organizational Performance

Edited by

Kweku-Muata Osei-Bryson
Virginia Commonwealth University, School of Business

Corlane Barclay
University of Technology, Jamaica

CRC Press
Taylor & Francis Group
Boca Raton London New York

CRC Press is an imprint of the
Taylor & Francis Group, an **informa** business

AN AUERBACH BOOK

MATLAB® is a trademark of The MathWorks, Inc. and is used with permission. The MathWorks does not warrant the accuracy of the text or exercises in this book. This book's use or discussion of MATLAB® software or related products does not constitute endorsement or sponsorship by The MathWorks of a particular pedagogical approach or particular use of the MATLAB® software.

First published in paperback 2024

Published 2015 by CRC Press
2385 NW Executive Center Drive, Suite 320, Boca Raton FL 33431

and by CRC Press
4 Park Square, Milton Park, Abingdon, Oxon, OX14 4RN

CRC Press is an imprint of Taylor & Francis Group, LLC

© 2015, 2024 Taylor & Francis Group, LLC

Version Date: 20150202

ISBN: 978-1-4822-1236-5 (hbk)
ISBN: 978-1-138-89425-9 (pbk)
ISBN: 978-0-429-16099-8 (ebk)

DOI: 10.1201/b18231

To my children: Baraka, Ngozi, Ibukun, and Nyamekye Osei

Kweku-Muata Osei-Bryson

To my Mom and Dad: Hermina I. Barclay and Caswell A. Barclay

Corlane Barclay

Contents

Preface

The significance of knowledge discovery and data mining (KDDM) is on the rise because it serves as the glue to supporting the successful deployment of organizational learning for improved decision making and competitiveness. The aim of this book *Knowledge Discovery Process and Methods to Enhance Organizational Performance* is to provide some meaning or significance to organizations and persons who may be less experienced in the application of KDDM activities.

Although the terms "data mining" and "KDDM" are sometimes used interchangeably, data mining is but one step in a series of steps in the KDDM process. Data mining is the process of extracting useful, relevant knowledge from any data repository, big or small, whereas the KDDM process is the coordinated multistep process of determining and delivering the business objectives by understanding the business and data, mining the data to identify interesting and previously unknown patterns. KDDM is generally viewed as an interdisciplinary field that intersects artificial intelligence, machine learning, statistics, and data mining; however, in the context of organizational implementation, this is further augmented by an intersection of project management; strategy; financial management; and other business, legal, privacy, ethical, and security considerations. Considerations of all these elements underline its dynamism and are necessary for maximizing of the benefits of KDDM initiatives.

The current landscape presents an opportunity to present multiple conversations on the strategies to enhance the effectiveness of KDDM implementations in organizations through discussion of diverse topics in the domain. This book consists of 17 chapters with wide coverage relating to strategies, models, and techniques relevant to the different stages of the KDDM process, including the business understanding, data understanding, modeling (or data mining), deployment, and evaluation stages; the application of different techniques to discover patterns; and presentation of the importance and critical success factors in managing KDDM initiatives, which are organized as follows:

- Section I begins with an overall introduction to the current state of discussions in KDDM followed by an introduction to the concept of KDDM and the presentation of various models or perspectives adopted in academia and industry to deliver data mining projects. An alternative model that attempts to address some of the shortcomings in previous approaches is also presented.
- Section II covers the development and application to techniques to help improve the efficiency and outcome of the phases of the KDDM. This includes a discussion of a technique for the formulation of clearer business objectives to better inform the direction of the project, the explication of the activities in the business understanding phase to illustrate the importance of a structured approach to completing core activities at the beginning of the project, and the presentation of a semiautomated evaluation approach to promote the efficacy of the evaluation phase.
- Section III commences with a conversation underlining the important role of data mining to the sustainability of businesses, followed by insights into the impact of poor-quality data on the successful implementation of these types of projects and concludes with a formulation of critical success factors in KDDM projects.
- Section IV considers the advantages of discovering new knowledge through the application of KDDM in multiple business situations. A survey of multiple applications of data mining in industries common in developing states is presented to underline the vast opportunities that exist for the adoption and use of KDDM. The use of multiple techniques, including cluster analysis and neural networks, to determine the source of relative heterogeneity for an investigator is proposed. The applications of data mining in organizational behavior domain to understand project managers' decision styles and secondary high school students' performance are also presented.
- Section V, the final section, puts forward alternative methods for deriving greater utility from data mining algorithms. A multiobjective analysis of postpruning phase to identify sub-tree, an integrated ensemble generation procedure for selecting classifiers and the formulation of a rank aggregation structure.

The book is intended for anyone with an interest in data mining and KDDM processes. This pool includes practitioners; academic researchers, including experienced researchers; and graduate and undergraduate students engaged in KDDM activities, particularly in the less developed and emerging countries. The conversations relating to different methods, techniques, and application of KDDM activities will be of particular interest to persons and organizations that are relatively less experienced in conducting KDDM initiatives. It will also showcase how to design and implement these initiatives.

We anticipate that this book will foster a closer examination of strategies that can help industry members and governments, especially those with little or no experience in this domain, to optimize the organizational value from knowledge discovery. This may be achieved in several ways: through the growth in the adoption and use of KDDM and not simply through data mining algorithms or models and the continued examination of the KDDM process itself in order to better address some of the challenges currently experienced and develop relevant solutions to address these concerns.

In closing, we wish to extend our heartfelt gratitude to the publishing team and its editors, contributors, reviewers, participants, family, and friends in helping to make this project of passion become a reality.

Kweku-Muata Osei-Bryson
Virginia Commonwealth University

Corlane Barclay
University of Technology

MATLAB® is a registered trademark of The MathWorks, Inc. For product information, please contact:

The MathWorks, Inc.
3 Apple Hill Drive
Natick, MA 01760-2098 USA
Tel: +1 508 647 7000
Fax: +1 508 647 7001
E-mail: info@mathworks.com
Web: www.mathworks.com

Editors

Kweku-Muata Osei-Bryson is a professor of information systems (IS) at Virginia Commonwealth University in Richmond, Virginia, where he also served as the coordinator of the IS PhD program during 2001–2003. He is also a visiting professor of computing at the University of the West Indies at Mona, Kingston, Jamaica. Previously, he was a professor of information systems and decision sciences at Howard University in Washington, DC. He has also worked as an IS practitioner in the industry and government. He holds a doctorate degree in applied mathematics (management science and information systems) from the University of Maryland at College Park, Maryland; an MS degree in systems engineering from Howard University; and a bachelor's degree in natural sciences from the University of the West Indies at Mona, Kingston, Jamaica.

His research areas include data mining, decision support systems, knowledge management, IS security, e-commerce, information technology for development, database management, IS outsourcing, and multicriteria decision making. He has published in various leading journals including *Decision Support Systems, Information Systems Journal, Expert Systems with Applications,* the *European Journal of Information Systems, Information Systems Frontiers, Knowledge Management Research & Practice, Information Sciences, Information & Management,* the *Journal of the Association for Information Systems,* the *Journal of Information Technology for Development,* the *Journal of Database Management, Computers & Operations Research,* the *Journal of the Operational Research Society,* and the *European Journal of Operational Research.* He serves as an associate editor of the *INFORMS Journal on Computing,* as a member of the editorial boards of the *Computers & Operations Research journal* and the *Journal of Information Technology for Development,* and as a member of the International Advisory Board of the *Journal of the Operational Research Society.*

Corlane Barclay is a business consultant and a full-time lecturer at the University of Technology, Jamaica, since 2009, where she has designed and successfully implemented the first and only wholly owned graduate program in information systems management, with five specializations, of the School of Computing and

Information Technology in 2011. She also served as a coordinator for this program between 2011 and 2012. She is a certified project manager, with a PMP® certification, with over 10 years of industry and government experience. She also holds a doctorate degree in information systems, an MS degree in information systems, and a bachelor's degree in management and accounting and law from the University of the West Indies, Mona campus. She is currently in the final year at the Norman Manley Law School, Mona, Kingston, Jamaica, completing the certificate of legal education, which prepares for admission to practice in the Commonwealth Caribbean territories.

Her research interests include cyber security and cybercrime, project performance and project success, technology and telecommunications law, information and communication technologies for development, and knowledge discovery and data mining models. She has published in several top-rated journals, including *Information Systems Frontiers, Project Management Journal*, the *International Journal of Production Economics*, and *Information for Technology Development*, and academic conferences such as ITU Kaleidoscope conference, Americas' Conference on Information Systems, and the Hawaii International Conference on System Sciences. She currently serves as part of the program committee for the Special Interest Group on ICT and Global Development—SIG GlobDev.

Contributors

Corlane Barclay
School of Computing & Information
    Technology
University of Technology Jamaica
Kingston, Jamaica

Ghazi Bel Mufti
LARIME
ESSEC
University of Tunis
Tunis, Tunisia

Waad Bouaguel
LARODEC, ISG
University of Tunis
Tunis, Tunisia

Edward Chen
University of Massachusetts
Lowell, Massachusetts

Andrew Dennis
Digicel Jamaica
Kingston, Jamaica

Mohamed Limam
LARODEC, ISG
University of Tunis
Tunis, Tunisia

and

Dhofar University,
Salalah, Oman

Patricia E. Nalwoga Lutu
Department of Computer Science
University of Pretoria
Pretoria, South Africa

Kweku-Muata Osei-Bryson
School of Business
Virginia Commonwealth University
Richmond, Virginia

Reza Salehzadeh
Department of Management
University of Isfahan
Isfahan, Iran

Sergey Samoilenko
Department of CS/CIS
Averett University
Danville, Virginia

Arash Shahin
Department of Management
University of Isfahan
Isfahan, Iran

Sumana Sharma
JPMorgan Chase & Co.
Wilmington, Delaware

Jerome Shepherd
School of Humanities and Social
  Sciences
University of Technology Jamaica
Kingston, Jamaica

Chapter 1

Introduction

Kweku-Muata Osei-Bryson and Corlane Barclay

Contents

Abstract: Knowledge is a key organizational resource and it is, therefore, no surprise that the methods to expose, engage, and harness this key resource have been growing, particularly in the highly competitive and data-rich contexts of recent years. Recently, the Rexer Analytics Data Miner 2013 Survey (Rexer 2013) reported that 85% of over 1250 data miners across 75 countries foresaw increases in the number of data mining projects. This survey also reported that such projects often face multiple challenges, including the continued low rate of deployment of the resulting models and new knowledge; huge resource requirements (e.g., money, time, and efforts) to complete knowledge discovery projects; and data management and model performance issues. These findings have significant implications for organizational knowledge discovery efforts including increasing the awareness of the role and benefits of using formal knowledge discovery and data mining (KDDM) process models for increasing the likelihood of success of these projects and utilizing a multidimensional approach in managing these projects.

Keywords: Knowledge discovery, Knowledge discovery and data mining (KDDM), data mining, organizational performance

What Is KDDM?

The academic conversations on KDDM started in the late 1980s and in the early 1990s, where opportunities of knowledge discovery in databases (KDD) were being observed. This period of *discovery* was crystallized during the first workshop on KDD in 1989, where there were reports on the viability of extracting different forms of knowledge from databases, and the experts from different areas, including machine learning, expert databases, knowledge acquisition, and fuzzy sets, were able to share their understanding and needs of organizational databases (Piatesky-Shapiro 1991). As a result, KDDM process models were designed to guide the management and implementation of these projects. The nine-step model developed by Fayyad et al. (1996a) is considered to be one of the seminal guides. Further academic (e.g., Cios et al. 2007; Sharma and Osei-Bryson 2010; Sharma et al. 2012) and practitioner (e.g., Shearer 2000) efforts continued in the succeeding decades.

The terms *KDD* and *KDDM* are used interchangeably and generally refer to a series of activities to discover or identify knowledge of domain(s) from databases. Fayyad et al. (1996a) describes this concept as "a non-trivial process of identifying valid, novel, potentially useful and understandable patterns in data." Hand et al. (2001) went further to say that, "it is the exploration of the data to find unsuspected relationships and to summarize the data in novel ways that are both understandable and useful to the data owner." This underlines the complex nature of the process while highlighting the opportunities for learning from the identification of new and useful knowledge or patterns in the data, and the importance of communicating the findings in a manner that business users understand. The KDDM process generally spans the activities to promote efficient access to data, applies specific algorithms to derive interesting patterns, and deploys and integrates the new knowledge in the organization to improve on its current way of operating. Data mining is one of the steps in the process and is considered as the application of specific algorithms to extract patterns or models from the data (Fayyad et al. 1996a).

KDDM can, therefore, be simplified into several basic activities that are supported by the general underlying principles of project management in the knowledge discovery project:

1. Development of a clear understanding of the organizational goals and objectives for the given project, that is, what the organization wishes to uncover from its data or wishes to achieve from the project.
2. Identification, analysis, and preparation of relevant data to facilitate computer-aided mining.
3. Application of algorithms to derive patterns and interestingness from the data.
4. Evaluation and selection of the most suitable models based on objectives.
5. Application and use of the new knowledge.

All the steps are important and necessary preconditions in creating the organization and having a successful project. As a result, many process models have been developed, which have originated from both academia and industry.

Why KDDM?

The importance of KDDM cannot be understated. The traditional method of turning data into knowledge relies on the manual analysis and interpretation (Fayyad et al. 1996a,b). This old way of doing things has significant implications for organizational growth and learning, as it means that there are delays in any useful knowledge discovery, limited efficiencies in the discovery process, and the lack of optimization of the value of the data, as proper computer-aided tool and process such as KDDM are not employed. It is not a panacea, however, and requires experienced personnel, sufficient resources, and other strategic considerations to aid in organizational growth.

The following are the two added benefits that engagement in KDDM can provide:

1. Improvement in the chance for success through due diligence in outlining certain requirements is necessary not only to deliver the results but also to trust the derived results.
2. Provision of a management tool or support to discover new approaches, perspectives, or ways of undertaking organizational operations such as a better understanding of its customer base, identifying revenue leakages or opportunities, and promoting innovation.

Opportunities for the Application of KDDM in Organizations

As the significance of KDDM becomes more widespread, the less experienced entities will need to invest more in these initiatives, if they wish to remain sustainable and better exploit their data asset. Studies have shown that despite challenges, there have been many successful applications of KDDM across multiple domains, including governments and businesses, where data mining techniques have been used to better understand consumers, reduce fraud, improve processes, and increase revenues. The viability of knowledge discovery has been recognized since the early years of data mining, where Piatetsky-Shapiro (1990) described that several companies have been exploring this strategy such as an airline company looking at patterns in its frequent flyer database, banks analyzing credit data to determine better rules for credit assessment and bankruptcy prediction, the government revenue-collection agency searching for patterns of tax cheating, and an automobile company developing a diagnostic expert system derived from car trouble symptoms and problems.

In addition, knowledge discovery has been used in medicine to predict the survivability of critical illnesses, minimize infections, and profile characteristics of certain lifestyle illnesses; in insurance, to predict customer churn and customer-relationship management to improve service levels; in manufacturing to improve fault detection; in education to aid in student performance and education adminis-tration; in agriculture to manage crop yields; and in telecommunications.

Despite the benefits of KDDM, one needs to be mindful of some of the short-comings that exist in the current KDDM process models. Therefore, due consider-ations for improvements include the following:

1. Exploration of strategies to develop detailed data collection guidelines, where the data may not be readily available, digitized, or computer manipulateable. This will help to improve the data quality and the achievement of business objectives.
2. Examination of perspectives to develop and identify measurable business and data mining objectives, and create a greater alignment between the two.
3. Greater integration of project management practices in the KDDM process, including project planning, risk management, and resource management.
4. Identification of approaches to evaluate the derived models to better deter-mine the suitability and alignment with business objectives.
5. Development of clear deployment strategies to safeguard knowledge integra-tion in the organization.

Purpose of This Book

The purpose of this book is to provide some meaning or significance to organiza-tions and persons who may be less experienced in the application of knowledge discovery and data mining activities.

We anticipate that this book will foster a closer examination of strategies that can help industry members and governments, especially those with little or no experience in KDDM, to advance the net benefits they receive from their knowl-edge discovery initiatives. This may be achieved through the growth in the adop-tion and the use of KDDM process models and not simply using data mining algorithms or models and the continued examination of the KDDM process itself in order to better address some of the challenges currently experienced and develop relevant solutions to address these concerns.

The book is intended for anyone with an interest in the data mining field and the KDDM process. This pool consists of practitioners; academic researchers, including experienced researchers; graduate; and undergraduate students engaged in KDDM activities, particularly in less developed and emerging countries. The conversations relating to the different methods, techniques, and application of KDDM activities will be of particular interest to persons and organizations that are relatively less experienced in conducting KDDM initiatives. It will also showcase how to design and implement these initiatives.

The rest of this book is organized into five main sections.

Section I presents theoretical foundations to the key concepts.

Chapter 2 provides a more in-depth discussion of KDDM and some of the leading models, including the nine-step model proposed by Fayyad et al. (1996a,b) and a multistep model in the form of Chapman et al. (2000).

Chapter 3 presents a KDDM model that addresses some of these shortcomings (such as checklist approach of describing the tasks and the limitation in capturing the dependencies that exist among the various tasks of the same and different phases) by prescribing tools for supporting each task as well as identifying and leveraging dependencies among tasks for semiautomation of tasks, wherever possible.

The next three chapters in Section II deal with the development and application of techniques to help in improving the efficiency and outcome of the phases of KDDM.

Chapter 4 proposes a technique for the formulation of clearer business objectives to better inform the direction of a data mining/KDDM project. This technique was primarily influenced by the principles of value-focused thinking, goal question metric method, and Specific, Measurable, Attainable, Realistic, and Time-Related (SMART) criteria.

Chapter 5 discusses the importance of the business understanding phase by explicating the activities of a project situated in the education domain. It is argued that despite the significance of the foundation stages of the KDDM process, an examination of the data mining literature revealed scant regard to the sharing of the *know-how* in regard to the execution and reporting of this phase.

Chapter 6 presents a semiautomated evaluation approach to promote the value of the evaluation phase of KDDM. It is suggested that a multicriteria evaluation framework requires the identification of relevant objectives, measures, and preference functions to enable the analysis and use of this information for improved semiautomated evaluation, and thereby relied on tools from multiple domains to address this issue.

The subsequent three chapters in Section III discuss the importance of KDDM activities to the project itself and their role in the organization and the important elements to achieve success.

Chapter 7 underlines the important role of data mining to the sustainability of businesses by way of a discussion of the history, importance, procedures, practical examples, and current issues surrounding data mining.

Chapter 8 provides insights into the impact of poor-quality data on the successful implementation of these types of projects by reiterating that poor-quality data will result in misleading information. The chapter also provides guidelines on the successful implementation of data quality assurance programs in KDDM activities.

Chapter 9 identifies several critical success factors in KDDM projects through the experience from a data mining project. The chapter outlines strategic and tactical success for factors such as project management practices, stakeholder commitment, data collection protocol, data availability and accessibility, clear deployment strategies, and experience and knowledge of the data mining team.

The succeeding five chapters in Section IV underscore the advantages of discovering new knowledge through the application of KDDM in multiple business situations and highlight the versatility of the KDDM approach to other organizational tasks.

Chapter 10 shares the application of data mining in multiple domains, and the availability of data mining tools, particularly open-source applications, to underline the significant opportunities that exist for small developing countries to invest in KDDM projects. This is especially relevant as these countries currently experience relatively low adoption rates of KDDM projects or are not fully utilizing the capabilities of the tools.

Chapter 11 presents and demonstrates a hybrid five-step methodology that involves the use of multidecision criteria analysis and data mining techniques such as cluster analysis and neural networks, allows an investigator to determine the source of relative heterogeneity.

Chapter 12 discusses the applications of data mining in organizational behavior domains using data collected by questionnaires.

Chapter 13 presents a data mining-based data analysis for identifying relationships between demographic characteristics of a project manager and his or her dominant decision style.

Chapter 14 uses the decision tree technique to extract useful predictive knowledge relating to secondary high school students' performance, particularly in the core subjects of mathematics and the English language.

Section V includes three chapters that consider alternative methods for deriving greater utility from data mining algorithms.

Chapter 15 presents a multiobjective analysis in the post-pruning phase to identify the best subtree, and proposes a procedure for obtaining the optimal subtree based on the user-provided preference and value function information.

Chapter 16 presents an integrated ensemble generation procedure for selecting classifiers to be included in an ensemble, which provide better performance than the individual classifiers.

Chapter 17 introduces the formulation of a rank aggregation structure using generic data mining algorithms to address some of the disadvantages in rank aggregation methods.

References

Chapman, P., Clinton, J., Kerber, R., Khabaza, T., Reinartz, T., Shearer, C., and Wirth, R. (2000). *CRISP-DM 1.0 Step-by-Step Data Mining Guide*. SPSS Inc.

Cios, K. J., Swiniarski, R. W., Pedrycz, W., and Kurgan, L. A. (Eds.) (2007). The knowledge discovery process. In *Data Mining: A Knowledge Discovery Approach* (pp. 9–24). Springer, New York.

Fayyad, U., Piatetsky-Shapiro, G., and Smyth, P. (1996a). From data mining to knowledge discovery: An overview. In *Advances in Knowledge Discovery and Data Mining*. Fayyad, U. M., Piatetsky-Shapiro, G., Smyth, P., and Uthurusamy, R. (Eds), AAAI/MIT Press.

Fayyad, U., Piatetsky-Shapiro, G., and Smyth, P. (1996b). The KDD process for extracting useful knowledge from volumes of data. *Communications of the ACM*, 39(11), 27–34.

Hand, D. J., Mannila, H., and Smyth, P. (2001). Principles of data mining. MIT press, Cambridge, MA.

Piatetsky-Shapiro, G. (1990). Knowledge discovery in real databases: A report on the IJCAI-89 Workshop. *AI Magazine*, 11(4): 68.

Rexer, K. (2013). RexerAnalytics 6thDataMiner Survey—2013, retrieved on July 14, 2014 from, http://www.rexeranalytics.com/Data-Miner-Survey-2013-Intro.html.

Sharma, S. and Osei-Bryson, K.-M. (2010). Toward an integrated knowledge discovery and data mining process model. *The Knowledge Engineering Review*, 25(01), 49–67.

Sharma, S., Osei-Bryson, K.-M., and Kasper, G. M. (2012). Evaluation of an integrated knowledge discovery and data mining process model. *Expert Systems with Applications*, 39(13), 11335–11348.

Shearer, C. (2000). The CRISP-DM methodology: The new blueprint for data mining. *Journal of Data Warehousing*, 5(4): 13–22.

FOUNDATIONS

I

1

FOUNDATIONS

Chapter 2

Overview of Knowledge Discovery and Data Mining Process Models

Sumana Sharma

Contents

Introduction

Application of data mining (DM) techniques is becoming increasingly important in modern organizations, which seek to utilize the knowledge that is embedded in the mass organizational data to improve efficiency, effectiveness, and competitiveness. The field of DM has gained unprecedented exposure with the exponential increase in data assets to the point where many firms are being presented with the challenge of mining "big data," which is rightly being regarded as an organization's most key asset, one that should be very well understood by organizational leaders and not just by data managers (Maynika et al. 2011).

Given this backdrop and the record growth in data assets across a wide variety of organizations, it is not surprising that in recent years, both DM practitioners and researchers have become more aware of the need for formal DM process models, which prescribes the journey from data to discovering knowledge. As noted by Kurgan and Musilek (2006) with regard to DM, "The general research trends were concentrated on the development of new and improved DM algorithms rather than on the support for other KD activities ... Before any attempt can be made to perform the extraction of this useful knowledge, an overall approach that describes how to extract knowledge needs to be established." Thus, a multi-industry collective of practitioners came together to develop the Cross Industry Standard Process for DM (CRISP-DM), which was further extended by researchers. The knowledge discovery and DM (KDDM) process has been described in various ways but essentially consists of the following steps: (1) application domain or business understanding (which includes the definition of DM goals); (2) data understanding; (3) data preparation; (4) modeling (data mining); (5) evaluation (e.g., evaluation of results based on DM goals); and (6) deployment.

In this chapter, we present an overview of the five leading KDDM process models, which have been proposed in the extant literature. These include a nine-step model proposed by Fayyad et al. (1996); a five-step model proposed by Cabena et al. (1998); a six-step model proposed by Cios et al. (2000), and a multistep model in the form of CRISP-DM (2003). We also discuss the model proposed by Berry and Linoff (1997), authors of the book *Data Mining Techniques for Marketing, Sales, and Customer Relationship Management*, who have done some early work in this area. Of these models, CRISP-DM has been proposed in the practitioner literature, whereas all the other models have been proposed in the academic literature. In Chapter 3, we will provide a more detailed discussion of another KDDM process model, the integrated KDDM process model of Sharma and Osei-Bryson (2010).

The Nine-Step Process Model

Fayyad et al.'s (1996) KDDM model consists of nine steps, which are outlined as follows:

1. *Developing and understanding the application domain*: This step includes learning the relevant prior knowledge and the goals of the end user of the discovered knowledge.
2. *Creating a target dataset*: Here, the data miner selects a subset of variables (attributes) and data points (examples) that will be used to perform discovery tasks. This step usually includes querying the existing data to select the desired subset.
3. *Data cleaning and preprocessing*: This step consists of removing outliers, dealing with noise and missing values in the data, and accounting for time sequence information and known changes.
4. *Data reduction and projection*: This step consists of finding useful attributes by applying dimension reduction and transformation methods, and finding invariant representation of the data.
5. *Choosing the DM task*: Here, the data miner matches the goals defined in step 1 with a particular DM method, such as classification, regression, clustering, and so on.
6. *Choosing the DM algorithm*: The data miner selects the methods to search for patterns in the data and decides the appropriate models and parameters of the methods to be used.
7. *Data mining*: This step generates patterns in a particular representational form, such as classification rules, decision trees, regression models, trends, and so on.
8. *Interpreting mined patterns*: Here, the analyst visualizes the extracted patterns, models, and the data based on the extracted models.
9. *Consolidating discovered knowledge*: The final step consists of incorporating the discovered knowledge into the performance system, documenting, and reporting it to the interested parties. This step may also include checking and resolving potential conflicts with previously believed knowledge.

The Four-Step Process Model

Berry and Linoff (1997) presented a four-step methodology consisting of the following steps: (1) identifying the problem; (2) analyzing the problem; (3) taking action; and (4) measuring the outcome. They also specify the following 11 steps to further describe their proposed approach:

1. Translate the business problem into a DM problem.
2. Select the appropriate data.
3. Get to know the data.
4. Create a model set.
5. Fix problems with the data.
6. Transform data to bring information to the surface.

7. Build models.
8. Assess models.
9. Deploy models.
10. Assess results.
11. Begin again.

The Five-Step Process Model

Step 1—Determination of business objectives: This step involves clearly defining the business problems or challenges. The minimum requirements are a perceived business problem or opportunity and some level of executive sponsorship. Expectations are usually established during this step in the process.

Step 2—Data preparation: Cabena et al. (1998) note that data preparation is the most resource-consuming step in the process, typically requiring up to 60% of the effort of the entire project. This step comprises the following three subtasks:

1. Data selection: This involves identifying all internal or external sources of information and selecting the appropriate data subset for the DM application.
2. Data preprocessing: Preprocessing of data includes studying the quality of the data to pave the way for further analysis and determining the kind of mining operation that will be possible and worth performing.
3. Data transformation: During data transformation, the preprocessed data is transformed to produce the analytical data model. This model is an informational data model, and it represents a consolidated, integrated, and time-dependent restructuring of the data selected and preprocessed from the various operational and external sources. Data transformation is a crucial phase as the accuracy and validity of the final result depend vitally on how the data analyst decides to structure and present the input.

Step 3—DM: This is the step in which the actual DM takes place. The objective is to clearly apply the selected DM algorithm or algorithms to the preprocessed data. The actual details of the DM step will vary with the kind of application that is under development. Although in the case of database segmentation, one or two runs of the algorithm may be sufficient, the development of a predictive model will be a cyclical process where the models will be repeatedly trained and retrained on sample data before being tested against the real database.

Step 4—Analysis of results: According to this process model, the analysis of results is inseparable from the DM step in that the two are typically linked in an interactive process. The specific activities in this step depend very much on the kind of application that is being developed. However, the main objective remains the same, that is, to interpret and to evaluate the output from the DM step.

Step 5—Assimilation of knowledge: This step closes the loop, which was opened when the business objectives were set at the beginning of the process. The objective now is to put into action the commitments made in the opening step, according to the new, valid, and actionable information from the previous process steps. The two main challenges in this step are as follows: (1) to present the new findings in a convincing, business-oriented way and (2) to formulate ways in which the new information can be best exploited.

Cross Industry Standard Process for DM

CRISP-DM (CRISP-DM 2003) is an industry-neutral, tool-neutral DM process model, which was conceived in the late 1996 by three leaders of the then-immature DM market: Daimler (then Daimler-Benz), SPSS (then ISL), and NCR. At the time, Daimler was ahead of other industrial and commercial organizations, as it had already gained experience in DM by applying it to its business operations. SPSS too had DM experience owing to the DM services it had been providing since the 1990s. It was also the first vendor to launch commercial DM work-bench called "Clementine" in 1994. NCR too brought in DM expertise owing to its experience of offering DM services through its teams of consultants and technology specialists, in order to deliver added value to its Teradata data ware-house customers.

In 1997, a consortium was formed with the goal of formalizing the experience of the various real-world organizations that had been practicing DM, in the form of a process model. One of the prime characteristics of this project was to focus on creating a nonproprietary and freely available model that would assist in execution of DM projects.

CRISP-DM describes the life cycle of a DM project in the form of six different phases, namely, business understanding, data understanding, data preparation, modeling, evaluation, and deployment (Figure 2.1). It also describes the tasks and activities that need to be carried out in each of these phases. A description of the six phases of the CRISP-DM process model is presented subsequently.

Phases of the CRISP-DM Process Model

Table 2.1 discusses the various phases of the CRISP-DM process model, which are explained as follows:

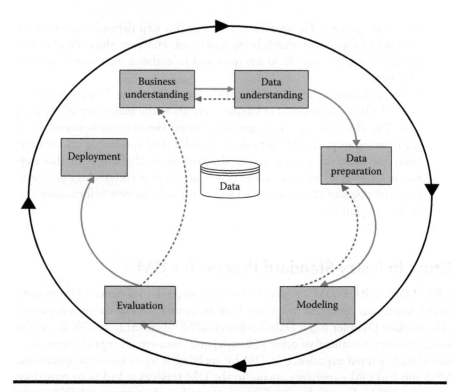

Figure 2.1 The CRISP-DM process model. (Data from CRISP-DM, Cross industry standard process for data mining 1.0: Step by step data mining guide, http://www .crisp-dm.org/, 2003.)

Phase 1—Business understanding: The initial phase focuses on understanding the project objectives and requirements from a business perspective, and then converting this knowledge into a DM problem definition and a preliminary plan designed to achieve the objectives.

Phase 2—Data understanding: This phase starts with an initial data collection and proceeds with activities in order to get familiar with the data, to identify data-quality problems, to discover first insights into the data, or to detect interesting subsets to form hypotheses for hidden information.

Phase 3—Data preparation: This phase covers all activities to construct the final dataset (data that will be fed into the modeling tool[s]) from the initial raw data. Data preparation tasks are likely to be performed multiple times and not in any prescribed order. Tasks include table, record, and attribute selection as well as transformation and cleaning of data for modeling tools.

Phase 4—Modeling: In this phase, various modeling techniques are selected and applied and their parameters are calibrated to optimal values. The CRISP-DM documentation points out that, typically, there are several techniques for the

Table 2.1 Phases, Tasks, and Outputs—CRISP-DM Process Model

Business Understanding	Data Understanding	Data Preparation	Modeling	Evaluation	Deployment
Determine business objectives • Background • Business objectives • Business success criteria	Collect initial data • Initial data collection report	Select data • Rationale for inclusion/exclusion	Select modeling technique • Modeling technique • Modeling assumptions	Evaluate results • Assessment of DM results with respect to business success criteria • Approved models	Plan deployment • Deployment plan
Assess situation • Inventory of resources • Requirements, assumptions, and constraints • Risks and contingencies • Terminology • Costs and benefits	Describe data • Data description report	Clean data • Data cleaning report	Generate test design • Test design	Review process • Review of process	Plan monitoring and maintenance • Monitoring and maintenance plan

(Continued)

Table 2.1 (Continued)   Phases, Tasks, and Outputs—CRISP-DM Process Model

Business Understanding	Data Understanding	Data Preparation	Modeling	Evaluation	Deployment
Determine DM goals • DM goals • DM success criteria	Explore data • Data exploration report	Construct data • Derived attributes • Generated records	Build model • Parameter settings model • Model description	Determine next steps • List of possible actions • Decision	Produce final report • Final report • Final presentation
Produce project plan • Project plan • Initial assessment of tools and techniques	Verify data quality • Data quality report	Integrate data • Merged data Format data • Reformatted data	Assess model • Model assessment • Revised parameter settings		Review project • Experience • Documentation

same DM problem type. Some techniques have specific requirements on the form of data and, therefore, stepping back to the data preparation phase is often necessary.

Phase 5—Evaluation: This phase of the project consists of thoroughly evaluating the model and review the steps executed to construct the model to be certain that it properly achieves the business objectives. A key objective is to determine if there is some important business issue that has not been sufficiently considered. At the end of this phase, a decision on the use of the DM results should be reached.

Phase 6—Deployment: Creation of the model is generally not the end of the project. Even if the purpose of the model is to increase knowledge of the data, the knowledge gained will need to be organized and presented in a way that the customer can use it. According to the CRISP-DM process model, depending on the requirements, the deployment phase can be as simple as generating a report or as complex as implementing a repeatable DM process across the enterprise.

Feedback Loops Described in the CRISP-DM Process Model

CRISP-DM model also describes various feedback loops to emphasize how certain phases should be revisited to leverage the new information or knowledge gained in the phase succeeding them. These have also been highlighted in Figure 2.1. For instance, although data preparation typically precedes modeling, there may be a need to revisit data preparation as a chosen modeling technique may require data to be prepared in a certain way.

CRISP-DM is the most detailed process of existing KDDM models. The documentation associated with CRISP-DM v1.0 is divided in two parts. The first part provides a description of the reference model, its phases, general tasks, and outputs. The second part called the "user guide" aims to provide detailed guidance about how to perform activities associated with each task.

That is, the user guide is expected to provide tools for implementing the vast number of activities suggested in the process model. However, the analysis of the user guide reveals that it does not meet its intended objective and only proposes a checklist of activities to be performed to accomplish the tasks associated with each phase. Tool support is only provided toward only two of the total 24 tasks mentioned in the model, and it appears that even these are not sufficient for efficiently executing the corresponding tasks. These are described as follows:

1. Tool support for the task of selecting modeling techniques (modeling phase): CRISP-DM v1.0 documentation (CRISP-DM 2003) includes some support toward the modeling phase by providing a list of modeling techniques relevant to various types of DM problems. However, it does not provide any support toward the selection of appropriate techniques. Clearly, the list of techniques

enumerated in the process model could be narrowed down further using output from previous tasks such as business objectives and DM objectives, but that it is not considered by the process model.

2. Tool support for the task of identifying divisions and manager's name and responsibilities (business understanding phase): Analysis of the foundational business understanding phase reveals the use of just one tool—an organizational chart—to identify divisions, manager's names and responsibilities etc. Clearly, organizations also need support for the diverse array of other activities associated with this important phase. Besides, the usefulness of organizational charts, primarily as a static entity, to identify organizational actors and their interrelationships can also be debated.

Six-Step Process Model

The process model proposed by Cios and Kurgan (2005) is shown in Figure 2.2.

Understanding the Problem Domain

In this step, one works closely with domain experts to define the problem and determine the project goals, identify key people, and learn about current solutions to the problem. It involves learning domain-specific terminology. A description of the problem including its restrictions is done. The project goals then need to be translated into the KDDM goals, and may include the initial selection of the potential DM tools.

Understanding the Data

This step includes collection of sample data and deciding the appropriate data, including its format and size. If background knowledge does exist, then some attributes may be ranked as more important. Next, we need to verify the usefulness of the data in respect to the KDDM goals. Data needs to be checked for completeness, redundancy, missing values, plausibility of attribute values, and so on.

Preparation of the Data

According to this process model, data preparation is the key step upon which the success of the entire knowledge discovery process depends; it usually consumes about half of the entire project effort. In this step, decisions regarding which data will be used as input for DM tools of step 4 are made. It may involve the sampling of data, running correlation and significance tests, data cleaning such as checking the completeness of data records and removing or correcting for noise, and so

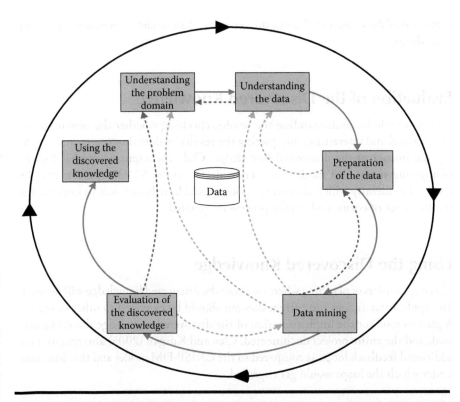

Figure 2.2   The KDDM process model. (Data from Cios, K. and L. Kurgan, Trends in data mining and knowledge discovery, In *Advanced Techniques in Knowledge Discovery and Data Mining*, N. Pal and L. Jain, Eds., Springer, pp. 1–26, 2005.)

on. The cleaned data can be further processed by feature selection and extraction algorithms (to reduce dimensionality), by the derivation of new attributes (say by discretization), and by the summarization of data (data granularization). The result would be new data records, meeting specific input requirements for the use of the potential DM tools.

Data Mining

This is also regarded as a key step in the knowledge discovery process. Although it is the DM tools that discover new information, their application usually takes less time than data preparation. This step involves the usage of the planned DM tools and the selection of the new ones. DM tools include many types of algorithms, such as rough and fuzzy sets, Bayesian methods, evolutionary computing, machine learning, neural networks, clustering, preprocessing techniques, and so on. This step involves the use of several DM tools on data prepared during step 3. First, the training and testing procedures are designed and the data model is constructed using one of the chosen DM tools; the generated data model is verified using testing procedures.

Evaluation of the Discovered Knowledge

This step includes understanding the results, checking whether the new information is novel and interesting, interpreting the results by domain experts, and checking the impact of the discovered knowledge. Only the approved models (results of applying many DM models) are retained. The entire KDDM process may be revisited to identify which alternative actions could have been taken to improve the results. A list of errors made in the process is prepared.

Using the Discovered Knowledge

This step consists of planning where and how the discovered knowledge will be used. The application area in the current domain should be extended to other domains. A plan to monitor the implementation of the discovered knowledge should be created, and the entire project documented. Cios and Kurgan (2005) also specify four additional feedback loops as compared to the CRISP-DM model and the situations under which the loops would get triggered.

Conclusion

Based on the discussion of KDDM process in the earlier sections, we identify some main components of the KDDM process.

1. Gathering background information about the problem to be addressed through DM.
2. Formulating (business and DM) objectives.
3. Formulating success criteria or evaluation criteria for the business and DM objectives.
4. Identifying relevant individuals (i.e., key stakeholders and project participants).
5. Understanding data and relationships between variables.
6. Integrating data in preparation for modeling.
7. Understanding DM problem type(s) to be addressed through modeling.
8. Analyzing characteristics of various modeling techniques.
9. Evaluating the output of modeling techniques to determine whether or not it meets the requirements.

References

Berry, M. and G. Linoff (1997). *Data Mining Techniques for Marketing, Sales and Customer Support*, New York, Wiley.

Cabena, P., P. Hadjinian et al. (1998). *Discovering Data Mining: From Concepts to Implementation*, Prentice Hall, Upper Saddle River, NJ.

Cios, K. and L. Kurgan (2005). Trends in data mining and knowledge discovery. In *Advanced Techniques in Knowledge Discovery and Data Mining*. N. Pal and L. Jain, Eds., Springer, pp. 1–26.

CRISP-DM. (2003). Cross industry standard process for data mining 1.0: Step by step data mining guide. Retrieved on October 01, 2007, from http://www.crisp-dm.org/.

Fayyad, U. M., G. Piatetsky-Shapiro et al., Eds. (1996). *Advances in Knowledge Discovery and Data Mining*, Menlo Park, CA, AAAI/MIT Press.

Han, J. and N. Cercone (2000). RuleViz: A model for visualizing knowledge discovery process. *The 6th ACM SIGKDD International Conference on Knowledge Discover and Data Mining*.

Kurgan, L. A. and P. Musilek (2006). A survey of knowledge discovery and data mining process models. *The Knowledge Engineering Review* 21(1): 1–24.

Maynika, J., C. Michael et al. (2011). Big data: The next frontier for innovation, competition and productivity. McKinsey Global Institute. Retrieved on July 08, 2014, from http://www.mckinsey.com/insights/business_technology/big_data_the_next_frontier_for_innovation.

Sharma, S. and K.-M. Osei-Bryson (2010). Toward an integrated knowledge discovery and data mining process model. *The Knowledge Engineering Review*, **25**(01): 49–67.

Chapter 3

An Integrated Knowledge Discovery and Data Mining Process Model

Sumana Sharma and Kweku-Muata Osei-Bryson

Contents

Abstract: Knowledge discovery and data mining (KDDM) process models describe the various phases (e.g., business understanding, data understanding, data preparation, modeling, evaluation, and deployment) of the KDDM process. They act as a roadmap for the implementation of the KDDM process by presenting a list of tasks for executing the various phases. The checklist approach of describing the tasks is not adequately supported by appropriate tools which specify *how* the particular task can be implemented. This may result in tasks not being implemented. Another disadvantage is that the long checklist does not capture or leverage the dependencies that exist among the various tasks of the same and different phases. This not only makes the process cumbersome to implement but also hinders possibilities for semiautomation of certain tasks. Given that each task in the process model serves an important goal and due to the dependencies even affects the execution of related tasks, these limitations are likely to negatively affect the efficiency and effectiveness of KDDM projects. This chapter proposes an improved KDDM process model that overcomes these shortcomings by prescribing tools for supporting each task as well as identifying and leveraging dependencies among tasks for semiautomation of tasks, wherever possible.

Keywords: Knowledge discovery and data mining (KDDM) process models, Limitations of KDDM models, Integrated KDDM, Formulating business objectives, Formulating data mining objective, Data mining success criteria

Introduction

Data has emerged as a newfound source of competitive advantage in an era where traditional bases of competition have largely evaporated (Davenport and Harris 2007). This competitive advantage is based on the knowledge gained from the analysis of data and has catapulted to the forefront fields such as data mining (DM) and knowledge discovery, which offer techniques and processes for extracting this knowledge. Knowledge discovery is widely acknowledged as an interactive and iterative multistep process ranging from the development of business (or domain) understanding, data understanding, data preparation, modeling (or DM), evaluation, and ultimately to the deployment (consolidation) of discovered knowledge. This process is embodied in the form of knowledge discovery and data mining (KDDM) process models that describe the steps/phases and tasks involved in the knowledge discovery process.

Our review of existing KDDM process models (Fayyad et al. 1996; Berry and Linoff 1997; Anand and Buchner 1998; Cabena et al. 1998; Cios et al. 2000; Han and Kamber 2001; CRISP-DM 2003; Cios and Kurgan 2005) reveals that they suffer from certain common deficiencies such as they often (1) present the complex knowledge discovery process in a checklist manner and (2) present a fragmented view of the KDDM process and do not explicate the various dependencies existent in the knowledge discovery process. A disadvantage of the latter is that it hinders the potential for semiautomation of tasks, affecting the efficiency with which the KDDM projects can be carried out. Some other limitations include the lack of support for execution of the various tasks (Charest et al. 2006) and the lack of attention toward the business understanding (BU) phase (Sharma and Osei-Bryson 2008), both of which have been highlighted in the literature.

This chapter aims to address the deficiencies of existing models (Fayyad 1996; Berry and Linoff 1997; Anand and Buchner 1998; Cabena et al. 1998; Cios et al. 2000; Han and Kamber 2001; CRISP-DM 2003) through an improved integrated model, which addresses the limitations of the existing process models, thereby improving the efficiency and effectiveness with which KDDM projects are currently carried out. The scope of the integrated model includes all phases of the KDDM process, except the deployment phase.

This chapter is organized as follows: in section "Overview of Relevant Literature," we provide an overview of the KDDM process models and a discussion on the limitations of KDDM models, which this chapter addresses through the proposed solution. In section "Design of an Integrated KDDM Process Model," we present the proposed solution and discuss how it achieves the set objectives. The final section summarizes the objectives and contributions of the research.

Overview of the Relevant Literature

In this section, we discuss (1) KDDM process models and their instances to describe the life cycle of KDDM projects and (2) the common deficiencies in the existing process models and the effect of these deficiencies on the efficiency and effectiveness with which KDDM projects are currently being executed.

KDDM Process Models and Examples

Several KDDM process models have been proposed (Fayyad 1996; Berry and Linoff 1997; Anand and Buchner 1998; Cabena et al. 1998; Cios et al. 2000; Han and Kamber 2001; CRISP-DM 2003; Cios and Kurgan 2005) that, while differing in their level of detail, describe the same sequence of phases from BU to deployment, to describing the life cycle of a KDDM project.

Limitations of KDDM Process Models

Our analysis of existing KDDM process models reveals that they suffer from certain common deficiencies. Subsequently, we discuss the various limitations and their effects on the efficiency and effectiveness with which KDDM process models are currently executed.

Description of the KDDM Process in a Checklist Manner

Existing KDDM process models typically describe the complicated KDDM process in terms of a valid checklist of steps (or tasks or activities) that, while providing at best a broad guideline, could be perceived as being very cost prohibitive to implement. For example, CRISP-DM (2003) recommends executing a total number of 288 activities, which when presented in a checklist approach, are likely to be intimidating to personnel involved in executing the project.

Fragmented View of the KDDM Process

Existing KDDM process models do not capture or highlight the important dependencies (i.e., interrelationships between the various steps, or between the various phases and tasks) existent in a typical KDDM process. Moreover, consider Figure 3.1 that represents the typical flow of any KDDM process. The most obvious dependency from this model is the phase–phase dependency resulting from the ordering of phases proposed by the model. These dependencies are critical as they cannot be reversed without leading to detrimental effects or even incapability of executing a particular phase. Because a phase really comprises various tasks, its output of a phase really comprises the output of the diverse array of tasks that lie within it. Therefore, it is important to also explicate and highlight the task-level dependencies, but these are not shown in Figure 3.1. This issue has not been addressed in the existing KDDM process models, although Cross Industry Standard Process for Data Mining (CRISP-DM) briefly alludes to the capturing of dependencies, but does not incorporate them in the design of the model.

The repercussion of not explicating various dependencies existent in the context of a KDDM project could lead to inefficient/ineffective implementation of projects. For example, the selection of a modeling algorithm without first clearly formulating the business objective(s) is an important task–task dependency, if neglected, can lead to the project take a completely different direction than is appropriate.

Fragmented View—A Hindrance to Semiautomation

Although for some time there was the assumption that only the task of implementation of DM methods (modeling phase) was amenable to automation (Berry and Linoff 2000), recently, however, researchers have realized that some of the

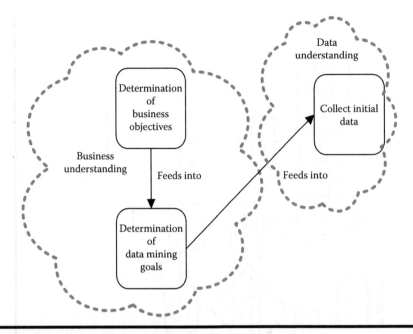

Figure 3.1 Explicating of dependencies as a first step toward enabling semiautomation.

other tasks, such as the selection of appropriate modeling techniques or algorithms (Bernstein et al. 2005), are also amenable to full or partial automation. Support for the automation of relevant aspects of the DM process, however, requires the specification of an integrated process model in which task–task dependencies have been explicated.

Continuing with the example presented above, we argue that the identification of dependency between two tasks such as a business and DM objective should be leveraged to drive the execution of the latter task. For instance, effort should be made to examine whether output of business objects can be used to semiautomate tasks, such as determination of DM objectives, that utilize it as its input (see Figure 3.2).

Lack of Support for the End-to-End KDDM Process

Existing KDDM models do not provide enough support toward *how* to implement the long list of tasks and activities suggested by them (Charest et al. 2006). Charest et al. (2006) note that existing process models "only provide general directives, however what a non-specialist really needs are explanations, heuristics and recommendations on how to effectively carry out the particular steps of the methodology." Therefore, it is necessary that the process models be complemented with appropriate tools and techniques for carrying out the various tasks in order to prevent or at least minimize the nonexecution of relevant tasks during the knowledge discovery process.

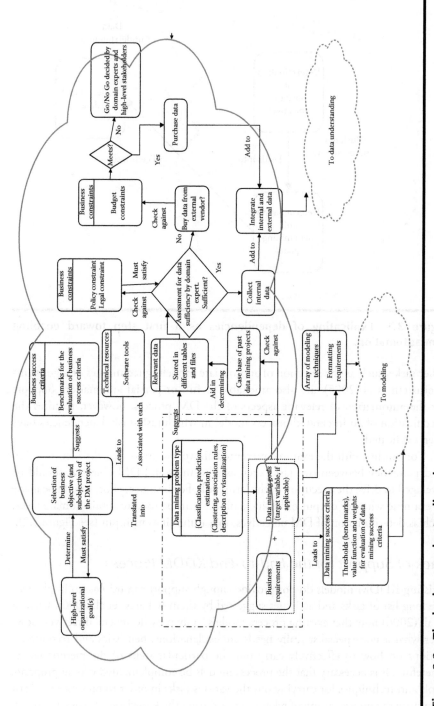

Figure 3.2 The business understanding phase.

Although it may appear that this issue is less problematic in case of the modeling phase that has benefitted from the rapid advancement in the development of a plethora of DM techniques. As noted by Simoudis et al. (1996) that a single DM technique is often insufficient for extracting knowledge from a dataset, the modeling phase requires careful selection of the techniques if the objectives of the project are to be accomplished (Pyle 2003). Therefore, support is needed to aid the user in selecting these techniques and the order in which they should be used if the KDDM project is to be effectively executed.

Lack of Adequate Attention toward the BU Phase

The importance of the BU phase, which includes making determinations about business and DM objects, assessing resources, and generating a project plan for the remainder of the project, cannot be overemphasized. However, our review of published DM case studies reveals that that the BU phase of KDDM projects is often implemented in an *ad hoc* manner (Sharma and Osei-Bryson 2008). We believe that the reason for such an unstructured approach is because of the general lack of support toward how the tasks of this phase can be implemented.

This issue has been highlighted and somewhat addressed by Pyle (2003), who describes how real-world business problems (to be addressed through DM) can be modeled. Although the author has not based his approach on any particular DM methodology, he discusses various tools to carry out many (though not all) of the activities prescribed under the BU phase of the CRISP-DM methodology. However, these are only presented in a linear fashion, with the description of each activity followed by a brief description of a proposed tool. The overall framework, which consists of nested sequences of action boxes, discovery boxes, technique boxes, and example boxes, is complicated to navigate, and may appear to be cumbersome or even cost prohibitive to actors involved in carrying out the critical BU phase.

Design of an Integrated KDDM Process Model

The objective of this study is to design an improved KDDM process model that addresses the deficiencies of existing models. Given that design is a goal-oriented activity (Simon 1996), the requirements that the proposed model should meet must be clearly outlined. These are also necessary for adequate evaluation of the proposed solution against the set requirements. The requirements that the proposed solution must address are described in Table 3.1.

Next, we describe how we designed the proposed solution in the form of the improved KDDM process model. The design of the proposed model incorporated treating each phase and its constituent tasks to understand the task–task dependencies existing among the various tasks of the same phase. The next step was to integrate

Table 3.1 Design Requirements for the Integrated KDDM Model

Issues Identified (As-Is Situation)	Design Requirements (To-Be Situation)
Description of the KDDM process in a checklist manner	Present a user-oriented coherent description of the KDDM process
Fragmented view of the KDDM process	Develop an integrated view of the KDDM process by explicating the various phase–phase and task–task dependencies
Emphasis on feedback loops prior to completely understanding the primary sequencing of phases and tasks in a KDDM process	Explicate sequencing of the various phases and their tasks before identifying feedback loops and establishing conditions under which the loops would get triggered
Fragmented view serves as a hindrance to building an integrated process model and *semiautomating* tasks	Leverage the dependencies explicated in the integrated process model to drive semiautomation of tasks
Lack of support for the end-to-end KDDM process	Prescribe approaches for offering decision support to all tasks described in the integrated KDDM model
Insufficient discussion and conspicuous lack of support toward the execution of the BU phase—the foundational phase of a KDDM process	Discuss the significance of the BU phase and uses the tasks recommended for this phase as the basis for developing the integrated model

the various phases together by linking the task–task dependencies existing among tasks of the various phases. The final step was to carefully analyze all the task–task dependencies (same phase and between different phases) to identify opportunities for leveraging the dependencies so identified through semiautomation. A simultaneous consideration was also to prescribe approaches and or tools for implementing each task of the KDDM process. In Table 3.2, we present the chief tasks of all the phases of the KDDM process, their output, and the tools that can be used for implementing the given task and an indication as to whether a given task can be a candidate for semiautomation.

BU Phase

We present in Figure 3.3 our explication of dependencies among the various tasks of this phase. In the remainder of this section, we describe how the various tasks of this phase could be implemented.

Table 3.2   KDDM Process: Phases, Tasks, Output, Tools, and Opportunities for Semiautomation

	Methods/Tools	*Repositories/ Sources*	*Output*
Business Understanding Phase			
Creation of business objectives (selection among a set of competing objectives)	Goal mapping, cognitive mapping, analytic hierarchy process (AHP)	DM projects base	Business objectives
Business objectives to business success criteria	Group support systems (GSS)	DM projects base	Business success criteria
Business objectives to data mining (DM) objectives	Value-focused thinking (VFT) and GSS	DM projects base	DM objectives
DM objectives to DM success criteria	Goal question metric (GQM) method	Cross-reference matrix (Tables 3.5 and 3.6)	Evaluation measures and thresholds for modeling phase
Determination of preference function[a]	Preference function elicitation tool (e.g., AHP)	Domain experts	Preference function to be used in the evaluation phase (e.g., weights for evaluation measures)
Determination of value functions for relevant evaluation measures[a]	Domain expert	Value function repository	Value function(s)
Identification of applicable data resources		Domain experts metadata repository	List of required datasets
Verification of data		Business rules base	List of available data

(Continued)

Table 3.2 (*Continued*)   KDDM Process: Phases, Tasks, Output, Tools, and Opportunities for Semiautomation

	Methods/Tools	*Repositories/ Sources*	*Output*
Identification of relevant personnel[a]		Ontologies, organizational charts, skills/ competency base	List of available personnel
Clarification of business requirements	Requirements elicitation tools	Domain experts	List of business requirements
Business objectives to financial constraints	GSS		
DM objectives to relevant modeling techniques		DM/MT cross-reference matrix (Table 3.8)	Relevant modeling techniques
Identifying benefits and risks from a business perspective[a]	GSS	DM projects base domain experts	Statement of expected benefits (tangible and intangible) and risks
Creation of contingency plans	GSS	DM projects base domain experts	Contingency plan for each risk situation
Estimation of data collection, implementation, and operational costs	Project management cost estimation tools	External data sources	Statement of expected costs
Cost–benefit analysis	Automated cost–benefit analysis tools	Domain experts DM projects base	Statement of costs and benefits
Data Understanding Phase			
Analyze data for anomalies, missing values, and outliers	DM software, basic statistical analysis	Domain expert(s)	Data quality report

Table 3.2 (*Continued*) KDDM Process: Phases, Tasks, Output, Tools, and Opportunities for Semiautomation

	Methods/Tools	Repositories/ Sources	Output
Analyze data to explore relationships among variables and exploring potential for derived attributes		Domain expert(s) and metadata repository	Data exploration report
Data Preparation Phase			
Create dataset for analysis		Domain expert(s)	Integrated dataset containing the relevant data
Format data in accordance with the first modeling technique[a]		Software tools base and domain expert(s)	Formatted modeling dataset
Modeling Phase			
Run models using first technique in the array of applicable techniques	DM software		Output of modeling technique
Run models using all applicable techniques	DM software	Cross-reference matrix (Tables 3.8 and 3.9)	Output of all relevant modeling techniques
Compare results of models output from different modeling techniques against DMSC set up earlier[a]	MS Excel	DMSC and domain experts	Model results assessed with respect to each DMSC

[a] Candidate tasks for semiautomation

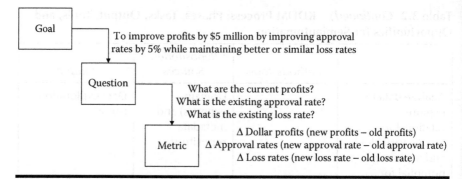

Figure 3.3 GQM approach for setting up of business success criteria.

Formulation of Business Objectives

The formulation of business objectives is a multistep process and requires collaboration among various high-level business stakeholders of the company. Doran (1981) proposed the Specific, Measurable, Attainable, Realistic, and Time-Bound (SMART) criteria (see Table 3.3) for evaluating the quality of business objectives. Of the five SMART criteria, the measurable and realistic criteria are implemented through separate KDDM tasks, namely, setting up of business success criteria and assessment of inventory of resources, respectively. This serves as a reminder that the setting up of business objectives is not a one-step process and needs to be revisited

Table 3.3 SMART Criteria for Evaluating Business Objectives

Criterion	Description
Specific	The business objective must clearly describe the objective of the project and should relate to one or more higher level organizational objectives.
Measurable	Concrete, clearly defined criteria should be laid down for measuring the attainment of the proposed business objective. These criteria are referred to as business success criteria and are described in the next task.
Attainable	The business objective must be agreed upon by the key stakeholders involved in the project.
Realistic	The business objective must be achievable within the constraints of the available resources, knowledge, and time.
Time-Bound	There should be clear deadlines for achievement of the business objective.

to finalize the well-thought through but preliminary business objectives that are set up at the end of the completion of this first task.

Consider the following illustrative example that involves the financial services company, Global Credit, that wishes to revise one of its outdated credit-scoring models as a means of meeting one of its organizational goals of improving profit.

The business objective of a DM project launched by the Credit Risk Division of Global Credit is "to improve profits over the Financial Year 2008–2009, by improving approval rates of sub prime customers by 5% while maintaining better or similar loss rates." Based on the past data analysis, it has been observed that a 5% increase in approval rate while maintaining similar loss rates leads to approximately $5 million increase in net profit assuming everything else remains constant.

This business objective satisfies the specificity criteria as it relates to at least one high-level organizational objective, in this case, improvement in profits. Lack of association between a business objective of a DM project and organizational objectives makes the business objective vague and ill formulated. The stated objective also specifies the timely criterion and specifies the time frame during which the business objective must be accomplished for the project to be considered successful.

If available, an exploration of the DM projects base (which is a repository of past DM projects) could be used to determine if a similar project has been conducted in the past and note must be taken of the various details of the project such as entities involved, solution chosen, benefits and contingencies, findings, and so on.

Setting Up of the Business Success Criteria

The goal question metric (GQM) approach (Basili and Weiss 1984) can be used to formalize business success criteria that specify how the outcome of the implementation of the business objective can be evaluated. The GQM approach proposes refining the overall goal (business objective in the case of a DM project) into a set of questions, and then refining the questions into a set of metrics, which could be objective or subjective in nature.

The metrics help to implement the measurability criterion associated with well-formulated business objective. We use the example presented earlier to show how the GQM approach can be used for setting up business success criteria. The metrics describe the business success criteria and must meet the threshold values specified in the statement of objectives. For instance, in the case of the example shown in Figure 3.3: (a) Δ dollar profits should be $\geq$ \$5 million; (b) Δ approval rate $\geq 5\%$; and (c) Δ loss rate ≤ 0, as the objective is to maintain better or similar loss rates.

Analysis of Inventory of Business Personnel and Other Business Resources

This task ensures that the business personnel, key high-level stakeholders, domain experts, and other organizational actors who will be part of the project team are available for the duration of the project. An organization ontology (Fox et al. 1998; Sharma and Osei-Bryson 2009), or an organization chart can play an important role in identifying the relevant personnel for data mining projects. An organizational chart can be used to locate particular individuals and their role in the hierarchy of an organization. With an organization ontology such as that of Sharma and Osei-Bryson (2009), the identification of agents or relevant personnel can be accomplished by simply navigating through the various links in the organizational ontology. Once identified, the domain experts and other key business personnel can be used to elicit information about relevant business resources such as business glossary and business metadata associated with the project.

Clarification of Business Requirements

All requirements of the project must be clarified through consultations with relevant business personnel. When the business objective is related to creating or refining models, an important aspect of requirements analysis should entail establishing details about whether or not an explanatory model is to be produced through the DM project. Requirements elicitation tools (Laguna et al. 2001) can be used to aid the execution of this task.

Clarification of Business Constraints

Assessment of business constraints such as policy, legal, and budgetary constraints as well as the availability of business personnel and business resources (described earlier) must be undertaken, as the potential solutions designed during the succeeding phases such as data preparation and modeling as well as tasks such as the identification of necessary data that are performed during the BU phase must be in accordance with the business rules laid down by the organization. Legal constraints may prohibit an organization from using certain variables in a certain manner and must be satisfied in the naming of solutions. Budgetary constraints are also an important type of business constraints and must present details about the budget allocated to the given project. The business and technical personnel can assess whether or not their needs in form of resources (personnel, data, tools, etc.) can be satisfied within the confines of the allocated budget.

Determination of DM Objective

A DM objective is often defined as the technical translation of the business objective but this definition by itself does not provide the user with enough guidance regarding the creation of a well-formulated DM objective. We propose using the technique of value-focused thinking (VFT) (Keeney 1996) to move from business objectives to DM objectives. VFT includes three types of objectives: fundamental objectives, means objectives, and strategic objectives. Fundamental objectives concern the ends that decision makers value in a particular decision context, whereas means objectives are the methods to achieve the ends. When we extend the decision frame to the decision context of an organization's entire existence, our ends objectives become strategic objectives. In the context of KDDM process, fundamental objectives are the business objectives, whereas means objectives are the DM goals. DM goals (e.g., development of a more accurate classification model) are methods to achieve the ends, that is, the business objective (e.g., improvement in profits). Within this context, it is important to determine whether any of the means objectives can be addressed using DM methods; if that is not the case, then DM techniques are not appropriate for addressing the given decision-making problem. Once it is established that the means objective can be formulated using DM techniques, a formal process toward the generation of a well-formulated DM objective should be employed. The first step of the process is to select the problem type best representing the proposed project. Each problem type involves certain features that must be taken into account to lead to a well-formulated DM project (see Table 3.4). The features of a well-formulated DM problem serve to confirm that the user has selected the correct DM problem type.

Table 3.4　Creation of Well-Formulated Data Mining Objectives

Type of Learning	Problem Types	Features of a Well-Formulated Data Mining Objective
Supervised (or directed)	Classification—if the goal is to classify unseen records into predefined classes	Entity to be classified and name of the target variable (types: binary, nominal, ordinal, and interval/continuous)
	Estimation—if the goal is to estimate the value of a continuous target variable	Name of the target variable (type: continuous)
	Prediction—if the goal is to classify or estimate but based on some future behavior or estimated future value	If classification: entity to be classified and name of the target variable (types: binary, nominal, ordinal, and interval/continuous) If estimation: name of the target variable (type: continuous)
Unsupervised (or undirected)	Clustering—if the goal is to divide records into several clusters or segments	Records or subset of records to be divided into clusters

(Continued)

Table 3.4 (*Continued*)   Creation of Well-Formulated Data Mining Objectives

Type of Learning	Problem Types	Features of a Well-Formulated Data Mining Objective
	Association rules—if the goal is to study implicative co-occurring relationship between two sets of binary-valued transactional database attributes.	Item set
	Description or visualization—if the goal is to explore or visually analyze the relationship between two of more variables	Set of variables to be explored using description or visualization techniques
Combination of undirected and directed with output of undirected data mining being used to drive directed data mining	Output of clustering can be used to drive directed data mining efforts such as classification, estimation, or prediction	Clustering: records or subset of records to be divided into clusters. Output of clustering to be used as input to classification or estimation. If classification: entity to be classified and name of the target variable (types: binary, nominal, ordinal, and interval/continuous) If estimation: name of the target variable (type: continuous)
	Output of association rules can be used to drive a directed data mining effort such as classification	Association rules: Item Set Classification: entity to be classified and name of the target variable (types: binary, nominal, ordinal, and interval/continuous)

Continuing with the example of Global Credit, here is how the DM objective can be formulated:

The business objective was set up as improving approval rates of subprime customers by 5%, while maintaining better or similar loss rates. The business and technical personnel involved in the project realize that this is a prediction problem, which requires the creation of a classification model that improves the rank ordering of credit card applicants as compared to the existing model. The DM objective, therefore, becomes to "predict (problem type) the probability of charge off (target variable) of sub prime credit card applicants (entity) within 12 months from the point of booking."

Setting Up of DM Success Criteria

DM success criteria (DMSC) are used to evaluate the results of implementation of modeling techniques. These criteria must be defined before the implementation of the modeling phase. We suggest using the GQM approach of Basili and Weiss (1984) to move from DM objectives to DMSC. In this case, the GQM approach can help translate the DM objective into a set of questions that can then be refined into a set of objective or subjective metrics. These metrics are the evaluation criteria that can be used for assessing the results of the modeling phase to establish whether or not the selected model was helping to accomplish the DM objectives of the project. DMSC influence the critical decision of whether or not a model should be deployed. Technical personnel in consultation with business users must be involved in setting up these criteria. Table 3.5 shows relevant evaluation criteria in the context of directed DM. We present only classification and estimation as instances of directed DM problems, as prediction can be modeled as either of these problems (Berry and Linoff 2000). Table 3.6 shows relevant evaluation criteria in the context of undirected DM problems. The criteria presented here are discussed in Redpath and Srinivasan (2003). The criteria associated with clustering (Osei-Bryson 2006) and association rules (Choi et al. 2005) can be used for evaluating the results from these modeling techniques.

Elicitation of Preference Functions and Creation of a Value Function

Techniques from the field of decision analysis can be adapted here. For example, given the need to evaluate generated models in the modeling phase, a composite score could be calculated for each model based on the preference function (e.g., the weighted sum of measures). Osei-Bryson (2004) proposed an approach for comparing and selecting the *optimal* decision tree (DT) model based on the preference and value functions specified by the domain expert(s). Choi et al. (2005)

Table 3.5   Data Mining Success Criteria for Directed DM

Problem Type	DMSC
Classification	Accuracy, precision, recall, profit and loss, lift, simplicity,[a] stability, speed, training time, and memory usage
Estimation	Mean square error, variance (standard deviation), simplicity,[a] stability, speed, training time, and memory usage

[a]   Simplicity is not relevant in case of nonexplanatory, black box models.

Table 3.6 DMSC for Undirected DM

Problem Type	DMSC
Clustering	Normalized cluster mean, variable importance vectors, and outliers and usefulness
Association rules	Lift, simplicity (rule length), support, confidence, recall, precision, interest factor, expected monetary factor, and incremental monetary factor
Description or visualization	Number of instances in dataset, number of dimensions, overlapping data instances, ability to reveal patterns in dataset, ability to reveal clusters of two or three dimensions, number of clusters present, amount of background noise, variance of clusters, ability to manipulate display automatically, and ease of use

presented approaches for prioritizing association rules. Osei-Bryson (2004) also presented an approach for selecting the most appropriate segmentation. In the preference function, assessment is to be done using a weighted sum, and then a technique such as the analytic hierarchy process (AHP) of Saaty (1991) could be used for to determine the relevant weights based on the input of domain experts. In Table 3.7, we present an example of the DMSC and the corresponding value functions and weights for a classification problem (where the business requirement is to produce an explanatory model) to illustrate the concepts of value functions, weights, thresholds, and composite score, which are involved for the evaluation framework of Osei-Bryson (2004). An organization could follow a similar methodology for other problem types such as prediction, estimation, clustering, and visualization.

Analysis of Applicable Data Resources

The business objective and DM objective provide a glimpse into the applicable data resources. The DM projects base can also be used to identify applicable data by searching for similar past projects. It is important to note that as business situations change, new variables may be needed based on the set DM objectives. Data on these new variables may be available to the organization or may need to be purchased from an external data vendor. In the former case, there will be a cost associated with extracting the data and ensuring that it will be available to relevant personnel for the duration of the project. In the latter case, there will be a cost associated with buying the data from an external vendor. The costs in both instances should be analyzed in accordance with the budget and should be approved before proceeding to the next task.

Table 3.7 DMSC for Classification Problems (BusReq = Explanatory)

Applicable DMSC (Description)	Value Function	Thresholds	Weights
Accuracy (proportion correctly classified)	(1−Test misclassification rate)	>0.75	0.60
Profit and loss (unequal misclassification costs)	(Avg. worst possible loss − Avg. loss of model)/(Avg. Worst possible loss − Avg. Best possible loss)	>0.75	
Lift (Cumulative%captured response at the kth decile)	(Model-baseline)/ (Exact-baseline)	>0	0.20
Stability (Visual inspection of the noncumulative%response lift chart)	Stability is binary, with 1 indicating a stable model and 0 indicating an unstable model	>0	0.15
Simplicity score (SIMPL) based on the number of rules (NR)	SIMPL = 0 If NR $\geq$ 2 or $\leq$13 SIMPL = (NR-2)/3 If NR $\in$ (2, 5) SIMPL = 1 If NR $\in$ [5, 8] SIMPL = (13-NR)/5 If NR $\in$ [9, 12]		0.05
Speed (run time)	Number of minutes	<25	
Training time (time taken to train the model)	Number of hours	<5	
Formula for creating composite score	(0.60 × accuracy score) + (0.20 × lift score) + (0.15 × stability score) + (0.05 × simplicity score)		

Analysis of Other Technical Resources (Personnel and Tools)

During this task, the lead technical personnel must analyze the available of other technical resources such as personnel and tools for implementing the problem type selected in the previous task. An organizational ontology, an organizational chart, or a skill and competency base can aid the technical stakeholders in quickly identifying the technical personnel most suited for the project. Analysis of tools can be simplified by storing the problem types supported by DM tools (such as SAS Enterprise Miner, SPSS Clementine, etc.) available to the organization. If no available tool support the selected problem type, then the relevant actors may propose the sourcing of a relevant tool to the project sponsor or other key high-level stakeholder who can then make the decision about whether or not the budget would support the purchase of a new tool and ensuing training and implementation costs.

Initial Assessment of Applicable Modeling Techniques

Generation of the DM model can involve the use of a single modeling technique, and/or an unsequenced combination of modeling techniques; and/or sequence(s) of modeling techniques. For the first two cases, characteristics of the DM project (i.e., its problem type, data type of the target variable, and the business requirement of whether or not an explanatory model is desired) can be used for identifying modeling techniques that are applicable (see Table 3.8). For the case that involves the use of sequence of modeling techniques (e.g., neural network followed by DT), the penultimate technique would be a black box technique (e.g., neural network,

Table 3.8 Applicable Modeling Techniques for Various DM Problem Types

Target Variable ╲ Problem Type	Classification	Prediction	Estimation
Binary	Logistic regression, classification tree, k-nearest neighbor, Naïve Bayes,[a] neural network,[a] support vector machines,[a] and genetic algorithm[a]	Logistic regression, classification tree, k-nearest neighbor, Naïve Bayes,[a] neural network,[a] support vector machines,[a] and genetic algorithm[a]	Not applicable
Ordinal	Ordinal logistic regression, classification tree, k-nearest neighbor, Naïve Bayes,[a] neural network,[a] support vector machines,[a] and genetic algorithm[a]	Ordinal logistic regression, classification tree, k-nearest neighbor, Naïve Bayes,[a] neural network,[a] support vector machines,[a] and genetic algorithm[a]	Not applicable

Table 3.8 (*Continued*)   Applicable Modeling Techniques for Various DM Problem Types

Problem Type / Target Variable	Classification	Prediction	Estimation
Nominal	Multinomial logistic regression, classification tree, k-nearest neighbor, Naïve Bayes,[a] neural network,[a] support vector machines,[a] and genetic algorithm[a]	Multinomial logistic regression, classification tree, k-nearest neighbor, Naïve Bayes,[a] neural network,[a] support vector machines,[a] and genetic algorithm[a]	Not applicable
Interval	Prompt user to discretize the target variable, then apply any of the classification techniques based on the number of bins	Regression, regression tree, k-nearest neighbor, Naïve Bayes,[a] neural network,[a] support vector machines[a]	Regression, regression tree, k-nearest neighbor, memory-based reasoning, and neural networks[a]

[a] Cannot be a final-stage modeling technique if business requirements demand an explanatory model.

support vector machines, and genetic algorithm) whose output could feed into the final technique of the pair (e.g., DT and logistic regression).

The identification of relevant modeling techniques could be done in the following manner:

1. Given characteristics of the DM project that were identified in the BU phase, use a cross-reference table such as Table 3.8 to:
   a. Identify modeling techniques relevant for the single technique and non-sequenced combinations approaches.
   b. Techniques identified in (1a) are the ones that are relevant for the final stage technique of the sequenced techniques approach.
2. Identify directed learning techniques that are applicable for the penultimate stage sequenced techniques approach by selecting DM techniques (e.g., neural network, support vector machines, and genetic algorithm) whose output could feed into the techniques identified in (1b).

The approach proposed earlier indicates that this task of generating a list of applicable techniques can be semiautomated. Our approach is different from that of Bernstein et al. (2005), who start at the level of the data itself and propose that the data type can be used for making decisions about the applicable techniques. Use of their approach can result in the enumeration of those techniques that clash with the business requirement. Therefore, even if these techniques were tried, the results would not eventually be accepted, resulting in inefficient usage of resources. Moreover, their approach results only in the enumeration of single techniques, and combination of techniques is not accommodated in their approach.

Data Understanding

During this phase the integrated dataset (consisting of internal and or external data) is to be explored and analyzed in order to: gain an understanding of gross properties of the data; identify data quality issues; and assess whether the available data is adequate to address the DM goals. A metadatabase could be used to identify relevant derived attributes. Figure 3.4 shows a schematic of the *data understanding* phase. Note that it also highlights that the phase received input from the *BU* phase and that the output of the phase is fed into the data preparation phase.

Data Preparation

During this stage the final dataset is constructed from the raw initial data. The dataset constructed should be evaluated by the domain expert for appropriateness and the need for any additional derived attributes should be reconsidered in light of the integrated data. Figure 3.5 shows a schematic of the data preparation phase, its relations with two preceding phases, namely, business and data understanding and its output to the modeling phase. The *modeling techniques base*, which stores the formatting requirements for the various techniques, should be used to format the data in accordance with the modeling techniques generated during the BU phase.

Modeling Phase

During this phase each modeling technique (or their combinations) would be applied to the formatted data. The results of the DM model application would then be assessed to find whether or not it needs the DMSC. Those models that meet the criteria should be stored in the list of acceptable models and the next modeling technique should be executed. Figure 3.6 shows a schematic of the *modeling* phase, its relation to two preceding phases, namely, *BU* and *data preparation*, and its output to the *evaluation* phase.

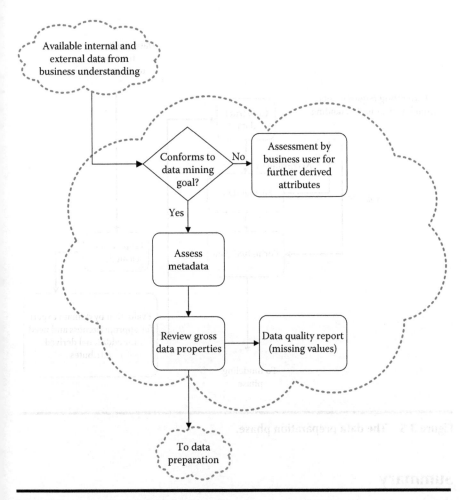

Figure 3.4 The data understanding phase.

Evaluation Phase

In the evaluation phase, the top-ranked models should be identified based on a composite score comprising of value functions and weights for the evaluation of the DMSC. This step of selection of the best model can be semiautomated.

Schematic of Integrated KDDM

In Figure 3.7, we present the schematic of our integrated KDDM process model. The figure shown here explicates some of the tasks (and their proposed execution) based on the discussion provided earlier.

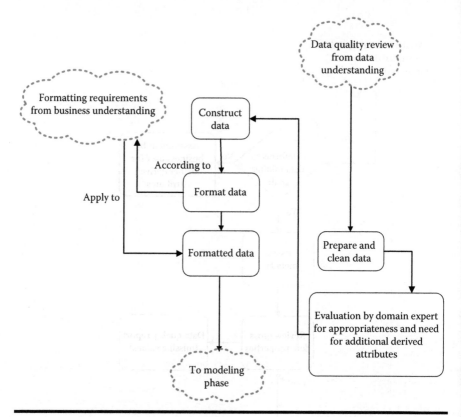

Figure 3.5   The data preparation phase.

Summary

Kurgan and Musilek (2006), who conducted a detailed review of existing KDDM models, noted that the future of KDDM process models lies in achieving the integration of the whole process. This chapter addresses an important research objective, namely, the creation of an improved KDDM process model, which is relevant to both academicians and practitioners. We identified significant limitations of existing KDDM process models (Fayyad 1996; Berry and Linoff 1997; Anand and Buchner 1998; Cabena et al. 1998; Cios et al. 2000; Han and Kamber 2001; CRISP-DM 2003), and designed an integrated KDDM process model to address these limitations. We discuss how the dependencies highlighted in the integrated model can be used for semiautomating the execution of six different tasks belonging to BU through the modeling phases. The semiautomation of proposed tasks is likely to result in more efficient and effective implementation of the knowledge discovery process. Further, we also propose techniques that can be used for providing decision support in the form of appropriate tools and techniques for the various tasks (excluding tasks

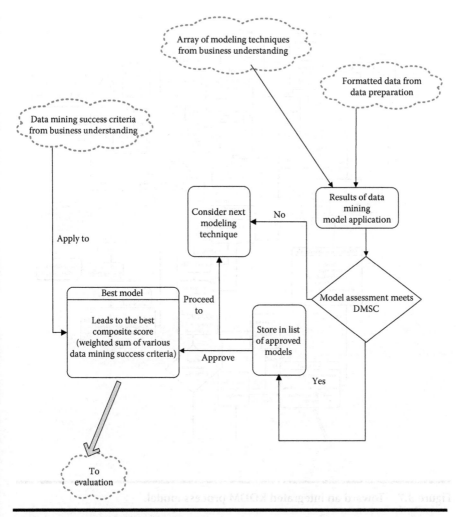

Figure 3.6 The modeling phase.

belonging to deployment phase) belonging to the integrated KDDM process model. The identification and description of relevant techniques can serve to ensure that all the tasks of the process model are executed and no task is inadequately executed due to the lack of support toward its implementation.

The proposed integrated KDDM process architecture can be used as a platform for executing different knowledge discovery projects across an organization. Future research should focus on identifying more candidate tasks for semiautomation, improvements to the KDDM artifact, development of an architecture to support the implementation of KDDM process, and implementation of the artifact in an organizational setting.

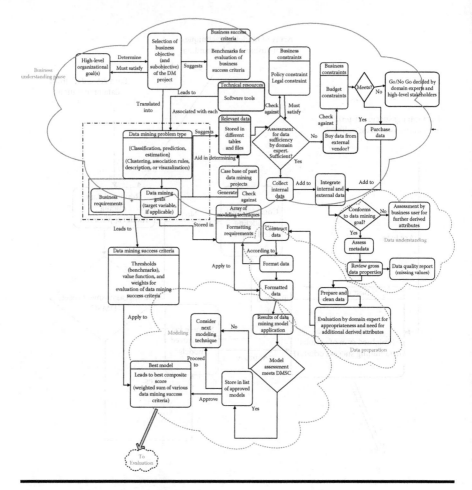

Figure 3.7 Toward an integrated KDDM process model.

Acknowledgment

Material in this chapter previously appeared in: "Toward an integrated knowledge discovery and DM process model," *The Knowledge Engineering Review* **25**, 49–67 (2010).

References

Anand, S. and A. Buchner (1998). *Decision Support Using Data Mining*. London, Financial Times Pitman Publishers.

Basili, V. R. and D. M. Weiss (1984). "A methodology for collecting valid software engineering data." *IEEE Transactions on Software Engineering* **10**(6): 728–738.

Bernstein, A., S. Hill et al. (2005). "Toward intelligent assistance for a data mining process: An ontology-based approach for cost-sensitive classification." *IEEE Transactions on Knowledge and Data Engineering* **17**(4): 503–518.

Berry, M. and G. Linoff (1997). *Data Mining Techniques for Marketing, Sales and Customer Support*, John Wiley & Sons, New York.

Berry, M. and G. Linoff (2000). *Mastering Data Mining: The Art and Relationship of Customer Relationship Management*, John Wiley & Sons.

Cabena, P., P. Hadjinian et al. (1998). *Discovering Data Mining: From Concepts to Implementation*, Prentice Hall, Upper Saddle River, NJ.

Charest, M., S. Delisle et al. (2006). "Intelligent data mining assistance via CBR and ontologies." *Proceedings of the 17th International Conference on Database and Expert Systems Applications*, Washington, DC.

Choi, D. H., B. S. Ahn et al. (2005). "Ranking discovered rules from data mining with multiple criteria by data envelopment analysis." *Expert Systems with Applications* **29**(4): 867–878.

Cios, K. and L. Kurgan (2005). "Trends in data mining and knowledge discovery." In *Advanced Techniques in Knowledge Discovery and Data Mining*. N. Pal and L. Jain (Eds.), Springer, New York, pp. 1–26.

Cios, K., A. Teresinska et al. (2000). "Diagnosing myocardial perfusion from PECTbull's-eye maps—A knowledge discovery approach." *IEEE Engineering in Medicine and Biology Magazine, Special Issue on Medical Data Mining and Knowledge Discovery* **19**(4): 17–25.

CRISP-DM. (2003). "Cross industry standard process for data mining 1.0: Step-by-step data mining guide." Retrieved January 10, 2007, from http://www.crisp-dm.org/.

Davenport, T. H. and J. G. Harris (2007). *Competing on Analytics*, Harvard Business School Press, Boston, MA.

Doran, G. T. (1981). "There's a S.M.A.R.T. way to write management goals and objectives." *Management Review (AMA Forum)* **70**(11): 35–36.

Fayyad, U. M., G. Piatetsky-Shapiro et al. (Eds.) (1996). *Advances in Knowledge Discovery and Data Mining*, AAAI Press, Menlo Park, CA.

Fox, M. S., M. Barbuceanu et al. (Eds.) (1998). "An organization ontology for enterprise modeling." *Simulating Organizations: Computational Models of Institutions and Groups*. AAAI Press, Menlo Park, CA, pp. 131–152.

Han, J. and M. Kamber (2006). *Data Mining: Concepts and Techniques*, Elsevier, Amsterdam, the Netherlands.

Keeney, R. L. (1996). *Value-Focused Thinking: A Path to Creative Decisionmaking*. Harvard University Press, 1996.

Kurgan, L. A. and P. Musilek (2006). "A survey of knowledge discovery and data mining process models." *The Knowledge Engineering Review* **21**(1): 1–24.

Laguna, M. A., J. M. Marqués et al. (2001). "A user requirements elicitation tool." *ACM SIGSOFT Software Engineering Notes Archive* **26**(2): 35–37.

Osei-Bryson, K.-M. (2004). "Evaluation of decision trees." *Computers and Operations Research* **31**: 1933–1945.

Osei-Bryson, K.-M. (2006). "Class notes: clustering Info 614—Graduate course in data mining." Virginia Commonwealth University, Richmond, VA.

Pyle, D. (2003). *Business Modeling and Data Mining*, Morgan Kaufmann Publishers, Boston, MA.

Redpath, R. and B. Srinivasan (2003). Criteria for a Comparative Study of Visualization Techniques in Data Mining. *IEEE 3rd International Conference on Intelligent Systems Design and Application*, Tulsa, Springer-Verlag, Berlin, Germany, August 10–13.

Saaty, T. L. (1991). "Response to holder's comments on the analytic hierarchy process." *The Journal of the Operational Research Society* **42**(10): 909–914.

Sharma, S. and K.-M. Osei-Bryson (2008). "Framework for formal implementation of the business understanding phase of data mining projects." *Expert Systems with Applications*, 1–10.

Sharma, S. and K.-M. Osei-Bryson (2009). Organization-ontology based framework for executing the business understanding phase of data mining projects. *Hawaii International Conference on Systems Sciences* **36**(2): 4114–4124.

Simon, H. A. (1996). *The Sciences of the Artificial.* MIT Press, Cambridge, MA.

Simoudis, E., B. Livezey et al. (1996). Integrating inductive and deductive reasoning for data mining. *Advances in Knowledge Discovery and Data Mining*. U. M. Fayyad, G. Paitetsky-Shapiro, P. Smyth, and R. Uthurusamy (Eds.), AAAI Press, Menlo Park, CA.

KDDM
TECHNIQUES

II

KDDM
TECHNIQUES

Chapter 4

A Novel Method for Formulating the Business Objectives of Data Mining Projects

Sumana Sharma and Kweku-Muata Osei-Bryson

Contents

Abstract: Formulation of business objectives is the first step in any data mining (DM) or knowledge discovery project. It is critical to correctly formulate the business objective because all the succeeding tasks in the project are directly dependent on it. Our analysis of the extant academic and practitioner literature reveals the lack of any specific approaches for formulating business objectives of DM projects. Based on some general approaches for formulating objectives such as, value-focused thinking, goal question metric method, and Specific, Measurable, Attainable, Realistic, and Time-Bound (SMART) criteria, we propose a novel method for formulating the business objective of a DM project. The step-by-step approach proposed in the method can also provide semiautomated assistance toward the development of a well-formed business objective. An illustrative example depicted through Microsoft Visio screenshots is used to describe how each step of the method can be implemented. The significance of the proposed method and its contributions are discussed.

Keywords: Formulating business objectives, method, data mining, knowledge discovery, goal question metric method, value-focused thinking, SMART criteria

Introduction

Modern business organizations operate in a highly competitive environment, in which it is critical that they have an in-depth knowledge about their internal operations, and the actions of both their competitors and business partners. This has lead to an increased interest in what is referred to as "business intelligence" (BI) activities, which aim to facilitate decision making that is based on data. In fact, data has emerged as a newfound source of competitive advantage in an era where traditional bases of competition have largely evaporated (Davenport and Harris 2007). In many organizations, knowledge discovery through data mining (DM) is an important component of BI activities. In recent years, DM practitioners and researchers have become aware of the need for formal knowledge discovery and data mining (KDDM) process models (e.g., Fayyad et al. 1996; CRISP-DM 2003; Cios et al. 2000; Cabena et al. 1998) that prescribe how organizations can sift through mountains of data to discover valuable nuggets of knowledge.

Most KDDM process models describe the process of knowledge discovery as comprising of multiple phases starting with the business understanding (BU) phase, and followed by data understanding, data preparation, modeling, and evaluation phases. BU phase is the foundational phase of any KDDM project. Being the foundational phase, the output of the BU phase (the chief output being the business objective) directly affects the remaining phases and the tasks contained therein. As can be seen from Figure 4.1, the BU phase is very critical, as the business objectives formulated during this phase affect other tasks in this phase (such as the technical or DM objectives and the project plan) as well as tasks in *all* the other phases (such as data understanding, data preparation,

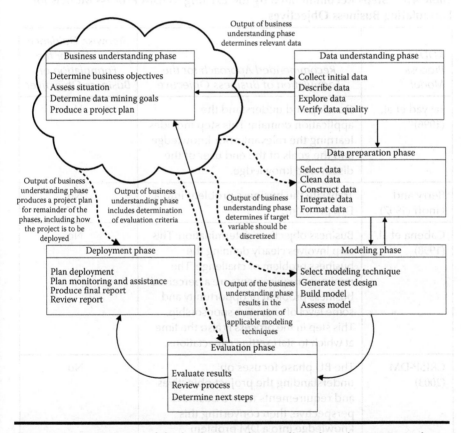

Figure 4.1 Importance of the business understanding phase in KDDM projects. (Data from Sharma, S. and Osei-Bryson, K.-M., *Expert Systems with Applications,* **36, 4114–4124, 2008.)**

modeling, evaluation, and deployment). Given such a direct dependency, any issues with the formulation of business objectives is likely to have a negative effect on the overall project quality and the effectiveness of the DM models so generated (Sharma and Osei-Bryson 2008).

One of the main tasks of the BU phase includes the formulation of business objectives. The importance of this task cannot be overemphasized, as it is the business objective of a project that determines the direction for the entire DM project. Our analysis of extant DM process models reveals that they do not provide explicit guidance toward formulation of business objectives. In Table 4.1, we summarize the approaches for formulating business objectives, as prescribed by five leading KDDM process models, including Fayyad et al. (1996), Cios and Kurgan (2005), CRISP-DM (2003), Berry and Linoff (1997), and Cabena et al. (1998). In each of

Table 4.1 Steps Recommended by the Existing KDDM Process Models for Formulating Business Objectives

KDDM Process Model	Recommended Approach for the Formulation of Business Objective	Stepwise Guidance Provided for the Formulation of Business Objective?
Fayyad et al. (1996)	Develop and understand the application domain: This step includes learning the relevant prior knowledge and the goals of the end user of the discovered knowledge.	No
Berry and Linoff (1997)	Translate the business problem into a DM problem.	No
Cabena et al. (1998)	Business objectives determination: This step involves clearly defining the business problem or challenge. The minimum requirements are a perceived business problem or opportunity and some level of executive sponsorship. This step in the process is also the time at which to start setting expectations.	No
CRISP-DM (2003)	The BU phase focuses on understanding the project objectives and requirements from a business perspective, then converting this knowledge into a DM problem definition and a preliminary plan designed to achieve the objectives.	No

Table 4.1 (*Continued*)   Steps Recommended by the Existing KDDM Process Models for Formulating Business Objectives

KDDM Process Model	Recommended Approach for the Formulation of Business Objective	Stepwise Guidance Provided for the Formulation of Business Objective?
Cios and Kurgan (2005)	Understand the problem domain: In this step, one works closely with domain experts to define the problem and determine the project goals, identify key people, and learn about current solutions to the problem. It involves learning domain-specific terminology. A description of the problem including its restrictions is done. The project goals then need to be translated into the KDDM goals, and may include the initial selection of potential DM tools.	No

these models, the description of a task such as formulation of business objectives, is at best, a broad guideline, and fails to guide the users in terms of *how exactly* this critical task can be executed.

Moreover, on surveying the literature, we found that while some techniques that have been proposed for formulation of objectives of projects (although not necessarily KDDM projects), such as value-focused thinking (VFT) (Keeney 1992), goal question metric (GQM) method (Basili and Weiss 1984), and Specific, Measurable, Attainable, Realistic, and Time-Bound (SMART) criteria (Doran 1981), these cannot be directly applied to formulate a well-formed business objective of a DM project. The VFT approach is geared toward encouraging the assessment of values relevant to the given context, so that objectives may be formulated in accordance with those consciously selected values. GQM was originally proposed by Basili and Weiss as an approach for software metrics and centers around the identification of the correct metrics, which can ultimately be used to improve the software development process as well as the software products themselves. SMART criteria serve as a checklist of important characteristics that should be found in a good objective (such as specificity, time-boundedness, etc.); however, it does not prescribe steps toward how exactly the objectives should be formulated. The research problem addressed by this chapter is: How to formulate a well-formed business objective of a DM project? To address this research problem, we propose a novel method that can be used to provide stepwise guidance to a user toward the process of formulating a *well-formed business objective*. In section "Theoretical Foundation," we discuss the theoretical underpinnings that guided the design of this method. In section "Proposed Method for Formulating a Business Objective," we describe our proposed method for formulating business objectives and explain how it can be implemented using a hypothetical example. The final section includes a discussion of the significance of the proposed method.

Theoretical Foundation

In this section, we present a description of the three methods that guided the development of our proposed method for formulating business objectives. These include VFT (Keeney 1992), GQM approach (Basili and Weiss 1984), and SMART criteria (Doran 1981).

Value-Focused Thinking

VFT considers the role of values in decision making and can be differentiated from conventional decision making, which focuses on the enumeration of alternatives. The concept of VFT was first proposed by Keeney (1992), who argues that conventional decision-making approaches are reactive in nature, as they emphasize the identification of alternatives ahead of the articulation of values that are important to the particular decision situation. VFT has found applications across a wide variety of decisions belonging to diverse domains, including environmental engineering (Hassan 2004), military operations (Keeter and Parnell 2005), homeland security (Pruitt 2003), tourism management (Kajanus et al. 2004), and systems engineering (Boylan et al. 2006), to name a few.

According to Keeney, it is important to make the values explicit and use them to guide the decision-making process. Keeney (1996) offers a methodology for creating and structuring values in the form of objectives and using the objectives to guide decision making. Keeney's work has helped to address an important gap in research, namely, the lack of support toward the formulation of objectives to characterize a decision situation. Keeney (1996) notes that while all experts on decision making agree that it is crucial to list your objectives, they are not specific about how to do it or how to use the objectives to guide your thinking. Keeney's work on VFT provides explicit guidance toward the formulation of objectives, an indispensable task in any decision-making situation.

VFT includes three different types of objectives: fundamental objectives, means objectives, and strategic objectives. Fundamental objectives concern the ends that decision makers value in a particular decision context, whereas means objectives are the methods to achieve the ends. Strategic objectives provide common guidance for more detailed fundamental objectives. Thinking about these different types of objectives can lead to enumeration of alternatives relevant to a decision situation. Keeney (1996) also contends that there is value in thinking about certain decision situations as opportunities rather than problems. He states that a decision opportunity can help alleviate problems or allow avoiding of future problems.

Keeney (1994) notes that, in many cases, it is difficult to conclude whether a given objective is a fundamental or a means objective. To overcome such issues, Keeney (1994) recommends applying the "why is that important?" (WITI) test to distinguish between fundamental and means objectives. If the decision maker answers that a particular objective is essential to a decision context, then that objective is a fundamental objective. If however, he or she says that a particular objective is important due to its implication for other objectives, then it is a means objective.

Goal Question Metric

GQM method (Basili and Weiss 1984; Basili and Rombach 1988) was proposed as a mechanism for defining and evaluating a set of operational goals using measurement metrics. This approach has been successfully applied toward the identification of defects in software engineering management (Birk et al. 1998; Van Rini and Berghout 1999). The GQM approach is generally used as an approach for determining *software metrics*; a software metric is a method for quantitatively determining the extent to which a software process or product possesses a certain attribute (Daskalantonakis 1992). However, it is salient to point out that the GQM approach emphasizes *goal-oriented measurement*. It recommends that the goals must be identified before the identification of metrics (Basili and Weiss 1984; Basili and Rombach 1988), because metrics are useful only when they are strongly interlinked to goals.

Specifically, the GQM approach consists of a top-down hierarchical structure consisting of three components: goals, questions, and metrics. A goal specifies the purpose of measurement, object to be measured, issue to be measured, and the view point from which the measure is taken. A goal can be refined into a set of questions that characterize the goal in a quantifiable way. Finally, each question can be refined into a set of quantitative and/or qualitative metrics. These metrics can be regarded as the evaluation criteria or success criteria for the stated objectives (Figure 4.2).

According to the GQM approach, each goal should include five facets of information, namely, object, purpose, focus, viewpoint, and context. The five facets and their examples are included in Table 4.2.

SMART Approach

The SMART acronym proposed by Doran (1981) is commonly recommended for setting objectives and is commonly used for forming objectives. The approach

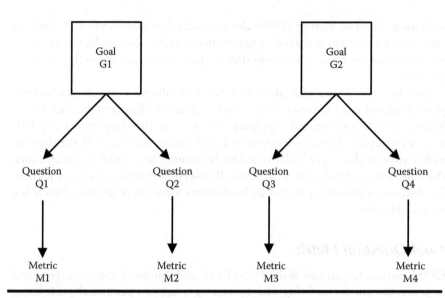

Figure 4.2 The GQM approach. (Data from Basili, V. R. and D. M. Weiss, *IEEE Transactions on Software Engineering*, 10, 728–738, 1984.)

Table 4.2 GQM Approach—Five Information Facets of Goals

Five Facets of Information to Formulate Goals	Example
1. *Object:* the product or process under study	Testing phase or the subsystem of an end product
2. *Purpose:* motivation behind the goal (why the goal is being pursued)	Better understanding, guidance, control prediction, and improvement
3. *Focus:* the quality attribute of the object under study	Reliability, effort, and error slippage
4. *Viewpoint:* perspective of the goal (from whose viewpoint is goal being formulated)	Project manager, developer, customer, and project team
5. *Context:* context or scope of the program	Project X and division B

Source: Basili, V. R. and D. M. Weiss, *IEEE Transactions on Software Engineering*, 10(6), 728–738, 1984.

underlying SMART suggests that objectives should be specific, measurable, achievable, relevant, and timely. The meaning of each criterion is presented in Table 4.3. An Internet search for SMART goals yields numerous websites dedicated to providing help with setting up SMART objectives, that is, objectives that satisfy all the characteristics described in Table 4.3. An Internet search for SMART goals also

Table 4.3   SMART Approach for Setting Up Objectives

Criterion	Description
Specific	The objective must lead to an observable action, behavior, or achievement
Measurable	The objective must be measurable throughout
Achievable	The business objective must be achievable within the constraints of the available resources, knowledge, and time
Relevant	The objective must be relevant to the organizational goals
Time-Bound	There should be clear deadlines for the achievement of the objective

Source: Doran, G. T., *Management Review (AMA Forum)*, 35–36, 1981.

reveals numerous templates and worksheets, which are available for providing assistance with setting up of SMART goals.

Proposed Method for Formulating a Business Objective

As discussed earlier, approaches such as VFT and GQM that have been proposed for the formulation of objectives are quite generic and cannot be directly applied toward the formulation of business objectives of DM projects. The SMART approach is more a way of assessing the *correctness* of objectives than a way of formulating objectives themselves. However, all three approaches do provide valuable guidance toward how to get started with the task of formulating business objectives. We utilized these approaches as guiding principles as we devised a more specific and detailed method to formulate business objectives of DM projects. Figure 4.3 presents a general outline of our method. Detailed description of the various steps is included as follows.

Step 1—Stimulating Discussion about Business Objectives: Applying VFT

Keeney (1992) highlighted that decision making often focuses on alternatives and only afterward addresses objectives or criteria to assess these alternatives. He labeled such reactive thinking as "alternatives focused thinking" and argued that such thinking takes away the control of the decision situation from the decision maker. Keeney

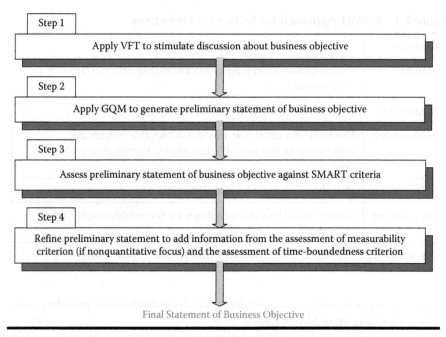

Step 1

Apply VFT to stimulate discussion about business objective

Step 2

Apply GQM to generate preliminary statement of business objective

Step 3

Assess preliminary statement of business objective against SMART criteria

Step 4

Refine preliminary statement to add information from the assessment of measurability criterion (if nonquantitative focus) and the assessment of time-boundedness criterion

Final Statement of Business Objective

Figure 4.3 Step-by-step approach for formulating business objective.

contended that because various alternatives are after all only a *means* to achieve *values*, it should be values that drive the decision-making process of selecting among alternatives and not vice versa.

It appears that DM projects also often suffer from alternatives-focused thinking. Berry and Linoff (2000) is a compilation of DM case studies, across diverse industries and using diverse DM modeling techniques. Study of each of these case studies reveals that often a brief description of a problem situation is quickly followed up by a discussion of alternatives in terms of what type of model (classification, estimation, prediction, association rules, etc.), or what type of DM technique (decision tree, neural network, regression, etc.), would best address the problem scenario at hand. There is typically no guidance provided toward how the business objective in the context of a DM project was or could be formulated.

Keeney (1996) acknowledges the same concern and asks that while "clear objectives are useful, how should they be created?" He defines an objective as a statement of something one wants to achieve in a particular decision context. He proposes that each statement of objectives must contain three features: a decision context, an object, and a direction of preference. In his work on VFT, Keeney discusses two types of objectives: fundamental objectives and means objectives. Fundamental objectives are ends that decision makers value in a particular decision context; means objectives are methods to reach toward those ends.

We posit that in the context of DM projects, fundamental objectives are the business objectives of the DM project. The DM objectives (the technical objectives) are the methods for accomplishing the business objectives or the ends. Consider the following commonly used DM objective as an example: predict which customers are most likely to respond to a promotional offer. Is this objective, a fundamental or means objective? In the absence of any approach, different individuals may categorize it differently.

Following the WITI test recommended by Keeney (1994), if the decision maker answers that a particular objective is essential to a decision context, then that objective is a fundamental objective. If, however, he or she says that a particular objective is important due to its implication for other objectives, then it is a means objective. With respect to the above example, a decision maker might answer that this objective is important because the company wishes to increase the response rate from customers, which in turn would mean that it is the desire to increase response rates that is the fundamental objective. By accurately predicting which customers are most likely to respond, the company can direct offers toward the customers most likely to apply for the offers, thereby accomplishing the fundamental objective of increasing response rates.

Keeney's approach provides a starting point for stimulating discussion toward setting up of business objectives and suggests that organizations ask what they value most in a particular decision context to formulate the objective. Although the importance of the approach cannot be undermined, it may be difficult to implement by business users involved in setting up the objective. More specifically, the business users may find it difficult to formulate the statement of business objective for their project using this approach. We posit that a modified GQM approach, described subsequently, should be utilized for a step-by-step guidance in formulating the business objectives.

Step 2—Creating a Well-Formulated Business Objective: Applying the GQM Approach

The GQM approach provides a process for setting goals, and measures for evaluating the goals, and is supported by specific methodological steps. In the context of DM projects, the approach can be applied to determine business objectives, DM objectives, and business success criteria (measures) for evaluating the business objectives. The latter two are discussed in the following sections, as they are independent tasks in the DM process.

In applying the approach, we had to adapt it for an entirely new context, knowledge discovery and DM. To the best of our knowledge, this is the first implementation of the GQM approach to formulate objectives (business and technical/DM) and success criteria of a DM project. Although we follow the tenets of the approach in formulating the objectives and success criteria, we also suggest some enhancements to the steps, which have been duly noted in the description.

Five Components of Business Objectives in the Context of DM Projects

According to the GQM approach, each goal should include five facets of information, namely, object, purpose, focus, viewpoint, and context.

Let us consider the five components of goals (business objectives) in the context of DM projects.

- *Purpose:* This signifies the motivation behind formulating the objective, or why the objective is being formulated. In the context of DM projects, purpose can be of the following five types:
  - Increase/improve
  - Decrease/reduce
  - Identify
  - Understand
  - Determine (hypothesis testing)
- *Object Name and Defining Characteristic:* Object is the entity under the study. Examples of objects can include the following:
  - Customers
  - Suppliers
  - Products
  - Employees
  - Transactions, etc.

  In selecting the object, it is important to provide further qualifying information in the form of the defining characteristic of the object. For instance, if the object is chosen as simply *customers*, it is may not be clear as to which customers of the firm are of interest and a resultant DM endeavor may be based on the entire customer base of the firm. However, the results of DM so obtained are likely to be diluted as it is well known that different types of customers behave differently. Therefore, when specifying the object, we must augment it by adding more information (see Table 4.4 for examples for various types of objects and their defining characteristics).

- *Focus:* Focus is the variable or the quality attribute of the entity under study, that is, what is being studied through the DM project. The focus of a DM project can be on a tangible or quantitatively measurable behavior, or on an intangible attribute. We provide examples of both types subsequently.
  - *Quantitative focus:* Such a focus variable can be measured in terms of percentage, rate, amount, and so on. For example, churn rate or loss rate of a CUSTOMER [OBJECT]
    - *Assuming constancy of other variables:* When focus is a quantitatively measured variable, other variables may have to be treated as constant. Constancy of other variables may or may not apply, but the user must be asked to provide this information, whenever applicable. For example, a credit card provider may be interested in increasing approval

Table 4.4   Objects and Their Defining Characteristics

Objects	Defining Characteristics
Customers	Wireless Internet customers Customers with tenure >1 Customers acquired though marketing channel Most loyal customers
Suppliers	Suppliers for eastern region Suppliers of small moving parts Suppliers of parts X
Products	Co-selling products Products from a particular line (baby care or feminine products)
Employees	Internal hires Part-time employees Full-time employees Contract employees Employees with tenure >5
Transactions	Transactions that occurred in last week/month/year Transactions valued at >$250

rates while maintaining the same loss rates. If the latter is not specified, DM models that lead to an increase in approval rate, but at the
cost of increasing bad rates may be created.

- *Qualitative focus:* Such a focus variable cannot be measured in terms of
percentage, rate, amount, and so on. For example, factors affecting the
motivation of EMPLOYEES [OBJECT]

**RELATION BETWEEN PURPOSE AND FOCUS
OF A BUSINESS OBJECTIVE**

Note that the focus of a business objective is closely related to the purpose of
the business objective. When the purpose is to *increase, decrease,* or *reduce,* the
focus is often on a quantitative variable. On the other hand, when the purpose is
to *identify"* or *understand,* the focus is typically on a qualitative variable. When
the purpose is hypothesis testing, the focus can be quantitative or qualitative
depending on what is being hypothesized. Table 4.5 shows examples of some
preliminary business objectives with three components, namely, purpose, focus,
and object (and their defining characteristic) identified.

Table 4.5 Examples of Preliminary Statements of a Business Objective (Purpose, Focus, and Object Identified)

Purpose	Focus/Issue	Object
Increase	Approval rates	• New credit card applicants • Customers acquired through alternate channels
Decrease/ Reduce	Loss/bad/charge-off	• Customers with tenure >2 • Subprime credit card customers
	Churn rate	• Handset customers
Identify	List of probable churners	• Customers with tenure >5
	List of responders to a new offer	• Prospective customers
	Factors affecting churn rate	• Handset customers
	Characteristics	• Most loyal customers
	List of yogurt lovers	• Overall customer population
	Co-selling products	• Complete line of products • Line of health and fitness products
	Occurrence of fraud	• Transactions >$250 • Online transactions >$150
Understand	Characteristics	• High-risk customers
	Factors affecting retention	• Existing customers with tenure >3 years
	Reasons behind charge-off	• Subprime credit card customers
Determine if	Difference in price sensitivity	• Frequent roamers versus other customers
	Difference in likelihood of response to a home equity offer	• Families with children versus others

- *Viewpoint:* Viewpoint reflects the entity from whose perspective the objective is being designed. For example, (1) project manager, (2) project team, (3) project sponsor, and so on.
- *Context:* Context represents the scope or the environment where the DM project is being carried out. For example, (1) a particular project (project "manage churn," project "retain customers") and (2) a particular division (Marketing division, Credit Risk Management division, Customer Relationship Management division).

Figure 4.4 shows how the five facets of information can be put together to create a preliminary statement of business objective of a DM project.

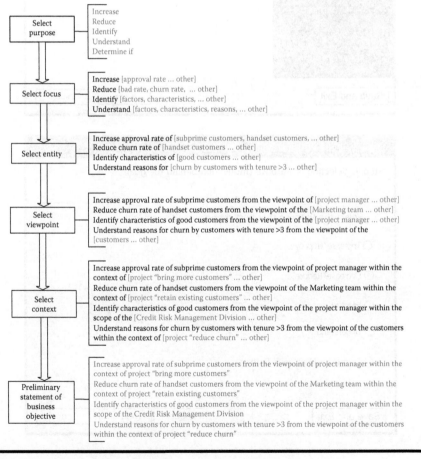

Figure 4.4   Formulating preliminary statement of business objective.

Screenshots for Assisting User in Formulating the Preliminary Business Objective

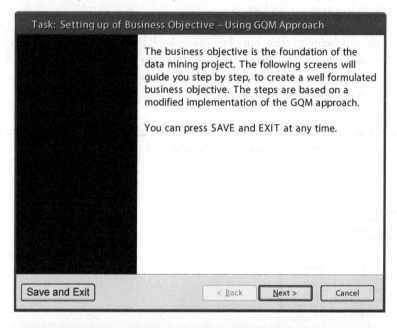

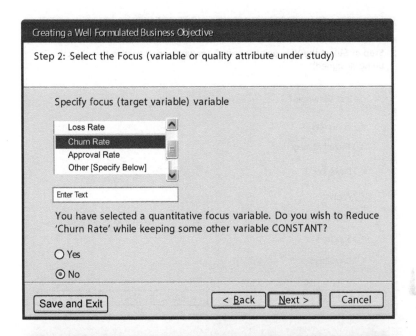

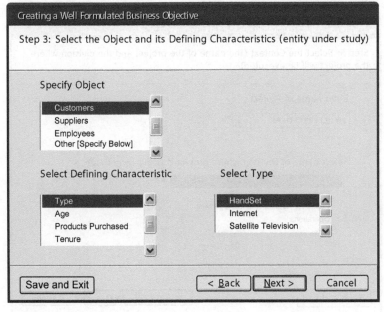

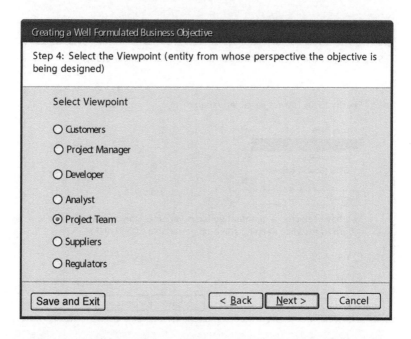

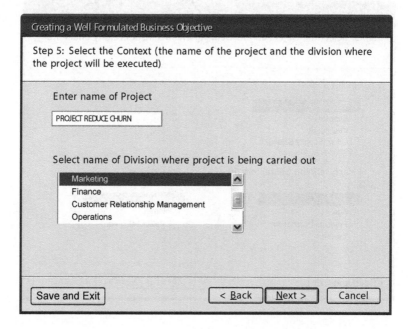

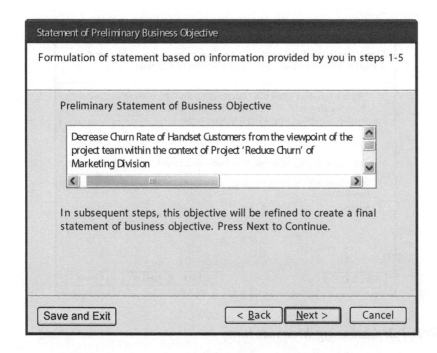

In the screenshot:

Statement of Preliminary Business Objective

Formulation of statement based on information provided by you in steps 1-5

Preliminary Statement of Business Objective

Decrease Churn Rate of Handset Customers from the viewpoint of the project team within the context of Project 'Reduce Churn' of Marketing Division

In subsequent steps, this objective will be refined to create a final statement of business objective. Press Next to Continue.

Save and Exit   < Back   Next >   Cancel

Step 3—Applying SMART Criteria and GQM Approach to Refine Statement of Preliminary Business Objective

The preliminary statement of business objectives formulated in steps 1 and 2 should be assessed against the various criteria underlying the SMART approach. The definitions of the five criteria underlying the SMART acronym can be found in Table 4.3.

Step 3-1: Assessing Specificity

The *specificity* criterion requires that the objective should lead to an observable action, behavior, or achievement. In the context of DM projects, such observable action is often specified in quantitative terms, such a percentage improvement in profit, percentage reduction in losses or charge offs, and so on. It could also be specified in nonquantitative terms such as improvement in customer's perception of the company's product(s), improvement in employee morale, and so on.

If the preliminary statement of business objectives does not satisfy the specificity criterion, then the steps related to the formulation of the objective should be repeated. This ensures that the objective will lead to a concrete identifiable outcome.

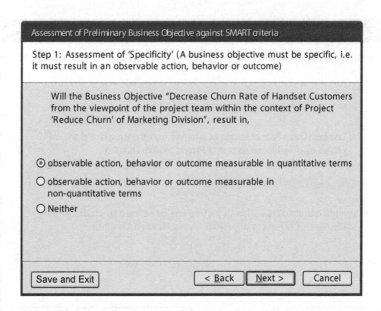

Step 3-2: Assessing Measurability

The assessment of measurability criterion helps to determine the business success criteria associated with the project. This criterion stipulates that the business objective must be measurable in quantitative or nonquantitative terms. This step ensures that the objective formulated is indeed measurable. Based on the focus variable (set up during the formulation of the objective), two situations arise: the focus variable is quantitative in nature or the focus variable is nonquantitative in nature.

- In case of *objectives with a nonquantitative focus*, the assessment of measurability should be performed by a domain expert who should set subjective criteria for assessing whether or not the objective was achieved.
- In case of *objectives with a quantitative focus*, step 2 of the GQM approach (refining questions into a set of quantitatively verifiable metrics) can be used for assessment of measurability.

Using the GQM Approach for the Assessment of Measurability for Objectives with a Quantitative Focus

The GQM approach proposes refining the overall goal (business objective in the case of a DM project) into a set of questions, and then refining the questions into a set of metrics that could be objective or subjective. Figure 4.5 shows an example of how questions and metrics can be formulated from a statement of business objective.

Note that the *questions* in the GQM approach are based directly on the focus variable or attribute. The metrics describe the business success criteria and must

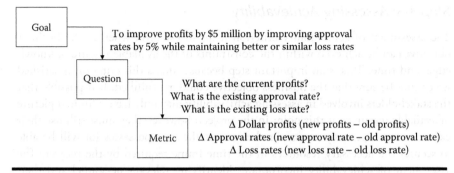

Figure 4.5   GQM approach for setting up of business success criteria.

meet the threshold values specified in the statement of objectives. For instance, in case of the example shown in Figure 4.5: (a) Δ dollar profits should be $\geq$ \$5 million; (b) Δ approval rate $\geq$ 5%; and (c) Δ loss rate $\leq$ 0, as the objective is to maintain better or similar loss rates. The sequence of steps is also summarized as follows:

- Select the existing and the desired values for the focus variable.
- The *delta* (or difference) between existing and desired values is a business success criterion.
- For example, if the existing value for charge-off rate is 5% and the desired value is 2%, then the business success criteria = (5–2)/5 = 60% reduction in the charge-off rate or Δ charge-off rate = 60%.
- Project will only be deemed as successful if it leads to a 60% reduction in the charge-off rate. Anything less than that will be deemed unsatisfactory.

Assessment of Preliminary Business Objective against SMART criteria

Step 2: Assessment of 'Measurability' (A business objective must be measurable in quantitative or non-quantitative terms)

Based on information provided during selection of FOCUS, the Business Objective "Decrease Churn Rate of Handset Customers from the viewpoint of the project team within the context of Project 'Reduce Churn' of Marketing Division", can be measured in quantitative terms.

Provide existing churn rate in %   5%

Provide desired churn rate in %   2%

Preliminary Business Success Criteria is   60%

   Δ Churn rate =

Save and Exit   < Back   Next >   Cancel

Step 3-3: Assessing Achievability

The assessment of achievability criterion helps to establish whether the business objective can be achieved within the constraints of the available resources, knowledge, and time. This is an important step because unless this criterion is satisfied we cannot be sure that the business objective could get fulfilled. It is possible that the stakeholders involved in assessing achievability may only have a limited picture of available resources at this point in the project; however, they must still use their expertise to consciously assess whether or not the firm possesses (or will be able to secure) the necessary resources in the time frame required by the project. The assessment of achievability incorporates identifying relevant personnel and their availability, which is regarded as an independent task in the DM process, and therefore discussed separately.

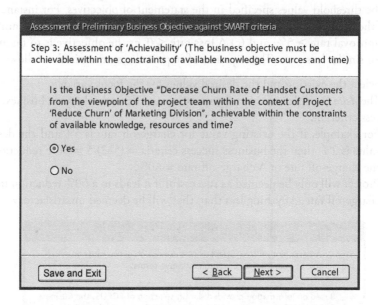

Step 3-4: Assessing Relevance

This criterion ensures that the business objective is relevant to a higher order organizational objective. Unless this is the case, the project cannot be regarded as useful for the organization, making it difficult to approve any funding for its execution. The stakeholders involved in assessing this objective must clearly specify the particular organizational objective that would be fulfilled if the business objective was carried out.

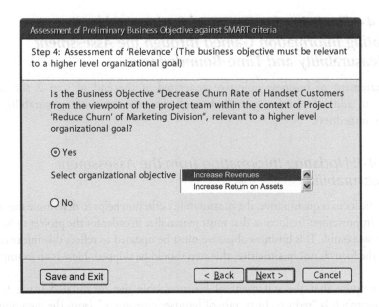

Step 3-5: Assessing Time-Boundedness

This criterion ensures that there is a clear timeline for the execution of the project and delivery of final results. Unless this criterion is satisfied, it will be difficult, if not impossible to track the progress of the project, to allocate critical resources. The information provided by stakeholders in assessing this criterion must be used in refining the preliminary business objective, to also reflect the time frame during which the project must be completed.

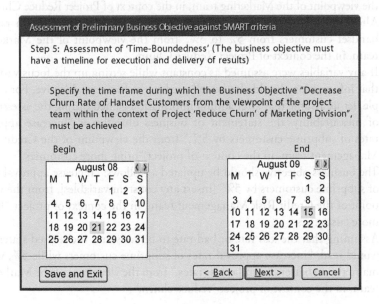

Step 4—Finalizing Statement of Business Objective: Updating Information Gained through the Assessment of Measurability and Time-Boundedness

The statement of business objective generated at the end of step 2 should be revised to add information gained through the assessment of measurability and time-boundedness.

Step 4-1: Updating Information from the Assessment of Measurability

When the focus is quantitative, the measurability criterion helps to determine the quantitative improvement/reduction that must materialize in order for the project to be considered successful. This business objective must be updated to reflect this information. When the focus is not quantitative, this step should be skipped. Here is an example:

■ Suppose that the statement of business objective formulated using GQM approach is "reduce churn rate of handset customers," from the viewpoint of the Marketing team, in the context of project "reduce churn."

■ Let us assume that the assessment of measurability reveals that the churn rate must be reduced by 2%, that is, from 5% to 3%.

■ The business objective should be updated as follows: "reduce churn rate of handset customers" [insert delta or desired and existing values for focus variable], from the viewpoint of the Marketing team, in the context of project "reduce churn."

■ The statement would read "reduce churn rate of handset customers by 2%," from the viewpoint of the Marketing team, in the context of Project Reduce Chum."

■ Alternatively, the business objective can be stated as 'reduce churn rate of handset customers from 5% to 3%,' from the viewpoint of the Marketing team, in the context of Project Reduce Chum.

■ If any variables were assumed as constant while setting up the focus variable, that information should also be reflected in the business objective. For example, let us assume that after adding information gained during the assessment of measurability, the statement of business objective is "increase approval rates of subprime customers by 5%," from the viewpoint of the Credit Risk Management team, in the context of project "bring more customers."

■ The business objective should be updated as follows: "increase approval rates of subprime customers by 5%" [insert any constant variables], from the viewpoint of the Credit Risk Management team, in the context of project "bring more customers."

■ Assuming that the loss rate or bad rate to be constant, the revised statement would read: "increase approval rates of subprime customers while 5%, while maintaining better or similar loss rates," from the viewpoint of the Marketing team, in the context of project "reduce churn."

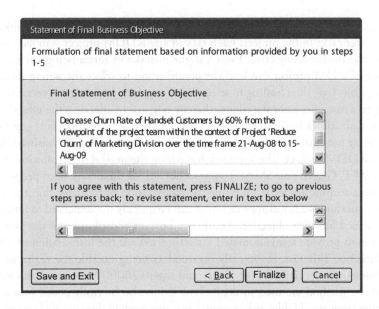

Step 4-2: Updating Information from the Assessment of Time-Boundedness

Review of the business objective so formulated reveals that it possesses all characteristics of a well-formulated business objective, except the time frame during which this objective must be accomplished for the project to be considered successful. This information is collected during the assessment of time-boundedness.

Let us assume that the assessment of time-boundedness revealed that the project must be accomplished over September 2008–August 2009. The business objective can be updated as follows. "reduce churn rate of handset customers by 2%," from the viewpoint of the Marketing team, in the context of project "reduce churn" over [insert time frame].

The final statement of business objective would read: "reduce churn rate of handset customers by 2%," from the viewpoint of the Marketing team, in the context of project "reduce churn" over September 2008–August 2009.

Discussion

A KDDM process model plays a significant role in the effective and efficient execution of KDDM projects. By its very definition, it is meant to assist the user through every single one of the multitude of tasks that underlie complex and iterative KDDM projects. A review of the existing KDDM process models reveals that they provide only general advice toward how the business objective, the first step of the KDDM project, can be implemented. This is a serious problem and is compounded by the fact that there exist numerous dependencies between the business objective and the later tasks in the project. Each task in any KDDM project is in fact dependent on the business objective. Even a slight mistake in formulating the business objective of a DM project can lead the organization to select the wrong technical (or DM) objective, thus leading to selecting wrong data, building imprecise models leading to erroneous interpretations, thereby negatively affecting the effectiveness of an organization's business decisions. This chapter fills an important gap in the literature by proposing a step-by-step approach for formulating the business objective of a KDDM project. The approach has strong theoretical underpinnings in the form of VFT, GQM, and SMART approaches. All of these have been proposed as appropriate techniques for stimulating the formulation of business objectives. The proposed method is a novel approach that can be quickly implemented to formulate a well-formed business objective. Another important contribution of the proposed method is to provide semiautomated assistance toward the formulation of a business objective. This task is typically regarded as being outside the realm of DM tasks that can be semiautomated (Berry and Linoff 2000). Microsoft Visio screenshots of the method are used to depict how it can also be easily coded into a programming language. Unlike earlier approaches, our method does not make any broad assumptions about the domain knowledge of the users involved in formulating the business objective and will be valuable to users with differing skill levels. Ultimately, the formulation of a well-formed business objective sets the stage for effective and efficient implementation of the remainder of the KDDM project and also for rigorous evaluation of the results to determine whether or not the chosen solution in the form of the DM model truly satisfies the business objective of the project.

References

Basili, V. R. and H. D. Rombach (1988). "The TAME project: Towards improvement–oriented software environments." *IEEE Transactions on Software Engineering* **14**(6): 758–773.

Basili, V. R. and D. M. Weiss (1984). "A methodology for collecting valid software engineering data." *IEEE Transactions on Software Engineering* **10**(6): 728–738.

Berry, M. and G. Linoff (1997). *Data Mining Techniques for Marketing, Sales and Customer Support,* New York: Wiley.

Berry, M. and G. Linoff (2000). *Mastering Data Mining: The Art and Relationship of Customer Relationship Management,* New York: Wiley.

Birk, A., S. Rini Van, and J. Janne (1998). "Business impact, benefit, and cost of applying GQM in industry: An in-depth, long-term investigation at Schlumberger RPS." *The 5th International Symposium on Software Metrics,* March 20–21, Bethesda, MD, p. 93.

Boylan, G. L., E. S. Tollefson et al. (2006). "Using value-focused thinking to select a simulation tool for the acquisition of infantry soldier systems." *Systems Engineering* **9**(3): 199–212.

Cabena, P., P. Hadjinian et al. (1998). *Discovering Data Mining: From Concepts to Implementation,* Upper Saddle River, NJ: Prentice Hall.

Cios, K., A. Teresinska et al. (2000). "Diagnosing myocardial perfusion from PECT bull's-eye maps—A knowledge discovery approach." *IEEE Engineering in Medicine and Biology Magazine, Special Issue on Medical Data Mining and Knowledge Discovery* **19**(4): 17–25.

CRISP-DM. (2003). "Cross industry standard process for data mining 1.0: Step-by-step data mining guide." Retrieved January 10, 2007, from http://www.crisp-dm.org/.

Daskalantonakis, M. (1992). "A practical view of software measurement and implementation experiences within Motorola." *IEEE Transactions on Software Engineering*, 18(11): 998–1010.

Davenport, T. H. and J. G. Harris (2007). *Competing on Analytics*, Boston, MA: Harvard Business School Press.

Doran, G. T. (1981). "There's a S.M.A.R.T. way to write management goals and objectives." *Management Review (AMA Forum)* **70**(11): 35–36.

Fayyad, U. M., G. Piatetsky-Shapiro et al. (Eds.) (1996). *Advances in Knowledge Discovery and Data Mining*, Menlo Park, CA: AAAI Press.

Hassan, O. A. B. (2004). "Application of value-focused thinking on the environmental selection of wall structures." *Journal of Environment Management* **70**(2): 181–187.

Kajanus, M., J. Kangas et al. (2004). "The use of value focused thinking and the A'WOT hybrid method in tourism management." *Tourism Management* **25**(4): 499–506.

Keeney, R. L. (1992). *Value Focused Thinking: A Path to Creative Decision Making*. Cambridge, MA: Harvard University Press.

Keeney, R. L. (1994). "Creativity in decision making with value-focused thinking." *Sloan Management Review* **35**: 33–41.

Keeney, R. L. (1996). "Value-focused thinking: Identifying decision opportunities and creating alternatives." *European Journal of Operations Research* **92**: 537–549.

Keeter, R. R. and G. Parnell (2005). *Applying Value-Focused Thinking to Effects Based Operations*, Operations Research Center of Excellence Technical Report DSE-BCR-0520 DTIC #: ADA 438165, West Point, NY: Department of System Engineering, US Military Academy at West Point.

Pruitt, K. A. (2003). *Modeling Homeland Security: A Value Focused Thinking Approach*. Ohio, Air Force Institute of Technology. Master of Science in Operations Research, p. 237.

Sharma, S. and K.-M. Osei-Bryson (2008). "Implementation of business understanding phase of data mining projects." *Expert Systems with Applications*, **36**(2:2): 4114–4124.

Van Rini, S. and E. Berghout (1999). *The Goal/Question/Metric Method*. Chicago, IL: McGraw-Hill Education.

Chapter 5

The Application of the Business Understanding Phase of the CRISP-DM Approach to a Knowledge Discovery Project on Education

Corlane Barclay

Contents

Abstract: Educational data mining (EDM), an emerging subdiscipline, is the process of discovering hidden patterns and knowledge within data from educational repositories (e.g., primary, secondary, and tertiary institutions) and making predictions. The study applies the Cross Industry Standard Process for Data Mining (CRISP-DM) methodology to undertake the set of coordinated steps toward discovering hidden patterns and knowledge in high school data in Jamaica. The initial stage of CRISP-DM is reported in this study, that is, the business understanding (BU) phase, which is reported to be the most significant phase in establishing a sound foundation on which the data mining (DM) project can be executed. Despite the importance of the BU phase, a survey of the DM literature shows there is scant regard to the execution and reporting of this phase. The study underlines the importance of applying a standardized process toward achieving useful results from the knowledge extraction process, while highlighting some important lessons in defining feasible business and DM goals. It also highlights the challenges in obtaining buy-in from data owners and the issue of data stored in different locations, which are some of the issues that ought to be accounted for during the BU phase. This study, therefore, provides significant implications for policy makers and educators, as they consider data analytics approaches to the *big data* phenomenon.

Keywords: Education data mining, data mining, CRISP-DM, education, business understanding, Jamaica

Introduction

Knowledge discovery and data mining (KDDM) activities can yield substantial benefits for any organization and in turn the country as a whole, especially as more and more decision makers are realizing its potential to enhance the decision-making process. For developing countries, in particular, it is imperative that they harness the potential benefits of KDDM to help achieve efficiencies and the development of goals. KDDM is the process of extracting interesting patterns and trends from large datasets (Mansingh et al. 2013). Educational data mining (EDM), a subarea of KDDM, "is an emerging discipline, concerned with developing methods for exploring the unique types of data that come from educational settings, and using those methods to better understand students, and the settings which they learn in" (IEDMS 2013). Understanding the steps involved in maximizing the effectiveness of the results from extracting the knowledge is crucial. Kurgan and Musilek (2006) shared that before making any attempt to perform knowledge extraction, an overall approach guiding how to extract the knowledge is essential. The initial stages can even be considered especially crucial as the understanding of the business objectives, exploring the data, and preparing of the data can impact the reliability of the results from the knowledge extraction process. For example, the first process, business understanding (BU), is sometimes considered to be one of the most important phases of the data mining (DM) process (Sharma and Osei-Bryson 2010). Despite these guidelines, there is a paucity of studies that report on the complete KDDM process or even the BU phase, but instead focus primarily on the knowledge extraction or mining process.

The research project applies the principles of the CRISP-DM process model to aid in profiling high school students' examination performance in Jamaica. The CRISP-DM is generally considered the most popular and most used KDDM process model. It consists of six steps, including the initial and crucial BU phase, which is the focus of this study. This phase consists of obtaining knowledge on the requirements needed to facilitate the successful implementation of the DM project. According to Sharma and Osei-Bryson (2010), BU activities are often implemented in an *ad hoc* manner. Additionally, the published DM case studies rarely provide a detailed description of how this phase can be formally implemented, which would serve as a guide to practitioners. This research underlined the importance of outlining clear business and DM objectives to help assure efficiency, reliability, and confidence in the subsequent phases. The application of standard reference model also facilitates the advantage of providing a clear roadmap for the successful application of each stage.

Examination of public records reveals that EDM is currently not being formally practiced in Jamaica or in other English-speaking Caribbean countries. It is, therefore, reasonable to suggest that there is relatively low adoption and application in the region and likely in other developing countries. However, as a country's education level is one of the principal criteria for national development (Chabbott and Ramirez 2006), it is important to find strategies to provide sustainable solutions, particularly with the effective use of Information and Communication Technologies (ICT). EDM is a viable means to explore and finds ways to understand the identification and improvement of strategies and methods to enhance the performance of students. The relevance of this study is further enhanced by an analysis of the literature that shows that there is no known study that examines educational data through DM from a Caribbean perspective.

In the English-speaking Caribbean countries, the educational system is modeled closely after the U.K. system. At the fifth form stage (i.e., 15–18 age group), students sit the Caribbean Examination Council (CXC), a regional examination for progression to the sixth form, university or work. Based on the reports from the last decade, there have been inconsistent and poor performances by students in core areas such as the English language and mathematics. In Jamaica, for example, the pass rate ranges from 16% to 40% and 28% to 65% for mathematics and English, respectively, based on media reports. Many theories have been put forward to explain, but none has adequately or effectively addressed the problem especially, as the poor performance still persists.

The study offers both research and practitioner contributions. The study contributes to the discourse of the application of standardized processes to KDDM, and extends the knowledge base of EDM. The final results of study are important to the government and educators, as it can help in informing and guiding educational policies and pedagogy to improve student experience and performance at the secondary school level. The study can also help bolster the knowledge level that currently exists on DM and its potential in segments of developing countries such as Jamaica where its application is currently limited. Additionally, the study illustrates the use and application of a process-based approach such as CRISP-DM in addressing important business and educational problems, especially those experienced by developing economies.

Research Background

An Overview of DM

DM is a discipline that allows for the analysis of large datasets with a view of discovering the unknown or indiscernible. Hand et al. (2001) explained that "data mining is the analysis of (often large) observational data sets to find unsuspected relationships and to summarize the data in novel ways that are both understandable and useful to the data owner." Balasubramanian and Umarani (2012) also explained that DM is the process of extracting knowledge from large datasets through the use of algorithms and techniques drawn from the fields of statistics, machine learning, and database management systems.

A large number of organizations have initiated and installed DM projects to leverage the strategic benefits of facilitating improved decision making, which may result in improved performances, increased profits, or understanding of business environment. According to Marbon et al. (2009), the number of DM project applications has increased enormously over the past few years. The multiple advantages of DM can be seen at both the organizational and country levels. For example, it can be used to identify successful marketing strategies to dominate interactive entertainment niches, improve management of product flow through and entire supply chain, detect fraud, and assess risks, among others (Marbon et al. 2009). Sayad and Balke (2000) further explained that DM has helped organization realize unprecedented profits margins. In turn, the country benefits from improved competitiveness.

The successful application of DM techniques to aid organizational decision making can be seen in many domains, which are as follows:

- Profiling Internet-banking users in Jamaica (Mansingh et al. 2013)
- Detecting credit card fraud (Brause et al. 1999; Chan et al. 1999)
- DM and Bayesian methods in biomedicine and health care, in particular critical care (Lucas 2004) and mining of healthcare data (Alonso 2002)
- DM in agriculture for yield prediction (Rub 2000)
- DM in education (Cortez and Silva 2008)
- Financial forecasting (Chun and Park 2006)
- Gene mapping (Kantardzic and Zurada 2005)

Application of Education DM

Applying DM in education is an emerging interdisciplinary research field also known as EDM and is concerned with developing methods for exploring the unique types of data that come from educational environments (IEDMS 2013). Baker (2010) explained that EDM is "the area of scientific inquiry centered on the development of methods for making discoveries within the unique kinds of data that come from educational settings, and using those methods to better understand students and the settings which they learn in." Therefore, the analysis and inquiry to enhance the stakeholders (e.g., students and teachers) experience and performance would form part of the goal of EDM.

Siemens and Baker (2012) explained that EDM has certain characteristics: it has strong origins in educational software, student modeling, and predicting course outcomes; has more emphasis on the description and comparison of the DM techniques used; and automated discovery is essential and, therefore, leveraging human judgment is a tool used to accomplish this goal. EDM can be classified into several approaches and techniques, including prediction, classification, regression, density estimation, clustering, relationship mining, association rule mining, correlation mining, sequential pattern mining, causal DM, distillation of data for human judgment, and discovery with models (Baker 2010).

Some of the applications of these techniques to fulfill the goals of an educational setting include the following:

- A case-study description of the application of several techniques to help in identifying students at risk and who may not have sufficient training (Merceron and Yacef 2005)
- Analysis of tutor–student interactions (Mostow et al. 2005)
- An examination of the effectiveness of an EDM method, learning factors analysis on improving the learning efficiency in the cognitive tutor curriculum (Cen et al. 2007)
- The application of DM in learning management systems and a case-study tutorial with the Moodle system (Romero et al. 2008)
- A comparison of several methods and techniques for classifying students based on their Moodle usage data and the final marks obtained in their respective courses (Romero et al. 2008)

Perspectives on Students' Performance

Several studies have put forward varying perspectives on the reason for poor examination performances. Socioeconomic variables, family size, instructors' styles, and cognitive skills of students are just some of the possible explanations. Harb and El-Shaarawi (2006) shared that factors that may affect students' performance include family size, which differs significantly among different ethnic and economic subgroups. Kennedy and Tay (1994), on the other hand, observed that the age of the student, study effort, and an alignment between students' learning style and instructor's teaching style all have positive effect on performance. Other factors identified include previous schooling, parents' education (Anderson and Benjamin 1994), family income (Devadoss and Foltz 1996), self-motivation and learning preferences (Aripin et al. 2003), and class attendance (Romer 1993).

Report on the Jamaican Experience

Historical data taken from multiple media reports from Jamaica show a poor performance record of students in certain subjects, including the English language and mathematics (see Table 5.1). The data show that for at least the last 10 years between 2002 and 2012, the average percentage of students who successfully sat the mathematics exam was a paltry 31.35% and for the English language, a slightly better but still an unacceptable 46%.

Educators and government ministers have put forward multiple reasons for the poor performance, which could be classified into instructor-based, student-based, infrastructural, and socioeconomic factors. Despite the possible reasons, to date there has been no feasible solutions to the continued lackluster examination results.

Table 5.1 CXC Mathematics and English Pass Rate

Year	English (Pass%)	Mathematics (Pass%)
2002	27.8	15.8
2003	25.3	16.7
2004	46	32
2005	54	36
2006	46	32
2007	45	35
2008	44	36
2009	42	37
2010	64.9	39.5
2011	63.9	33.2
2012	46.2	31.7
Average	45.92%	31.35%

DM Process Models

There are several DM or KDDM process models available that provide some guidance on how to execute DM projects. KDDM process model specifies the phases for producing, deploying, and using DM models, and provides a structure for organizing the DM effort by describing the tasks involved in DM. A KDDM process model consists of a set of processing steps to be followed by practitioners when executing KDDM projects. Such a model describes procedures that are performed in each of the steps, primarily used to plan, work through, and reduce the cost of any given project (Fayyad et al. 1996b). Further, a process approach provides a mechanism for conducting DM in a systematic, disciplined, and structured manner, which can increase the likelihood of getting accurate and reliable results (Sharma and Osei-Bryson 2010), and also improve the level of understanding by the team of the linkages of business and DM goals to the chosen knowledge extraction models. In short, establishing standards for DM is essential especially as it enables effective decision support. Consequently, the use of standards will help to ensure that the process of DM is reliable and repeatable, especially for those persons who are not experts in the field (Mansingh et al. 2013). This guide is even more apt in organizations and countries where DM is still a novel discipline, for example, in Jamaica and the rest of the Caribbean.

The de facto standard industry model is the CRISP-DM (Chapman et al. 2000) while the Select, Explore, Model, Modify, and Assess (SEMMA) (SAS 2013) is another approach. Other models have been developed by researchers (Cios et al. 2000; Fayyad et al. 1996a, 1996b; Sharma and Osei-Bryson 2010). Fayyad et al. (1996b) initially proposed nine steps that included inter alia developing and understanding the application domain, creating target dataset to interpreting minded patterns, and consolidating discovered knowledge. Their model has been attributed as the main foundation from which many perspectives have been derived. The CRISP-DM proposed six steps that are BU, data understanding, data preparation, modeling, evaluation, and deployment. BU is concerned with understanding the project and business requirements and translating these into formulating the DM initiative. Sharma and Osei-Bryson (2010) build on the CRISP-DM model to primarily explicate the substeps and highlight the interconnection between tasks that could in turn aid in semiautomation or efficiency process. Cios et al. (2000) proposed six steps that included understanding the problem domain and data, preparing the data evaluation, and using the discovered knowledge. Additional analysis of some KDDM models developed before 2006 can be found in Kurgan and Musilek (2006).

Research Methodology—CRISP-DM

This study applies the CRISP-DM approach. CRISP-DM was developed by a collection of practitioners from multiple industries after the practitioner community became aware of the need for formal DM process models that prescribe the journey from data to knowledge discovery. Although the original model has been further extended (Sharma and Osei-Bryson 2010), the original model is applied here because of its seminal nature and its steps are generally representative of the activities necessary to implement these projects.

The phases of the CRISP-DM approach include understanding the business problem, capturing and understanding data, applying DM techniques, interpreting results, and deploying the knowledge gained in operations (Chapman et al. 2000) (see Figure 5.1). Figure 5.2 identifies the set of tasks and outcome in each phase of CRISP-DM. The iterative six process steps are explained as follows:

> *Business understanding.* This is the initial phase of the process model where the focus is on understanding the business/research objectives and requirements from a business/research perspective. This knowledge is then converted into a DM problem definition and a preliminary plan designed to achieve the objectives. Consequently, an assessment of the business situation, determination of the DM goals and success criteria, and the DM project plan are outlined.
>
> *Data understanding.* This phase is concerned with obtaining knowledge on and about the data to be explored. It commences with an initial data collection and continues with activities to describe and explore the data, to identify data quality problems, or to discover initial insights into the data. The data can be collected from multiple repositories or developed from manual data, interviews, or from other sources.

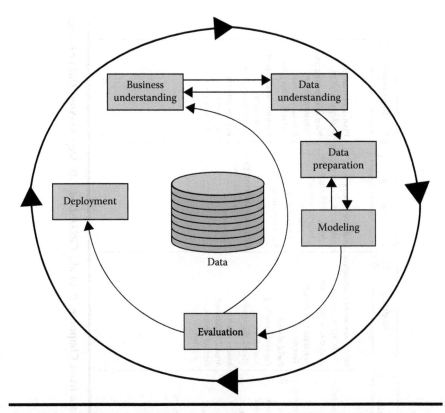

Figure 5.1 CRISP-DM. (Data from Chapman, P. et al., *CRISP-DM 1.0: Step-by-Step Data Mining Guide*, 2000.)

Data preparation. In this phase, the raw data is converted to the format that is required by the modeling tool. The focus in this phase is to select, cleanse, construct, integrate, and format data. This phase is dependent on a thorough understanding of the previous steps to be able to select appropriate attributes to achieve the business and DM goals. Common DM software tools also help in the preparation and/or transformation of data to facilitate modeling phase.

Modeling. In this phase, the information from the previous stages is used to identify the set of applicable DM techniques. This process is semiautomated with software tools such as RapidMiner or SAS Enterprise Miner. The process involves selection of modeling techniques; generation of test design; building of particular models, which involves setting of parameters; and assessing the model.

Evaluation. The results from the DM results are evaluated against the business objectives and success criteria. For example, the top models (e.g., the top two or three from the set of best models) from the modeling phase are evaluated based on the business/research objectives and those that are seen as adding value to the decision makers (Mansingh et al. 2013).

Business understanding	Data understanding	Data preparation	Modeling	Evaluation	Deployment
Determine business objectives *Background* *Business objectives* *Business success criteria*	**Collect initial data** *Initial data collection report*	**Select data** *Rationale for inclusion/ exclusion*	**Select modeling techniques** *Modeling technique* *Modeling assumptions*	**Evaluate results** *Assessment of data mining results with respect to business success criteria* *Approved models*	**Plan deployment** *Deployment plan*
Assess situation *Inventory of resources* *Requirements, assumptions, and constraints* *Risks and contingencies* *Terminology* *Costs and benefits*	**Describe data** *Data description report*	**Clean data** *Data cleaning report*	**Generate test design** *Test design*	**Review process** *Review of process*	**Plan monitoring and maintenance** *Monitoring and maintenance plan*
Determine data mining goals *Data mining goals* *Data mining success criteria*	**Explore data** *Data exploration report*	**Construct data** *Derived attributes* *Generated records*	**Build model** *Parameter settings* *Models* *Model descriptions*	**Determine next steps** *List of possible actions* *decision*	**Produce final report** *Final report* *Final presentation*
Produce project plan *Project plan* *Initial assessment of tools and techniques*	**Verify data quality** *Data quality report*	**Integrate data** *Merged data* **Format data** *Reformatted data* **Dataset** *Dataset description*	**Assess model** *Model assessment* *Revised parameter settings*		**Review project** *Experience documentation*

Figure 5.2 Generic tasks and outputs of CRISP-DM. (Data from Chapman, P. et al., *CRISP-DM 1.0: Step-by-Step Data Mining Guide*, 2000.)

Deployment. Results of the model are presented to the decision maker/user to help improve their knowledge of the data, so that the models can be used in a decision-making environment.

Application of CRISP-DM: BU

The target group for this DM project is students who have taken CXC examinations, which include mathematics and English. Schools from the metropolitan capital and the rural areas will be randomly selected to participate in the study. According to the Ministry of Education's School Profiles 2012–2013 Report, Jamaica has 164 high schools across the 14 parishes and are classified as secondary, technical, and agricultural (MoE 2012). These students would generally be in the range of 15–18 years on taking these examinations during the fourth or fifth year of high school. The overall business objective of this research project is to obtain an understanding of the characteristics or profile of students who perform well and those who perform poorly in CXC mathematics and English. The business problem was the persistently poor performance by high school students in these subjects, as indicated in Table 5.1.

Determine Business Objectives

In an effort to grasp the full extent of the problem, extensive examination of the literature surrounding education in Jamaica was done. This included various research papers done on the topic, transcripts of interviews done with the current and former education ministers, other articles done by various stakeholders within the education sector, and whitepapers. It must be noted that our examination of the literature was not exclusively around or about student failing mathematics and the English language, but rather, focused on the wider education system as it exists in Jamaica. We also relied on anecdotal evidence and our own experiences to inform our understanding of the research problem.

Business Objectives

The specific objectives of the project are as follows:

1. To increase pass rate in mathematics and the English language.
2. To understand the characteristics of the students who fail in mathematics and the English language, in order to mitigate (where possible) against those characteristics and improve the performance in both subjects.
3. To maintain the privacy and security of the data throughout the phases.

It is important to note that the achievement of these objectives will be fully realized or assessed during the evaluation and deployment stages of the project. Additionally, general project objectives such as conformance to budget, time, and scope are also considered.

Business Success Criteria

The business success criteria describe the criteria for a satisfactory or successful outcome of the project from a business viewpoint. In other words, the business success criteria are the basis for the determination of achievement of the business objectives. This involves incorporating objective and measurable outcome to the identified business objectives. The technique espoused in the project performance development framework (PPDF) can be applied to determine the objectives and criteria/measures of the KDDM project (Barclay and Osei-Bryson 2010). In the PPDF, principles from operation research and software engineering are applied to aid in the development and structuring of clear objectives and measures that are aligned with the stakeholders' expectations. From this, the measures or criteria include the following:

1. Improvement in pass-rate percentages (a 5% increase, at minimum, on the average rate) in mathematics and the English language. Specific percentages will be dependent on the deployment strategies as a result of consultations with the education stakeholders.
2. Identification of the characteristics or profile of students (e.g., at minimum, three unique characteristics) who are likely to obtain passes in the English language and mathematics at the CXC level.
3. Identification of characteristics that links certain demographic factors and student performance or pass rate.
4. The attainment of satisfactory results from a security assurance assessment tool that is either developed or adopted for the project.

Situation/Domain Assessment

A preliminary assessment of the situation revealed that the data that resides at the high schools were largely paper based and stored in an *ad hoc* manner. This would have significant implications for the data collection and coding exercise along with the project schedule and costs.

Inventory of Resources

To complete this study, the following resource requirements were identified:

1. Technical personnel, project manager, DM analysts, research assistants, and data entry personnel
2. Access to student and examination data for the period 2008–2013
3. RapidMiner software for data preparation and mining
4. Visual Basic Suite to aid in data preparation
5. Computers to facilitate processing and execution of tasks
6. Microsoft Office Suite

The personnel roles were identified based on the core activities necessary to execute the project. RapidMiner was chosen primarily because it was freely available and had the requisite features to achieve the project's objectives. Similarly, Visual Basic Suite and Office were chosen because of familiarity among the team and their availability for use. Hardware capacity to perform the tasks would be necessary and computers already in the possession of the team were identified. Data is crucial and as such the initial plan was to collect data from schools in the city and rural areas as indicated earlier. The minimum span of three years was identified as providing a good base sample for interrogation and to improve considerations for the feasibility of data collection.

Requirements, Assumptions, and Constraints

The key requirement is access to data that is not readily available or easily accessible based on the current situation in the schools in Jamaica. To enable success, it is assumed that there will be sufficient resources to collect and code the data and that the high schools will be willing to participate and share their data. Financial considerations will be met primarily by the project team; however, there is still a constraint in the availability of funds to facilitate timely collection and coding of data. Access to the DM software, the open source RapidMiner software drastically reduced project costs and eliminated any issue of feasibility and availability in this area. The major constraint included the issue of collecting or getting access to data from schools in all parishes, and the form of data that is available, that is, being largely paper based. Legal constraint in sharing the data was also considered and found to be a minimal risk.

Risks and Contingencies

Risks relate to any positive or negative uncertainty, whereas contingences are any suitable responses to the identified risks. Some of the risks identified were the unwillingness to share data, unavailability of some aspects of the data, unavailability of sufficient personnel to complete specific tasks, and data integrity in coding paper-based records. To help overcome this, participants were informed of the benefits of the project and the adoption of research and legal ethics where data privacy and security assurance protocols would be adhered to. Where the data was unavailable that risk was accepted and schedule was extended to facilitate any shortage in resources. To improve data integrity quality checks, such as reviews, were integrated in the collection and coding activities.

Terminology

A glossary of business and DM terminology to facilitate knowledge elicitation and learning was compiled. The business component was concluded upon the completion of the data collection exercise. Some of the technical terms described were those relating to performance-based criteria such as *lift* and *accuracy*.

Costs and Benefits

The main costs associated with this project were related to the traveling costs for personnel to visit the schools island-wide and the acquisition of computers. Expected benefits were translated primarily to nonmonetary and range from short to long term. Consequently, there is anticipated improvement in operational efficiencies in schools' approach to student performance, general improvements in students' performance in specific subjects, and improvements in data management and increased knowledge in DM and KDDM processes.

Determine DM Goals

DM Goals

DM goals refer to technical representation of the business objectives. In other words, these goals describe the project objectives in technical terms. The DM goals identified are as follows:

1. To predict the type of students who will be likely to pass mathematics and/or the English language given the performance trends over the last two to three years, student demographics and other subjects taken and passed.
2. To find significant clusters that identify the characteristics that are likely to facilitate the pass or fail of certain subjects, including mathematics and/or the English language.

DM Success Criteria

The DM criteria describe the guage for accepting the result from a particular model or use case. The criteria serves as the thresholds or measurements of the DM algorithms that are acceptable to the user, which when evaluated determines if the results it extracted is useful and can be deployed in the organization. The DM success criteria for the objectives are defined in the context of accuracy, precision, and lift for classification types and normalized cluster means, outliers, and variable importance vectors for clustering. The specific measures are linked with the type of data mining algorithm. Therefore, 80% level of accuracy in predicting students likely to pass mathematics is an example of success criteria for this project. The selection of suitable algorithms determines the measures and thresholds, that is, the criteria that are acceptable to the stakeholders. This activity is done after the identification and agreement of the business objectives to ensure alignment between both. Similar principles in identifying business success criteria are applied in identifying DM success criteria.

Produce Project Plan

Project Plan

The project is slated to be completed within six months. The milestones are based on the CRISP-DM process, where the completion of the BU phase and initial data collection are classified as key phases, for example. Table 5.2 shows some of the key activities planned in this project. Note that some aspects of data understanding phase were included, as based on the context of this project, it was necessary to understand the data to better facilitate planning of the project.

Table 5.2   Extract of Project Activities (BU Phase)

Key Activities	Duration (Weeks)	Dependencies (Task #)	Resources Required (Roles)
1. Determine goals and objectives	1	–	Business analyst, data analyst, and project manager
2. Determine criteria and measures	1	1	
3. Assess project feasibility (assess situation)	1	1	Project manager and business analyst
4. Cost/benefit analysis	1	1,2,3,4	Project manager and business analyst
5. Identify resources	1	1	Project manager and business analyst
6. Identify study's participants	1		Project manager and business analyst
7. Develop glossary	1	10	Business analyst, data analyst, and project manager
8. Develop/ disseminate letters of permission	3	1	Project manager and business analyst
9. Obtain software/ hardware	4	2,3,3	Project manager
10. Initial data collection	2	6	Research assistant
11. Initial data entry and coding	4	10	Data entry personnel

Initial Assessment of Tools and Techniques

The software tools identified were deemed suitable for use throughout the phases of the project. Directed and undirected DM techniques were chosen based on the business and DM goals. Continuous assessment and necessary changes or corrective actions are planned throughout the project.

Subsequent Phases of the Project

Data Understanding

Data that included students' demographic information, academic performance, and financial information were targeted as the basis for analysis and discovering knowledge. Some initial data were collected from schools located in Kingston, the largest metropolitan area in Jamaica. Initial assessments of the records stored on the papers were done to determine an appropriate method for extracting the information and transforming it to digital form. The data was subsequently entered directly into a spreadsheet using a prescribed format. The data included school name, student name, subjects taken and results, and parish residence, among other variables. This data was assessed by the team for errors, gaps, and inconsistencies or integrity violations. Missing values relating to demographic data were verified with the original data and the schools and were revised wherever necessary. Missing values relating to subjects were verified for accuracy and where it was accurately a null value it was taken to mean a subject not taken by students.

The initial data collection efforts were hampered by the unwillingness of many schools to share data due to general fear and privacy concerns, this despite our contingency plans at the BU phase. Additionally, the data to facilitate effective decision analysis were stored in disparate locations and offices, and were predominantly paper based. Consequently, alternative plans will be made to get more suitable data, that is, revisiting the BU phase. This experience underlined the iterative steps in the KDDM process.

Data Preparation

The initial data will be initially prepared using MS Excel to fit the requirements of the RapidMiner software. Subjects not taken by students were given a number that fell outside the range of the given examination results. Therefore, illustratively where 1 = distinction, 2 = credit and 3 = pass, and so on, and, therefore, 9 = not taken. Data validity will be managed through multiple persons conducting checks and reviews for completeness and accuracy. Unnecessary attributes will be removed from the overall dataset, leaving only those attributes relevant to the current problem being analyzed.

Modeling

Multiple DM techniques will be used to classify and predict the data including both directed and undirected techniques. Several DM techniques may be applicable to a given dataset to fulfill a particular DM objective, for example, for objectives that require prediction, both decision trees and logistic regression can be used (Osei-Bryson and Giles 2006).

Evaluation

Based on the results, the models will be evaluated against the project (business and DM) objectives and associated success criteria. The models that best accomplish these requirements will be chosen for deployment, that is, the top two or three models will be used. For example, the decision tree model that best represents the requirements will be selected and used as a basis to aid predictive analysis in the deployment phase. Additionally, the preceding steps will be reviewed to identify opportunities for improvement along with the determination of next steps will be undertaken to determine if the project proceed to the next stage or previous steps.

Deployment

Deployment plan will include dissemination of the results to the expected users of extracted knowledge. Therefore, it is anticipated that the results of this project will be shared with government and school officials to help improve their knowledge of the factors that may impact students' performance in mathematics and English. Specifically, the Ministry of Education as well as the CXC, which are mandated with the responsibility of the education sector and the CXC exams, respectively, would be ideal candidates for the DM results.

Concluding Remarks

The importance of DM will continue to grow especially as the volume of data continues to grow at a rapid rate. To obtain real value from the DM projects, a disciplined and structured process must be employed from the beginning to end of the project. This study concentrated on the BU phase of a DM project in the educational domain where a critical issue is one of students' persistently poor performances in the core subjects of mathematics and English in Jamaica. The study underlined that BU phase is nontrivial and is essential to the successful execution of the subsequent phases since it minimizes rework and enables the achievement of the business and DM objectives.

Reports have shown that students perform poorly in mathematics and English at the CXC level in Jamaica, and despite this trend no sustainable solutions have been found. We contend that applying DM process in a standardized form can uncover some previously unknown patterns that can inform government and school officials to help improve their knowledge of the factors that may impact students' performance in these and possibly other subjects. This study reports on the crucial first step in completing this important initiative of improving knowledge on or about students' examination performance at the CXC level in Jamaica. The research offers significant value as there is limited application of structured process approach to DM national level and likely at the regional level. The research contribution is in the form of an illustrated application of the underreported BU phase of KDDM to a known national problem. The research also provides a novel value-adding exploration of an important topic, that is, academic performance of students in a developing country context that resonates with policy makers, educators, and researchers. The study demonstrates the application of a KDDM process model, CRISP-DM, as a framework for social science research. It is hoped that this study will aid in extending the discourse on the use and application of KDDM approaches to specific problems in Jamaica and other developing economies in particular.

Additional activities within this project include further explication of the derivation of business and DM objectives and the identification of techniques to aid in this process, share the application of the CRISP-DM to other stages of the project including the reporting of the final results. Future research includes application of the KDDM approach to other sectors, other areas of education and levels, including primary and tertiary.

References

Alonso, F., Caraça-Valente, J. P., González, A. L., and Montes, C. (2002). Combining expert knowledge and data mining in a medical diagnosis domain. *Expert Systems with Applications*, 23(4), 367–375.

Anderson, G. and Benjamin, D. (1994). The determinants of success in university introductory economics courses. *Journal of Economic Education*, 25(2), 99–119.

Aripin, R., Mahmood, Z., Rohaizad, R., Yeop, U., and Anuar, M. (2003). Students' learning styles and academic performance. *The 22nd Annual SAS Malaysia Forum*, July 15, Kuala Lumpur Convention Center, Kuala Lumpur, Malaysia.

Baker, R. (2010). *Data Mining for Education. International Encyclopedia of Education* (3rd Edn). Oxford: Elsevier.

Balasubramanian, T. and Umarani, R. (2012). Classification: An analysis technique in data mining for health hazards of high levels of fluoride in potable water. *European Journal of Scientific Research*, 78(3), 384–394.

Barclay, C. and Osei-Bryson, K. M. (2010). Project performance development framework: An approach for developing performance criteria & measures for information systems (IS) projects. *International Journal of Production Economics*, 124(1), 272–292.

Brause, R., Langsdorf, T., and Hepp, M. (1999). Neural data mining for credit card fraud detection. *Proceedings of the 11th IEEE International Conference on the Tools with Artificial Intelligence* (pp. 103–106). IEEE.

Cen, H., Koedinger, K. R., and Junker, B. (2007). Is over practice necessary? Improving learning efficiency with the cognitive tutor through educational data mining. *Frontiers in Artificial Intelligence and Applications*, 158, 511.

Chabbott, C. and Ramirez, F. O. (2006). Development and education. In M. T. Hallinan, ed. *Handbook of the Sociology of Education* (pp. 163–187). Springer, New York.

Chan, P. K., Fan, W., Prodromidis, A. L., and Stolfo, S. J. (1999). Distributed data mining in credit card fraud detection. *Intelligent Systems and their Applications, IEEE*, 14(6), 67–74.

Chapman, P., Clinton, J., Kerber, R., Khabaza, T., Reinartz, T., Shearer, C., and Wirth, R. (2000). *CRISP-DM 1.0: Step-by-Step Data Mining Guide*, SPSS Inc.

Chun, S. H. and Park, Y. J. (2006). A new hybrid data mining technique using a regression case based reasoning: Application to financial forecasting. *Expert Systems with Applications, 31*(2), 329–336.

Cios, K. J., Teresinska, A., Konieczna, S., Potocka, J., and Sharma, S. (2000). A knowledge discovery approach to diagnosing myocardial perfusion. *Engineering in Medicine and Biology Magazine, IEEE, 19*(4), 17–25.

Cortez, P. and Silva, A. (2008). Using data mining to predict secondary school student performance. Retrieved from http://repositorium.sdum.uminho.pt/bitstream/1822/8024/1/student.pdf (accessed July 7, 2014).

Devadoss, S. and Foltz, J. (1996). Evaluation of factors influencing student class attendance and performance. *American Journal of Agricultural Economics, 78*(3), 499–507.

Fayyad, U., Piatetsky-Shapiro, G., and Smyth, P. (1996a). From data mining to knowledge discovery in databases. *AI Magazine, 17*(3), 37.

Fayyad, U., Piatetsky-Shapiro, G., and Smyth, P. (1996b). Knowledge discovery and data mining: Towards a unifying framework. *Paper presented at the KDD Conference*. Vol. 96, pp. 82–88.

Hand, D. J., Mannila, H., and Smyth, P. (2001). *Principles of Data Mining (Adaptive Computation and Machine Learning)*. Cambridge, MA: MIT Press.

Harb, N. and El-Shaarawi, A. (2006). Factors affecting students' performance. MPRA Paper No. 13621.

International Educational Data Mining Society (IEDMS). (2013). Educational data mining. Retrieved January 4, 2014, from www.educationaldatamining.org.

Kantardzic, M. and Zurada, J. (2005). *Next Generation of Data-Mining Applications*. Wiley-IEEE Press.

Kennedy, P. and Tay, R. (1994). Students' performance in economics: Does the norm hold across cultural and institutional settings? *Journal of Economic Education, 25*(4): 291–301.

Kurgan, L. A. and Musilek, P. (2006). A survey of Knowledge Discovery and Data Mining process models. *Knowledge Engineering Review, 21*(1), 1–24.

Lucas, P. (2004). Bayesian analysis, pattern analysis, and data mining in health care. *Current Opinion in Critical Care, 10*(5), 399–403.

Mansingh, G., Rao, L., Osei-Bryson, K.-M., and Mills, A. (2013). Profiling internet banking users: A knowledge discovery in data mining process model based approach. *Information Systems Frontiers*, 1–23. Doi:10.1007/s10796-012-9397-2.

Marbon, O., Mariscal, G., and Segovia, J. (2009). A data mining and knowledge discovery process model. Retrieved January 4, 2014, from http://cdn.intechopen.com/pdfs/5937/InTechA_data_mining_amp_knowledgediscovery_process_model.pdf.

Merceron, A. and Yacef, K. (2005). Educational data mining: A case study. In *Artificial Intelligence in Education: Supporting Learning through Socially Informed Technology* (pp. 467–474). Washington, DC: IOS Press.

Ministry of Education (MoE). 2012. Jamaica student profiles 2012–13. Retrieved January 4, 2013, from http://moe.gov.jm/sites/default/files/Profile%202012.pdf.

Mostow, J., Beck, J., Cen, H., Cuneo, A., Gouvea, E., and Heiner, C. (2005). An educational data mining tool to browse tutor-student interactions: Time will tell. *Proceedings of the Workshop on Educational Data Mining, National Conference on Artificial Intelligence*, pp. 15–22.

Osei-Bryson, K. M. and Giles, K. (2006). Splitting methods for decision tree induction: An exploration of the relative performance of two entropy-based families. *Information Systems Frontiers, 8*(3), 195–209.

Romer, D. (1993). Do students go to class? Should they? *Journal of Economic Perspectives, 7*(3),167–174.

Romero, C., Ventura, S., Espejo, P. G., and Hervás, C. (2008). Data mining algorithms to classify students. *Proceedings of Educational Data Mining*, pp. 20–21.

Romero, C., Ventura, S., and García, E. (2008). Data mining in course management systems: Moodle case study and tutorial. *Computers & Education, 51*(1), 368–384.

Ruß, G. (2009). Data mining of agricultural yield data: A comparison of regression models. In Advances in Data Mining: Applications and Theoretical Aspects (pp. 24–37). Berlin; Heidelberg, Germany: Springer.

SAS. (2013). SAS Enterprise Miner—SEMMA. Retrieved December 20, 2013, from http://www.sas.com/offices/europe/uk/technologies/analytics/datamining/miner/semma.html.

Sayad, S. and Balke, S. (2000). *Data Mining Online Book*. Retrieved from www.saedsayad.com.

Sharma, S. and Osei-Bryson, K.-M. (2010). Toward an integrated knowledge discovery and data mining process model. *The Knowledge Engineering Review, 25*(01), 49–67.

Siemens, G. and Baker, R. S. (2012). Learning analytics and educational data mining: Towards communication and collaboration. In: *Proceedings of the 2nd International Conference on Learning Analytics and Knowledge*. pp. 252–254. Vancouver, British Columbia, Canada: ACM.

Chapter 6

A Context-Aware Framework for Supporting the Evaluation of Data Mining Results

Kweku-Muata Osei-Bryson

Contents

Abstract: For many data mining projects, the evaluation phase of the knowledge discovery and data mining (KDDM) process is a challenging one for various reasons. Given this challenge, several studies have presented techniques that could be used for the semiautomated evaluation of data mining results. When taken together, these studies suggest the possibility of a common multicriteria evaluation framework. In this chapter, we present such a framework that utilizes and integrates a pair of established tightly coupled techniques (i.e., value-focused thinking [VFT] and the goal question metric [GQM] methods) as well as established techniques from multicriteria decision analysis (MCDA), in order to explicate and utilize context information to facilitate semiautomated evaluation.

Keywords: Context, data mining process, KDDM, evaluation, decision analysis, multicriteria decision analysis, post-processing

Introduction

Knowledge discovery and data mining (KDDM) is a multiple phase process that essentially consists of the following steps: business (or application domain) understanding, which includes definition of business and data mining (DM) goals; data understanding; data preparation; data mining(or modeling); evaluation (EV; e.g., evaluation of results based on DM goals); and deployment (Kurgan and Musilek 2006). For many DM tasks, the EV phase is a challenging one for various reasons. For example, with regard to decision tree (DT) induction, although the performance measures may be clear (e.g., accuracy, simplicity, and lift), challenges include the need to evaluate a large number of DTs. Gersten et al. (2000) noted that with regard to setting parameter values, there is "no practicable approach to select ... the most promising combinations early in the process" and as such "it is necessary to experiment with different combinations" but "it is very hard to compare that many models and pick the optimal one reliably." Given this challenge, Osei-Bryson (2004) proposed an approach for comparing and selecting the *optimal* DT model given preference and value functions specified by the domain expert(s) are defined beforehand. Choi et al. (2005) and Chen (2007) presented approaches for prioritizing association rules. Osei-Bryson (2005, 2010) also presented approaches for selecting the most appropriate segmentation. Overall, these works describe techniques that could be used for the semiautomated evaluation of DM results. When taken together, they suggest the possibility of a common context-aware multicriteria framework for evaluating the results of DM that accommodates multiple performance measures, supports adequate DM experimentation and the nonburdensome semiautomated evaluation of results from the application of DM techniques. The use of such a multicriteria evaluation framework, however, requires that relevant objectives, measures, and preference function be identified.

This implies that the context of the DM problem is particularly important for the EV phase of the KDDM process. The stakeholders, business objectives (BOs), DM objectives (DMO) and associated performance measures, and the preference function are the major elements in the context of the particular DM problem, with the stakeholders' perspectives being a major factor for determining other elements. Given the identification and definition of the objectives, associated measures and preference function, a multicriteria approach could be used to automatically determine the ranking of the DM results during the EV phase. Several studies, including Osei-Bryson (2004, 2005, 2007, 2008, 2010), Choi et al. (2005), and Chen (2007), have offered this type of context-aware multicriteria approach for post-processing. However, apart from Osei-Bryson (2010), the solution methods of those studies were not explicitly situated within the context of KDDM process models and none (including Osei-Bryson 2010) described how the implications of a given problem context could be explicated in a manner that would facilitate the evaluation of DM output.

In this chapter, we present a KDDM process model based on the common context-aware multicriteria framework for evaluating DM results that includes the explication of business and DMO and performance measures. Our research problem can be considered to involve context-aware support for the selection of *a limited set of the "best"* models (Zopounidis and Doumpos 2002) in order to reduce the cognitive burden on the domain experts in the EV phase of the KDDM process.

Description of Proposed Framework

Description of the Process

In this section, we will describe our extended KDDM process for doing context-aware evaluation. Our description covers the business understanding (BU), modeling (i.e., DM phase), and EV phases, and assumes that activities that are equivalent to other phases (e.g., data understanding and data preparation steps) are done in the usual manner (see Table 6.1).

Sharma and Osei-Bryson (2010) in an earlier work explicated the major links and outputs between the phases of the KDDM process model (e.g., see Figure 6.1). Assuming that the stakeholders, BOs, DMO and associated performance measures, and the preference function are the major elements of the context of a given DM problem, this context would be explicated in the BU, and utilized in later phases of the KDDM process. Given the activities listed in Table 6.1, outputs of the BU phase would include the set of performance measures (i.e., substeps BU:b, d, e), preference function (i.e., substep BU:j), and value functions (i.e., substep BU:k). Given the preference function (e.g., including weights, if relevant) and the set of

Table 6.1 Steps of Adjusted DM Process Model

Phase	Tasks
Business understanding (BU)	1. Identify stakeholders.
	2. Define business goals and success criteria.
	3. Learn current solutions and domain terminology.
	4. Use hybrid VFT method to translate business goals into actionable DM goals (i.e., DM goals and non-DM goals). If none of the goals can be considered to be a DM goal, the given business problem is not a DM problem.
	5. Use the goal question metric method to generate DM performance measures that correspond to DM goals along with corresponding thresholds (that will be used to evaluate DM success criteria).
	6. Do preliminary identification of relevant data.
	7. Select specific DM methods (e.g., regression, DT induction, and clustering) plus their parameter settings for use in the modeling (i.e., DM) phase.
	8. Determine whether available DM software offer adequate facilities for applying the selected DM methods.
	9. Assess whether available DM software can directly or indirectly provide data for all the identified DM MO performance measures.
	10. Elicit preference functions from domain experts (e.g., weights obtained using the AHP) that will be used in the evaluation step for comparing models.
	11. Elicit from domain experts value functions that may be relevant for some measures and DM methods (e.g., trapezoidal value functions for simplicity).
Data mining (DM)	1. Apply to the prepared data, each DM method that was selected in the BU phase.
	2. Record the resulting data that corresponds to the DM performance measures elicited in the BU phase.

Table 6.1 (*Continued*) Steps of Adjusted DM Process Model

Phase	Tasks
Evaluation (EV)	Evaluation of the generated knowledge from the business perspective: 1. Exclude models that do not satisfy the relevant threshold for any of the performance measures. 2. For each model, use the preference function to generate a composite performance score for that model. 3. Rank models in descending sequence based on the composite score.

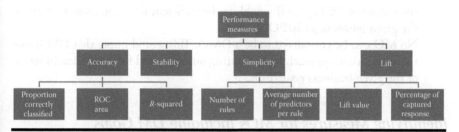

Figure 6.1   An hierarchy of measures for evaluating DTs.

DM performance measures it is then possible to use multicriteria decision-making (MCDM) techniques such as the Analytic Hierarchy Process (AHP) to do automatic ranking in the EV phase of the multiple DM models that would have been generated in the DM phase.

Generating DM Goals from BOs

Several approaches could be used to identify the appropriate set of DMO that correspond to a given set of BOs. One such approach is the value-focused thinking (VFT), proposed by Keeney (1992, 1996), that provides explicit guidance on the formulation of objectives, an indispensable task in any decision-making situation. VFT has been applied across a wide variety of domains (Kajanus et al. 2004) and systems engineering (Boylan et al. 2006).

VFT assumes three different types of objectives: fundamental objectives (FOs), means objectives (MO), and strategic objectives. FOs concern the ends that decision makers value in a particular decision context, whereas MOs are the methods to achieve the ends. Strategic objectives provide common guidance for more detailed FOs.

VFT can be done in a top-down or bottom manner, with our focus being on the former. In a top-down approach MOs are obtained from FOs by determining for each FO all the immediate lower level things that must be done satisfactorily (i.e., MO) in order to achieve the given FO. Lower level MOs can be obtained for next higher level MOs in a similar manner. The result is a network of objectives with the FOs at the root level and a set of MOs at the leaf level. Each leaf level MO can be considered to be equivalent to an actionable goal.

VFT can be used to provide a formal process to go from the BOs to the DMOs. For our purposes, the BOs are the FOs, whereas each leaf level MO may be a DMO. Now, it is possible that for a given FO (i.e., BO), not each associated MO would be a DMO. Therefore, let us consider the following three possibilities that could occur:

1. Each MO is a DMO. This would imply that the output of DM by itself would be sufficient for evaluation in terms of the given business goals/BOs.
2. Some MOs are DMOs while others are not DMOs. This would imply that the output of DM by itself would not be sufficient for evaluation in terms of the given business goals/BOs.
3. No MO can be considered to be a DMO. This would imply that DM is not the appropriate approach for generating output useful for evaluation in terms of the given business goals/BOs.

Identifying Measures for MOs Including DM Goals

Overview on the Goal Question Metric Method

Goal question metric (GQM) method (Basili and Weiss 1984; Basili and Rombach 1988) is a formal approach for generating appropriate measures for a given set of goals. It has been applied in various areas (Basili and Weiss 1984; Basili et al. 1994; Esteves et al. 2003). GQM involves the development of a top-down hierarchical structure consisting of three components: goals, questions, and metrics. A *goal* (e.g., DMO) can be refined into a set of *questions*, each of which can be refined into a set of quantitative and/or qualitative *metrics*. Our use of the GQM method begins with a set of specified goals that are the leaf level MOs, which result from the application of the VFT method. Next for each goal, relevant questions would be elicited from relevant stakeholders. Finally, for each question, relevant metrics would be identified.

Illustration of the GQM Method

There are several possible goals for a clustering exercise. In this chapter, for the purpose of illustration, we will focus on three clustering goals (Table 6.2):

1. *Segmentation should exclude outliers*: This problem has several applications, including the sample heterogeneity status test for data envelopment analysis (e.g., Samoilenko and Osei-Bryson 2008).

Table 6.2 Metrics Resulting from the Application of GQM Method to Illustrative Goals

Goal	Question(s)	Metric
Segmentation should exclude outliers	• What are the characteristics of an outlier cluster? (One simple approach would involve a threshold (i.e., $\tau_{Outlier\_Size}$) on the size of an outlier cluster.) • What is the maximum number of outlier clusters that should be in an "acceptable" segmentation?	• Number of outlier clusters
Segmentation should include a pair of clusters that provide the lowest and highest means for each variable	• Is there a pair of clusters that in the segmentation provides the smallest and largest means for all the variables?	• Let $\rho_{(k1, k2)}$ be the proportion of variables for which clusters (C_{k1}, C_{k2}) provides the minimum and maximum mean values • $\rho_{t(*, *)} = Max \{\rho_{(k1, k2)}:$ $k_1 \neq k_2\}$ is the performance of the given segmentation t, where $\rho_{t(*, *)} \in [0,1]$ with 1 being the ideal value
Segmentation should include user-specified variables as important discriminating variables	• How similar is the discriminating variables of the segmentation to the user-specified variables?	• Cosine of the importance vector of the segmentation to the user-specified importance vector

2. *Segmentation should include a pair of clusters that provide the lowest and highest means for each variable:* An example of this problem is a theory-building study (Wallace et al. 2004) where the interest was in finding clusters that provide the characteristics that could be used to describe low-, medium-, and high-risk projects.

3. *Segmentation should include user-specified variables as important discriminating variables:* There are several reasons why this goal may be important to users. For example, as noted by Huang et al. (2005): "It is well-known that an interesting clustering structure usually occurs in a subspace defined by a subset of

the initially selected variables. To find the clustering structure, it is important to identify the subset of variables." Then this could also be relevant for theory-building exercises.

Some Measures for DM Problems

In the previous section, we presented an approach for generating performance measures for DM problem, and offered an illustration as to how this approach could be applied to generate metrics for a clustering problem. In this section, we provide some previously proposed performance measures for evaluating DTs and association rules. We also present corresponding hierarchies of measures. The fact that a set of relevant performance measures (e.g., Tables 6.3 and 6.4; Figure 6.1) related

Table 6.3 Description of Measures for Evaluating

Measure	Description
Accuracy	The most commonly used accuracy measure for problems with discrete targets is the *proportion correctly classified*; for problems with interval targets it is the R-*squared*, or the average squared error is often used.
	For problems with binary target variables and a specified target event, various combinations of *sensitivity* and *specificity* have also been considered as measures of accuracy including the *area under the ROC curve*
Loss or profit	Used instead of accuracy if either there is unequal misclassification cost (i.e., loss) for the different target events or there is unequal classification gain (i.e., profit) for the different target events. The objective is to maximize profit or minimize loss. Focus could be on all target events or target event in top ρ percent
Simplicity	In situations when the rules are to be applied by human beings rather than computers, there is the concern that the DT should be interpretable, thus facilitating ease of use. Thus, this measure is based on the following: • The number of rules in the DT. • The average number of predictor variables of the corresponding rules.
Stability	This measure concerns our interest that there should not be much variation in this *accuracy rate* when a predictive model (e.g., DT) is applied to different datasets. Thus, at a minimum one might expect that there should not be much variation in predictive accuracy of the given predictive model on the validation dataset when compared to that for the training dataset.

Table 6.3 (*Continued*) Description of Measures for Evaluating

Measure	Description
Lift	This set of measures concerns the relative improvement over the baseline that is provided by the given DT and is relevant for problems with binary target variables. It is used in database marketing applications, and much of the terminology arises from this application. Thus, a *responder* is an individual who responded positively to an offer. However, this performance measure is also relevant for other applications. There are multiple lift measures, two of which are outlined below: • *Captured lift response*: "What is the relative importance over the base line in terms of the probability of the target event?" In a good model, the lift will be greater than 1 decile that is smaller than the prior probability of the target event. • *Percentage of captured lift response* answers the question: "What percentage of total responders are in a bin?"

Table 6.4 Description of Some Measures for Evaluating Association Rules

Measure	Description
Support(A ⇒ B)	• Prob(A ∩ B)
Confidence(A ⇒ B)	• Prob(A ∩ B)/Prob(A)
Confidence(A ⇒ B)	• *Confidence*(A ⇒ B)/Prob(A)
Reliability(A ⇒ B)	• *Confidence*(A ⇒ B) – Prob(B)
Recency(A ⇒ B)[a]	• The time trend of a rule between time intervals • A higher value implies a higher worth of attention to a rule • This factor can be measured with the attribute of the *degree of change* in *Support*
Interest factor(A ⇒ B)[a]	• The ratio between the joint probability of two variables with respect to their expected probabilities under the independence assumption
Expected monetary value (A ⇒ B)[a]	• The expected profit after buying a product X is equal to the probability of buying Y, given X multiplied by the profit of Y
Incremental monetary value (A ⇒ B)[a]	• Expected profit minus the profit you would expect to receive due to the natural course of a customer's purchasing

[a] Data from Choi, B. et al., *Expert Systems with Applications*, 29, 867–878, 2005.

to the given DM objectives can be generated for a given DM problem suggests that a common framework that includes MCDA techniques could be used to evaluate and generate the DM models.

Overview on MCDM Problems

In formal terms, MCDM problems are said to involve the prioritization of a set of alternatives in situations that involve multiple, sometimes conflicting criteria. MCDM problems may be addressed informally or formally. In the informal approaches while there might be acknowledgment that multiple criteria are involved, there is either no formal identification of the relevant criteria, or no formal approach to evaluation, or no formal approach to the synthesis of each alternative's criteria ratings. Thus, unarticulated, implicit decision-making procedures are used to determine the ranking of the alternatives. In some cases, the use of these informal approaches amounts to pretending that a multiple criteria decision is in fact a single-criteria decision. It is, therefore, advisable to use formal approaches for addressing MCDM problems.

While any formal model will suffer from the disadvantage of screening out some aspects of the decision-making problem, all alternatives can be treated consistently, evaluations can be reviewed, and the basis for the ranking of the alternatives can be articulated and justified within the context of the model. Various formal techniques have been proposed, including the weighing model, which is a popular formulation for MCDM and other problems (e.g., Hodgkin et al. 2004; Ngai 2003; Park and Han 2002; Bryson 1999), that have relative simplicity and intuitive appeal. In our illustrative example, we will utilize on the weighing model formulation.

MCDM problems often have no single alternative that provides the best value for each criterion. Rather for each problem, there is a set of alternatives that are said to be *nondominated*. An alternative is nondominated if there is no other alternative that outscores it with regard to each criterion. Given that MCDM problems do not, in general, have an objectively unique *best* alternative, then procedures for addressing these problems cannot *solve* them. Rather, such procedures aid the decision maker(s) in analyzing the given decision-making problem, and facilitate the identification of a ranking of the alternatives that is consistent with the decision maker's beliefs in the importance of the various criteria. Such a procedure is thus often referred to as being a multiple criteria decision aid (MCDA). Multiple criteria decision aids that are based on the weighing model formulation to MCDA follow the general procedure outlined below:

1. Identification of the relevant criteria, and structuring of the relationships between these criteria
2. Determination of the importance ratings (or weights) for the relevant criteria

3. Specification of feasibility threshold values for the criteria
4. Determination of the score for each criterion for each alternative
5. Elimination of alternatives that do not satisfy the criteria feasibility threshold values
6. Computation of the composite score for each alternative as the weighted sum of the alternative's scores with regard to the criteria
7. Computation of ranks for alternatives based on their composite scores

A Preference Function: The Weighting Model

The weighting model formulation will involve implicitly computing each DM Model M_k's composite score as the weighted sum of its performance with regard to the individual measures. Thus, for given DM model "M_k," the composite score would be $s_k = \sum_{j \in J} v_{kj} w_j$, where v_{kj} and w_j are the value and weight of performance measure "j", respectively, for model M_k for the given evaluation problem. Given a pair of generated DM models, M_h and M_k are our set of weights and M_h would be preferable to M_k if $s_h > s_k$.

The weighing model obviously requires the specification of a set of non-negative weights for our performance measures. Various approaches are available for generating weights w_j from the subjective inputs of evaluators, both for individual and group decision-making contexts, and for situations where the inputs are precise or imprecise including those that involve the use of pairwise comparison matrices (e.g., Saaty 1980; Bryson 1995; Bryson et al. 1995; Bryson and Joseph 1999, 2000; Choo and Wedley 2004). Some of these techniques have been previously used to address various other problems in computer science and information systems (e.g., Monti and Carenini 2000; Ngai 2003; Osei-Bryson 2004; Park and Han 2002).

The use of these weight vector generation techniques requires estimates of the relative importance of pairs of performance measures, and result in a weight vector that is a synthesis of the input pairwise comparison information. A pairwise comparison matrix is $N \times N$ matrix $A = \{a_{ij}\}$, where a_{ij} is a positive rational number that is the numerical equivalent of the relative importance of object "i" compared to object "j." The pairwise comparison matrix A is said to be consistent if for each triple of objects (i, j, k), the equality $a_{ij} = a_{ik} a_{kj}$ holds; otherwise, it is said to be inconsistent. Now because the matrix A is sometimes inconsistent, it is necessary to measure its level of inconsistency in order to determine if the resulting weight vector "w" will be meaningful. Consistency measures have been proposed by various researchers (e.g., Saaty 1980; Bryson 1995; Salo and Hämäläinen 1997; Osei-Bryson 2006). Some commercial MCDM software (e.g., Expert Choice) provides tools for elicitation of pairwise comparison data from evaluator(s), after which the associated consistency measure and weight vectors are automatically generated.

Illustrative Example

Overview on the Illustrative Problem and Dataset

Our illustrative problem involves the clustering of the *Asia* magazine dataset. This illustrative dataset contains business-related data (e.g., number of employees; various measures of sales, assets, equity, and profit) for 1996 on 1000 companies that was compiled by *Asiaweek* magazine.

Application of the Evaluation Framework

BU Phase

Steps BU:b–BU:e
We will assume that:

- The clustering goals are the same as those described in section "Illustration of the GQM Method," namely, segmentation should exclude outliers; segmentation should include a pair of clusters that provide the lowest and highest means for each variable (i.e., *Max:Min*); and segmentation should include user-specified variables as important discriminating variables (i.e., *variable importance*).

- The corresponding measures are those described in Table 6.2, namely, *Max:Min Proportion* $\rho_{t(*, *)}$ for the *Max:Min* goal and $\cos(w, v^t)$ for the *variable importance* goal.

- The thresholds for *Max:Min Proportion* $\rho_{t(*, *)}$ and $\cos(w, v^t)$ are both 0.70. For the outlier goal, only segmentations that have no outlier clusters are to be considered.

- The target preference vector for the *variable importance* goal is displayed in Table 6.5.

Steps BU:f–BU:i
The relevant DM technique is clustering. The available DM software is SAS Enterprise Miner. It was decided to generate several segmentations by varying the following two parameters: similarity measure (i.e., least squares, mean absolute deviation [MAD], Newton, and modified Ekblom–Newton) and variable transformation method (i.e., none, range, and standard deviation). The *Max:Min* goal requires that each segmentation involves at least three clusters. It was decided that each segmentation would have three clusters.

Table 6.5 Variable Importance Goal: Target Preference Vector *w*

Target	(0.111,0.013,0.000,0.034,0.000,0.000,0.091,0.149,0.000,0.180,0.211,0.115, 0.0978,0.000,0.000,0.000,0.000,0.000)

Step BU:j

- The preference function is $s_t = \omega_{MM} * \rho_{t(*, *)} + \omega_{VI} * \cos(w, v^t)$, where ω_{MM} and ω_{VI} are the weights for the *Max:Min* and *variable importance* goals, respectively. It should be noted that as all the segmentations have to be nonoutlier segmentations, it is not necessary to explicitly include a weight for the outlier goal.
- The domain expert(s) used the AHP to generate the normalized weight vector, ($\omega_{MM} = 0.55$; $\omega_{VI} = 0.45$) for the Max:Min and variable importance clustering goals.

Step BU:k

For each clustering goal, the scores for each measure is to be standardized to take their values from the [0,1] interval.

DM Phase

Step DM:a—Apply Clustering to Generate the Segmentations

Table 6.6 displays the parameter settings associated with the five segmentations of our illustrative example.

Step DM:b—Record the Performance Measures for each Segmentation

Given that the five segmentations have been generated, the scores of each segmentation for the *Max:Min* and variable importance goals can be calculated and recorded. Tables 6.7, 6.8, 6.9a, and 6.9b displays the relevant scores and some intermediate results.

EV Phase

Step EV(a): Exclude Models That Do Not Satisfy All Thresholds

All five segmentations satisfy the thresholds for all clustering goals.

Table 6.6   Parameter Settings for Segmentations

			Result	
Label	Similarity Measure	Transform Method	Sizes of Clusters	Outliers
DS3	MAD	Standard Deviation	514,122,364	No
ER3	EK	Range	498, 115,387	No
ES3	EK	Standard Deviation	498, 115,387	No
LS3	LS	Standard Deviation	517,56,425	No
NS3	NT	Standard Deviation	384,365,251	No

EK, modified Ekblom–Newton; LS, least squares; MAD, mean absolute deviation; NT, Newton.

Table 6.7 Detailed Results of Max:Min Procedure on Segmentation DS3

Variable	Clusters	
	Min	Max
SALES1	C1	C2
SALES2	C2	C3
NETPROF1	C1	C2
ASSETS1	C1	C2
ASSETS2	C2	C1
EQUITY1	C1	C2
EQUITY2	C2	C1
EMPLOY1	C1	C2
EMPLOY2	C2	C1
$\rho_{DNS3(C1,C2)} = 8/9 = 0.889$; $\rho_{DNS3(C2,C3)} = 1/9 = 0.111$		
$\rho_{DNS3(*,*)} = $ Max $\{\rho_{DNS3(C1,C2)}, \rho_{DNS3(C2,C3)}\}$ $= $ Max $\{0.889, 0.111\} = 0.889$		

Table 6.8 Scores of Segmentations: Max:Min Goal

Label	Max:Min Proportion $\rho_{t(*,\,*)}$
DS3	1.000
ER3	0.889
ES3	1.000
LS3	0.875
NS3	0.750

Step EV(b): Compute Composite Scores for Segmentations

The composite scores (i.e., $s_t = 0.55 * \rho_{t(*,\,*)} + 0.45 * \cos[w, v']$) of the segmentations are automatically calculated (see Table 6.10).

Step EV(c): Rank Segmentations Based on Composite Scores

The segmentations are ordered in descending sequence based on their composite scores (see Table 6.10).

Table 6.9a   Example—Variable Importance Vector for DS3

Variable	Relative Weights
SALES1	0.2271
SALES2	0.2513
SALES3	0.0000
NETPROF1	0.2026
NETPROF2	0.0000
NETPROF3	0.0000
ASSETS1	0.2513
ASSETS2	0.4074
SALEPER1	0.0000
EQUITY1	0.1884
EQUITY2	1.0000
EMPLOY1	0.2843
EMPLOY2	0.2742
PROFPER	0.0000
MARKTCAP	0.0000
PROFTAS1	0.0000
PROFTAS2	0.0000
PROFTAS3	0.0000

Table 6.9b   Variable Importance Goal: Scores of Segmentations

Label	Variable Importance Vector v^t	$\cos(w, v^t)$
DS3	(0.227,0.154,0.000,0.203,0.000,0.000,0.251,0.407,0.000,0.188, 1.000,0.284,0.274,0.000,0.000,0.000,0.000,0.000)	0.899
ER3	(0.344,0.124,0.000,0.159,0.000,0.000,0.202,1.000,0.000,0.493, 0.901,0.567,0.415,0.000, 0.000,0.000,0.000,0.000)	0.969
ES3	(0.143,0.000,0.000,0.177,0.000,0.189,0.168,0.394,0.000,0.151, 1.000,0.368,0.000,0.000, 0.000,0.000,0.000,0.000)	0.816

(Continued)

Table 6.9b (*Continued*)   Variable Importance Goal: Scores of Segmentations

Label	Variable Importance Vector v^t	$cos(w, v^t)$
vLS3	(0.588,0.000,0.000,0.135,0.000,0.000,0.546,0.345,0.000,1.000, 0.910,0.432,0.426,0.000,0.000,0.000,0.000,0.000)	0.950
NS3	(0.000,0.000,0.000,0.270,0.000,0.000,0.181,0.549,0.000,0.214, 1.000,0.202,0.272,0.000,0.402,0.000,0.000,0.000)	0.830

Table 6.10   Results of Application of Step EV(c)

Label	Max:Min Proportion $\rho_{t(*,*)}$	Variable Importance $cos(w, v^t)$	Composite Score
DS3	1.000	0.899	0.955
ER3	0.889	0.969	0.925
ES3	1.000	0.816	0.917
LS3	0.875	0.950	0.909
NS3	0.750	0.830	0.786

Conclusion

The KDDM process is a multiple phase process that includes the BU, DM, and evaluation (e.g., evaluation of results based on DM goals), and deployment (Kurgan and Musilek 2006). Although modern commercial DM software simplifies the execution of the DM phase, for many DM problem types and instances, the EV phase can be a challenging one for various reasons. The KDDM process models can, however, be extended in a manner that reduces this challenge. In this chapter, we have presented a formal approach for the context-based evaluation by domain expert(s) of DM results that is based on DM process models such as Cross Industry Standard Process for Data Mining (CRISP-DM). Our framework utilizes and integrates a pair of established tightly coupled techniques (i.e., VFT and the GQM) as well as established techniques from MCDA, in order to explicate and utilize context information. This framework offers a semiautomated multistep multicriteria-based decision-support process that facilitates the domain expert's efforts for selecting the *best* model in a manner that is not cognitively burdensome while being consistent with the specified DM goals.

Acknowledgment

Materials in this chapter previously appeared in: "A context-aware data mining process model based framework for supporting evaluation of data mining results," *Expert Systems with Applications* **39:1**, 1156–1164 (2012).

References

Basili, V., Caldiera, G., and Rombach, H. (1994) "The goal question metric approach," *Encyclopedia of Software Engineering*.

Basili, V. R. and Rombach, H. D. (1988) "The TAME Project: Towards improvement–oriented software environments." *IEEE Transactions on Software Engineering* **14:6**, 758–773.

Basili, V. and Weiss, D. (1984) "A methodology for collecting valid software engineering data," *IEEE Transactions on Software Engineering* **10:6**, 728–738.

Boylan, G. L., Tollefson, E. S., Kwinn, M., and Guckert, R. (2006) "Using value-focused thinking to select a simulation tool for the acquisition of infantry soldier systems," *Systems Engineering* **9:3**, 199–212.

Bryson, N. (1995) "A goal programming for generating priority vectors," *Journal of the Operational Research Society* **46**, 641–648.

Bryson, N., Mobolurin, A., and Ngwenyama, O. (1995) "Modelling pairwise comparisons on ratio scales," *European Journal of Operational Research* **83**, 639–654.

Bryson, N. (K.-M.) and Joseph, A. (1999) "Generating consensus priority point vectors," *Computers & Operations Research* **26**, 637–643.

Bryson, N. (K.-M.) and Joseph, A. (2000) "Generating consensus priority interval vectors for group decision making in the AHP," *Journal of Multi-Criteria Decision Analysis* **9:4**, 127–137.

Chen, M.-C. (2007) "Ranking discovered rules from data mining with multiple criteria by data envelopment analysis," *Expert Systems with Applications* **33**, 1110–1116.

Choi, B., Ahn, B., and Kim, S. (2005) "Prioritization of association rules in data mining: Multiple criteria decision approach," *Expert Systems with Applications* **29**, 867–878.

Choo, E. and Wedley, W. (2004) "A Common Framework for Deriving Preference Values from Pairwise Comparison Matrices," *Computers & Operations Research* **31**, 893–908.

Esteves, J. M., Pastor, J., and Casanovas, J. (2003) "A goal/question/metric research proposal to monitor user involvement and participation in ERP implementation projects," *Proceedings of the 2003 Conference of the Information Resources Management Association*, Philadelphia, PA.

Gersten, W., Wirth, R., and Arndt, D. (2000) "Predictive modeling in automotive direct marketing: tools, experiences and open issues," *Proceedings of the 6th ACM SIGKDD International Conference on Data Mining and Knowledge Discovery*, 398–406.

Hodgkin, J., Pedro, J., and Burstein, F. (2004) "Quality of Data Model For Supporting Mobile Decision Making," *Proceedings of the 2004 IFIP TC8/WG8.3 International Conference: Decision Support in an Uncertain and Complex World*, 372–379.

Huang, J., Ng, M., Rong, H., and Li, Z. (2005) "Automated variable weighting in k-means type clustering," *IEEE Transactions on Pattern Analysis and Machine Intelligence* **27:5**, 657–668.

Kajanus, M., Kangas, J., and Kurtilla, M. (2004) "The use of value focused thinking and the A'WOT hybrid method in tourism management," *Tourism Management* **25:4**, 499–506.

Keeney, R. L. (1992) *Value-Focused Thinking: A Path to Creative Decision Making*. Cambridge, MA: Harvard University Press.

Keeney, R. L. (1996) "Value-focused thinking: Identifying decision opportunities and creating alternatives." *European Journal of Operational Research* **92**, 537–549.

Kurgan, L. and Musilek, P. (2006) "A survey of knowledge discovery and data mining process models," *The Knowledge Engineering Review* **21:1**, 1–24.

Monti, S. and Carenini, G. (2000) "Dealing with the expert inconsistency in probability elicitation," *IEEE Transactions on Knowledge and Data Engineering* **12:4**, 499–508.

Ngai, E. (2003) "Selection of web sites for online advertising using the AHP," *Information and Management* **40**, 233–242.

Osei-Bryson, K.-M. (2004) "Evaluation of decision trees: A multi-criteria approach," *Computers & Operations Research* **31:11**, 1933–1945.

Osei-Bryson, K.-M. (2005) "Assessing cluster quality using multiple measures," *The Next Wave in Computing, Optimization, and Decision Technologies* 371–384.

Osei-Bryson, K.-M. (2006) "An action learning approach for assessing the consistency of pairwise comparison data," *European Journal of Operational Research* **174:1**, 234–244.

Osei-Bryson, K.-M. (2007) "Post-pruning in decision tree induction using multiple performance measures," *Computers & Operations Research* **34:11**, 3331–3345.

Osei-Bryson, K.-M. (2008) "Post-pruning in regression tree induction: An integrated approach," *Expert Systems with Applications* **34:2**, 1481–1490.

Osei-Bryson, K.-M. (2010) "Towards supporting expert evaluation of clustering results using a data mining process model," *Information Sciences* **180**, 414–431.

Park, C.-S. and Han, I. (2002) "A case-based reasoning with the feature weights derived by analytic hierarchy process for bankruptcy prediction," *Expert Systems with Applications* **23:3**, 255–264.

Saaty, T. (1980) *The Analytic Hierarchy Process: Planning, Priority Setting, Resource Allocation*, McGraw-Hill, New York.

Salo, A. and Hämäläinen, R. (1997) "On the measurement of preferences in the analytic hierarchy process" (and comments by V. Belton, E. Choo, T. Donegan, T. Gear, T. Saaty, B. Schoner, A. Stam, M. Weber, B. Wedley), *Journal of Multi-Criteria Decision Analysis* **6**, 309–343.

Samoilenko, S. and Osei-Bryson, K.-M. (2008) "Increasing the discriminatory power of DEA in the presence of the sample heterogeneity with cluster analysis and decision trees," *Expert Systems with Applications* **34:2**, 1568–1581.

Sharma, S. and Osei-Bryson, K.-M. (2010) "Towards an integrated knowledge discovery and data mining process model," *Knowledge Engineering Review* **25:1**, 49–67.

Wallace, L., Keil, M., and Rai, A. (2004) "Understanding software project risk: A cluster analysis," *Information & Management* **42**, 115–125.

Zopounidis, C. and Doumpos, M. (2002) "Multicriteria classification and sorting methods: A literature review," *European Journal of Operational Research* **138**, 229–246.

KDDM AND ORGANIZATIONAL PERFORMANCE

III

KDDM AND ORGANIZATIONAL PERFORMANCE

Chapter 7

Issues and Considerations in the Application of Data Mining in Business

Edward Chen

Contents

Abstract: This chapter discusses the importance, procedures, practical examples, and current issues surrounding data mining. Data mining is an imperative part of doing business in today's economy. In the wake of the global financial crisis of 2008–2009, businesses of all industries and sizes are looking for ways to increase efficiency and decrease expenses. With the advancement of information and communication technology devices and data analytics software, data mining has emerged as a solution tool kit for organizations. Properly employing the practice of data mining techniques may lead to added sales, decreased operational expenses, and increased profits. A case analysis of a company applying data mining in various business problems is examined, along with a review on a leading data mining software, Waikato Environment for Knowledge Analysis (Weka). Observations on data mining's key positive and negative features and issues are also discussed in this chapter.

Keywords: Data mining, big data, data analytics, Weka, privacy

Introduction

Is this wireless customer about to change to another cell phone company? Is it time to send this chicken to slaughter or should she be left to produce eggs for another season? Should the diapers be farther from or closer to the beer? These may appear to be completely random questions but they can all be solved through the use of data mining. Data mining is the collection, refinement, analysis, and interpretation of raw data. This process is used in a myriad of industries to solve countless questions in an effort to increase sales and efficiency while decreasing cost (Hand et al. 2001; Han et al. 2011).

One of the key steps in data mining is the collection of raw data. This can be done in any number of ways depending on the industry. For example, in the retail industry, data mining is often seen in the form of loyalty cards, which log all purchases made by a consumer in conjunction with their demographic information. Alternatively, in the healthcare industry, patient information is taken at the time of admission. In some industries, this information can be taken from the consumers against their will or without their knowledge at all. Regardless of how it is assembled, all data collected is pooled together into what is known as "raw data." Raw data is data that has not been edited or, by industry standards, is not *clean*. The data is considered raw because it may have inconsistencies, duplicate entries, format errors, or other data quality issues. Once these issues are resolved the data is then known as "clean data" (IBM 2010; Witten et al. 2011).

After the data is *cleaned*, it can then be analyzed or entered into data mining software such as Weka. This software will then analyze the data by a set of parameters. From there, the software will draw conclusions that the individual can interpret and decide how the data can best be used. The conclusions drawn from the decision-making software can help to determine business practices such as merchandise placement in a store. The determination is made by identifying which demographic is most likely to buy a specific product together with any number of other goods at a retail center.

Upper management can then take that information and use it to the business' advantage. For example, the most popular items could be separated in the store, so that the customer is likely to pick something else up on their way from popular product section. This information can also allow management to know which items the store should have readily available or in stock at all times. In the case of our farmer who questioned, "Is it time to send this chicken to slaughter or should she be left to produce eggs for another season?" data may determine each chicken's potential profitability in laying eggs for another season versus going to slaughter. This could be determined by the chicken's age, feeding habits, health, current egg output, or any number of variables. The potential of data collected and the implications it can draw are truly limitless. Aggarwal et al. (2012) list the standard data mining process from problem definition, data exploration, data preparation, monitoring, evaluation, to deployment. The cycle will repeat itself from start to finish as data mining is a never-ending process (Aggarwal et al. 2012).

Emerging Trend of Data Mining

In the third century B.C., it was widely held that the libraries in Alexandria were the pinnacle of human data collection. Today, if the sum of the world's current data were distributed evenly to every human around the world, each individual would possess more than 350 times the information stored in Alexandria's library (Cukier and Mayer-Schoenberger 2013). Not surprisingly, this number grows larger each day. It is estimated that the world's data volume doubles every 20–36 months (Witten et al. 2011). How has such an exponential growth been possible? And, even more, how is all this data stored and assessed? In one word: digital. Today, only 2 percent of the world's data is analog or handwritten. This number is down from 75 percent in the year 2000 (Cukier and Mayer-Schoenberger 2013). A key reason for the exponential growth of digitally storing data is the drastically reduced cost in storing data using digital media storage solutions. Today, to store every song ever recorded, you only need a flash drive valued at $600 (Di Domenico and Nunan 2013).

Due to the lower cost of storing data, information that was once previously discarded is now saved. For instance, hospitals once discarded 90 percent of their older medical records. Today, everything can be saved for an eternity because of the lowered cost and convenience of digital software (Di Domenico and Nunan 2013). Another added benefit of digital media storage solutions is that it only takes up a fraction of the space that traditional paper-filing systems require. Additionally, answers can be found on digital systems in just a fraction of a second (IBM 2010; Pearlson and Saunders 2013).

The main reason for the increase in world data supply is technological advancement such as the invention of computing devices, digital storage, monitors, and so on. (Hilbert and López 2011). With these advancements, it has become easier to work with project team members virtually and keep large pools of data. In the days before computers, individuals preferred working with the smallest amount of data possible because their ability to gather, analyze, and process that data was limited. Hand typing and physically moving and reading through huge stacks of paper was time consuming and cumbersome (Linoff and Berry 2011). However, this trend has been reversed with the increase in storage and processing capacity. As little as two decades ago, these large pools of data were processed with complex decision-making algorithms that either did not exist or had to be done manually. Today, people prefer to work with the largest datasets possible in order to give them the most accurate results. This has led to more accurate and precise results than ever before. With the rapid spike in technology, we get a rapid spike in the world's recorded data (Cukier and Mayer-Schoenberger 2013).

Inquiry of Data Mining

The first references to data mining were found in the 1960s, although the official term was created in the 1990s. It began with the storing of data on computers, tapes, and disks. In the 1980s, the next evolutionary step occurred with the introduction of relational databases and structured query languages (SQL). This gave the data a structure, which allowed for easier interpretation and faster access to data analysts. In the 1990s, data warehousing was introduced. This was made possible by online analytic processing and multidimensional databases. Data warehousing is a central repository of data that is created by integrating data from one or more sources. This data is used to create trending reports for senior management, such as annual and quarterly comparisons. The final stage of the data mining evolutionary process is what is currently known as "data mining." Each step of the data mining process is built on the previous step (Kantardzic 2003).

The increase in data volume and data mining technology can be attributed to metrics that International Business Machines (IBM) calls "velocity" (IBM 2010) and Di Domenico and Nunan (2013) call them as "variety." Velocity refers to the speed in which large data pools can be processed and analyzed. In the not-so-distant past, large pools of data took too long to process and as a result they were not desirable to work with. The data pools also had high margins of error. In stark contrast, today's super computers can read everything ever written about a subject throughout the history of humanity in just a matter of minutes. This increase in speed, efficiency, and accuracy has made data mining more cost-effective. Regarding variety, traditionally, data could only be stored in limited ways through binary numbers translated into a series of bits called "zeroes" and "ones." Today, data can be stored and processed in any way imaginable. Free text, images, videos, speech, and code can all be easily saved and processed by modern computers and modern data mining devices (Di Domenico and Nunan 2013).

With this sharp increase in data storage, there comes a need of proper methods to process it. That is where data mining comes into play. All the raw data in the world is not nearly as valuable as just a fraction of data that has been cleaned, mined, and analyzed. Data mining has soared in popularity in recent years with the increased computer power previously mentioned. In order to increase sales and efficiency while reducing cost, the desire for businesses, health care, and government to practice data mining is at an all-time high with the trend expected to continue (Baesens et al. 2009; Au et al. 2012).

What Can Data Mining Do for Business?

Data mining roots fall into three categories: classical statistics, artificial intelligence, and machine learning. Statistics are the foundation of most technologies on which data mining is built. Regression analysis, standard deviation, standard distribution, standard variance, discriminant analysis, cluster analysis, and confidence intervals are all used to study data. Artificial intelligence uses a different approach to statistics. It attempts to apply human thought-like processing to statistical problems. Machine learning focuses on prediction based on known properties in the data. An example of this is how an email program can identify what is spam and what is not.

Data mining uses a technique called "modeling" to help analyze the data to predict what may happen based on the type of information. Modeling is the act of building a model based on the data inputted from known variables and then applying that information to other situations that are not known. An example of this would be with a marketing manager who may be looking for what customers to target for a new product. The marketing manager may take sales data for a similar product and be able to determine the age group, sex, demographics, income level, race, and education level of prospective buyers. This can greatly increase their chances of the product being a success, as this will allow them to concentrate their marketing efforts to target customers that the model predicts will more than likely become actual customers.

Each of these following actions can be better explained with a question, because data mining is intended to answer those questions. Many of these questions will be asked and answered in examples throughout this chapter.

Reporting
> Question: "What happened?" Data mining captures raw data and allows decision makers to look back at exactly what happened during a certain time frame.

Analyzing
> Question: "Why did it happen?" This question is answered with the results that come from data mining. When data mining takes place, the results are given to key decision makers who can then determine the root cause of success or failure.

Predicting
> Question: "What will happen?" One of the most wonderful features of data mining is its ability to forecast. Analysts can use data mining to predict future trends based on past performance.

Operationalizing
> Question: "What is happening now?" This question is achieved using real-time data. Many industries use real-time data to determine inventory levels, direct purchasing behavior, and coordinate sales activities.

Data mining offers a unique view into industries and organizations. It also permits business leaders to have a clearer view of the past than ever before because past data can be analyzed to offer a more vibrant view of the future. Data mining strives to present information to managers that can help them find ways to increase their top and bottom lines through increased efficiency and decreased expenses (Ogut et al. 2008; Lee 2013).

Data Mining Tools

Data models are built using analytical software. Some of the better known software packages include SAS by SAS Institute, SPSS by IBM, and R by R Foundation. There are many other software packages that specialize in specific types of analysis. Some of the softwares are open source, which allow them to be modified from its original device, whereas others are not. For example, R is an open-source software that allows the user to write custom statistical program, but SAS is not (Han et al. 2011).

Most data mining software can be classified into three categories: (1) traditional data mining tools, (2) dashboards, and (3) text mining tools. Traditional data mining programs help companies establish data patterns and trends using a number of complex algorithms and techniques. Most traditional programs handle a variety of data, while some are designed to handle just one database type. Dashboards reflect data changes and show updates on the screen, often in a form of a chart or table. This enables a company to measure its performance. It also allows the user to access historical data to compare company performance with the past. Text mining tools are able to mine data from different kinds of text. These tools scan content and convert data into a format compatible with the tools database. Other applications and programs such as Microsoft Excel can also be used for data mining purposes. Analyst can use pivot tables in the spreadsheet to review complex data in a simplified format (Han et al. 2011; Linoff and Berry 2011).

Weka as a Data Mining Tool

This chapter discusses Weka as a principal source of data mining software for a number of reasons. First, Weka was one of the first large-scale data mining software programs developed. Second, Weka is free, many university students and other researchers with shallow pockets often use it for their data mining research and publications. Third, Weka is written in Java and can be used on any operating system (Witten et al. 2011). Finally, there are a lot of tutorials and self-help YouTube videos surrounding Weka. Thus, Weka becomes a popular data mining tool due to its nonexistent cost, ease of use, and widespread distribution.

Weka was founded in 1993 and was created at the University of Waikato in New Zealand. The name "Weka" is derived from Waikato Environment for Knowledge Analysis. The project was established on a grant from the New Zealand Foundation for Research, Science, and Technology. A machine-learning program was chosen for the research because researchers felt that machine learning could assist with New Zealand's agriculture industry. Since that time, subsequent and more modern versions of Weka have been frequently released, permitting Weka to remain as current data mining software (Frank et al. 2005; Witten et al. 2011).

Why Use Weka?

One of the best features of Weka is that it is an open-source software and is free for public use. It is a general-purpose data mining tool for small businesses, university research students, and any individuals or businesses looking to analyze data on a budget. Weka also has reached a high level of acceptance among data miners because of its simplistic user interface. Many early data mining programs were command based but Weka was not, so its software dashboard is of particular use to early learners of the program. When Weka was created, it was written in Java (Bouckaert et al. 2010). Java applications have become a standard practice today. The Weka designers have shown great foresight at the time that Weka was first written. The Java-based code allows Weka to be run on any major operating systems. The world's most popular operating systems, such as Linux, Windows, and iOS, all support Weka (Witten et al. 2011). Weka has a loyal and passionate online community. Active Weka community users have created a Weka Wiki, where they have established forums for Q&A, blogging, and troubleshooting scenarios (Bouckaert et al. 2010).

Weka's Key Features

Weka's main work area is aptly named the "workbench." The majority of data mining takes place at the workbench. The main powerhouse at the workbench is an interface called "Explorer." Explorer is the tool chest to Weka's workbench. Here, users can find all commands and menus from which to work. Explorer guides users step-by-step prompting them along the way to decide which type of algorithm they would like to establish. Even for novice users, there is a help feature that will explain all the buttons and their uses in the data mining process (Witten et al. 2011).

A convenient feature of Weka is that the algorithms know what sequential order they belong in. If you choose several different algorithms, you can select to have them learn from each other. Weka will order them appropriately in the sequence of increasing complexity. You can then save this sequence and apply it to any other dataset. Weka also has features for advanced users, so that they can create their own algorithms (Hall et al. 2009). To stay current, Weka is linked online to servers that update the program automatically as new programs are constantly written and shared. The individual user can also create their exclusive algorithm on Weka for personal use or share it with the Weka community (Witten et al. 2011).

Issues in Data Mining

Ethical Issues

No one likes the idea of being spied on. When one thinks of spying, often the first thought is of a man standing in an alley with a trench coat and binoculars. However, spying can occur at the corporate and government level as well, not just corporation on corporation and government on government, but with these entities spying on everyday citizens. Today, firms and governments collect as much data as possible about average everyday individuals. An individual's demographics and purchase patterns are a very valuable asset when placed in the right hands. This can happen without the consumer's knowledge or consent. Sensitive personal data may be ended into the wrong hands or used unethically, illegally, or discriminatorily (Milne 2000).

Google searches, Internet cookies, shopper loyalty cards, and a plethora of other devices can be used to collect data from unsuspecting or even suspecting individuals. Although it has been discussed that these collections can offer countless advantages to firms, it can also harm the individual whose data has been harvested and minded. Society is well aware of security compromises that private and public entities have led to leaks of private information. This information, even if cleaned of personal data, can still be traced back to the individual. There have been reports of companies releasing private data cleansed of personal information for demonstrations with good intentions but analysts or hackers were still able to trace back the information to the individuals who had their names blocked. Aside from personal data thievery, in addition, personal data can be used discriminatorily (Hand 2006).

In banking, for instance, gender and race can be used to calculate risk of default for a potential borrower. This would be highly illegal so it is unlikely that this practice is done formally. There is no way to determine if banks and corporations do analysis like this behind closed doors for their own internal analysis (Dahlan et al. 2002). Today, the vast majority of loans are decided electronically but a person decides those loans that are on the fence. Humans could be subjected to illegally obtained statistics that the bank has developed internally. Likewise, one would not think that a zip code is used in a discriminating way for a loan application decision. But a banking institution could determine a neighborhood's racial background or socioeconomic status and cast a broad brushstroke on an individual just based on the location of their primary residence (Witten et al. 2011).

Quality and Availability of Data

It is no question that the availability and quality of data are a constant issue. Finding enough raw data for the analysis to find conclusive trends can take years of accumulation and *scrubbing*. As in statistics, there must be overwhelming amounts of information collected to support a claim and for that claim to carry serious validity (Elragal and El-Gendy 2013). That is why so many businesses allow the use of reward cards or customer loyalty cards. The price paid to the consumer in the form of discounts is miniscule in comparison to the value of the information collected. This raw information, when processed appropriately, is worth a lot to the company because of what they can do with the findings. That is why there is always a strong push for all retailers to issue loyalty cards. Upper management is hungry for their analysts to come up with cost-saving or sales-increasing plans from the raw data that these programs provide. As scarcity of data is a big concern, so is the quality of data (Witten et al. 2011; Elragal and El-Gendy 2013).

The frequently used expression, "garbage in, garbage out," holds true for data mining. If poor data is inserted into data mining machines, then the results are as useless as the raw data itself. That is why data is initially called "raw data" and raw data is then cleaned to become "clean data." Only clean data can be input into the system to create a proper hypothesis. If raw data is input and this data is corrupt or inaccurate, then the conclusions created will not be accurate. Inaccurate results generated from data mining will not help upper-level managers to do their jobs right in terms of planning strategies for the corporation. This will have devastating effects on the firm's top and bottom lines. Thus, it is absolutely critical to ensure that the data collected for data mining is reliable, clean, and accurate. Poor-quality data leads to poor conclusions, which lead to poor decisions (Watts et al. 2009; Han et al. 2011).

Because most data mining projects pull from multiple sources and are enormous, there are often duplicate records, incomplete records, corrupted data, and formatting errors. Formatting errors can be something as simple as the date written inconsistently throughout the data. Incomplete records may be an entry that failed to fill out all the required fields for the transaction. Another example of data *noise* would be two different product codes used to identify the same product, or the wrong store code used for the sale of a product at a particular store. These all may seem like trivial errors but if this uncleaned data is used for analysis, it will produce inaccurate results. It is also critical for data to be clean because if it is not, then those who process and interpret the data will not trust it. The entire exercise will have been a waste of time (Shankaranarayanan and Cai 2006; Han et al. 2011).

Data Mining Applications

Throughout the course of this section, practical examples of data mining will be described in an effort to explain the real value that data mining can offer business owners and managers.

In the Sports Industry

Data mining has recently come into the spotlight with the 2011 film, *Moneyball*. This film is based on a true story. The manager of a struggling baseball team, the Oakland A's, must compete in the Major League with a budget roughly one-third of other big market teams. In 2002, the A's general manager, Billy Beane, used a baseball's version of data mining tool called "Sabermetrics" for the first time on a large scale of sport data. Sabermetrics is a statistical analysis program to record and analyze each player's historical performance.

Prior to 2002, talent acquisition in professional sports was still done the old-fashioned way, with seasoned scouts and an accurate account of several key statistics. However, that was not going to work for much longer for small market teams. In 2002, the Oakland A's, with a salary budget of around $40 million, were forced to compete with the likes of the New York Yankees who had budgets three times that size.

In order to compete without the traditional, expensive talent acquired by those big market teams, Beane sought to find undervalued players by focusing on key statistics such as hitting and base percentage as opposed to scouting recommendations and trivial facts such as pitching speed, stolen base percentage, and player physique (Schumaker et al. 2010). As a result, Beane was able to compose an unconventional roster of players resulting in a low budget team. Despite all odds, the team was able to win the AL West with a .636 win percentage. Beane continued this performance up for the following five years, averaging a per win cost of about $800,000 less than the New York Yankees. This outstanding achievement caught the attention of professional sports teams around North America and as a result teams in all sports use various versions of Sabermetrics (Schumaker et al. 2010).

In the Pharmaceutical Industry

Similar to most industries, the history of data storage, collection, and processing in the pharmaceutical industry began with data written by hand or typewriter on a collection of note cards that were stored at a central location. Prior to the 1970s, most science research companies had their own libraries where they kept critical information such as chemical components, melting points, reactions, and so on. As technology advanced, the storage of scientific information maintained pace, putting information on microfilm and on the enormous-sized early computers of the 1960s (Balakin and Ekins 2010).

There are not many industries that have as many variables and individual data items like the healthcare industry. There are countless medications available just over the counter, not to mention the prescription drugs that pharmaceutical companies must study before creating a new drug with minimal side effects. Fortunately for the industry and humanity, data mining has made this daunting challenge slightly more bearable (Ordones et al. 2006).

Drug manufacturers are able to get general medical information from pools of applicants and volunteers. They save this medical information to create databases and run averages on numerous variables such as race, sex, physical fitness, medical history, allergies, and so on. With all this information stored in a database, the pharmaceutical industry is able to take their information and develop new drugs that will alleviate the most symptoms with the least side effects (Setoguchi et al. 2008). This would have been exponentially more difficult even 30 years ago as all of this information was previously stored with pen and paper on little note cards. Now a simple click of a button can let a computer run a program test to determine if the new drug will be successful. This is just one of the very simple ways in which data mining is helping the pharmaceutical industry (Setoguchi et al. 2008).

One of the most basic yet most valuable features of data mining is the decision tree (Utgoff 1989; Biggs et al. 1991). Decision trees start with a question and split with arrows going in different directions. Each arrow displays different answers to each question. The answer you choose is the direction that you should take and this will often lead to another question, and another, and so on. Eventually, you will arrive at the correct course of action. This works particularly well with the pharmaceutical industry (Balakin and Ekins 2010). When creating a new drug or determining if two different drugs are compatible with each other, a simple decision tree can help. The questions at the top of the tree start out broad and eventually become more specific as one moves down the tree into the branches. Pharmacists and chemists can then determine the likelihood of a reaction with a different drug or medical condition (Balakin and Ekins 2010). Although this is the simplest example of data mining in the pharmaceutical industry, it shows how much data mining can help this complex and highly regulated industry. Increasingly complex and sophisticated levels of data mining are currently one of the biggest driving forces in the pharmaceutical industry (López-Vallverdú et al. 2012).

In Customer Service

Data mining has proven itself time and time again in the realm of customer service. Customer service is arguably one of the areas of data mining that has the highest amount of raw data to work with. That does not mean that there is little work to do in preparing the customer data. Rather, there is a fair amount of research to go into the raw data before the results are applicable. In the realm of customer service, it is important to get these facts and figures right. If inaccurate information is provided and solutions are implemented based on wrong information, customers could be put off by the poor decisions made (Chen et al. 2012a).

For example, a supermarket chain in Texas was trying to determine which, if not all products at all stores, should be advertised in Spanish and English (Linoff and Berry 2011). Language is a factor to be certain for marketing a product. If you advertise one product in just English but it is popular to Spanish speakers, then you are shutting both the company and the product off to a large demographic. On the other hand, if you advertise in Spanish and English and the product is not popular with Spanish speakers, then you are fruitlessly wasting money on advertising. Data mining was put into action to answer this riddle by this Texas supermarket chain.

To figure out this dilemma without using racial information on the individual level, the grocery chain used demographics on the city level around the stores in question. The grocery chain chose to study stores that had either very high concentrations of Spanish speakers or very low concentrations of Spanish speakers. They would take products that did very well in the Spanish-speaking areas and subtract the popularity from the high English-speaking stores. The products that did well in Spanish stores were only the products that should be advertised in Spanish. On the contrary, the products that did well in the English-speaking stores and that did not do well in the Spanish-speaking stores should not be advertised in Spanish (Linoff and Berry 2011).

A few conclusions of this data mining exercise are very interesting. For example, English speakers preferred beef as their meat of choice, whereas Spanish speakers selected pork. For snacking, English speakers scored high with potato chips, whereas Spanish speakers had higher markings on corn chips (Linoff and Berry 2011). In the end, the main point of this exercise was met and the grocery store was able to determine what advertisements to run for which foods in which language and in which markets. This marketing and customer service information was able to be deciphered all because of the valuable information learned from raw data that was data mined (Hui and Jha 2000).

A Data Mining Case at ABC Belting

ABC Belting is a firm that manufactures lightweight, European style conveyor belts. The conveyor belts are commonly used at the supermarket check-out or on an exercise treadmill. To respect the company's identity, the case firm will be referred to as ABC Belting in this chapter. ABC Belting is at an exciting time in its history as it just recently turned 50 and is one of the largest belting firms in the world. ABC Belting has seven branches around the world, of which three subdivisions manufacture belts and the other four subdivisions operate as fabrication and distribution centers. The U.S. branch recently began to use data mining to calculate a number of factors in sales, customer service, and quality (Au et al. 2012).

Order History Analysis

ABC Belting started its data analysis with a customized order entry system that recorded all the different fabrication specifications as the customer requested in the purchase of their conveyor belts. After several years of acquiring this information, ABC Belting was then able to run a program in Weka that did basic analyses, such as the fabrication of the most common belt type and typical sizes. The company took an additional step to forecast demand at different times of the year. Through many years of analyses, ABC found that certain products were seasonal and consistently performed much better at different times of the year. With this finding, ABC Belting was able to know what branches needed which products at what times. In turn, the production managers around the globe can coordinate for *just in time* arrival of raw materials to make the different belt types (Chen and Shen 2005).

After acquiring this information and making purchasing and production changes at several manufacturing branches, ABC Belting was able to reduce their inventory levels of raw materials by 5 percent and of finished goods by 10 percent. This reduction of inventory in raw materials and finished products allowed the capital that was once tied up in inventory to be put into areas of the operation that would yield higher returns. Additionally, the slabs of conveyor belting that were reduced from the inventory previously occupied around 30 square feet each. With the excess inventory no longer taking up space, this has freed up more manufacturing and fabrication space in the ABC warehouses, leading to more productivity (Colicchia et al. 2010). Another area where ABC Belting benefited from data mining was with the analysis of return good authorizations (RGAs).

RGA Analysis

With a sophisticated RGA program in place, ABC Belting was able to analyze which departments, fabrication methods, or customers were causing the most frequent and costly RGAs. The program allowed for individual steps of the fabrication process to be identified in an RGA in conjunction with the fabricator that worked on the process and for which client and on which day of the week along with other variables (Khan et al. 2008). The company was able to find several interesting features.

After the data analysis, ABC was able to determine that one customer in particular was ordering belts for a very complex application and was constantly requesting an RGA when the belt failed. When ABC Belting sales representatives learned of this instance, they contacted the customer and discovered that the customer was ordering the wrong belt for the application. By recommending the proper belt, ABC Belting was able to prevent approximately $10,000 in RGAs per year just in this single case.

Another way in which the mining of the RGA information helped ABC Belting was with a trend analysis. ABC found that belts manufactured on one of the production lines at a certain time of the year were failing in a very specific way. The problem was reported to engineers and they found out at that time of the year the cooling lines operate at a different temperature because they are fed by a city water line. In order to combat the fluctuating temperature throughout the year, a water temperature control device was installed and the manufacturing process error was corrected. This quotation system was yet another beneficial case of the mining of big data at ABC Belting.

Quotation Analysis

The quotation system, like the order entry system, kept track of all the quotes versus orders received and was able to compare them down to every variable, product, size of belt, fabrication method, time of year, and so on. ABC Belting deduced which fabrication methods or products were overpriced or underpriced (Leopoulos and Kirytopoulos 2004). Now, when a salesperson is quoting a belt in a highly competitive market, they must use a Weka program. The sales person types in the parameters of the quote and Weka will tell the salesman the likelihood of the customer accepting the order given the parameters. When the answer is not favorable, the salesman can then alter the parameters of the quote, and adjust the pricing for the various fabrication services. When Weka agrees that the salesman is likely to accept the order by making appropriate margins, the salesman can then send the quote according to the Weka program's suggestions. As a result of this process, ABC Belting saw a 400 percent increase in business from a customer that was previously buying a very small amount of belts from them.

These data mining programs were working so well at ABC Beltings' American, Canadian, and Italian branches that they were going to implement the program at every branch around the world. Although this may be viewed as a small victory for a company in just one out of sight industry, the progress of data mining is very encouraging. This case of data mining at ABC Belting may be applied to thousands of companies around the world to increase production efficiency and the quality of customer service.

Implications and Lessons Learned

The rapid expansion of technology that hangs over the head of data mining has been ongoing since the 1990s. Over the past few decades, technology has evolved rapidly. Products are becoming obsolete after they are produced, packaged, and shipped to customers. Competition is fierce in the IT industry. If you are not creating the next best application, then it is likely that someone else will. In order to "keep up with the Jones's," IT companies must continue to invest significant portions of their budgets in R&D to stay on top of the current market. This can lead to thin profits, especially, as consumers expect to pay less and less for today's top technologies.

As we continue to strive toward advancements in technology, information becomes more abundant and data mining and analytical methods will continue to evolve to help businesses process raw data into usable information. Businesses will explore new niches, whereas advertisers will target potential customers with more precision. It may become so common and practical that the average computer user would be able to use data mining to assist with common issues such as finding the best price for a potential car or analyzing the most practical way to complete a task in real time. As technology advances, we may also see computers discover new medical treatments to a fatal disease. Companies will even be able to profile consumers into health risk insights simply by gathering their social media, smartphone, and purchasing activities. They will use these data sources to develop a complete profile of each consumer applicant.

Recent advances in technology, such as e-commerce, smartphones, and social networking, are generating new types of data on a scale never seen before—a phenomenon known as "big data." The increased amount of data in the world has created many new job opportunities for business analytics. Though there is no job category for business analytics or data analytics in the Bureau of Labor Statistics (BLS) Occupational Outlook Handbook, BLS realizes the new job creation and publishes a recent report, "Working with Big Data," in the Fall 2013 *Occupational Outlook Quarterly Online*. BLS indicates in the report that there will be significant opportunities for big data analytics and business analytics professionals well into the future (Bureau of Labor Statistics 2013).

In order to attempt to keep up with the demand, universities are developing masters programs dedicated to analytics. Northwestern University and DePaul University created masters in science in predictive analytics; Stanford University has a masters in science in computer science with a specialization in information management and analytics; and Bentley University has a master of science in marketing analytics. Many other schools also have similar programs. These students that enroll in these programs will have a distinct advantage over their co-worker who may have not. These individuals will have better credentials for pursuing higher-level roles in a company.

Privacy issues are becoming more and more of a concern in today's society. Average citizens are becoming weary of big brother looking over their back. Even corporations have had privacy concerns that have raised the eyebrows of citizens. More so of a concern than corporate spying, individuals are concerned about their corporations servers being hacked or accidentally leaking out personal information. There is an entirely different level of privacy concerns about information that is collected by retailers. These concerns are related to what the retailers do with the information that is collected and raise awareness about the prevalence of cookie usage in general. This concern over privacy in cookie use has long been an issue. As more and more of our personal information is stored electronically by businesses and government agencies, the risk of identity theft increases greatly (Son and Kim 2008; Smith et al. 2011; Stoica et al. 2013).

Large-scale breaches happen very frequently. Recent cases of data breach happened at TJ Maxx, Target, and Neiman Marcus have impacted millions of consumers. Hacker's schemes of using malware to compromise payment information storage systems are getting more sophisticated every day. According to the report, the invasive code poses a threat to retailers because it is incredibly difficult to trace. As individuals, we must protect ourselves and give our information only to trusted entities. But even still, there is risk of information being lost, misused, or stolen. It is imperative that credit information is checked regularly. Businesses, on the other hand, have a corporate responsibility to constantly strive to improve protection measures to safeguard consumers' personal information (Smith 2009).

It is critical for individuals to read privacy rights when first signing on to a new service contract and reread them as new versions are published. Consumers must be proactive in knowing what they are permitting those companies to do with their data. In addition to preserving privacy rights, it is equally as important to monitor personal and business credit reports on a routine basis. It is impossible to know if someone has opened a credit card in your name until it becomes too late. With identity theft on the rise, individuals must take it upon themselves to protect their identity by frequently checking their user profile and transaction statements to make sure that nothing is compromised. These simple measures can do a great deal in protecting the individual and the small business from privacy invasions surrounding big data (Chen et al. 2012b; LaValle et al. 2011).

Conclusion

Advancements in technology and the alarming increase of information triggered the growth of data mining. Data mining is defined as the computer-assisted process of digging through and analyzing enormous sets of data and then extracting the meaning of the data. We learned that businesses utilize that information to predict future trends. As technology improves and new methods are discovered for analyzing data, organizations will develop new and innovative ways to use that data to help them achieve organizational objectives.

We also learned about different methods related to data mining such as big data and business analytics and what their uses are. It was also found that many industries utilize data mining methods and that in the future those numbers will continue to grow. Due to this many schools have developed masters programs centered around analytics as the demand for professionals with these skills will continue to rise.

Data mining plays a central role as a competitive weapon in today's industries. Its role will only continue to grow. Data mining is used to win games, produce better drugs, segment marketing, decrease expenses, increase profits, and customize order as seen at ABC Belting. In an era with so much competition domestically and globally, all firms are striving to be a millisecond faster, a penny cheaper, and just hair better. This is not expected to dissipate in the near future. Data mining is forming as a new discipline for years to come. The use of data mining will continue to grow as companies look to streamline their businesses and use advanced data analytics to determine strong and weak points in their operations. The widescale applicability of data mining to countless industries and services of all shapes and sizes makes it a very adaptable practice. The demand for data mining professionals is growing, as data mining applications have been rapidly implemented by organizations.

The possibility of great success in data mining practice does not come completely risk free. Constant fears of privacy concerns can be a great potential hindrance to the adoption of big data analytics and data mining programs. Due to unrelated government espionage in our homeland and abroad, citizens across the globe are becoming more sensitive to the idea that someone is tracking what they are doing at all times. Organizations must be conscientious of this concern of privacy. For firms that hold customer data, they must be vigilant to safeguard their customers' information from hackers and malicious employees.

Given current trends of data explosion, it appears that big data and data mining are gaining momentum to becoming imperatives in businesses. Thus, organizations must be mindful of the risks previously explained in order to maintain high levels of trust and confidence from consumers. As we enter into a day where almost everything is recorded electronically and digitally, data security and privacy issues have become of utmost importance in businesses here and around the world.

References

Aggarwal, N., Amit, K., Harsh, K., and Vaishali, A. (2012). Advances in engineering software. *Science Direct, 47*(1), 164–169.

Au, S., Duan, R., and Jiang, W. (2012). A data mining framework for product and service migration analysis. *Annals of Operations Research, 192*(1), 105–121.

Baesens, B., Mues, C., Martens, D., and Vanthienen, J. (2009). 50 years of data mining and OR: Upcoming trends and challenges. *Journal of the Operational Research Society, 60*(1), 16–23.

Balakin, K. V. and Ekins, S. (2010). *Pharmaceutical Data Mining: Approaches and Applications for Drug Discovery.* Hoboken, NJ: Wiley.

Biggs, D. B., De Ville, B., and Suen, E. (1991). A method of choosing multi-way partitions for classification and decision trees. *Journal of Applied Statistics, 18*(1), 49–62.

Bouckaert, R. R., Frank, E., Hall, M. A., Holmes, G., Pfahringer, B., Reutemann, P., and Witten, H. (2010). WEKA—Experiences with a Java open-source project. *Journal of Machine Learning Research, 11*(9), 2533–2541.

Bureau of Labor Statistics (2013). Working with big data. *Fall 2013 Occupational Outlook Quarterly Online*. Retrieved November 15, 2013, from http://www.bls.gov/careeroutlook/2013/fall/art01.pdf.

Chen, D., Sain, S. L., and Guo, K. (2012a). Data mining for the online retail industry: A case study of RFM model-based customer segmentation using data mining. *Journal of Database Marketing & Customer Strategy Management, 19*(3), 197–208.

Chen, H., Chiang, R. H., and Storey, V. C. (2012b). Business intelligence and analytics: From big data to big impact. *MIS Quarterly, 36*(4), 1165–1188.

Chen, Y. L. and Shen, C. C. (2005). Mining generalized knowledge from ordered data through attribute-oriented induction techniques. *European Journal of Operational Research, 166*(1), 221–245.

Colicchia, C., Dallari, F., and Melacini, M. (2010). Increasing supply chain resilience in a global sourcing context. *Production Planning and Control, 21*(7), 680–694.

Cukier, K. and Mayer-Schoenberger, V. (2013). The rise of big data. *Foreign Affairs, 92*(3), 27–40.

Dahlan, N., Ramayah, T., and Koay, A. H. (2002). Data mining in the banking industry: An exploratory study. *Proceedings of the 2002 International Conference of Internet Economy and Business*. September 17–18, Kuala Lumpur, Malaysia.

Di Domenico, M. L. and Nunan, D. (2013). Market research and the ethics of big data. *National Journal of Market Research, 55*(4), 1–13.

Elragal, A. and El-Gendy, N. (2013). Trajectory data mining: Integrating semantics. *Journal of Enterprise Information Management, 26*(5), 516–535.

Frank, E., Hall, M. A., Holmes, G., Kirkby, R., Pfahringer, B., and Witten, I. H. (2005). WEKA: A machine learning workbench for data mining. In O. Maimon and L. Rokach (Eds.), *Data Mining and Knowledge Discovery Handbook: A Complete Guide for Practitioners and Researchers*, Berlin, Germany: Springer, 1305–1314.

Hall, M., Frank, E., Holmes, G., Pfahringer, B., Reutemann, P., and Witten, I. H. (2009). The Weka data mining software: An update. *ACM SIGKDD Explorations Newsletter, 11*(1), 10–18.

Han, J., Kamber, M., and Pei, J. (2011). *Data Mining: Concepts and Techniques*. 3rd Edition. Waltham, MA: Morgan Kaufmann Publishers.

Hand, D. (2006). Protection or privacy? Data mining and personal data. *Proceedings of the 10th Pacific-Asia Conference, PAKDD*, Lecture Notes in Computer Science, vol. 3918, Singapore, April 9–12, pp. 1–10.

Hand, D. J., Mannila, H., and Smyth, P. (2001). *Principles of Data Mining*. Cambridge, MA: MIT Press.

Hilbert, M. and López, P. (2011). The world's technological capacity to store, communicate, and compute information. *Science, 332*(6025), 60–65.

Hui, S. C. and Jha, G. (2000). Data mining for customer service support. *Information & Management, 38*(1), 1–13.

IBM Corporation (2010). *CRISP-DM 1.0: Step-by-step data mining guide*. IBM White Paper YTW03084 GBEN IBM Corporation, Somers, NY. Retrieved December 1, 2013, from http://www.the-modeling-agency.com/crisp-dm.pdf.

Kantardzic, M. (2003). *Data Mining: Concepts, Models, Methods, and Algorithms*. Hoboken, NJ: Wiley.

Khan, O., Christopher, M., and Burnes, B. (2008). The impact of product design on supply chain risk: A case study. *International Journal of Physical Distribution and Logistics Management, 38*(5), 412–432.

LaValle, S., Lesser, E., Shockley, R., Hopkins, M. S., and Kruschwitz, N. (2011). Big data, analytics and the path from insights to value. *MIT Sloan Management Review, 52*(2), 21–32.

Lee, P. M. (2013). Use of data mining in business analytics to support business competitiveness. *The Review of Business Information Systems, 17*(2), 53–58.

Leopoulos, V. N. and Kirytopoulos, K. A. (2004). Risk management: A competitive advantage in the purchasing function. *Production Planning and Control, 15*(7), 678–687.

Linoff, G. and Berry, M. A. (2011). *Data Mining Techniques: For Marketing, Sales and Customer Relationship Management.* Indianapolis, IN: Wiley.

López-Vallverdú, J. A., Riaño, D., and Bohada, J. A. (2012). Improving medical decision tree by combining relevant health-care criteria. *Expert Systems with Applications, 39*(14), 11782–11791.

Milne, G. R. (2000). Privacy and ethical issues in database/interactive marketing and public policy: A research framework and overview of the special issue. *Journal of Public Policy & Marketing, 19*(1), 1–6.

Ogut, A., Kocabacak, A., and Demirsel, M. T. (2008). The impact of data mining on the managerial decision-making process: A strategic approach. *Journal of American Academy of Business, Cambridge, 14*(1), 137–143.

Ordones, C., Ezquerra, N., and Santana, C. A. (2006). Constraining and summarizing association rules in medical data. *International Journal of Knowledge Information Systems, 9*(3), 259–283

Pearlson, K. and Saunders, C. (2013). *Managing and Using Information Systems.* 5th Edition. New York: Wiley.

Schumaker, R., Soleiman, O., and Chen, H. (2010). *Sports Data Mining.* New York: Springer.

Setoguchi, S., Schneeweiss, S., Brookhart, M. A., Glynn, R. J., and Cook, E. F. (2008). Evaluating uses of data mining techniques in propensity score estimation: A simulation study. *Pharmacoepidemiology and Drug Safety, 17*(6), 546–555.

Shankaranarayanan, G. and Cai, Y. (2006), Supporting data quality management in decision-making, *Decision Support Systems, 42*(1), 302–317.

Smith, G. (2009). Data mining: How hackers steal sensitive electronic information. *The Journal of Corporate Accounting & Finance, 20*(4), 23–26.

Smith, H. J., Dinev, T., and Xu, H. (2011). Information privacy research: An interdisciplinary review. *MIS Quarterly, 35*(4), 989–1016.

Son, J. Y. and Kim, S. S. (2008). Internet users' information privacy-protective responses: A taxonomy and a nomological model. *MIS Quarterly, 32*(3), 503–529.

Stoica, M., Trif, S., and Visoiu, A. (2013). Security solutions for privacy preserving improved data mining. *Informatica Economica, 17*(3), 157–169.

Utgoff, P. E. (1989). Incremental induction of decision trees. *Machine Learning, 4*(2), 161–186.

Watts, S., Shankaranarayanan, G., and Even, A. (2009). Data quality assessment in context: A cognitive perspective. *Decision Support Systems, 48*(1), 202–211.

Witten, I. H., Frank, E., and Hall, M. A. (2011). *Data mining: Practical Machine Learning Tools and Techniques.* Burlington, MA: Morgan Kaufmann Publishers.

Chapter 8

The Importance of Data Quality Assurance to the Data Analysis Activities of the Data Mining Process

Patricia E. Nalwoga Lutu

Contents

Abstract: The data used for a data mining project may be automatically collected by computer systems or electronic equipment and stored in special files (e.g., server log files), or, the data may be generated from organizational transactions and stored in operational databases, or, it may be data that has been preprocessed, integrated, and loaded into a data warehouse. Given that the results of data mining are typically used to support decision making, it goes without saying that if poor-quality data is used for data mining, the results obtained will provide misleading information to the decision makers. The purpose of this chapter is to discuss the impact of poor-quality data on data mining projects, provide a discussion on data quality assurance, some guidelines on how organizations faced with poor-quality data can ensure that in the short term they are able to apply knowledge discovery and data mining (KDDM) while they embark on data quality assurance programs.

Keywords: Data mining, data quality, data quality assurance, data quality framework, capability maturity model, CRISP-DM

Introduction

From a general perspective, Hand et al. (2001) have defined data mining as the analysis of (often large) observational datasets, to find unsuspected relationships, and to summarize the data in novel ways that are both understandable and useful to the data owner. Most commonly, usefulness translates into assisting the data owners to make informed decisions. From a purely business perspective, Simoudis (1996) has defined data mining as the process of extracting valid, previously unknown, comprehensible, and actionable information from large databases and using it to make crucial business decisions. The above definitions of data mining indicate that the results of data mining are predominantly used to support decision making. Many highly sophisticated statistical methods, computational algorithms, and software tools currently exist for the description and summarization of data, as well as the creation of descriptive models and predictive models that can be used to provide useful insights to data owners (Hand et al. 2001; Guidici 2003; Witten et al. 2011; Linoff and Berry 2013). Given that the results of data mining are used to support decision making, it is essential that the information obtained from data mining activities should be correct and accurate. It goes without saying that if poor-quality data is used for summarizing data or creating descriptive and predictive models, regardless of how sophisticated the methods, algorithms, and tools are, the resulting models will provide misleading results to the decision makers. Many writers (e.g., Caballero 2008; Newman and Logan 2008; Loshin 2010) have argued that organizations should treat data as a strategic asset, so that they can obtain maximum value from the data.

The Cross Industry Standard Process for Data Mining (CRISP-DM) model (Shearer 2001; IBM 2011) is commonly used to guide the activities for data mining projects. This model consists of six phases, two of which are dedicated to the understanding and preparation of the data to be used for a data mining project. It was often reported in the early literature on data mining (between 1995 and 2005) that as much as 90% of a data mining estimated project duration and resources were typically spent on the understanding and preparation of the data (Shearer 2001). This was due to the fact that the quality of the data in the databases, where data for data mining projects was extracted from, was often very poor. Since the mid-1990s, there have been many efforts (by researchers and organizations) aimed at improving the quality of the data that is stored in the databases for operational systems as well as data warehouses. To this end, several data quality frameworks for data quality assessment, data quality improvement, and data quality assurance have been reported in the literature (e.g., Ryu et al. 2006; Caballero 2008; Newman and Logan 2008; Loshin 2010; Berti-Equille et al. 2011) and have been adopted by many organizations. When there is a culture of data quality assurance in an organization, the quality of the data used in data mining can be *trusted*. This should result in the reduction of the time spent on data understanding and data preparation, and a reduction in the chances of abandoning a data mining project due to poor-quality data.

The purpose of this chapter is to discuss the impact of poor-quality data on data mining projects, review the literature on data quality assessment and data quality assurance, and provide some guidelines on how organizations faced with poor-quality data can ensure that in the short term they are able to apply knowledge discovery and data (KDDM), while they embark on data quality assurance programs. The section "Data Mining Application Domains and Processes" discusses application domains for data mining and the data mining process. The section "Data for Data Mining Projects" discusses the sources of data for data mining projects and data quality problems associated with this data. The section "Data Quality Assurance" discusses assurance of data quality. The section "Management of Data Quality Assurance Programs" discusses how data quality assurance programs are managed. The section "Discussion and Recommendations" provides recommendations for data quality assurance to support data mining projects. The final section concludes the chapter.

Data Mining Application Domains and Processes

Data mining for economic development may be viewed in terms of the value that data mining applications provide to decision makers in business environments and in the public sector. Application domains of data mining and process models for conducting data mining projects are briefly discussed in this section.

Application Domains for Data Mining

There are many application areas where data mining has traditionally been applied. In the business sector these areas include credit scoring (Hand 1997; Sharma and Osei-Bryson 2009), credit card fraud (Chan and Stolfo 1998), forensic data mining for the prediction of telephone fraud (Fawcett and Provost 1997), computer network intrusion detection (Lee and Stolfo 2000), web usage mining for analyzing and predicting customer purchases behavior (Guidici 2003; Theusinger and Huber 2000; Kohavi et al. 2004), customer relationship management (Guidici 2003; Kohavi et al. 2004), and market (shopping) basket analysis (Guidici 2003). These applications of data mining are most commonly used by large business organizations in the so-called developed economies.

In the public sector, applications of data mining to support decision-making activities include health care (Koh and Tan 2005), education (Luan 2002; Bellazzi and Zupan 2008), and the mining of official statistics data (Hassani et al. 2014). One application of data mining in health care is the analysis of clinical data to determine the most effective and cost-effective treatments for patients (Koh and Tan 2005; Bellazzi and Zupan 2008). A second type of application in healthcare management activities is the tracking of chronic illnesses and epidemiology (Koh and Tan 2005). A third type of application is fraud detection in medical insurance claims (Koh and Tan 2005). Applications of data mining in the educational sector have been reported by Luan (2002) and Romero and Ventura (2007). Luan (2002) has discussed the use of data mining in institutional research activities for purposes of analyzing student data on course registration and performance. Romero and Ventura (2007) have discussed the use of data mining to analyze data generated from student usage of web-based courses. This analysis can be used to create recommender systems that guide students to those pages that can provide the most useful content based on the student's needs. Hassani et al. (2014) have reported that, in recent years, National Statistical Institutes around the world have started applying data mining methods to official statistical data in addition to the traditional methods of statistical data analysis.

All the foregoing applications of data mining involve the analysis of structured data that is sourced from within the organization. More recently, Web 2.0 technologies and social media services, for example, Twitter (2014) and Facebook (2014) have given rise to massive amounts of data which are generated by the public. This type of data, commonly called the "big data," is stored by the social media service organizations and is available to organizations that wish to conduct analysis activities such as data mining. Current trends in the mining of this unstructured data include sentiment analysis (Jansen et al. 2009; Bifet and Frank 2010; Wakade et al. 2012), which involves the use of text-mining methods to determine whether the public has expressed positive or negative sentiments toward the products and/or services provided by an organization. For these types of data mining applications the data is obtained from external sources.

Process Models for Data Mining

The data mining literature (e.g., Shearer 2001; Guidici 2003; Sharma and Osei-Bryson 2009) indicates that in business organizations, data mining tends to be a project-oriented activity. A business case is identified and then consultants/data analysts are recruited to work on the project. This is in contrast to online analytical processing analysis that organizations with data warehouses conduct on a continuous basis to monitor business performance. However, it should be noted that there are some types of models, for example, predictive models that are used continuously after deployment. Two data mining process models that are commonly used in data mining projects are CRISP-DM (Shearer 2001; IBM 2011) and the Sample, Explore, Modify, Model, Assess (SEMMA) process model from the SAS Institute (SAS 2013). SEMMA process model is specific to the SAS Enterprise Miner tool and specifies activities for data understanding, data preparation, modeling, and model evaluation. The CRISP-DM is a general-purpose process model that is not tied to any specific statistical software product. This process model has gained widespread adoption, and consists of six phases, namely, business understanding, data understanding, data preparation, modeling, evaluation, and deployment. These phases are depicted in Figure 8.1. The business

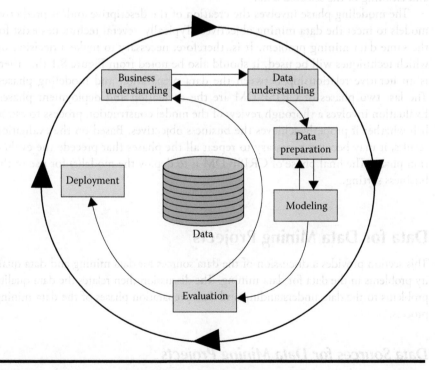

Figure 8.1 **The phases of CRISP-DM. (Adopted from Shearer, C., _Journal of Data Warehousing_, 5, 13–22, 2001.)**

understanding phase focuses on understanding the project objectives from a business perspective, converting this understanding into a data mining problem definition, and then developing an initial plan for achieving the objectives.

It goes without saying (but it should be noted from Figure 8.1) that data is at the core of data mining activities. The importance of the data is emphasized by the fact that two phases: data understanding and data preparation are dedicated to the preprocessing of data. The data understanding phase starts with an initial data collection and proceeds with activities to get familiar with the data, to identify data quality problems, to discover first insights into the data, and to detect interesting subsets to form hypotheses for hidden information. It should also be noted from Figure 8.1 that there is an *iterative* relationship between the data understanding and business understanding phases, that is, the outputs of the data understanding phase lead to a refinement of the business understanding phase and vice versa (Sharma and Osei-Bryson 2009). The data preparation phase covers all activities to construct the final dataset (data that will be fed into the modeling tools) from the initial raw data. Shearer (2001) has observed that data preparation tasks are likely to be performed multiple times, and not in any prescribed order. Tasks include the selection of database tables, records, and attributes as well as the transformation and cleaning of the selected data.

The modeling phase involves the creation of the descriptive and/or predictive models to meet the data mining objectives. Typically, several techniques exist for the same data mining problem. It is, therefore, necessary to make a decision on which techniques will be used. It should also be noted from Figure 8.1 that there is an iterative relationship between the data preparation and modeling phases. The last two phases of CRISP-DM are the evaluation and deployment phases. Evaluation involves a thorough review of the model construction process to establish whether it properly achieves the business objectives. Based on the evaluation results, it may become necessary to repeat all the phases that precede the evaluation phase. The final phase of CRISP-DM is to deploy the model(s) for use in the business setting.

Data for Data Mining Projects

This section provides a discussion of the data sources for data mining and data quality problems in the data for data mining. The discussion then relates the data quality problems to the data understanding and data preparation phases of the data mining process.

Data Sources for Data Mining Projects

Applications of data mining may be divided into various categories based on the type of data that is used for the project. Five of these categories are discussed here.

The first category are those projects where the data is automatically collected by computer systems. Examples of these are the creation of predictive models for computer network intrusion detection (Lee and Stolfo 2000) and click stream analysis (Theusinger and Huber 2000) to determine the navigation behavior of website visitors. These data mining applications use data that is stored in the server log files. The second category of applications are those that use data that is automatically generated by instruments/equipment and then stored in specialized databases. Examples of this category of applications are telecommunications applications that use call detail records generated by telecommunications equipment to create models for fraud detection (Fawcett and Provost 1997). A second example is the analysis of medical data that is generated by medical equipment (Hand et al. 2001).

The third category are those applications that use data stored in the operational systems of an organization. A classic example is the use of a transactional database to conduct market (shopping) basket analysis (Hand et al. 2001; Guidici 2003). An example from the educational sector is the analysis of student data on course registration and performance data in conducting institutional research activities (Luan 2002). The fourth category are applications that use integrated data stored in an enterprise data warehouse or departmental data marts. Examples of business applications include customer segmentation for customer relationship management (Guidici 2003), credit scoring by financial institutions (Hand 1997; Guidici 2003), and recommender systems for online shoppers (Hand et al. 2001). One example from the healthcare sector is the analysis of clinical data stored in a data mart to determine the most effective and cost-effective treatments for patients (Koh and Tan 2005; Bellazzi and Zupan 2008). The fifth category are applications that use data obtained from external sources. It is very common nowadays for organizations to obtain data from social media services such as Twitter and Facebook for purposes of analyzing public sentiment about the products and services provided by the organization.

Data Quality Problems

In the application domains of data mining, there is no *perfect* or problem-free data that analysts can just pick up and use for summarization and modeling activities. This is made explicit by the fact that CRISP-DM approach specifies two phases for data understanding and data preparation. Hand et al. (2001) have made a distinction between two types of data that are used for (statistical) data analysis. Experimental data is data that is specifically collected for primary analysis based on an experimental design for answering specific questions. The experimental design includes a specification of the data to be collected and how the data should be collected. On the other hand, observational data is data that was collected for some purpose and then later on the data owners decide to conduct (secondary) statistical data analysis such as data mining on this data. This is the root cause of data quality problems for data mining projects. The term "data quality" (or information quality) has been defined in literature as "fitness for use by data consumers" (Wang and Strong 1996; Lin et al. 2007). In the early days of data mining, the data understanding and data preparation phases were notoriously difficult, mostly due to data quality problems. In 2001, Shearer (2001) reported that industry-accepted estimates for these phases were approximately 75%–90% of the estimated project duration. It is the author's opinion that currently this is also very likely to be the case for any organization that is initiating a data mining project (from operational data) for the first time.

The discussion of the last section has pointed out that data for data mining projects may be generated by computer systems or electronic equipment and then stored in special files. Second, data may be generated from organizational activities, for example, business transactions and then stored in operational databases or data warehouses of an organization. Third, data may be obtained from external sources such as social media services. When data is collected by computer systems (e.g., server log data), or by instruments/equipment (e.g., medical instruments or satellite image data), there may be some errors due to noise. These types of errors can be handled using statistical methods, for example, outlier detection methods. When data is captured by people using data entry screens for information systems, many problems (e.g., incorrect values, missing values, and meaningless default values) arise. This is the case for business operational systems, public healthcare systems for administrative data and clinical data (Koh and Tan 2002), and in general, data that is entered into information systems by users in the public sector organizations.

Data warehousing involves extraction, transformation, and loading (ETL), where data is extracted from disparate internal operational systems as well as external systems, staged (cleaned), and then loaded into the enterprise data warehouse or departmental data mart. One might expect that, if data for a data mining project is sourced from a data warehouse, then the data is problem free. However, there have been reports in the literature, of many failed data warehousing projects. One main reason for failed projects is due to the poor quality of the data in operational systems, which no amount of staging could overcome. In 2007, Gartner predicted that more than 50% of data warehousing projects would have limited acceptance, or would be outright failures due to data quality problems. Since the mid-1990s, many organizations have become aware of the strategic value of the data that they collect, and as a result, data quality assurance has become a standard practice in many organizations (Newman and Logan 2008; Loshin 2010). Data that is sourced externally may be from organizations that have data quality assurance practices in place. Again, it should be emphasized that such data is observational data that is collected for some other purpose. As an example, social media data such as Twitter data (tweets) is generated by the public for purposes of expressing personal opinions. This data requires extensive preprocessing before it can be used by text mining algorithms (Wakade et al. 2012).

Data Preparation and Data Understanding Activities

It was previously observed that there is no *perfect* data waiting to be mined. The purpose of the data understanding and data preparation phases is to get the data to a level (of quality) that is appropriate for data mining. Data that is generated by computer systems is stored in server log files, proxy log files, and client log files. Server and proxy log files store data that records all the interactions with a server, for example, a web server. Romero and Ventura (2007) have provided examples of client log files for web-based educational applications. For such applications there is one client log file for each client (student). This file contains information about the interactions of the client with the system. For these types of data, the data quality problems are minimized as data is automatically generated and stored. However, it is still important to be keenly aware of the fact that this is observational data, that is, it is not collected in log files for purposes of data mining.

The data preparation phase involves four activities, namely, data cleaning, data construction, data integration, and data formatting (Shearer 2001). Romero and Ventura (2007) have discussed the data preprocessing activities for data stored in log files for web-based applications. They have observed that data cleaning is one of the major data preparation activities for log file data. Data cleaning involves the removal of irrelevant items and log entries that are not needed for the data mining activities. Data transformation and enrichment (equivalent to data construction) involves the derivation of new attributes from existing ones, conversion of numeric attributes to nominal or ordinal attributes (discretization), and providing meaning to references contained in the log files. Data integration involves the integration and synchronization of data from different log files and possibly other sources. A full discussion of data preprocessing activities for log file data may be found in Romero and Ventura (2007).

Data that is sourced from data warehouses or departmental data marts is expected to have minimal quality problems, as it has been subjected to the ETL process. However, many researchers have observed that it is not always the case that such data is of a reliable level of quality. A standard practice in data warehousing is to record metadata about the ETL process and the data. This metadata should provide data analysts with useful information during the data understanding phase. Data preparation activities still need to be conducted as this is also observational data.

Data that is sourced from operational systems is usually the most problematic. Common problems with this data include incorrect values, missing values, default (e.g., null) values, and attribute names that differ from one system to another. If these problems exist (and most commonly they do), they should be identified during the data understanding phase (Shearer 2001). During the data preparation phase, it has been recommended by Shearer (2001) and Guidici (2003) that data analysts should select clean subsets of the data in the data cleaning step prior to conducting the subsequent steps for data preparation. A major problem with selecting clean subsets of the data is that the resulting datasets may not be sufficiently representative for the data mining objectives. As an example, suppose that the data mining objective is to conduct customer segmentation to meet the business objectives of identifying homogeneous customer groups for marketing purposes. If the clean subsets of the data are not (statistically) sufficiently representative of the customer base, then the data mining and business objectives cannot be met using the selected data. This would lead to the abandonment of the data mining project. In recent years, many organizations have embarked on data quality assurance programs to improve the quality of data stored in operational systems, data warehouses, and data marts. Data quality assurance is discussed in the next two sections.

Data Quality Assurance

It was stated in the last section that data quality has been defined in literature as "fitness for use by data consumers" (Wang and Strong 1996; Lin et al. 2007). Data quality assurance involves organizational activities whose purpose is to ensure that at all times, the data stored in an organization's databases is of an acceptable quality. This section provides a discussion on the reasons why data quality assurance is important and the data quality frameworks used for data quality assurance.

The Need for Data Quality Assurance

The modern business organization needs to conduct timely data analysis to support decision making. Given that the decisions made based on the data analysis results can affect the short-term and long-term survival of a business, it is important for the data in the information systems to be of high quality. Other types of organizations, for example, the health care and educational sectors also need to conduct timely data analysis to support decision making. In the case of the healthcare sector, the analysis of poor-quality data to support decision making can lead to life-threatening outcomes. Since the mid-1990s, two types of activities for solving data quality problems in operational databases and data warehouses have been proposed by researchers. These are (1) the adoption of data quality frameworks to manage data quality and (2) the use of capability maturity models to assess the management activities for data quality assurance.

Loshin (2010, ch. 3) has advised that data quality assurance should start with the formulation of a data quality strategy. The purpose of a data quality strategy is to direct an organization to take steps that will reduce the business impact of poor-quality data to an acceptable level. A strategy may be defined as a long-term plan designed to achieve a specific objective. According to Loshin (2010, ch. 3), the process of formulating a data quality strategy should include the identification of various aspects, including (1) key success objectives, (2) evaluation of variables to be used in the measurement of success, (3) establishment of information quality expectations, (4) development of a governance model for overseeing success, and (5) development of protocols for ensuring that policies and procedures for maintaining high-quality data are followed by the stakeholders across the organization. Identification of these aspects of data quality assurance enables an organization to clearly specify a data quality framework and to continuously and effectively manage the data quality assurance/improvement practices based on a data quality maturity model.

Data Quality Frameworks

Loshin (2010, ch. 3, p. 37) has observed that a data quality framework defines management objectives that are consistent with key success objectives and the enterprise expectations for quality data and information either through integration of services or through the collaborative implementation of data governance policies and procedures. Loshin (2010, ch. 3, p. 37) has further observed that a data quality framework should additionally include the specification of metrics based on data quality dimensions, acquisition of technologies to support data quality management activities, and the incorporation of organizational and industry standards. Currently, there exists a large body of literature on data quality frameworks. This includes English (1999), Wang et al. (2001), Pipino et al. (2002), Shankaranarayanan and Cai (2006), Berti-Equille et.al (2011), and many more.

Data Quality Dimensions

Table 8.1 shows the general dimensions of data quality as defined by Wang and Strong (1996) and extended by Michnik and Lo (2009). The intrinsic data quality dimension refers to the degree to which data values are in conformance with the actual or true values (Wang and Strong 1996). This dimension denotes features that belong to the internal characteristic of data, namely, accuracy, objectivity, believability, and credibility (Michnik and Lo 2009).

The contextual data quality dimension refers to the degree to which the data is applicable to, or pertains to the task of a data user (Wang and Strong 1996). This dimension highlights the requirement that data quality must be considered within the context of the task at hand, that is, information must be relevant, timely, complete, and appropriate so as to add value (Michnik and Lo 2009). Michnik and Lo (2009) view this category as consisting of four subdimensions, namely, relevance, value added, timeliness, completeness, and amount of information provided by the data. The representational data quality dimension refers to the degree to which the data is represented in a clear and intelligible manner (Wang and Strong 1996). This dimension represents the need for information systems to present information in a way that is interpretable, easy to understand, concise, and consistently presented to the users (Michnik and Lo 2009). Michnik

Table 8.1 Data Quality Dimensions

Category of Data Quality	Subdimensions	Definition
Intrinsic data quality	Accuracy	Free from error
	Objectivity	Corresponding to objective reality
	Believability	Within the range of possibility or probability
	Reputation	Overall quality as judged by people in general
Contextual data quality	Relevance	Having a traceable and logical connection to the matter at hand
	Value-added	Being a product whose value has been increased through processing
	Timeliness	Being available at the right time (when needed)
	Completeness	Having all the necessary elements
	Amount of information	Containing a useful quantity of information
Representational data quality	Interpretability	Extent to which it is easy to explain the meaning
	Ease of understanding	Extent to which it is easy to understand the meaning
	Concise representation	Brevity of expression. Free from unnecessary details
	Consistent representation	Freedom from variation or contradiction
Accessibility data quality	Access	Permission, liberty, or ability to obtain
	Convenience	Conduciveness to comfort or ease of use
	Security	Measures taken to guard against sabotage, crime, or attack

Source: Michnik, J., and Lo, M.C., *European Journal of Operational Research*, 195, 850–856, 2009.

and Lo (2009) have proposed four subdimensions, namely, interpretability, ease of understanding, concise representation, and consistent representation. The accessibility dimension of data quality refers to the degree to which the data is available and obtainable (Wang and Strong 1996). It represents the need for information systems to be accessible but secure (Michnik and Lo 2009). Michnik and Lo (2009) view this category as comprising of three subdimensions, namely, access, convenience, and security.

Intrinsic data quality is essential for data mining projects because the summarization, creation of descriptive, and predictive models from data that is inaccurate, lacking objectivity, believability, and credibility will produce models that provide misleading information to decision makers. Contextual data quality is essential for data mining projects. Based on the business objectives established during the business understanding phase of the CRISP-DM model, it should be straightforward for the analysts to establish the levels of contextual data quality during the data understanding and data preparation phase. The subdimensions listed in Table 8.1 should guide the analysts to make the right decisions. Representational data quality is essential for data mining projects. Attempting to analyze data that is difficult to interpret and understand due to poor representation cannot lead to a timely and successful outcome. Statisticians have a golden rule that one should not attempt to analyze data that one cannot understand. When representational data quality is poor, this will lead to very large amounts of time being dedicated to the data understanding phase of the CRISP-DM model, worse still, to the cancellation of the project. Accessibility data quality is important for data mining projects. All the data for the project must be conveniently accessible to the analysts. At the same time, the data should have a history of being stored securely, so that its integrity is not questionable.

Data Quality Assessment

Data quality assessment consists of activities to establish the presence and extent of data quality problems. Several data profiling and quality assessment tools have been reported in the literature. These tools enable data analysts to get a quick understanding of the problems present in the data stored in a database (or a file). An example of such a tool is the *profiler* (Kandel et al. 2012), which supports exploratory analysis and understanding of data anomalies using statistical methods. A data analyst can use the profiler to establish missing data (records or attributes), erroneous data, inconsistent data, extreme values, and violations of primary key constraints for database tables. Specialized data quality assessment tools exist for some application domains where data analysis is conducted on a routine basis. Examples of such tools are the routine data quality assessment tool and data quality audit tool provided by the World Health Organisation (2011) for the management of data quality programs in public health information systems. Data profiling tools can be very useful in the data understanding phase of a data mining project. These tools are also very useful in the initial stages of establishing data quality assurance programs and for continuous monitoring of data quality levels. In addition to standard statistical methods for data quality assessment, data quality mining (DQM) has been reported in the literature as a useful method of data quality assessment (Hipp et al. 2001; Hassani and Anari 2005; Hassani et al. 2014). Hassani et al. (2014) have stated that DQM is defined as the application of data mining techniques for data quality measurement. The goal of DQM is to detect, quantify, explain, and correct data quality deficiencies in very large databases.

For continuous data quality assessment, it is important to formulate specific metrics to use in establishing the levels of data quality as part of a data quality framework. Loshin (2010, ch. 3, p. 39) has made the following observation: "One cannot improve something that cannot be measured." Therefore, for data quality assurance practices, measurement is an essential activity. The data quality dimensions, discussed in the previous section, specify data quality expectations. These dimensions are used as a basis for defining measures/metrics for the evaluation of the extent to which data quality expectations are met. Metrics are commonly subdivided into subjective and objective metrics. Subjective metrics reflect the needs and experiences of the stakeholders: the data collectors, custodians, and consumers (Pipino et al. 2002). After the definition of the metrics for assessment, the subjective and objective metrics are used to measure the levels of data quality. The last step involves comparing the measured levels (low or high) of data quality based on the subjective and objective assessments (Pipino et al. 2002). It should be noted that Pipino et al. (2002) have reported that, based on their experience, a *one-size-fits-all* set of metrics is not an appropriate solution for data quality assessment.

Pipino et al. (2002) have reported that many organizations, for example, health care, finance, consumer product companies, and banking institutions use questionnaires to measure subjective data quality. Motjolopane and Lutu (2012) have also reported the use questionnaires in the subjective assessment of the quality of banking supervision data. The questions in the questionnaires are based on the subjective assessment metrics, which are in turn derived from the data quality dimensions presented in the last section. Pipino et al. (2002) have also discussed three types of objective assessment measures, namely, *simple ratio*, *min* (minimum) or *max* (maximum) operation, and *weighted average*. The *simple ratio* is commonly used to measure exceptions. It is computed as the number of undesirable outcomes divided by the number of total outcomes subtracted from 1, so that 1 represents the most desirable score and 0 the least desirable score. The *min* or *max* operation is used for dimensions that require the aggregation of multiple data quality variables (indicators). The variable values are normalized first and then the *min* or *max* operation is applied. The *min* operation conservatively assigns the data quality dimension the lowest value among the indicators. The *max* operation optimistically assigns the data quality dimension the highest value among the indicators. An alternative to the *min* operation is the use of the *weighted average*, which is appropriate for the multivariate case. In order to ensure that the rating is normalized, each weighting factor should be between 0 and 1 and the weighting factors should add up to 1. Pipino et al. (2002) have advised that appropriate usage of a *weighted average* requires a good understanding of the importance of each variable to the evaluation of the dimension.

During the initial stages of a data quality assurance program subjective metrics can be used to quickly assess the extent of the data quality problems in the organization's data. The results of the analysis of the subjective assessment provides useful information in support of a business case for a data quality assurance program. When a data quality assurance program is in place and the subjective and objective metrics are used on a routine basis, a comparative analysis needs to be performed between the results of the subjective and objective assessments. Pipino et al. (2002) have stated that the most desirable outcome of data quality assessment is when it is established that both subjective assessment and objective assessment rank the data quality as being high. The second most desirable outcome is when there is agreement that the data quality is low. The most undesirable outcome is when there is a discrepancy between the subjective and objective assessments. When such discrepancies arise, an organization needs to determine the reasons for the discrepancies. It is very common for the data quality to be assessed as being poor both subjectively and objectively. When this happens, an organization needs to embark on a program for the management of data quality assurance activities. Several data quality assurance capability maturity models have been proposed as useful tools to guide organizations in the management of data quality assurance programs. These models are discussed in the next section.

Management of Data Quality Assurance Programs

The capability maturity model (CMM) is a management tool that defines the levels of organizational refinement in conducting profit-generating activities (Loshin 2010, ch. 3, p. 42). Some activities where CMMs are routinely applied include software development, programmer development, and project management. This section provides a discussion of CMMs for data quality assurance programs and the implications of the maturity levels to data mining projects.

Data Quality Capability Maturity Models

Several CMMs for data quality assurance practices have been proposed in the literature. Loshin (2010) has provided a specification of the data quality maturity model (DQMM) based on the CMM developed by the Software Engineering Institute at Carnegie Mellon University (Baker et al. 2007). Caballero et al. (2008) have proposed the Information Quality Management Maturity Model (IQM3) based on the CMM Integrated (CMMI) also developed by the Software Engineering Institute at Carnegie Mellon University (Baker et al. 2007). Newman and Logan (2008) have reported the Gartner Enterprise Information Management (EIM) maturity model.

The DQMM presented by Loshin (2010) defines five levels of maturity, called initial, repeatable, defined, managed, and optimized. At the initial level, the data quality assurance processes are largely informal and reactive. The problems that arise due to poor-quality data are severe, require immediate attention and often require significant roll-back and rework. Due to a lack of information sharing there is no ability to repeat success in solving data quality problems. At the repeatable level, there are some organizational management and information-sharing practices. These practices are supported by some process discipline, mostly in recognizing good practices and attempting to repeat them in similar situations. Organizational management is in terms of governance, documentation of processes, plans, and standards.

At the defined level, a framework for determining responsibility and account-ability for data quality is in place and accountability is monitored by an organi-zational governance board. Good practices for data quality assurance are well documented and an enterprise-wide data quality team meets regularly to discuss data quality issues. At the managed level, the data quality program incorporates business impact analysis with the ability to express data quality expectations and measure conformance to those expectations. Data quality assurance is proac-tive as quality problems are identified early in the information workflow. At the optimized level, the data quality maturity governance framework is in place. Enterprise-wide performance measures are used to identify opportunities for strategic improvement of data quality. Digital dashboards are used throughout the organization for continuous process monitoring of the data life cycle (Loshin 2010, ch. 3).

The IQM3 proposed by Caballero et al. (2008) also consists of five levels of maturity, namely, (1) initial, (2) defined, (3) integrated, (4) quantitatively man-aged, and (5) optimizing. The definitions for these levels largely correspond to the levels presented by Loshin (2010). The Gartner EIM maturity model discussed by Newman and Logan (2008) consists of six maturity levels, namely, (0) unaware, (1) aware, (2) reactive, (3) proactive, (4) managed, (5) effective. Levels 0 and 1 of the EIM maturity model correspond to level 1 (initial) of the Loshin CMM and Cabarello IQM3. Levels 2 through 5 of the EIM correspond to levels 2 through 5 of the Loshin data quality CMM and Cabarello information quality IQM3. Data quality CMMs provide systematic guidelines for organizations to manage and improve the management of their data quality assurance programs. Newman and Logan (2008) have advised that programs for the management of data quality assur-ance practices require a defined budget, charter, and resource plan. They also require a sustained effort that may take an organization several years to achieve. Newman and Logan (2008) have further observed that in 2008, there were only a few organi-zations that had advanced beyond the lower levels (levels 0, 1, 2) of the EIM CMM. This is very likely still the case today.

Implications of Data Quality Capability Maturity Models for Data Mining

Based on the discussion of data quality CMMs the following observations can be made. If an organization is at the initial level of capability maturity, it is risky to conduct data mining projects. It has been observed that at this level, the problems that arise due to poor-quality data are severe and often require significant roll-back and rework. The implication here is that the data owners either do not have any idea of the magnitude of their data quality problems or are aware of the data quality problems but have not made any effort to address these problems. It would, therefore, be very unwise to spend significant resources on the business understanding, data understanding, and data preparation phases of the data mining project and then abandon the project.

If an organization is at the repeatable level of capability maturity it makes sense to conduct data mining projects as there is some experience of data sharing and organizational management practices in terms of governance, documentation of processes, plans, and standards. The presence of such practices should make it easier for meaningful outputs from the business understanding phase of the data mining project as the data owners are more aware of the extent of their data quality problems. Therefore, an organization that is at the initial level should first conduct activities to get themselves to the repeatable level before attempting any data mining activities.

If an organization is at the defined, managed, or optimized level of capability maturity it should be fairly straightforward for data analysts to conduct data mining projects. At the defined level, an organization will most likely have a culture of data analysis using data that has been extracted, cleaned, transformed, integrated, and stored in an enterprise data warehouse or a collection of departmental data marts. At the managed level and optimized level, data quality problems should be minimal, so that data for data mining projects can be sourced directly from operational systems, from the enterprise data warehouse or from departmental data marts. However, as noted earlier, there are very few organizations that have advanced to these higher levels of capability maturity (Newman and Logan 2008).

Regardless of the capability maturity level, an organization should be able to conduct data mining projects if the source of the data is not the operational systems of the organization. Examples of such projects include creating predictive models for network intrusion detection, click stream analysis to identify browsing patterns of website visitors with a view to improving website design, and analysis of medical images. Data mining projects that depend on externally sourced data can also be conducted regardless of the capability maturity level of an organization. These include the analysis of satellite image data to study climate changes, and using social media data such as Twitter and Facebook data for sentiment analysis. For these types of projects, quality data is obtained through (possibly intensive) data preprocessing activities, which depend on the data mining objectives.

Discussion and Recommendations

This chapter has provided a discussion of the importance of data quality assurance for data mining projects. The discussion has been located in the context of data mining projects that use the CRISP-DM process model. Various examples of applications of data mining have been provided, the sources of data for these projects have been discussed, and various reasons have been highlighted on why the data quality of these sources may be poor. Two major reasons for the poor quality of data in organizational information systems are that (1) data entered by humans into computer information systems is commonly filled with errors and (2) data mining projects use observational data, which is data that was collected for some other purpose. Almost all the literature on data quality points to the fact that organizational data should be treated as a strategic asset. Data quality assessment, data quality frameworks, and data quality CMMs have been discussed in this chapter. These frameworks and maturity models have the potential to enable organizations to collect, store, and analyze quality data on a continuous basis. Needless to say, the application of data mining methods using high-quality data provides accurate and useful insights for purposes of decision making.

As reported by Newman and Logan (2008) most organizations will find themselves at level 0 (unaware), level 1 (aware), or level 2 (reactive) of the Gartner EIM maturity model, which corresponds to level 1 (initial) or level 2 (repeatable) of the CMM-based maturity models. It should be a straightforward matter to use a data quality CMM to establish the capability maturity level for the organization. Newman and Logan (2008) have advised that if an organization is at level 0 (unaware) of the EIM maturity model, the planners should informally educate the IT and business (organization) leaders on the potential value of formulating a data quality assurance strategy and data quality assurance program, and on the risks of not having such a program. Norman and Logan (2008) have further advised that if an organization is at level 1 (aware) of the EIM maturity model, the planners should formally present data quality assurance strategies to senior management. In order to make a convincing business case to senior management, it is suggested that planners should conduct a preliminary assessment of the current levels of data quality in the organization's information systems. The use of data profiling tools can be very useful at this stage. This should be followed by selecting the appropriate data quality dimensions based on the list presented in section "Data Quality Assurance," then defining data quality assessment metrics for subjective and objective assessment, as discussed in the same section. Assessment of the data quality should then be done using the guidelines provided by Pipino et al. (2002) and summarized in section "Data Quality Assurance." A report that details the extent of the data quality problems in concrete terms should go a long way to support the business case for a data quality assurance program.

Formulation of objective measures as discussed by Pipino et.al (2002) can be a complicated task, as it requires an intimate understanding of the variables that should be used to compute the data quality indicators. On the other hand, subjective assessment is a fairly straightforward activity. Motjolopane and Lutu (2010) have provided an example of a questionnaire that can be used for the subjective assessment of data quality. The questionnaire is based on the data quality dimensions that were discussed in section "Data Quality Assurance." Subjective assessment can be especially useful as an initial/starting step in establishing the depth and extent of data quality problems. Norman and Logan (2008) have also advised that the data quality assurance strategy should be linked to other business strategies. Given that data mining provides business intelligence, which supports decision making at the operational, tactical, and strategic levels of management, it should be easy for planners to link the benefits of data quality assurance to the benefits of data mining and business intelligence.

From a research perspective, there is a small but growing body of literature on data quality mining (DQM). Several authors (e.g., Hipp et al. 2001; Hassani and Anari 2005; Hassani et al. 2014) have argued that DQM methods can be used to measure and explain data quality deficiencies and to correct deficient data. There have also been proposals in the literature for the extension of knowledge discovery in databases process models to incorporate a data quality phase (Hipp et al. 2001). These emerging areas of research should gradually make significant contributions toward data quality assessment and data quality assurance practices in support of effective knowledge discovery and data mining.

Conclusions

It has been argued in this chapter that many highly sophisticated statistical methods, computational algorithms, software tools, and widely adopted process models currently exist for data mining. Given that the results of data mining are used to support decision making, it is essential that the information obtained from data mining activities should be correct and accurate. The impact of poor-quality data on data mining projects has been discussed. A review of the literature on data quality assessment and data quality assurance has been provided. Some guidelines have been provided on how organizations faced with poor-quality data can ensure that in the short term they are able to conduct data mining projects, while they embark on long-term data quality assurance programs.

References

Baker, E.R., Fisher, M.J., and Goethert, W. (2007) Basic principles and concepts for achieving quality, Software Engineering Institute Technical Note CMU/SEI-2007-TN-002, Software Engineering Institute.

Bellazzi, R. and Zupan, B. (2008) Predictive data mining in clinical medicine: Current issues and guidelines, *International Journal of Medical Informatics*, vol. 77, pp. 81–97.

Berry, M.J.A. and Linoff, G.S. (2000) *Mastering Data Mining: The Art and Science of Customer Relationship Management.* John Wiley & Sons, New York.

Berti-Equille, L., Comyn-Wattiau, I., Cosquer, M. et al. (2011) Assessment and analysis of information quality: A multidimensional model and case studies. *International Journal of Information Quality,* vol. 2, no. 4, pp. 300–323.

Bifet, A. and Frank, E. (2010) Sentiment discovery in Twitter streaming data. In: B. Pfahringer, G. Holmes, and A. Hoffmann (eds.), *Lecture Notes in Artificial Intelligence (LNAI)* vol. 6332, pp. 1–15, Springer-Verlag, Berlin, Germany.

Caballero, I., Caro, A., Calero, C., and Piattini, M. (2008) IQM3: Information quality management maturity Model. *Journal of Universal Computer Science,* vol. 14, no. 22, pp. 3658–3685.

Chan, P. and Stolfo, S. (1998) Toward scalable learning with non-uniform class and cost distributions: A case study in credit card fraud detection. *Proceedings of the 4th International Conference on Knowledge Discovery and Data Mining.* AAAI.

English, L. (1999) *Improving Data Warehouse and Business Information Quality: Methods for Reducing Costs and Increasing Profits,* Wiley, New York.

Facebook (2014) Facebook. http://www.Facebook.com.

Fawcett, T. and Provost, F. (1997) Adaptive fraud detection. *Data Mining and Knowledge Discovery,* vol. 1, pp. 291–316.

Guidici, P. (2003) *Applied Data Mining: Statistical methods for Business and Industry,* Wiley, Chichester.

Hand, D.J. (1997) *Construction and Assessment of Classification Rules,* Wiley, Chichester.

Hand, D.J., Manila, H., and Smyth, P. (2001) *Principles of Data Mining.* MIT Press, Cambridge, MA.

Hassani, H. and Anari, M. (2005) Using data mining in data quality improvement. *Proceedings of the 55th Session International Statistical Institute,* April 5–12, Sydney, Australia, The International Statistical Institute.

Hassani, H., Saporta, G., and Silva, E.S. (2014) Data mining and official statistics: The past, the present and the future. *Big Data,* vol. 2, no. 1, doi:10.1089/big.2013.0038.

Hipp, J., Güntzer, U., and Grimmer, U. (2001) Data quality mining—Making a virtue a necessity. *Proceedings of the 6th ACM SIGMOD Workshop on Research Issues in Data Mining and Knowledge Discovery,* May 2001, New York.

IBM (2011) *IBM SPSS Modeler CRISP-DM Guide,* IM Corporation. Available at: ftp://public .dhe.ibm.com/software/analytics/spss/documentation/modeler/14.2/en/CRISP_DM.pdf.

Jansen, B.J., Zhang, M., Sobel, K., and Chowdry, A. (2009) Micro-blogging as online word of mouth branding. *Proceedings of the 27th International Conference Extended Abstracts on Human Factors in Computing Systems,* April 2009, Boston, MA, pp. 3856–3864.

Kandel, S., Parikh, R., Paepcke, A., Hellerstein, J.M., and Heer, J. (2012) Profiler: Integrated statistical analysis and visualisation for data quality assessment. *Proceedings of the International Working Conference on Advanced Visual Interfaces (AVI '12),* May 21–25, Capri island, Italy, pp. 547–554.

Koh, H.C. and Tan, G. (2005) Data mining applications in healthcare. *Journal of Healthcare Information Management,* vol. 19, no. 2, pp. 64–72.

Kohavi, R., Mason, R.J., and Zheng, Z. (2004) Lessons and challenges from mining retail e-commerce data. *Machine Learning,* vol. 57, pp. 83–113.

Lee, W. and Stolfo, J. (2000) A framework for constructing features and models for intrusion detection systems. *ACM Transactions on Information and System Security,* vol. 3, no. 4, pp. 227–261.

Lin, S., Gao, J., Koronios, A., and Chanana, V. (2007) Developing a data quality framework for asset management in engineering organisations, *International Journal of Information Quality*, 1(1), pp. 100–126.

Linoff, G.S. and Berry, M.J.A. (2013) *Data Mining Techniques: For Marketing, Sales, and Customer Relationship Management*, 3rd Edition, Wiley, New York.

Loshin, D. (2010) *The Practitioner's Guide to Data Quality Improvement*, 1st Edition, Morgan Kaufman, Burlington, MA.

Luan, J. (2002) Data mining and its applications in higher education, *New Directions for Institutional Research*, no. 113, pp. 17–36.

Michnik, J. and Lo, M.C. (2009) The assessment of the information quality with the aid of multiple criteria analysis, *European Journal of Operational Research*, vol. 195, pp. 850–856.

Motjolopane, R. and Lutu, P.E.N. (2012) Improving data quality in the banking supervisory data of Southern Africa central banks. *Electronic Journal of Information Systems in Developing Countries*, 50, January 2012. http://www.ejisdc.org.

Newman, D. and Logan, D. (2008) Gartner introduces the EIM maturity model. *Gartner Research*, ID number: G000160425.

Pipino, L.L., Lee, Y.W., and Wang, R.Y. (2002) Data quality assessment. *Communications of the ACM*, vol. 45, no. 4, pp. 211–218.

Romero, C. and Ventura, S. (2007) Educational data mining: A survey from 1995 to 2005, *Expert Systems with Applications*, vol. 33, pp. 135–146.

SAS (2013) *Data mining from A to Z: Better insights, new opportunities*. SAS White Paper. http://www.sas.com/en_us/offers/sem/data-mining-2273479/register.html (accessed on November 14, 2014).

Shankaranarayanan, G. and Cai, Y. (2006) Supporting data quality management in decision-making, *Decision Support Systems*, vol. 42, pp. 302–317.

Sharma, S. and Osei-Bryson, K.-M. (2009) Framework for formal implementation of the business understanding phase of data mining projects. *Expert Systems with Applications*, vol. 36, pp. 4114–4124.

Shearer, C. (2001) The CRISP-DM model: The new blueprint for data mining, *Journal of Data Warehousing*, vol. 5, no. 4, pp. 13–22.

Simoudis, E. (1996) Reality check for data mining. *IEEE Expert*, vol. 11, no. 5, pp. 26–33.

Theusinger, C. and Huber, K.-P. (2000) Analyzing the footsteps of your customers—A case study by ASK|net and SAS Institute GmbH, *Proceedings of WEBKDD*. SAS Institute, GMBH, Heidelberg, Germany.

Twitter (2014). Twitter. http://www.twitter.com.

Wakade, S., Shekar, C., Liszka, K.J., and Chan, C.-C. (2012) Text Mining for Sentiment Analysis of Twitter Data, *International Conference on Information and Knowledge Engineering*, pp. 109–114.

Wang, R., Ziad, M., and Lee, Y. (2001) *Data Quality*, Kluwer Academic Publishers, London.

Wang, R.Y. and Strong, D.M. (1996) Beyond accuracy: What data quality means to data consumers. *Journal of Management Information Systems*, vol. 12, no. 4, pp. 5–34.

Witten, I., Frank, E., and Hall, M. (2011) *Data Mining: Practical Machine Learning Tools and Techniques*, 3rd Edition, Morgan Kaufmann, Boston, MA.

World Health Organisation (2011) Manual on use of routine data quality assessment (RDQA) tool for TB monitoring. WHO Press, Geneva, Switzerland. http://whqlibdoc.who.int/publications/2011/9789241501248_eng.pdf.

Chapter 9

Critical Success Factors in Knowledge Discovery and Data Mining Projects

Corlane Barclay

Contents

Abstract: The interest in knowledge discovery and data mining (KDDM) has grown especially with the current hype surrounding "big data." These types of projects provide unique challenges especially in terms of the demand for multidisciplinary skills throughout the KDDM process. It is therefore important to appreciate the set of critical success factors (CSFs) that impact the successful implementation of these projects. This study identifies some strategic and tactical factors using the action research approach. The study is situated in an educational data mining project experience where the factors are observed and adopted throughout the various stages. This critical reflection revealed that project management factors such as project planning, risk management, and stakeholder commitment are crucial when combined with tactical factors such as clear and aligned business and KDDM objectives, getting the right data, being knowledgeable with the appropriate software tools and data mining tasks, and facilitating continued dialog with end users to enable deployment of new knowledge. This research contributes to the planning and decision-making process through the identification of key considerations in the deployment of these types and similar KDDM projects.

Keywords: Critical success factors, project management, knowledge discovery and data mining, educational data mining, action research

Introduction

Critical success factors (CSFs) are important knowledge for decision making and learning in any organizations. According to Rockart (1979), CSFs are important performance factors that must receive continuous attention of management if an organization is to remain competitive. Similarly, they are preconditions to the successful attainment of organizational activities. Today, the information needs of organizations continue to grow with evolving customer requirements and technological and business landscapes. As a result, there is the creation of a wide array of data, small and big data that call for close interrogation of the data to enable transformation to information and knowledge via knowledge discovery and data mining (KDDM) or data mining projects. These KDDM projects are specifically targeted to help achieve organizational strategic objectives through the extraction of interesting patterns from the data for organizational decision support (Anand and Büchner 1998; Fayyad et al. 1996a). However, although there is little empirical statistics available, reports show that these projects have their share of challenges and have experienced limited success in businesses. Further, an analysis of industry shows that the organizational experiences include low deployment rates, difficulty in accessing data or "dirty data," and ill-defined business and data mining objectives. Therefore, it becomes necessary to investigate what are some of the CSFs in KDDM projects.

Formal Problem Definition

The identification of CSFs as an area is well studied in academic literature; for example, Butler and Fitzgerald (1999) identified generic and collective success factors for information system (IS) development process, Belassi and Tukel (1996) proposed a framework to classify the critical factors and outlined the impact of these factors on project performance, Westerveld (2003) proposed a Project Excellence Model, Baccarini and Collins (2003) identified factors critical to success of projects, Fortune and White (2006) proposed CSFs within the context of a system model, and Chow and Cao (2008) examined success factors in agile software projects. However, the evolving dimensions and complexities of projects require continued assessment to help ensure that organizations remain competitive, particularly within specific contexts. Closer analysis of literature also revealed that relatively little research has focused on data mining projects, except for researchers such as Hilbert (2005), Nemati and Barko (2003), and Jaesung Sim (2003) who examined factors within defined contexts. Consequently, it is seen that empirical analysis of factors contributing to successful deployment of KDDM projects is currently limited. Nemati and Barko (2003) observed that there was a paucity of empirical work relating to factors influencing the implementation of organizational data mining technologies, and the landscape has not changed significantly since that time.

Research Justification

The opportunity to position the research in a developing context cannot be undervalued because the application of KDDM projects is still in their formative stages of development and practice in these economies. Although the research is situated within a developing country context, its value can be extended to similar projects and experiences in organizations and countries with different levels of maturity in deploying KDDM initiatives.

CSF method is an important means for supporting strategic and tactical decision-making method including IS planning and requirements analysis (Boynton and Zmud 1984). Therefore, this study provides value in terms of understanding some of the key elements in planning KDDM projects and determining the business and data mining objectives necessary to facilitate the coordinated set of process activities through to deployment. In short, the research can provide some guidance on approaches to achieve successful execution and deployment of KDDM projects.

Purpose and Research Approach

The purpose of this research is to identify CSFs through the examination of a single KDDM project within the education realm from the domain understanding phase to the deployment phase of activities. The study highlights how project management (PM) principles are essential throughout the KDDM process cycle and the benefits of having a structured process to help assure the quality of the knowledge extracted for supporting business decisions. The principles of action research are adopted as appropriate because according to Meyer (2000) action research strength lies in its focus on providing solutions to practical problems and its ability to empower practitioners through engagement with the research and development activities. Therefore, in this context, key success factors are identified which help guide the subsequent deployment activities in the educational data mining (EDM) initiative. Additionally, one of the goals of action research is to provide practical knowledge that is useful for practitioners (Reason and Bradbury 2001), such as data mining and project practitioners, which is the goal of this research through the identification of CSFs in KDDM projects. It is expected that the results will translate into improved effectiveness and efficiency in managing these projects and improve success rates across multiple domains.

The rest of the chapter is organized as follows: Dimensions of success and CSFs are introduced, the nature and characteristics of KDDM projects are discussed, and the KDDM process is briefly outlined in section "Research Background"; the action research method that is adopted in this study to underscore its research validity is outlined in section "Research Approach: Action Research"; the findings are presented and discussed within the framework of a KDDM project in section "Findings: CSFs"; and the conclusion is provided in section "Concluding Remarks."

Research Background

Nature of KDDM Projects

KDDM projects can be described as any temporary initiative to mine or extract knowledge from predetermined datasets to aid organizational decision making through the application of appropriate project management and knowledge discovery methodologies. These projects have been shown to positively diverse domains, including customer relationship management, fraud detection and prevention, risk management, manufacturing quality improvement, healthcare quality improvement, and law enforcement and homeland security (IBM 2010).

An analysis of the literature shows a growing body of work on models that provide direction on activities to execute data mining projects, where the foundation was established in the early 1990s. A KDDM process model consists of a set of processing steps to be followed when executing KDDM initiatives (Kurgan and Musilek 2006). Two key models representing both academia and industry are the Cross Industry Standard Process for Data Mining (CRISP-DM) model (Chapman et al. 2013) and the seminal nine-step perspective of Fayyad et al. (1996a, 1996b).

CRISP-DM is a six-step process (Figure 9.1) (Chapman et al. 2013): business understanding focuses on understanding the project objectives and requirements from a business perspective, and then converting this knowledge into a data mining problem definition and a preliminary plan designed to achieve the objectives. Data understanding commences with an initial data collection and proceeds with activities that enable analysts to become familiar with the data, identify data quality

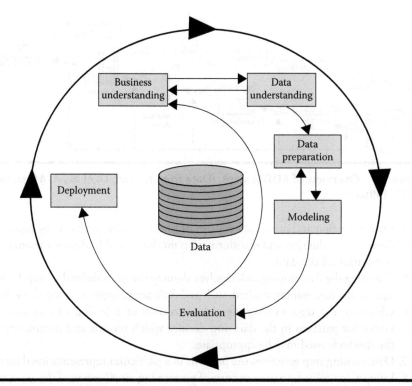

Figure 9.1 CRISP-DM. (Data from Chapman, P. et al., *CRISP-DM 1.0: Step-by-Step Data Mining Guide*, 2013.)

problems, discover first insights into the data, and/or detect interesting subsets to form hypotheses regarding hidden information. Data preparation covers all activities needed to construct the final dataset from the initial raw data. Modeling includes various modeling techniques that are selected and applied, and their parameters are calibrated to optimal values. Evaluation involves evaluation of the model and review of the steps executed to create it; to be certain, the model properly achieves the business objectives. Deployment involves applying "live" models within an organization's decision-making processes.

Fayyad et al (1996a, 1996b) introduced an iterative nine-step process to mining data (Figure 9.2):

1. Developing and understanding the application domain include learning the relevant prior knowledge and the goals of the end.
2. Creating a target dataset involves selection of a subset of variables (attributes) and data points (examples) that will be used to perform discovery tasks.
3. Data cleaning and preprocessing consists of removing outliers, dealing with noise and missing values in the data, and accounting for time sequence information and known changes.

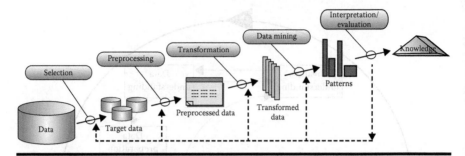

Figure 9.2   Overview of KDDM steps. (Data from Fayyad, U. et al., *AI Magazine*, 17, 37, 1996a.)

4. Data reduction and projection consists of finding useful attributes by applying dimension reduction and transformation methods, and finding invariant representation of the data.
5. Choosing the data mining task involves aligning the goals defined in step 1 with a particular data mining method, such as classification, regression, and clustering.
6. Choosing the data mining algorithm consists of selection of methods to search for patterns in the data and decides which models and parameters of the methods used may be appropriate.
7. Data mining step generates the patterns in a particular representational form.
8. Interpreting mined patterns consists of performing visualization of the extracted patterns and models, and visualization of the data based on the extracted models.
9. Consolidating discovered knowledge consists of incorporating the discovered knowledge into the performance system, and documenting and reporting it to the interested parties.

Dimensions of Success

Success may mean different things to different stakeholders and vary based on context (Cooke-Davies 2002). According to the Association for Project Management [APM (2013)], project success is the satisfaction of stakeholders' needs and is measured by the success criteria as identified and agreed at the start of the project. Although there is an ongoing debate on the dimensions, there is a growing trend to consider perspectives beyond the traditional approach of conformance to time, cost, and quality requirements (Barclay 2008; Barclay and Osei-Bryson 2010). Researchers have broadly categorized success into the process of completing the activity and the outcome. For example, Collins and Baccarini (2004) distinguished between *PM success* and *product success*, where PM success focuses on the project process and satisfying stakeholder objectives, including adherence to time and cost requirements, and product success is centered on the project's product and meeting the stakeholders' needs. It is posited that the view or dimensions of success impacts CSFs. Accordingly Lim and Mohamed (1999) suggested that CSF could be classified within the framework of the stages of the project life cycle at the micro and macro levels.

CSFs for Projects

CSFs are groups or categories of key jobs or activities that must be done exceedingly well for a company to be successful (Bullen and Rockart 1981; Rockart 1979). Similarly within a project context, it is those tasks or considerations that must be done well for the project to be successful. The analysis of CSFs has been in multiple contexts within the IS and business domains. Butler and Fitzgerald (1999) outlined that the CSF approach has been employed in areas and contexts such as IS development, strategic IS planning, data administration, IS function evaluation, IS executives, and requirements planning. The findings have shown CSFs to be broadly related to areas of executive support, stakeholder management and commitment, PM requirements, product quality, and client acceptance. Table 9.1 highlights a summary of some of the key literature and their findings.

CSFs for Data Mining Projects

Hermiz (1999) stated that there are four CSFs for any data mining project: (1) having a clearly articulated business problem that needs to be solved and for which DM is a proper tool; (2) insuring that the problem being pursued is supported by the right type of data of sufficient quality and in sufficient quantity for DM; (3) recognizing that DM is a process with many components and dependencies—the entire project cannot be "managed" in the traditional sense of the business world; (4) planning to learn from the DM process regardless of the outcome, and understanding, that there is no guarantee that any given DM project will be successful. Also, in an IBM white paper (IBM 2010), they suggested that practitioners should start with a strategic end in mind, line up the necessary resources, and define an executable data mining strategy to help increase the likelihood of implementing a successful data mining project. Similarly, formulating a well-defined business or research problem and assembling quality representative data sources are critical to the overall success of any data mining project (SAS 2013).

Nemati and Barko (2003) in a cross-sectional survey derived from the square-root framework (Atkinson 1999) to determine the relationship among project factors affecting organizational data mining implementation found that smaller organizations with little or no organizational data mining experience were subject to less favorable project outcome. Some of the key factors to favorable outcome included project-related factors such as shorter timeliness, few resources, and reduced project scope. Experts from the study further noted that viewing organizational data mining as an iterative process, properly selecting tools and algorithms, and possessing an in-depth knowledge of the industry and business are factors that positively impact the favorable implementation of these projects. The findings underlined the importance of the application of the complete KDDM process in the delivery of data mining projects.

Table 9.1 Summary of Literature

Literature	Factors	Dimensions
Andersen et al. (2006)	Strong project commitment, early stakeholder influence, stakeholder endorsement of project plans, and rich project communications	• Stakeholder • PM process
Bryde and Robinson (2005)	Minimization of project cost and duration (contractors' perspective) and satisfaction of stakeholders needs (clients' perspective)	• Stakeholder • PM process
Cooke-Davies (2002)	Twelve hard and soft factors that are mainly tied to organizational, project, and program practices	• Stakeholder • PM process
Dvir et al. (2003)	A well-designed initiation phase is the most important factor in project success; formal design and planning documents are instrumental in meeting project time and budget constraints	• PM process
Pinto and Slevin (1999)	Project mission, top management, project schedule/plan, client consultation, personnel, technical tasks, client acceptance, monitoring and feedback, communication, and troubleshooting	• Stakeholder • PM process • Client acceptance • Executive support
Kerzner (1987)	Project manager's leadership, commitment to planning and control, project manager's selection criteria, executive commitment to project management, organizational adaptability, and corporate understanding of project management	• Stakeholder • PM process • Client acceptance • Executive support

Research Approach: Action Research

Action research methodology is adopted in this research as an appropriate approach to attain the key research objective, that is, to identify CSFs in KDDM projects and address problems in deploying these types of projects. This is accomplished through the lens of a single EDM project based in the Caribbean. Susman and Evered (1978) noted that action research is useful for generating knowledge for use in solving problems that members of the organizations face. Rapoport (1970) outlined that action research goal is to contribute to both the practical concerns of stakeholders in an immediate problematic situation and the goals of social science by joint collaboration within a mutually acceptable ethical framework. Susman and Evered (1978) augmented these goals to include the development of self-help competencies of people facing problems. In other words, action research provides an interactive collaborative process for solving problems grounded in acceptable ethical principles. The cyclical process through continuous interaction with the social system includes diagnosing, action planning, action taking, evaluating, and specifying learning (Susman and Evered 1978).

Action research is a well-established research method and has increased importance for ISs (Baskerville 1999). It is one potential avenue to improve the practical relevance of IS research (Baskerville and Myers 2004), and is seen as the "touchstone of most good organizational development practice" (Van Eynde and Bledsoe 1990). The researcher generates new social knowledge about a social system, while at the same time attempting to change it (Lewin 1946; Peters and Robinson 1984). Its cyclical nature provides iteration of intervention and reflection that provides a rich opportunity for learning.

These characteristics motivate the use of this methodology in this research to enhance the practices in managing and deploying KDDM projects through the identification of key factors for success.

Research Process

Knowledge was obtained from informal and formal interviews, participant observation, and review of documents. The research setting was a single KDDM project focused on mining educational data on and about examination performance from students applying to a university in a Caribbean country, Jamaica. The strategy employed in deriving the CSFs is shown in Figure 9.3. The cyclical process of action research was applied at each stage of the project. Therefore, the five stages of the diagnosing, action planning, action taking, evaluating, and specifying learning were applied to all steps in the KDDM process to identify CSFs as part of the learning.

Diagnosing involves the identification and definition of an improvement opportunity or a general problem to be solved in the client organization. Therefore, the improvement opportunity for the overall project is the application of the KDDM process to educational data to predict students' performance in certain core subjects. An analysis of the CSFs in executing this project was considered because there were little or no benchmark or best practices to apply in this particular context, that is, education sector in the country. The issues and challenges were identified or diagnosed at each stage of the project process based on observations and interviews, and solutions were proposed and evaluated, which then formed the basis for the initial set of CSFs.

Action planning involves the consideration of alternative courses of action to attain the improvement or solve the problem identified. In determining the objective of the project, general courses of action were identified in relation to the best strategy to apply to achieve the objective. This includes the identification of KDDM process models, how they would be executed, and the software applications that are used.

Action taking involves the selection and realization of one of the courses of action considered in the previous stage. The specific courses of action were selected

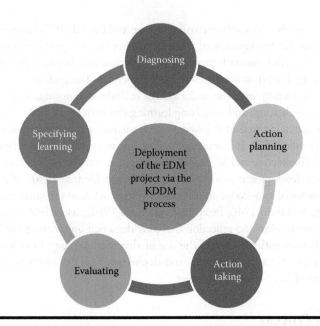

Figure 9.3   Research process.

based on consensus of the project team. As a result, the CRISP-DM and PM methodologies to deploy the project from start to completion were undertaken.

Evaluating involves the study of the outcomes of the selected course of action. Evaluation was undertaken at each stage of the KDDM process, which helped to identify any issues and success factors. In other words, an analysis of the courses of action taken throughout the life of the project and the results was done to help determine key factors for success. Lessons were applied to successive rounds in the process. The process of developing the CSFs was decomposed into four cycles described in Figure 9.4 and formed a subset of the research process (Figure 9.3).

Specifying learning involves the study of the outcomes of the evaluating stage. The key lessons from the process were identified based on the evaluating action taken throughout the project, including the postmortem analysis of the completed project.

Project Background

The target group for this KDDM project is students who have taken high-school leaving examinations and have applied to the tertiary institution in Jamaica. The country has been experiencing low pass rates in English language and mathematics among high-school students for over a decade. This suggests that there have been no sustainable solutions and traditional methods of analysis were not working. The project was therefore motivated by a need to better understand the characteristics of students' performance in the high-school leaving examination so as to enable improved focus on areas that can improve performance and to apply KDDM

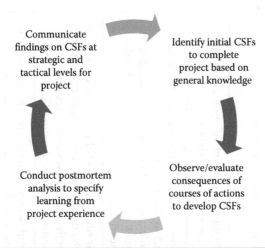

Figure 9.4   Process of developing CSFs.

within the context to identify any interesting and previously unknown patterns. A project of this nature was a first due to the relative low adoption of KDDM and even lower with any focus on education datasets. The strategic business objective was identified as determining the possible indicators to the students' performances in final examination from which can the key decision makers in the education sector can be informed. The project lasted over 6 months and included all the phases of CRISP-DM except a formal deployment stage. There were three core members of the project team with roles consisting of project manager and data analysts.

The findings from the study were collected through interviews with project team members and education stakeholders. The findings indicated that getting the right data and completing the project were paramount business objectives; observations of the project experience throughout the phases where action research process was manifested and learning of the factors that had a positive impact on the project was noted; postmortem analysis at the end of the project; and formal development and categorization of the CSFs into categories (Figure 9.4).

Findings: CSFs

CSFs in this context are considered to be any element or experience from the project that has been shown to have a positive impact on the project outcome. The CSFs are classified into two broad categories: strategic and tactical CSFs. Strategic CSFs refer to the general PM factors that are critical in successfully delivering the KDDM project. Tactical CSFs refer to the specific factors that are critical in executing the different phases of the KDDM process cycle, which in this instance is the CRISP-DM process.

In identifying the CSFs, the action research cycle was applied and resulted in learning of the factors essential to the successful completion of this project (see Table 9.2

Table 9.2 CSFs in KDDM

KDDM/Project Process	Diagnosing	Action Planning and Taking	Evaluating and Specifying Learning
General PM	Delays in the initial stages	Identify process models to guide execution Adopt the CRISP-DM and PM approaches to guide project	Adoption of a KDDM approach supported by PM methodology for an efficient and effective delivery of DM project
	Lack of buy-in and support from the education stakeholders	Initiate discussion with key stakeholders and meeting with data owner to discuss access to data	• Obtain commitment and buy-in from data owners to prevent delays. • Accessibility to data, regardless of the forms of data, is a prerequisite to better data understanding • Project leadership in both PM and KDDM issues is vital in navigating project and its uncertainties
Business understanding	Unclear business objectives	Develop objectives based on guidelines within the context of project goal	Clear set of business objectives sets the tone for the development of the data mining objectives and serves as the basis for evaluating the achievement of same
Data understanding	Difficulty in gaining access to right data	Request access to data to many institutions island-wide, highlighting the benefits of sharing the data	• Identification of data repositories and how access will be granted is not a taken-for-granted task. • Right data in the right form is critical for project execution and timely delivery • Privacy and security concerns ought to be managed

	Lack of sufficient formal guide in the collection of data	Access to data, highlighted that data had to be in the right form and often was not digitized. Therefore, a formal approach was necessary to ensure data quality. However, for this project, the strategy was revised to use more readily available and manipulatable dataset	Data collection guide for data mining required especially where there is no available digitized data. However, available datasets still require guidelines for accessibility and data transformation
Data preparation	Data quality concerns in data—missing and inconsistent data	Develop approach for addressing missing attributes and inconsistent data; for example, removal of records	• Improved accounting of missing attributes, etc. necessary for assuring data quality • Need to develop strategies for any missing data at onset. • Any errors found in data must be communicated to data keeper to correct/update database
	Additional preparation needed at commencement of modeling stage	Apply corrections and updates to eliminate errors in data file	Ensure that prepped data is compatible with software requirements Highlight the iterative nature of this activity, along with others in the KDDM process
Modeling	Access to right software tools	Perform search of available and suitable tools and select based on needs and constraints	Team must be knowledgeable with specific or chosen data mining software and data mining techniques and how their use can achieve business objectives

(Continued)

Table 9.2 (*Continued*)   CSFs in KDDM

KDDM/Project Process	Diagnosing	Action Planning and Taking	Evaluating and Specifying Learning
	Selection of appropriate modeling tasks and use cases	Training to develop competencies and skills in software and data mining techniques	"Know-how" and "know-about" prevent delays in the project, or adjustment in schedule where sufficient time for training at the beginning of the project is done
Evaluation	Clear measureable objectives	Iterative development of objectives	Clear measureable objectives that are aligned to the type of results from the modeling phase
Deployment	Limited deployment	Continued dialog with stakeholders	• End-user involvement impacts deployment rate • Limited acceptance and use of data mining results because of limited awareness and involvement among stakeholders. • Partnership with business area leading the deployment strategy may be one way of promoting deployment and use. • Continued open dialog with stakeholders/end users to improve deployment rate

where the issues are organized according to the CRISP-DM phases). Some of the problems identified or diagnosed during the project included delays in the initial stages, that is, commencement of the business understanding phase of the project; difficulty in gaining access to or collecting the right data; management of data quality; lack of clear business objectives necessary to inform the data mining objectives and aid the evaluation phase; selection and development of suitable models or use cases aligned with the business objectives; issues in the preparation of the data that match the requirements of the data mining software; and limited deployment opportunities to the users. The number of issues encountered may be attributed to the limited data mining experience within the team and limited resources available for executing the project. However, the experience underscored the necessity of certain factors to enhance a favorable outcome in the delivery of the data mining project.

The courses of actions taken to resolve each of the problem encountered during the KDDM phases will be discussed.

Strategic CSFs—PM

One of the key observations was the taken-for-granted aspect of project planning and management at the initial stage of the project. The project team members were keen to get started and "jump" into performing tasks, however, without due consideration for the activities within the steps often resulted in unnecessary work. After multiple discussions and delays, the team was forced to take a step back and apply the general guide for completing a project and deploying a data mining initiative. To stem the delays, the identification and selection of a disciplined approach to execute was identified. The CRISP-DM was selected because of its wide application and ease of use. This was supported by basic PM approach. The selection resulted in a turnaround in the project in which the team was able to deliver the project within time while achieving the stated objectives.

Stakeholder support was critical in executing the project. The data owners provided access to the data and a project champion understood the vision of the project and was able to share that with other stakeholders to obtain their buy-in. While speaking to the data owners or keepers, in this instance, who were the educational institutions, they expressed reservations in sharing the data due to concerns over privacy and confidentiality, despite assurances of ethical use of data. This exacerbated the data collection efforts. It was observed that in instances where there were low level of technology maturity within the secondary schools, for example, largely manual processes, there were difficulties in fully grasping made or understanding the benefits of data mining. The shift to university data alleviated this issue and the project champion was able to influence the data owner at the university to provide access to the data; this was communicated to the data keepers in the technology department, who provided a copy of the data based on our requirements, that is, online application data for 5 years.

The learning process underlined the importance of stakeholder buy-in and commitment, and even the understanding combined with the identification of a project champion in moving the project forward.

A robust feasibility and risk assessment is necessary to help identify the key issues in managing the KDDM project. This is best applied during the business understanding phase. The challenges experienced underline the importance of identifying legal and technical feasibility in particular. Legal considerations because the data owners are concerned about whether the sharing of student data will contravene any laws or breach confidentiality and technical considerations because knowledge of suitable software applications and the CRISP-DM process were limited at the project onset. Therefore, for less experienced team members, identification of any technical risks and corresponding response strategies is vital. Similarly, less mature or experienced data owners may be more concerned about privacy and legal concerns, which also have to be addressed through confidential agreements, privacy persevering algorithms, and awareness of the way in which the data will be used and reported.

It was also observed that the project team's ability to adapt to change or response swiftly to changes in the project significant impact their ability to complete the project on time given the agreed project objectives. Despite adequate planning, unforeseen challenges may arise, and it is therefore important to be flexible, with positive attitude to facilitate adapting to changes. With an alternate outlook, faced with the multiple changes, the team could have decided to abandon the project.

Tactical CSFs—KDDM Process

The business understanding phase was considered the most frustrating phase by the project team members. There were multiple iterations in the initial phases of the project that contributed to delays. Although the CRISP-DM considers an iterative process, it was observed that the difficulty in formulating the business and objectives severely impacted the quality of the project and resulted in reworks. Sharma and Osei-Bryson (2009) noted the limited guidance in formulating business objectives of data mining projects. The lack of sufficient guidance may have hindered the team initially. Action planning and taking activities included a better understanding of the goals of the project through additional research and interviews with domain experts. The objectives were subsequently simplified and written in a manner that the achievement or nonachievement could be objectively assessed. The importance of measureable and feasible business and data mining objectives and criteria became more apparent during the evaluation phase.

The data collection phase was riddled with difficulties mainly due to a combination of lack of initial data and the unwillingness of the data owners to share the data, where some expressed fear of privacy breaches. The experience highlighted that data from secondary schools were in disparate areas with no clear data policy for future analysis. Additionally, the nondigitized data, that is, paper records, made transformation into the right form challenging. This underscored the necessity for clear data collection methodology that considered data not yet available in databases and data warehouses, which is a reality for many organizations. An amalgamation of these issues resulted in a shift in collection strategy to identification and selection of a particular university where the application data was digitized and the data owner, i.e., the university's executive was willing to share the data. It also underscored the importance of accessibility and availability of the right data, in the right form, at the right time because it cannot be taken for granted.

The data preparation phase activities underlined the iterative nature of maintaining data quality and preparing the data for modeling. In the context of the execution of the data mining project, data quality dimensions of completeness and accuracy of the data were paramount. The data collected, although in electronic form, had many incidences of missing or inconsistent attributes. For example, there were multiple ways of accepting grades for subjects taken (i.e., both numeric and alphabetic representations). The decision was made to remove records with missing data and fix inconsistent data as a means to preserve data quality. The experience underlined the importance of database maintenance and quality control methods to safeguard the integrity of the data. Therefore, the lesson was that quality management in the data collection and maintenance processes helps to minimize data quality concerns during the actual project.

With respect to the modeling phase, a significant portion of time was spent in trying to identify suitable data mining software and becoming knowledgeable in using it. Additionally, identification of the appropriate data mining tasks and associated features was primarily experimental during the initial stages. Open-source alternatives were identified to resolve the issue of software tools and RapidMiner was subsequently selected because of its popularity and available manual and guide. The team members were allocated extra time to learn the features of RapidMiner as part of the action-taking process.

The evaluation phase was relatively less challenging given the type of objectives defined earlier in the project, and the models and results derived from the modeling stage. For example, the accuracy threshold in using decision trees was met, and therefore model result was accepted by the team.

The deployment phase may be considered ongoing because no formal deployment task was undertaken in this project. However, it was diagnosed that open dialog with the parties most interested in the results is imperative; otherwise, there is a risk of the new knowledge not being put into use (Figure 9.5).

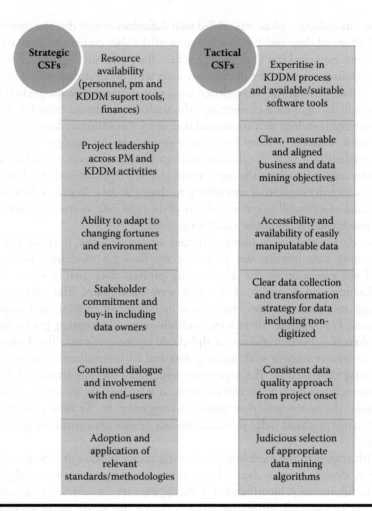

Figure 9.5   CSFs in KDDM.

Concluding Remarks

The chapter examines some of the key factors that impact the successful delivery of KDDM project. A single project was evaluated using the action research approach to diagnose the issues, outline the courses of actions, and specify the learning to identify the set of CSFs. The CSFs were categorized into strategic and tactical to reflect the PM and KDDM activities, respectively. The study found that use of the PM approach to execute the project was critical, support of the data owners and other stakeholders, and identification of the right data and software tools were important. In short, PM and KDDM best practices are important to the success of KDDM initiatives. This underscores the importance of all the steps and not just the data mining or modeling phase. Another key finding was that data collection was difficult and highlighted the need for more formal guidelines to properly manage this activity because the KDDM process models implicitly assume that data is readily available. This may prove helpful for organizations that are less mature in KDDM activities.

These initial findings have implications for practitioners, in particular, as they plan their KDDM initiatives. The less experienced team and organizations are at risk of less successful undertakings, and it is therefore important to note some of the CSFs. From a research perspective, it is envisioned that this study can extend the discourse of factors that hinder and aid the multiple KDDM initiatives that organizations may undertake, as KDDM becomes increasingly important where the search for value from data ensues.

References

Anand, S. S. and Büchner, A. G. (1998). *Decision Support Using Data Mining*. London: Financial Times Management.

Association for Project Management. (2013). *APM Body of Knowledge Definitions*, 5th edition, http://www.apm.org.uk/sites/default/files/Bok%205%20Definitions.pdf.

Atkinson, R. (1999). Project management: Cost, time and quality, two best guesses and a phenomenon, its time to accept other success criteria. *International Journal of Project Management, 17*(6), 337–342.

Baccarini, D. and Collins, A. (2003). Critical success factors for projects. In Brown, A. (ed.), Surfing the Waves: Management Challenges, Management Solutions, *Proceedings of the 17th ANZAM Conference*, Fremantle, Western Australia, December 2–5, 2003. Faculty of the Built.

Barclay, C. (2008). Towards an integrated measurement of IS project performance: The project performance scorecard. *Information Systems Frontiers, 10*(3), 331–345.

Barclay, C. and Osei-Bryson, K. M. (2010). Project performance development framework: An approach for developing performance criteria and measures for information systems (IS) projects. *International Journal of Production Economics, 124*(1), 272–292.

Baskerville, R. L. (1999). Investigating information systems with action research. *Communications of the AIS, 2*(3es), 4.

Baskerville, R. and Myers, M. D. (2004). Special issue on action research in informaton systems: Making IS research relevant to practice foreword. *Management Information Systems Quarterly, 28*(3), 2.

Belassi, W. and Tukel, O. I. (1996). A new framework for determining critical success/failure factors in projects. *International Journal of Project Management, 14*(3), 141–151.

Boynton, A. C. and Zmud, R. W. (1984). An assessment of critical success factors. *Sloan Management Review (pre-1986), 25*(4), 17–27.

Bullen, C. V. and Rockart, J. F. (1981). A primer on critical success factors. Centre for Systems Research, Sloan Management Centre, MIT, Cambridge, MA.

Butler, T. and Fitzgerald, B. (1999). Unpacking the systems development process: An empirical application of the CSF concept in a research context. *The Journal of Strategic Information Systems, 8*(4), 351–371.

Bryde, D. J. and Robinson, L. (2005). Client versus contractor perspectives on project success criteria. *International Journal of Project Management, 23*(8), 622–629.

Chapman, P., Clinton, J., Kerber, R., Khabaza, T., Reinartz, T., Shearer, C., and Wirth, R. (2013). *CRISP-DM 1.0: Step-by-Step Data Mining Guide,* 2000. SPSS Inc.

Chow, T. and Cao, D.-B. (2008). A survey study of critical success factors in agile software projects. *Journal of Systems and Software, 81*(6), 961–971.

Collins, A. and Baccarini, D. (2004). Project success—A survey. *Journal of Construction Research, 5*(02), 211–231.

Cooke-Davies, T. (2002). The "real" success factors on projects. *International Journal of Project Management, 20*(3), 185–190.

Dvir, D., Raz, T., and Shenhar, A. J. (2003). An empirical analysis of the relationship between project planning and project success. *International Journal of Project Management, 21*(2), 89–95.

Fayyad, U. M., Piatetsky-Shapiro, G., and Smyth, P. (1996a). From data mining to knowledge discovery in databases. *AI Magazine, 17*(3), 37.

Fayyad, U. M., Piatetsky-Shapiro, G., and Smyth, P. (1996b). Knowledge discovery and data mining: Towards a unifying framework. *Paper presented at the KDD,* vol 96, pp. 82–88.

Fortune, J. and White, D. (2006). Framing of project critical success factors by a systems model. *International Journal of Project Management, 24*(1), 53–65.

Hermiz, K. B. (1999). Critical success factors for data mining project. *Information Management.* Retrieved from http://www.information-management.com/issues/19990201/164-1 .html?pg=2 (accessed June 30, 2013).

Hilbert, A. (2005). Critical success factors for data mining projects. In Baier, D., Decker, R., and Schmidt-Thieme, L. (eds.), *Data Analysis and Decision Support. Studies in Classification, Data Analysis, and Knowledge Organization* series (pp. 231–240). Berlin, Germany: Springer.

IBM. (2010). Planning successful data mining projects. *IBM Software Business Analytics.* Retrieved from http://www-01.ibm.com/common/ssi/cgi-bin/ssialias?infotype=SA& subtype=WH&htmlfid=YTW03088USEN (accessed June 30, 2013).

Kerzner, H. (1987). In search of excellence in project management. *Journal of Systems Management, 38*(2), 30–39.

Kurgan, L. A. and Musilek, P. (2006). A survey of Knowledge Discovery and Data Mining process models. *Knowledge Engineering Review, 21*(1), 1–24.

Lewin, K. (1946). Action research and minority problems. *Journal of Social Issues, 2*(4), 34–46.

Lim, C. and Mohamed, M. Z. (1999). Criteria of project success: An exploratory re-examination. *International Journal of Project Management, 17*(4), 243–248.

Meyer, J. (2000). Using qualitative methods in health related action research. *British Medical Journal, 320*(7228), 178–181.

Nemati, H. R. and Barko, C. D. (2003). Key factors for achieving organizational data-mining success. *Industrial Management & Data Systems, 103*(4), 282–292.

Peters, M. and Robinson, V. (1984). The origins and status of action research. *The Journal of Applied Behavioral Science, 20*(2), 113–124.

Pinto, J. K. and Slevin, D. P. (1987). Balancing strategy and tactics in project implementation. *Sloan Management Review, 29*(1), 33–41.

Rapoport, R. N. (1970). Three dilemmas in action research with special reference to the Tavistock experience. *Human Relations, 23*(6), 499–513.

Reason, P. and Bradbury, H. (Eds.). (2001). *Handbook of Action Research: Participative Inquiry and Practice.* Thousand Oaks, CA: Sage.

Rockart, J. F. (1979). Chief executives define their own data needs. *Harvard Business Review, 57*(2), 81.

SAS. (2013). SAS Enterprise Miner—SEMMA. Retrieved December 20, 2013, from http://www.sas.com/offices/europe/uk/technologies/analytics/datamining/miner/semma.html.

Sharma, S. and Osei-Bryson, K. M. (2009). Framework for formal implementation of the business understanding phase of data mining projects. *Expert Systems with Applications, 36*(2), 4114–4124.

Sim, B. J. (2003). Critical success factors in data mining projects. Thesis. University of North Texas, Denton, TX.

Susman, G. I. and Evered, R. D. (1978). An assessment of the scientific merits of action research. *Administrative Science Quarterly, 23*(4), 582–603.

Van Eynde, D. F. and Bledsoe, J. A. (1990). The changing practice of organisation development. *Leadership & Organization Development Journal, 11*(2), 25–30.

Westerveld, E. (2003). The Project Excellence Model®: Linking success criteria and critical success factors. *International Journal of Project Management, 21*(6), 411–418.

APPLICATIONS
OF KDDM

VI   APPLICATIONS
      OF KDDM

Chapter 10

Data Mining for Organizations: Challenges and Opportunities for Small Developing States

Corlane Barclay

Contents

Abstract: Knowledge discovery through data mining facilitates deeper insights into understanding an organization's operations and environment. An analysis of the literature revealed the limited use and application of knowledge discovery or data mining techniques in small economies despite the advanced development and reporting of this technology in other economies. This may be explained in part by limitation of resources and a general lack of awareness of the benefits of knowledge discovery initiatives to the business and government sectors. It is suggested that greater investments in data mining in key sectors such as sports, agriculture and fisheries, manufacturing, mining, and government administration can yield positive economic benefits for small developing states, including Jamaica. This chapter provides a synthesis of the literature of the application of data mining across multiple domains such as medicine, insurance, banking and finance, and education, and shares some of the top open-source data mining tools (e.g., RapidMiner, Waikato Environment for Knowledge Analysis [Weka], KNIME, and R). This is motivated by the need to improve awareness of the opportunities that exists from investing in data mining projects and identify some of challenges that if not properly managed can derail knowledge discovery efforts.

Keywords: Knowledge discovery, data mining, knowledge discovery and data mining, open-source applications, developing states

Introduction

With the continued growth of structured and unstructured data knowledge discovery and data mining (KDDM) provides even more exciting opportunities for organizations to improve their operational efficiencies and better serve the needs of their internal and external customers. According to industry statistics, the volume of global business data doubles every 1.2 years and over 2.7 zetabytes of data currently exists in the digital universe. Fayyad et al. (1996c) contended that advances in the collection of data and advances in computerization of business transactions have created a need for tools that can automatically and intelligently transform the data into knowledge. As a result, for over two decades, researchers have observed that businesses can derive advantages by applying data mining (DM) solutions to obtain value from the use of the discovered knowledge. The results are seen in recent literature, where DM solutions have been used to enhance customer relationships and gain or maintain competitive advantage in mature markets. Mitchell (1999), for example, observed that DM is helpful in analyzing medical outcomes, detecting credit card fraud, predicting customer behavior, predicting personal interests of Internet users, and optimizing manufacturing processes.

Given the promise of KDDM, it is still puzzling the relatively low rate of adoption of KDDM solutions in small developing states such as Jamaica and the rest of the English-speaking Caribbean. For the purposes of the study, KDDM refers to any knowledge discovery project that relies on DM techniques. An assessment of the industries that significantly contributes to the GDP in these economies such as tourism, agriculture, and manufacturing are still relying on traditional methods to support their tactical and strategic decisions. Fayyad et al. (1996c) observed that the traditional method of turning data into knowledge relies on manual analysis and interpretation. This practice has implications for the ability to harness organization knowledge due to delays in the analysis and the reliance on these manual methods, thereby impacting competitiveness and sustainability.

The purpose of this chapter is to help initiate engagement of local and regional industry players in the discussion of the current applications of KDDM and how it has been applied in multiple industries, and the beneficial value that can be gained from these investments and in turn emphasize how this solution can be applied in small developing states. This is undertaken through a synthesis of some of the leading researches on the use and application of KDDM across multiple domains, including medicine, banking and insurance, customer relationship management (CRM), manufacturing, agriculture, telecommunication, and sports combined with an overview of some of the top free DM software tools. The study offers both practical and research significance. For instance, government may be informed on development of policy approaches to invest in KDDM projects or adopt an open-source thrust that encompasses DM tools. Industry members can be informed on the current environment and developments in the field that would be useful to apply to aid efficiencies and competitiveness. The research also seeks to engender continued exploration of suitable KDDM tools in less developed economies.

The rest of the chapter presents an overview of KDDM and DM, an introduction to some of the open source of free DM tools in use, and an analysis of the literature of its application across industries, and shows how these benefits may be applied to similar industries, taking into considerations limitations including resource challenges.

DM and KDDM

DM is the process of mining or extracting interesting patterns from the data. In other words, it is the application of specific algorithms for extracting meanings or patterns from data (Fayyad et al. 1996a). It is the process of extracting previously unknown, valid, and actionable information from large databases and then using the information to make crucial business decisions (Cabena et al. 1996). DM is considered one step in the KDDM process that entails a series of activities necessary to manage the alignment of DM objectives to the organizational business objectives and deploy the new knowledge for application. Previous works have primarily focused on the DM step; however, the other process steps are equally if not more important for the successful application of KDDM in practice (Faayad et al. 1996b). Therefore, for organizations the ability to extract knowledge and meaning from their data requires judicious application of all the process steps. This section will discuss the major DM tasks and two seminal processes that support KDDM activities.

DM Tasks

There are many approaches in the application of algorithms for extracting meaning from the data. Researchers have provided different forms of taxonomy. The top-level tasks are often classified into descriptive and predictive; however, in practice, applications will generally provide combinations of both. Visualization is also useful for providing insightful representations from the various tasks. Prediction involves some variables or fields in the database to predict unknown or future values of variables of interest and focuses on levels of accuracy in the predictive model. Descriptive goal focuses on understanding the underlying data-generating process to find human-interpretable patterns describing the data. These top-level goals may be achieved by multiple approaches (Figure 10.1).

Predictive Methods

Classification is generally considered supervised learning. It is one of the most common learning models in DM (Ahmed 2004). It maps or classifies a data item into one of several predefined classes (Hand 1981; Fayyad et al. 1996a). In other words, it is the task of providing certain structure or classification based on utilization of datasets. An example is a telecommunication company using different predefined classes to automatically determine the type of data or voice plan customers and prospective customers should receive.

Regression analysis is a statistical technique that estimates and predicts relations between variables. Instances of regression algorithms are simple linear, multiple

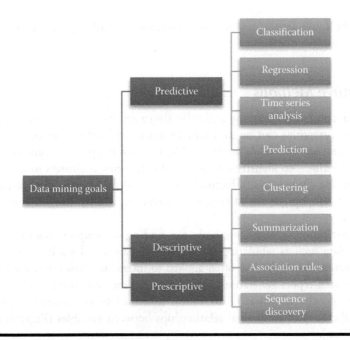

Figure 10.1 Basic data mining goals.

linear, fuzzy, and logistic. In DM, regression is used to predict unseen data based on continuous training data. Regression maps a data item to a real-valued prediction variable. It aims to find a function that models the data with the slightest error. Some examples include estimating the probability that a patient will survive given the results of a set of diagnostic tests, predicting consumer demand for a new product as a function of advertising expenditure, and predicting time series where the input variables can be time-lagged versions of the prediction variables (Fayyad et al. 1996b). Therefore, predicting the customer demand for new banking, telecommunication, or agricultural products is an example.

Time series analysis consists of identifying time-lagged versions of the prediction variable. For example, R describes time series decomposition and time series forecasting, where the time series is decomposed into trend, seasonal, cyclical, and irregular components, and forecasting entails forecasting future events based on known past data. An example is a bank forecasting loan application trends based on past data, where the trends would be based on different forms of structure, including period of the year, or based on events.

Prediction identifies a model or a set of models that can be used to predict some response of interest, for example, a credit card company identifying transactions likely to be fraudulent or an insurance company identifying customers likely to have high number of claims.

Descriptive Methods

Clustering consists of grouping and collecting a set of objects into similar classes. Clustering categories can be mutually exclusive and exhaustive or consist of a richer representation, such as hierarchical or overlapping categories (Fayyad 1996a). The aim is to identify a finite set of categories or clusters to describe the data (Jain and Dubes 1988). Examples include identifying or discovering similar clusters, subpopulations of telecommunication, and banking or supermarket customers.

Summarization involves methods for finding a compact description for a subset of data such as tabulating the mean and standard deviations for all fields. Summarization techniques are often applied to interactive exploratory data analysis and automated report generation. More advanced methods involve the derivation of summary rules (Agrawal et al. 1996), multivariate visualization techniques, and the discovery of functional relationships between variables (Zembowicz and Zytkow 1996).

Association rules look for relationships or associations between variables. The goal of association is to establish relationships between items that exist together in a given record (Mitra et al. 2002). Market basket analysis and cross-selling programs are typical examples for which association modeling is usually adopted (Fayyad et al. 1996a). Therefore, an example is where rice and sugar are purchased and 90% of the time chicken is also purchased in the supermarket.

Sequence discovery is the identification of associations or patterns over time. Its goal is to model the states of the process generating the sequence or to extract and report deviation and trends over time (Mitra et al. 2002). It is closely related to association; however, the key difference is that related items are spread over time. An example is where salary payments are lodged to the bank and 85% of the time full withdrawals are done within a week of the lodgment.

KDDM Process

The steps in the KDDM process invariably span the analysis of the organization's needs to mining to the deployment of new knowledge. It can be described as "the nontrivial process of identifying valid, novel, potentially useful, and ultimately understandable patterns in data" (Fayyad et al. 1996a). A process-centric approach not only promotes meaningful application of the DM methods but provides considerations for the supporting activities necessary to achieve the business objectives through the knowledge discovery process. As indicated earlier, all the steps are important to discovering knowledge and exploiting the subsequent value.

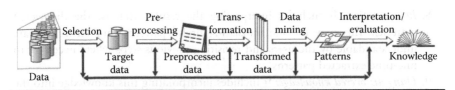

Figure 10.2   Overview of KDD process. (Data from Fayyad, U. M. et al., *Advances in Knowledge Discovery and Data Mining*, 1996a.)

Consequently, researchers have devised different sets of activities to describe the full end-to-end process of mining and deploying new knowledge to the organization. Two common methods will be discussed: the Cross Industry Standard Process for DM (CRISP-DM) (Chapman et al. 2000) and the KDD process as described by Fayyad et al. (1996a) because of their seminal nature.

KDD Process

According to Fayyad et al. (1996a), the KDD process is interactive and iterative. It consists of nine steps (Figure 10.2), which are summarized as follows:

1. *Learning the application domain:* It includes relevant prior knowledge and the goals of the application.
2. *Creating a target dataset:* It includes selecting a dataset on which discovery is to be performed.
3. *Data cleaning and preprocessing:* It includes basic operations to ensure data quality, such as removing noise or outliers where appropriate, deciding on strategies for handling missing data fields, and accounting for time sequence information and known changes, as well as deciding database management system (DBMS) issues (e.g., data types, schema, and mapping of missing and unknown values).
4. *Data reduction and projection:* It includes finding useful features to represent the data and using dimensionality reduction or transformation methods to reduce the effective number of variables under consideration.
5. *Choosing the function of DM:* It includes deciding the purpose of the model derived by the DM algorithm (e.g., summarization, classification, regression, and clustering).
6. *Choosing the DM algorithm(s):* It includes selecting method(s) to be used for searching for patterns in the data and determining which may be most appropriate.
7. *DM:* It includes searching for patterns given the objectives in a particular representational form, including classification rules or trees, regression, clustering, sequence modeling, and so on.

8. *Interpretation:* It includes interpreting the results, that is, the discovered patterns. This may include translating useful patterns into terms that are understandable by the users and revisiting previous steps where necessary to fine-tune extracted patterns.
9. *Using discovered knowledge:* It includes incorporating this knowledge into the organization or performance system. This may include taking actions based on the knowledge, documenting it or reporting it to interested parties, and conducting further analysis to resolve any possible conflicts.

CRISP-DM Process

The CRISP-DM process consists of six iterative steps (Chapman et al. 2000) (Figure 10.3), which are summarized as follows:

1. *Business understanding:* It focuses on understanding the objectives and requirements from a business perspective, and then converting this knowledge into a DM problem definition and a preliminary plan designed to achieve the objectives.

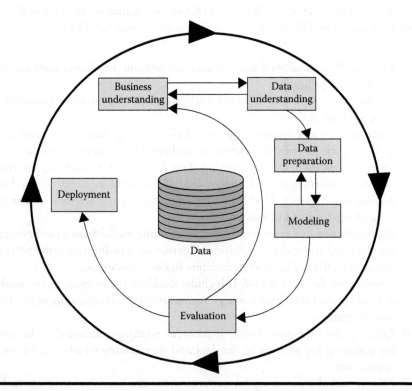

Figure 10.3   CRISP-DM. (Data from Chapman, P. et al., *CRISP-DM 1.0: Step-by-Step Data Mining Guide*, 2000.)

2. *Data understanding:* It commences with initial data collection and then enhancement of understanding by exploring the data to identify any data quality problems, discover first insights into the data, and/or detect interesting subsets to form hypotheses regarding hidden information.

3. *Data preparation:* It covers all activities needed to construct the final dataset and may require multiple cycles. Tasks include table, record, and attribute selection, as well as transformation and cleaning of data for modeling tools.

4. *Modeling:* It involves the selection and application of various modeling techniques and includes calibrating their parameters to optimal values.

5. *Evaluation:* It involves evaluating the model(s) and reviewing the steps executed to create it to ensure that the model properly achieves the business objectives. At the end of this phase, a decision on the use of the DM results is reached.

6. *Deployment:* It involves actual use or adoption of discovered knowledge. Depending on the requirements, this may range from generating a report to implementing a repeatable DM process across the enterprise.

DM Software Tools/Applications

There are commercial and open-source or free versions of software applications that are useful for modeling and managing KDDM projects. Rexer 2013 Data Miner Survey reported that users identified ease of use and costs as key distinguishing considerations in choice of tools (Rexer 2013). Few of the commercial versions include Salford Systems Data Mining Suite, IBM SPSS Modeler, and SAS Enterprise Miner that provides a graphical user interface (GUI) front end to the Sample, Explore, Modify, Model and Assess (SEMMA) process. However, the freely available applications will be the focus of this section as it is believed that this helps to eliminate the initial financial investment that may prove to be challenging for some organizations and therefore provide the requisite impetus for small or less mature organizations to more readily adopt open-source DM packages.

The number of open-source DM applications is growing, and each provides its own set of DM tasks and advantages. Industry literature identifies over 30 open-source DM packages. Also, KDnuggets.com currently provides a list of over 20 free or shareware packages. Some of the top applications include RapidMiner, KNIME, R, Weka, and Orange (Table 10.1). Others include ML-Flex, Databonics, KEEL, and AlphaMiner, to name a few. It is observed that many of these applications have their origins in the university community. Also, some of these free applications also have commercial versions available (e.g., RapidMiner). The interfaces for these applications are generally GUI and menu driven, which facilitate ease of use and cater to different levels of users ranging from novices to experts (Figures 10.4 through 10.8).

Table 10.1 Summary of Selected Top Free Data Mining Software

DM Application	Website	Description
RapidMiner	http://rapidminer.com/	It is an open-source application for both business and research. It provides an integrated environment for machine learning, data mining, text mining, predictive analytics, and business analytics. It runs on multiple platforms.
Weka	http://www.cs.waikato.ac.nz/ml/weka/	It is a collection of machine learning algorithms for data mining tasks for both researchers and practitioners.
KNIME	https://www.knime.org/	It is a data mining software that is designed as a teaching, research, and collaboration platform, which enables simple integration of new algorithms and tools.
Orange	http://orange.biolab.si/	It is a machine learning and data mining suite for data analysis. It runs on multiple platforms.
R	http://www.r-project.org/	It is a free software environment for statistical computing and graphics. It compiles and runs on a wide variety of UNIX platforms, Windows, and Mac OS X.

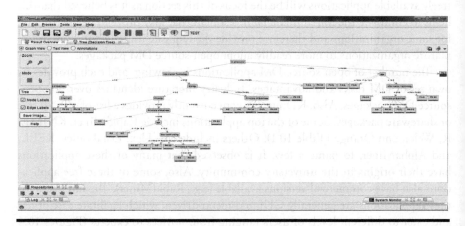

Figure 10.4 RapidMiner screenshot of decision tree.

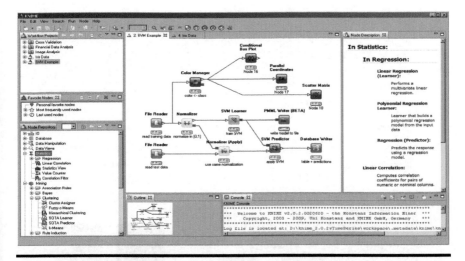

Figure 10.5   KNIME workbench with a small example workflow. (Data from Berthold, M. R. et al., *AcM SIGKDD Explorations Newsletter,* **11(1), 26–31, 2009.)**

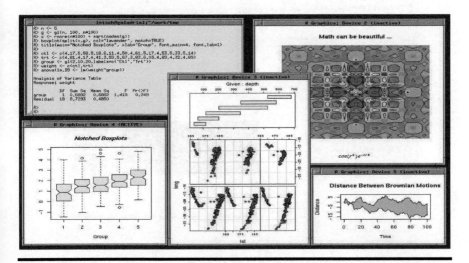

Figure 10.6   R—Unix desktop. (Data from http://www.r-project.org, ©**R foundation.)**

RapidMiner

RapidMiner is one of the most popular DM software applications. It provides software, solutions, and services in the fields of predictive analytics, DM, and text mining. According to KDnuggets.com, it is the leading open-source system for KDDM. It is used for business, industrial, and research applications, and supports the steps in the KDDM process. According to its website, RapidMiner runs on every major platform and operating system, and has a powerful and intuitive GUI

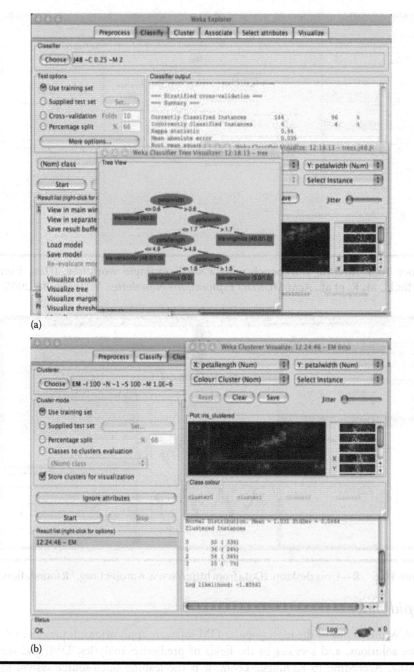

Figure 10.7 Weka—(a) classify panel (b) Cluster Panel. (Data from http://www. cs.waikato.ac.nz/~ml/weka/gui_explorer.html.)

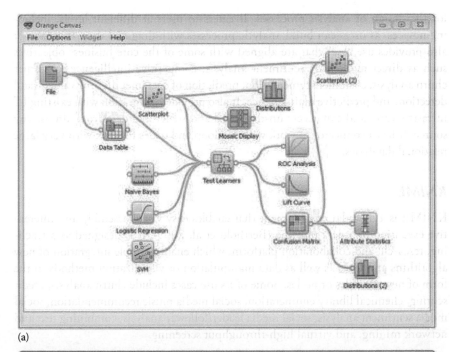

(a)

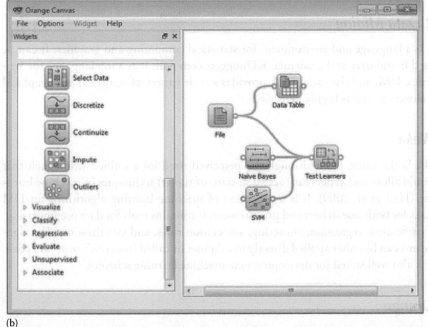

(b)

Figure 10.8   Orange—Canvases. (Data from http://orange.biolab.si/docs/latest/.)

for the design of analysis processes. It caters to users at different levels, including novices, as users can build analytic processes with drag and drop interface. It also provides use cases that are aligned with some of the core business objectives such as direct marketing, sentiment analysis, competitive intelligence, customer churn analysis, customer segmentation, prediction of customer lifetime value, fraud detection, and predictive maintenance. It also provides integration with existing IT infrastructures and can access unstructured and structured data from almost any source. It has a connector to work with Hadoop and scales to work with very large relational databases.

KNIME

KNIME is a modular environment that enables easy visual assembly and interactive execution of a data pipeline (Berthold et al. 2009). It is designed as a teaching, research, and collaboration platform, which enables simple integration of new algorithms and tools as well as data manipulation or visualization methods in the form of new modules or nodes. Some of its use cases include churn analysis, credit scoring, chemical library enumeration, social media music recommendation, social media sentiment analysis, social media leader/follower analysis, combining text and network mining, and virtual high-throughput screening.

R Data Mining

R is a language and environment for statistical computing and graphics. It can be used in industry and academia. KDnuggets.com polls it as a top language for analytics, DM, and data science. R provides a wide variety of statistical and graphical techniques, and is highly extensible.

Weka

The Weka came about through the perceived need for a unified workbench that would allow researchers easy access to state-of-the-art techniques in machine learning (Hall et al. 2009). It is a collection of machine learning algorithms for DM tasks for both researchers and practitioners. It contains tools for data preprocessing, classification, regression, clustering, association rules, and visualization. The algorithms can be either applied directly to a dataset or called from one's own Java code. It is also well suited for developing new machine learning schemes.

Orange

Orange is a machine learning and DM suite for data analysis through Python scripting and visual programming (Demšar et al. 2013). It is intended for both experienced users and programmers, as well as for students of DM. Orange runs on multiple platforms including Windows, Mac OS X, and Linux, and has coverage of most of standard data analysis tasks and includes add-ons for bioinformatics and text mining.

Application of KDDM

Based on studies that have highlighted the benefits of KDDM across multiple domains in different regions, it is fair to suggest that this solution has value, when applied correctly, in all sectors of business, government, and education. A survey of the literature shows that KDDM applications have been used to better understand consumers, help to reduce fraud, improve processes, and increase revenues; according to Chien and Chen (2008), it has also been to use improve personnel selection and enhance human capital. Some of the industry especially relevant to the Caribbean will be discussed herein, including medical and health industry, banking and financial services, agriculture, government and public administration, manufacturing, telecommunication, and sports.

Medicine and Health

According to Esfandiari et al. (2014), medical DM is the "Extraction of implicit, potentially useful and novel information from medical data to improve accuracy, decrease time and cost, construct decision support system with the aim of health promotion." Essentially, it involves the application of DM in the medical domain to achieve certain goals. Given the vast volume of data being generated, it is virtually impossible to process data by physicians using traditional techniques (Esfandiari et al. 2014). Therefore, in the quest to improve patient care, treatment, and diagnosis, several studies have been done to aid the sector. Esfandiari et al. (2014) observed in their comprehensive literature on DM in medicine that the primary business objectives were to improve efficiency and decrease human error, decrease cost and time, enhance medical decision support systems, and extract hidden knowledge. Multiple diseases, including different forms of cancer, cardiovascular disease, heart disease, leukemia, and general health care, were investigated. The DM applications were across the various medical tasks of treatment, screening, diagnosis, prognosis, monitoring, and management. They further noted that diagnosis is the most DM usage, and by contrast monitoring has received little effort.

Some examples of specific categories of medical DM are as follows:

■ Prediction of breast cancer survivability (Delen et al. 2005)
■ Control of infections in hospitals (Brossette et al. 1998) and general health care (Obenshain 2004)
■ The development of DM algorithms for predicting survival of coronary heart disease patients (Xing et al. 2007)
■ Investigation of chronic diseases prognosis and diagnosis system integrating DM and case-based reasoning (Huang et al. 2007)

- The detection, analysis, and evaluation of risks potentially existing in clinical environments (Tsumoto and Hirano 2010)
- The exploration of a medical claim fraud/abuse detection system (Ortega et al. 2006)

Within the Caribbean context, similar opportunities are available for KDDM projects to include the aspects of treatment, diagnosis, screening, diagnosis, and other areas of medical tasks. Considerations should be given to the application of KDDM to diseases that affect a high number of the population or have a high mortality rate as a means of aiding descriptive and predictive capabilities. Some of these include hypertension, cancer, sickle cell anemia, and heart disease. Extending the application to other health-related areas, including prescription and drug use, and at-risk population (e.g., disabled, children, and senior citizen care) offers a viable opportunity for health sector reform.

Banking and Financial Services

Fraud detection is one popular objective explored in the banking and financial services industry; however, DM application has multiple other uses. Bhasin (2006) stated that banks can use DM as a competitive tool. He further added that leading banks are using DM tools for activities such as customer segmentation and profitability, credit scoring and approval, predicting payment default, marketing, and detecting fraudulent transactions. Ngai et al. (2011) in their review of literature on financial fraud detection classified the categories of financial fraud, that is, bank fraud, insurance fraud, securities and commodities fraud, and other related financial fraud. Their findings revealed that DM techniques have been applied most extensively to the detection of insurance, corporate, and credit card fraud, and provided prospects for added exploration in mortgage fraud, money laundering, and securities and commodities fraud. Other applications in banking include predicting bank performance, specifically in the context of commercial banks in Taiwan (Lin et al. 2009), and profiling customers such as in the Internet-banking domain (Ravi et al. 2007; Mansingh et al. 2013).

Similarly, applications in different forms of insurance are seen, including property, health, and life insurance. In a recent IBM white paper, it was suggested that insurers lose millions each year through fraudulent claims, and thus there is an opportunity for companies to apply DM techniques to target claims with the greatest likelihood of adjustment, improve audit accuracy, and save time and resources (Insurance technology.com 2010). Dal Pozzolo et al. (2010) examined the prediction of insurance claim, in particular "Bodily Injury Liability Insurance" claim payments based on the characteristics of the insured customer's vehicle. Analysis of customer retention and insurance claim patterns (Smith et al. 2000) and clustering technique for risk classification and prediction of claim costs in the automobile insurance industry were also performed (Yeo et al. 2001).

Customer Relationship Management

CRM is generally described as comprising a set of processes and enabling systems supporting a business strategy to build long-term, profitable relationships with specific customer base (Ling and Yen 2001). It consists of the dimensions of customer identification, customer attraction, customer retention, and customer development (Kracklauer et al. 2004). It is relevant not only to marketing departments or agencies but also to business development area of any organization. Therefore, the application of DM to CRM directly applies to the business operations and measures to attract customers and build lasting relationships. Ngai et al. (2009) in their review of DM CRM literature found applications in various areas such as complaints management, loyalty program, one-to-one marketing, lifetime value, cross- and up-selling, and direct market segmentation.

Anecdotal evidence suggests that in Jamaica and other small developing states, CRM is typically not adopted outside of the larger organizations, and even then predictive or descriptive analytics are not generally applied to better understand customer segments. Therefore, there is a definite opportunity to examine through DM how businesses may properly identify customer segments, attract customers, manage complaints, and reduce customer churn.

Government/Public Administration

Slobogin (2008) observed that the government's ability to obtain and analyze recorded information about its citizens through DM has expanded enormously over the past decade. This was taken in the context of the United States and is also likely true for other more developed nations. The story may be distinctly different for developing states where public administration processes are largely manually intensive despite disparate e-government initiatives. Micci-Barreca and Ramachandran (2004) shared that DM offers many valuable techniques for increasing the efficiency and success rate of tax collection, which is one important area that requires reform in several developing states.

Improvement in tax administration is an objective that is investigated in multiple areas, including fraud detection. Micci-Barreca and Ramachandran (2004) discussed improving tax administration with DM where it details an actual tax compliance application. Kirkos et al. (2007) undertook the investigation of DM techniques for the detection of fraudulent financial statements (Kirkos et al. 2007). Wu et al. (2012) considered how DM can be used to enhance tax evasion detection performance. Similarly, Yu et al. (2003) examined DM application issues in fraudulent tax declaration detection and illustrated through a case study about building a fraudulent tax declaration detection system using decision tree classification algorithm.

Other applications observed included the focus on crime management. For example, the application of semantic association identification and knowledge discovery for national security applications where a prototypical demonstration was presented in the context of an aviation security application of significance to national security (Sheth et al. 2005) and the presentation of a general framework for crime DM that draws on experience gained with the Coplink project (Chen et al. 2004).

Cate (2008) argued that there is a need for legal framework in government DM and suggested that there is wide agreement about both the need to restore some limits on the government's use of personal data and the form that those limits should take. It is clear that the balance of privacy, national security, and operational efficiencies are principal concerns especially with the ease of data manipulation through technological advancements. This, however, should not deter governments from making the first step in utilizing DM applications to enhance public administration. It is argued that judicious use of data may help to increase efficiencies across agencies, increase revenue through improved strategies of collection and management, and improve national security.

Agriculture

Agriculture is a key part of the economy of many small developing states, particularly in the Caribbean. This area impacts not only food and food distribution but also health and medicinal industry. Therefore, DM provides an exciting opportunity for further growth and development in agriculture and related industries. An examination of the literature shows studies that have used DM to explore food/drink preference, soil quality, gene discovery, and pest management, to name a few:

- Modeling wine preferences by data mining from physicochemical properties (Cortez et al. 2009)
- Modeling soil visible–near infrared diffuse reflectance spectra and assessing the interpretability of the results (Rossel and Behrens 2010)
- Examining several strategies to improve the quality of the soil map models generated by rule induction (Moran and Bui 2002)
- Applying Naïve Bayes DM technique for classification of agricultural land soils (Bhargavi and Jyothi 2009)
- DM with neural networks for wheat yield prediction (Ruß et al. 2008)
- Examining the role of DM for gene discovery (Mahalakshmi and Ortiz 2001)

Education

Discovery of knowledge to aid in all stages of education, that is, preschool, primary, secondary, and tertiary, would be beneficial to any economy. Research in the area has seen applications predominantly at the secondary and tertiary levels. Educational DM (EDM) is considered an emerging discipline and can be described as developing methods for exploring the unique types of data that come from educational settings and using those methods to better understand students and the settings which they learn in (educationaldatamining.com). Some of the general questions that can be asked include who are the students taking the most credit hours, who are the ones likely to return for more classes, who are the persisters at our university and college, and what type of courses can we offer to attract more students? (Luan 2002a). For developing states such as Jamaica, questions may include who are the students failing or passing particular subjects and who are the students matriculating to higher education?

Romero and Ventura (2010) in their review of EDM considered the stakeholders or actors and some of their wide range of objectives include understanding students' learning and behavior, understanding the types of students that require support, predicting performance, evaluating courseware, maintaining student learning, evaluating the structure of course content and its effectiveness in the learning process, enhancing educational program offerings, and determining the effectiveness of the distance learning approach. This finding underlines the importance of communicating with the business users to understand their needs and thus be better able to develop suitable models to address their concerns or needs. Some of the actual applications of EDM include using DM to monitor and predict community college students' transfer to 4-year institutions and predict the possibility of return to school for every student currently enrolled at a community college in Silicon Valley (Luan 2002a, 2002b); the application of DM in learning management systems and a case study tutorial with the Moodle system (Romero et al. 2008); and the use of a recommendation system based on DM techniques to help students to take decisions on their academic itineraries, that is, to provide support for the student to better select how many and which courses to enroll in, having as the basis the experience of previous students with similar academic achievements (Vialardi et al. 2009).

From the literature, it is evident that insights from data within the institutional ecosystem can aid stakeholders in the development of the educational sector. Opportunities to predict student performance and therefore develop suitable policies and curriculum changes to reflect the realities of the system, application of suitable learning styles for different segments of students, and general improvements in administration are hidden in datasets in many schools.

Manufacturing

DM is now used in many different areas in manufacturing engineering to extract knowledge for use in predictive maintenance, fault detection, design, production, quality assurance, scheduling, and decision support (Harding et al. 2006). Studies have considered areas of production processes, control, maintenance, and CRM. It was further observed that there has been a significant growth in the number of publications in some areas of manufacturing, such as fault detection, quality improvement, manufacturing systems, and engineering design. By contrast, other areas such as CRM and shop floor control have received comparatively less attention from the DM (Harding et al. 2006).

The manufacturing sector in Jamaica has been on the decline for a number of years based on industry reports. The application of suitable techniques to inform decision makers on areas of revenue leakages and inefficiencies provides an avenue for exploring in helping to provide renewal in the competitive nature of this sector. Other countries may explore the common uses such as fault detection and quality assurance in improving competitiveness.

Telecommunications

According to Weiss (2005), the telecommunications industry was one of the first to adopt DM technology. He further stated that the telecommunication companies utilize DM to improve their marketing efforts, identify fraud, and better manage their telecommunication networks. Some examples include prediction of customer churn (Wei and Chiu 2002), prediction of telecommunication switch failures (Weiss and Hirsh 1998), and fraud detection through the employment of dynamic clustering and deviation detection (Alves et al. 2006).

In the Caribbean, the telecommunication sector is vibrant where rapid technological changes are causing industry players to rethink their business models, for example, the recent rift between telecom providers and Voice over Internet Protocol services; an application of DM techniques including time series-based analysis can help to inform players on the level of impact of certain events, the business areas affected, and how customer churn may be managed.

Sports Management

A scan of the literature shows relatively limited application of DM techniques in sports. One notable example was the use of a Bayesian classifier created to predict Cy Young Award winners in American baseball (Smith et al. 2007), where the award is given to the best pitchers annually. Despite the low application, there are still vast opportunities for decision makers in the Caribbean especially to employ KDDM in areas of football, soccer netball, cricket, track, and field. Analysis to aid the prevention of sport injuries, analysis of competitors, prediction of performance, analysis of game performance, and prediction of future performance are just some of the objectives that can achieved using DM techniques.

Discussion

The previous sections highlight some of the many potential applications of KDDM to businesses and governments in small developing states and the availability of both commercial and open-source applications that can be explored for suitability to context. Relevant sectors including nontraditional areas such as sports management and entertainment have significant data for knowledge discovery efforts and are worth exploring. In an effort to improve economically, it is important to adopt nontraditional means to extract new knowledge in all sectors of the economy. It is suggested that less mature organization such as those in developing states may undertake certain actions to begin to reap some of the benefits of KDDM. It is important to note that although KDDM offers many potential advantages to organizations, it is not a panacea. Barclay (2013) highlighted some strategies business that can consider in helping to translate data into knowledge:

■ View data as an asset. When data is stored in disparate databases or not stored at all, this hinders growth. Many organizations are still relying on manual forms of data (source). This would require assembling data in an organized fashion and digitizing the data to facilitate data collection and integration.
■ Maintain data security and assurance. Data security assurance relates to the maintenance of security, privacy, confidentiality, integrity and availability of data. It is argued that maintaining data security assurance from data collection to disposal is important in providing confidence in data quality and security.
■ Foster research and innovation. The growth of the industry is facilitated by exploration and development of new KDDM tools and processes to better meet the needs of the users.
■ Apply sound KDDM principles. This is similar to the observation made by Fayyad that not only the DM step but all steps are crucial to extracting knowledge for the business

Despite the many successful applications, there are, however, incidences of failed DM projects. This may be attributable to general project management issues, general stakeholder dissatisfaction, or DM issues. It is therefore important to apply due diligence across the full process to help manage the risks. Fayyad et al. (1996a) highlighted some challenges such as missing data, nonstandard and other nonnumeric forms of data, managing changing data and knowledge, and integration and understandability of the patterns generated. Missing data relates to missing attributes from records in the database and may occur as a result of operator error and actual system and measurement failures, or from a revision of the data collection process over time. Nonstandard and multimedia data generation is increasing and requires new and alternative methods of knowledge discovery. Nonstandard data may include nonnumeric, nontextual, geometric, and graphical data, as well as nonstationary, temporal, spatial, and relational data, and a mixture of categorical and numeric fields in the data. Multimedia includes free-form multilingual text as well as digitized images, video, and speech and audio data (Fayyad et al. 1996a). Integration with other applications is beneficial because according to Fayyad et al. (1996a) stand-alone discovery system may not be very useful. Understandability of patterns is necessary for the user and knowledge application. Some solutions include graphical representations, rule structuring, natural language generation, and techniques for visualization of data and knowledge. Rapidly changing or nonstationary data may make previously discovered patterns invalid. This underlines the need to have continuous assessment of the data, rules, and results to ensure accuracy and validity.

Other challenges that may be encountered during the KDDM project include nonuse or limited deployment of discovered knowledge, data collection issues, limited awareness of KDDM, and lack of or limited stakeholder buy-in or commitment. Projects may produce interesting models that reveal new knowledge; however, this may not be deployed in the organization due to multiple reasons such as resource constraints and lack of integrated systems that make changes difficult. Limited awareness of KDDM may be due to limited use and application across organizations, which may be as a result of reluctance to change or availability of skilled personnel. At times, there may be limited buy-in due to inability to communicate benefits in a way that they can understand, fear, or comfort with the status quo.

Concluding Remarks

This chapter underlines the opportunities for more adoption and use of DM applications. Challenges such as resource constraints are noted, however, with adequate planning some of the issues may be alleviated. The chapter synthesizes some of the top open-source DM applications and highlights how DM has been applied across multiple industries, including medicine, banking and finance, agriculture, and education. This study is motivated by the need to improve awareness of the benefits and opportunities of DM and KDDM in less mature organizations. It is envisioned that this study can help in bringing out change in the operations of many businesses as they begin to make the shift from the traditional methods of decision support tools to more advanced and timely methods such as KDDM to achieve competitiveness. The public sector is usually large with opportunities for reform, and the introduction of KDDM to various departments and sectors may be helpful in achieving economic development over time.

The study provides a glimpse into the opportunities and advantages that application of KDDM can provide. It is not a panacea, however, and with careful application, it is envisioned that the development synergies with industry to participate in DM projects in multiple domains, academia involvement with development of skills in machine learning, and development of suitable DM and/or KDDM tools that may better fit the circumstances of the domain and promote the development of DM software tool developments.

References

Agrawal, R., Mannila, H., Srikant, R., Toivonen, H., and Verkamo, I. (1996). Fast discovery of association rules. In U. Fayyad, G. Piatetsky-Shapiro, P. Smyth, and R. Uthurusamy (Eds.), *Advances in Knowledge Discovery and Data Mining* (pp. 307–328). AAAI Press, Menlo Park, CA.

Ahmed, S. R. (2004). Applications of data mining in retail business. *Information Technology: Coding and Computing*, 2, 455–459.

Alves, R., Ferreira, P., Belo, O., Lopes, J., Ribeiro, J., Cortesao, L., and Martins, F. (2006). Discovering telecom fraud situations through mining anomalous behavior patterns. *Proceedings of the ACM SIGKDD Workshop on Data Mining for Business Applications* (pp. 1–7). New York: ACM Press.

Barclay, C. (2013). Maximizing the value of data: Making the business case for Knowledge Discovery in Data Mining. *Presentation at the 2013 Jamaica Computer Society Conference.* Unpublished paper.

Berthold, M. R., Cebron, N., Dill, F., Gabriel, T. R., Kötter, T., Meinl, T., Ohl, P., Thie, K., and Wiswedel, B. (2009). KNIME—The Konstanz information miner: Version 2.0 and beyond. *AcM SIGKDD Explorations Newsletter*, 11(1), 26–31.

Bhargavi, P. and Jyothi, S. (2009). Applying Naive Bayes data mining technique for classification of agricultural land soils. *International Journal of Computer Science and Network Security*, 9(8), 117–122.

Bhasin, M. L. (2006). Data mining: A competitive tool in the banking and retail industries. *The Chartered Accountant*, 588–594.

Brossette, S. E., Sprague, A. P., Hardin, J. M., Waites, K. B., Jones, W. T., and Moser, S. A. (1998). Association rules and data mining in hospital infection control and public health surveillance. *Journal of the American Medical Informatics Association*, 5(4), 373–381.

Cabena, P., Hadjinian, P., Stadler, R., Verhees, J., and Zanasi, A. (1998). *Discovering Data Mining: From Concepts to Implementation.* Prentice Hall.

Cate, F. H. (2008). Government data mining: The need for a legal framework. *Harvard Civil Rights-Civil Liberties Law Review (CR-CL)*, 43(2). Available at SSRN: http://ssrn.com/abstract=1151435.

Chapman, P., Clinton, J., Kerber, R., Khabaza, T., Reinartz, T., Shearer, C., and Wirth, R. (2000). *CRISP-DM 1.0: Step-by-Step Data Mining Guide.* SPSS Inc.

Chen, H., Chung, W., Xu, J. J., Wang, G., Qin, Y., and Chau, M. (2004). Crime data mining: A general framework and some examples. *Computer*, 37(4), 50–56.

Chien, C. F. and Chen, L. F. (2008). Data mining to improve personnel selection and enhance human capital: A case study in high-technology industry. *Expert Systems with Applications*, 34(1), 280–290.

Cortez, P., Cerdeira, A., Almeida, F., Matos, T., and Reis, J. (2009). Modeling wine preferences by data mining from physicochemical properties. *Decision Support Systems*, 47(4), 547–553.

Dal Pozzolo, A., Moro, G., Bontempi, G., and Le Borgne, D. Y. A. (2010). Comparison of data mining techniques for insurance claim prediction. Doctoral dissertation, PhD thesis, University of Bologna, Italy.

Delen, D., Walker, G., and Kadam, A. (2005). Predicting breast cancer survivability: A comparison of three data mining methods. *Artificial Intelligence in Medicine*, 34(2), 113–127.

Demšar, J., Curk, T., and Erjavec, A., Gorup, Č., Hočevar, T., Milutinovič, M., and Zupan, B. (2013). Orange: Data mining toolbox in python. *Journal of Machine Learning Research*, 14(1), 2349–2353.

Esfandiari, N., Babavalian, M. R., Moghadam, A. M. E., and Tabar, V. K. (2014). Knowledge discovery in medicine: Current issue and future trend. *Expert Systems with Applications*, 41(9), 4434–4463.

Fayyad, U. M., Piatetsky-Shapiro, G., and Smyth, P. (1996a). From data mining to knowledge discovery in databases. *AI Magazine*, 17(3), 37.

Fayyad, U. M., Piatetsky-Shapiro, G., and Smyth, P. (1996b). The KDD process for extracting useful knowledge from volumes of data. *Communications of the ACM*, 39(11), 27–34.

Fayyad, U. M., Piatetsky-Shapiro, G., Smyth, P., and Uthurusamy, R. (1996c). *Advances in Knowledge Discovery and Data Mining*, AAAI/MIT Press.

Hall, M., Frank, E., Holmes, G., Pfahringer, B., Reutemann, P., and Witten, I. H. (2009). The WEKA data mining software: An update. *SIGKDD Explorations Newsletter*, 11(1), 10–18.

Hand, D. J. (1981). *Discrimination and Classification*. Wiley Series in *Probability and Mathematical Statistics*, Chichester: Wiley, 1.

Harding, J. A., Shahbaz, M., and Kusiak, A. (2006). Data mining in manufacturing: A review. *Journal of Manufacturing Science and Engineering*, 128(4), 969–976.

Huang, M. J., Chen, M. Y., and Lee, S. C. (2007). Integrating data mining with case-based reasoning for chronic diseases prognosis and diagnosis. *Expert Systems with Applications*, 32(3), 856–867.

Insurance technology.com. (2010). Using data mining to detect insurance fraud, retrieved July 20, 2014, from http://www.insurancetech.com/whitepaper/Customer-Insight-Business-Intelligence/Analytics/using-data-mining-to-detect-insurance-frau-wp128932 5070284?articleID=170800009.

Jain, A. K. and Dubes, R. C. (1988). *Algorithms for Clustering Data*. Prentice-Hall, Inc.

Kirkos, E., Spathis, C., and Manolopoulos, Y. (2007). Data mining techniques for the detection of fraudulent financial statements. *Expert Systems with Applications*, 32(4), 995–1003.

Kracklauer, A. H., Mills, D. Q., and Seifert, D. (2004). Customer management as the origin of collaborative customer relationship management. In *Collaborative Customer Relationship Management* (pp. 3–6). Springer, Berlin; Heidelberg, Germany.

Lin, S. W., Shiue, Y. R., Chen, S. C., and Cheng, H. M. (2009). Applying enhanced data mining approaches in predicting bank performance: A case of Taiwanese commercial banks. *Expert Systems with Applications*, 36(9), 11543–11551.

Ling, R. and Yen, D. C. (2001). Customer relationship management: An analysis framework and implementation strategies. *Journal of Computer Information Systems*, 41(3), 82–97.

Luan, J. (2002a). Data mining and its applications in higher education. *New Directions for Institutional Research*, 2002(113), 17–36.

Luan, J. (2002b). Data mining and knowledge management in higher education—Potential applications. *Paper presented at the 42nd Annual Forum for the Association, for Institutional Research* (19pp.), June 2–5, Toronto, Ontario, Canada.

Mahalakshmi, V. and Ortiz, R. (2001). Plant genomics and agriculture: From model organisms to crops, the role of data mining for gene discovery. *Electronic Journal of Biotechnology*, 4(3), 9–10.

Mansingh, G., Rao, L., Osei-Bryson, K.-M., and Mills, A. (2013). Profiling internet banking users: A knowledge discovery in data mining process model based approach. *Information Systems Frontiers*, 1–23, doi:10.1007/s10796-012-9397-2.

Micci-Barreca, D. and Ramachandran, S. (2004). Improving tax administration with data mining. *White Paper*. Elite Analytics LLC, 13pp.

Mitchell, T. M. (1999). Machine Learning and Data Mining. *Communications of the ACM*, 42(11), 30–36.

Mitra, S., Pal, S. K., and Mitra, P. (2002). Data mining in soft computing framework: A survey. *IEEE Transactions on Neural Networks*, 13, 3–14.

Moran, C. J. and Bui, E. N. (2002). Spatial data mining for enhanced soil map modelling. *International Journal of Geographical Information Science*, 16(6), 533–549.

Ngai, E. W. T., Hu, Y., Wong, Y. H., Chen, Y., and Sun, X. (2011). The application of data mining techniques in financial fraud detection: A classification framework and an academic review of literature. *Decision Support Systems*, 50(3), 559–569.

Ngai, E. W. T., Xiu, L., and Chau, D. C. (2009). Application of data mining techniques in customer relationship management: A literature review and classification. *Expert Systems with Applications*, 36(2), 2592–2602.

Obenshain, M. K. (2004). Application of data mining techniques to healthcare data. *Infection Control and Hospital Epidemiology*, 25(8), 690–695.

Ortega, P. A., Figueroa, C. J., and Ruz, G. A. (2006). A medical claim fraud/abuse detection system based on data mining: A case study in Chile. *DMIN*, 6, 26–29.

Ravi, V., Carr, M., and Sagar, N. V. (2007). Profiling of internet banking users in India using intelligent techniques. *Journal of Services Research*, 6(2), 61–73.

Rexer, K. (2013). RexerAnalytics 6th Data Miner Survey—2013, retrieved on July 14, 2014, from http://www.rexeranalytics.com/Data-Miner-Survey-2013-Intro.html.

Romero, C. and Ventura, S. (2010). Educational data mining: A review of the state of the art. *IEEE Transactions on Systems, Man, and Cybernetics, Part C: Applications and Reviews*, 40(6), 601–618.

Romero, C., Ventura, S., and García, E. (2008). Data mining in course management systems: Moodle case study and tutorial. *Computers & Education*, 51(1), 368–384.

Rossel, R. A. and Behrens, T. (2010). Using data mining to model and interpret soil diffuse reflectance spectra. *Geoderma*, 158(1), 46–54.

Ruß, G., Kruse, R., Schneider, M., and Wagner, P. (2008). Data mining with neural networks for wheat yield prediction. In *Advances in Data Mining. Medical Applications, E-Commerce, Marketing, and Theoretical Aspects* (pp. 47–56). Springer, Berlin, Germany.

Sheth, A., Aleman-Meza, B., Arpinar, I. B., Bertram, C., Warke, Y., Ramakrishanan, C., and Kochut, K. (2005). Semantic association identification and knowledge discovery for national security applications. *Journal of Database Management*, 16(1), 33–53.

Slobogin, C. (2008). Government data mining and the fourth amendment. *The University of Chicago Law Review*, 75(1), 317–341.

Smith, K. A., Willis, R. J., and Brooks, M. (2000). An analysis of customer retention and insurance claim patterns using data mining: A case study. *Journal of the Operational Research Society*, 532–541.

Smith, L., Lipscomb, B., and Simkins, A. (2007). Data mining in sports: Predicting Cy Young award winners. *Journal of Computing Sciences in Colleges*, 22(4), 115–121.

Tsumoto, S. and Hirano, S. (2010). Risk mining in medicine: Application of data mining to medical risk management. *Fundamenta Informaticae*, 98(1), 107–121.

Vialardi, C., Bravo, J., Shafti, L., and Ortigosa, A. (2009). Recommendation in higher education using data mining techniques. *International Working Group on Educational Data Mining. Proceedings of the International Conference on Educational Data Mining (EDM)*, Cordoba, Spain, July 1–3, 2009.

Wei, C. and Chiu, I. (2002). Turning telecommunications call details to churn prediction: A data mining approach. *Expert Systems with Applications*, 23(2), 103–112.

Weiss, G. M. (2005). Data mining in telecommunications. In O. Maimon and L. Rokach (Eds.), *Data Mining and Knowledge Discovery Handbook* (pp. 1189–1201). Springer, New York.

Weiss, G. M. and Hirsh, H. (1998). Learning to predict rare events in event sequences. In R. Agrawal and P. Stolorz (Eds.), *Proceedings of the 4th International Conference on Knowledge Discovery and Data Mining* (pp. 359–363). AAAI Press, Menlo Park, CA.

Wu, R. S., Ou, C. S., Lin, H. Y., Chang, S. I., and Yen, D. C. (2012). Using data mining technique to enhance tax evasion detection performance. *Expert Systems with Applications*, 39(10), 8769–8777.

Xing, Y., Wang, J., Zhao, Z., and Gao, Y. (2007). Combination data mining methods with new medical data to predicting outcome of coronary heart disease. *International Conference on Convergence Information Technology*, November, pp. 868–872. IEEE.

Yeo, A. C., Smith, K. A., Willis, R. J., and Brooks, M. (2001). Clustering technique for risk classification and prediction of claim costs in the automobile insurance industry. *Intelligent Systems in Accounting, Finance and Management*, 10(1), 39–50.

Yu, F., Qin, Z., and Jia, X. L. (2003). Data mining application issues in fraudulent tax declaration detection. *International Conference on Machine Learning and Cybernetics*, Vol. 4, November, pp. 2202–2206. IEEE.

Zembowicz, R. and Zytkow, J. (1996). From contingency tables to various forms of knowledge in databases. In U. Fayyad, G. Piatetsky-Shapiro, P. Smyth, and R. Uthurusamy (Eds.), *Advances in Knowledge Discovery and Data Mining*, 329–351. AAAI Press, Menlo Park, CA.

Chapter 11

Determining Sources of Relative Inefficiency in Heterogeneous Samples Using Multiple Data Analytic Techniques

Sergey Samoilenko
and Kweku-Muata Osei-Bryson

Contents

Abstract: Data envelopment analysis (DEA) is widely used by researchers and practitioners alike to assess relative performance of decision-making units (DMUs).
Commonly, the difference in the scores of relative performance of DMUs in the
sample is considered to reflect their differences in the efficiency of conversion of
inputs into outputs. In the presence of scale heterogeneity, however, the source of
the difference in scores becomes less clear, for it is also possible that the difference in
scores is caused by heterogeneity of the levels of inputs and outputs of DMUs in the
sample. In this chapter, we present and demonstrate a hybrid five-step methodology
that involves the use of DEA, cluster analysis, and neural networks, and that allows
an investigator to determine the source of relative heterogeneity.

Keywords: Cluster Analysis, neural nets, data envelopment analysis, relative efficiency,
heterogeneous samples.

Introduction

Data envelopment analysis (DEA) is a widely used nonparametric analytic tool (e.g.,
Asmild et al. 2007; Chen and van Dalen 2010; Doyle and Green 1994; Gillen and
Lall 1997; Khalili et al. 2010; Khouja 1995; Shao and Lin 2001), which is commonly applied in the research and practitioner communities to determine the relative efficiencies of the *decision-making units* (*DMUs*). Any entity that receives a
set of inputs and produces a set of outputs could be designated as a DMU; thus,
any group of such entities could be subjected to DEA. As a result, this method
has been applied to evaluate productivity and performance of airports (Gillen and
Lall 1997; Martin and Roman 2001; Pels et al. 2001), efficiency of US Air Force
maintenance units (Charnes et al. 1985), hospitals (Grosskopf et al. 2001; Gruca

and Nath 2001; Kirigia et al. 2001; Sola and Prior 2001), university departments (Beasley 1990), schools (Bessent and Bessent 1980; Grosskopf and Moutray 2001; Portela and Thanassoulis 2001; Santos and Themido 2001), and counties (Raab and Lichty 1997), as well as to compare industries and sectors (Sueyoshi and Goto 2001; Navarro and Camacho 2001; Murillo-Zamorano and Vega-Cervera 2001; Mathijs and Swinnen 2001), banks (Mukherjee et al. 2001; Sathye 2001; Kuosmanen and Post 2001; Hartman et al. 2001; Lin et al. 2009; Schaffnit et al. 1997), products and services (Doyle and Green 1991; Hollingsworth and Parkin 2001; Johnston and Gerard 2001), computers (Doyle and Green 1994), regulations (Piot-Lepetit et al. 2001; Gronli 2001), strategic decision making (Demirbag et al. 2010), and technologies (Khouja 1995; Shao and Lin 2001; Ramanathan 2001; Pare and Sicotte 2001).

One of the fundamental assumptions of DEA is that all DMUs in the sample are *functionally similar* in the sense that all DMUs receive the same *number* and the same *type* of inputs and outputs. The compliance with this assumption is enforced by defining a common *DEA model*, according to which the evaluation of the relative efficiency of every DMU in the sample takes place. DEA treats a DMU as a collection of inputs and outputs, without any regard to the actual process by which conversion of inputs into outputs takes place; instead, the process of conversion is treated by DEA as a "black box" common to all DMUs in the sample. Another fundamental assumption of DEA is that a set of DMUs is *homogeneous* in the sense that all DMUs are "alike" and thus directly comparable. Compliance with this important assumption of *homogeneity* of the sample is not enforced in DEA and usually resides under implicit purview of the decision maker. We suggest that two factors are important for the assumption of homogeneity of DMUs to hold. The first factor, *semantic homogeneity*, refers to the common meaning that is assigned to all DMUs in the sample by the decision maker. Compliance with this factor is straightforward. The second factor, *scale homogeneity*, refers to the *levels* of inputs and outputs of each DMU in the sample. In the absence of perfect scalability, the compliance with the second factor is problematic, for the decision maker must ensure that the levels of inputs and outputs are not affecting the functional similarity of DMUs in the sample.

However, in many situations, the sample of DMUs is a sample of convenience. It is possible, under such circumstances, that an investigator conducts DEA using a sample consisting of DMUs that are functionally similar, semantically homogeneous, yet heterogeneous in terms of the levels of inputs and outputs, which would mean that the validity of the resulting relative efficiency scores would be questionable because the *homogeneity* assumption holds only partially.

We must note that we are not drawing attention of the reader to the obvious case where scale heterogeneity arises simply due to the differences in the scale of the transformation of inputs into outputs, with all other factors being constant. The scale heterogeneity could be easily countered through the use of a scaling factor. Instead, we are interested in the cases where scale heterogeneity arises because of a more complex, not clearly obvious, scaling pattern that makes creation of any accurate subcategorization problematic. Let us consider an example of a comparison of a group of hospitals ranging in size from small to large. Clearly, the significant differences in the levels of inputs and outputs of such hospitals, whatever they might be, are important in themselves. However, it is also possible that such heterogeneity of the levels of inputs and outputs is reflective of the differences among the other important dimensions that are not accounted for by the DEA model. In many cases, a large hospital is a very different enterprise, from a standpoint of quality, complexity, and technological sophistication, than a small hospital.

Let us take this example further and consider that a smaller hospital A turned out to be relatively less efficient than a larger hospital B. Based on the results of the DEA of such *scale heterogeneous* sample of hospitals, the decision maker interested in improving efficiency of hospital A would face two possible options. The first option is to reduce the level of relative inefficiency of hospital A by improving the efficiency of the process by which inputs are converted into outputs. However, one cannot rule out that a lower level of relative efficiency of a hospital A is due to the comparatively lower level of inputs that it receives. Consequently, the second option is to reduce the level of relative inefficiency of hospital A by affecting the level of *scale heterogeneity*, that is, to change the existing level of inputs. The question becomes, then, what option is to be pursued? Considering this, in our study we aim to investigate the following research question: *How to account for the differences in the relative efficiency scores of the DMUs in the sample in the presence of scale heterogeneity associated with a complex and nonobvious scaling pattern?*

Our inquiry relies on the assumption that the difference in the relative efficiencies of the DMUs in a scale heterogeneous sample could arise from the two sources. The first source reflects the difference in the *transformative capacity* of the DMUs, which reflects the "true" difference in the relative efficiencies of the DMUs in terms of the conversion of the set of inputs into the set of outputs. The second source reflects scale heterogeneity of the DMUs in the sample and is indicative of the difference in the *levels* of inputs and outputs associated with a complex and nonobvious scaling pattern.

We suggest that the assumption of homogeneity of a sample of DMUs should not be taken for granted, but explicitly tested for. The reader may note that this position is similar to what applies in statistical analysis where there is explicit testing of the normality assumption. Consequently, in the situation where an investigator needs to perform DEA, we suggest a multistep methodology that is an extension of our previous work aimed at increasing the discriminatory power of DEA (Samoilenko and Osei-Bryson 2008). In order to present our methodology, we structure this chapter as follows: A brief overview of some common approaches of combining DEA with cluster analysis (CA) and neural networks (NNs) is provided in section "DEA with CA and NNs." An overview of the component techniques utilized in our methodology is offered in section "Description of the Methodology." An application of the methodology on an illustrative dataset is provided in section "Illustrative Example." A brief conclusion is presented in section "Discussion and Conclusion."

DEA with CA and NNs

CA and DEA

Clustering is a popular data mining technique (e.g., Ben-Dor and Yakhini 1999; Benfield and Raftery 1992; Cristofor and Simovici 2002; Dhillon 2001; Fisher 1997; Huang 1997; Okazaki 2005; Rai et al. 2005; Wallace et al. 2004), which involves the partitioning of a set of objects into a useful set of mutually exclusive clusters such that the similarity between the observations within each cluster (i.e., subset) is high, whereas the similarity between the observations from different clusters is low.

The approach of using CA with DEA is not novel to this research (Hirschberg and Lye 2001; Lemos et al. 2005; Marroquin et al. 2008; Meimand et al. 2002; Schreyögg and von Reitzenstein 2008; Sharma and Yu 2009; Shin and Sohn 2004). In general, CA could be incorporated with DEA in two distinct ways. The first approach is to apply CA to the results of DEA with the purpose of constructing multiple reference subsets from the original set of DMUs (Meimand et al. 2002; Bojnec and Latruffe 2007). Another approach calls for limiting a comparison of each DMU to its reference subset. As a result of this approach, the efficiency score of a DMU is defined not by an efficient subset of all DMUs, also called a *peer group*, but only by an efficient subset of its *peer subgroup*. Consequently, in the presence of scale heterogeneity of the sample, this approach will result in isolation of the multiple homogeneous subsets (Azadeh et al. 2007), and then in comparing each DMU only with the appropriate subset consisting of its peers within the subset. Although the use of this method offers obvious benefits, the shortcoming of this approach is that the relative efficiency of a DMU could only be determined in reference to its subset peer group, rather than to the sample as a whole.

Similar to the above-mentioned approaches, our study proposes a solution to conducting DEA of a scale heterogeneous dataset by means of using CA. Unlike the other approaches, our method does not require explicit partitioning of the sample of DMUs into multiple peer groups, a large dataset, or any external to DEA data, such as "external comparators" mentioned by Dyson et al. (2001) and used by Sarrico and Dyson (2000). Instead, our method aims at identifying and taking into consideration the presence of heterogeneous subsets without actually dividing the sample. As a result, our approach is not incongruent with one suggested by Dyson et al. (2001), where grouping of DMUs into homogeneous subsets is based on management information; furthermore, we suggest that our method could aid the decision maker's judgment by increasing available to her additional information provided by the results of CA. Consequently, similarly to the approach of Athanassopoulos and Thanassoulis (1995), our method results not in physical, but rather in *logical partitioning* of the otherwise intact dataset that is subjected to DEA.

NNs and DEA

NN modeling aims to develop a black box model (i.e., an artificial NN) of the unknown complex relationships in the data. This data mining method is particularly appropriate when there is no known mathematical formula that relates the input and output variables, and prediction is more important than explanation. It has been extensively used by researchers (Bu et al. 2003; Choi and Yoo 2001; Crestani and van Rijsbergen 1997; Harb and Chen 2005; Lu et al. 1996; Pao and Sobajic 1991; Vai and Xu 1995).

Using NN in conjunction with DEA is also not novel to this investigation. Combination of DEA and NN in one study started with the work of Athanassopoulos and Curram (1996), who extended the comparison of DEA with corrected ordinary least-squares methods (Banker et al. 1993) to the comparison of DEA with NN. For the purposes of estimating efficiency frontiers, NN could be perceived as a possible alternative (Azadeh et al. 2007; Costa and Markellos 1997; Santin and Valino 2000; Santin et al. 2004; Wang 2003), or as a complement to DEA (Angelidis and Lyroudi 2006; Celebi and Bayraktar 2008; Emrouznejad and Shale 2009; Mostafa 2009; Pendharkar and Rodger 2003; Wu 2009; Wu et al. 2006).

We believe that NN can augment rather than replace DEA, and in our methodology, we employ NN as a complementary to DEA technique. What differentiates our approach, however, is that we use NN for the purposes of simulating the values of outputs of DEA model based on which scores of the relative efficiency of DMUs will be calculated, and not for the purposes of classifying DMUs in terms of the relative efficiency (e.g., Wu 2009), or predicting the scores of relative efficiency of DMUs (e.g., Emrouznejad and Shale 2009), or preprocessing of the data prior to DEA (Celebi and Bayraktar 2008).

The fact that DEA and NN lack the explanatory power to provide insights regarding the *mechanism of transformation* does not negate the capability of these methods to provide inquirers with the insights regarding the *results of transformation*. The black box approach used by both methods fits the purpose of our study well, for we are not trying to determine *how* scale heterogeneity affects relative efficiency of DMU; instead, we are interested in the *presence* of the effect. This brief overview of such complex subject as NN cannot do justice to the topic. Thus, we direct the interested reader to Bishop (1995) for a comprehensive treatment of the subject.

Description of the Methodology

The proposed methodology helps an investigator to address two potential problems that arise when conducting DEA. The first problem is associated with a possible nonhomogeneous environment of DMUs (Dyson et al. 2001), which, due to its complexity, cannot be dealt with by simple inclusion of environmental variables in the DEA model. For example, if we are to compare two hospitals in different states in the United States, in order to account for a possible heterogeneity of their environment, we would need to include some sort of environmental variables reflecting the differences in social, political, environmental, legal, and cultural environments. Dyson et al. (2001) acknowledge that such environmental variables, especially in the service sector, could be difficult to identify, define, and measure. Furthermore, even if it is possible to completely account for the differences in the environment of DMUs and include the environmental variables into the DEA model, this approach will result in a possibly significant increase in the number of inputs and output. This, in turn, would lead to the lower level of discrimination (Dyson et al. 2001). Although the authors suggested that this problem can be dealt with by increasing the number of DMUs in the sample, such increase could bring an additional source of nonhomogeneity in the sample, which would have to be dealt with by inclusion of new types of environmental variables with all the consequences. The proposed use of NN in our methodology, however, allows an investigator to capture the impact of the specific environment for each logical subgroup without actually including any environmental variables in the DEA model.

The second problem is associated with the available return-to-scale assumptions of DEA. Let us revisit our earlier example and compare two hospitals in terms of their relative efficiency of the production of revenues from the sale of a new type of service—a novel plastic surgery. The product life cycle model informs us that such *sales* curve is S shaped (Hauser et al. 2005; Mahajan et al. 1995; Rogers 2003; Sultan et al. 1990; Van den Bulte and Stremersch 2004). It is commonly accepted that the models that produce S-shaped curves (e.g., logistic curve model or Gompertz model) contain areas of increasing, constant, and decreasing return to scale. Using DEA to compare relative efficiency of two hospitals in such situation will require an investigator to impose two additional assumptions. First, it will be required to assume that our two hospitals are in the same phase of the *sales* curve (e.g., introduction, growth, maturity, or decline). Second, it will be required to assume that the estimate of the relative efficiency provided by DEA holds for the duration of the *sales* curve. Our approach utilizes NN to simulate the position of a DMU in more than one point on the *sales* curve; thus, the first assumption can be relaxed. Furthermore, by performing DEA of the simulated data, we can obtain multiple scores of the relative efficiency for each DMU, which will allow us to relax the second assumption. Furthermore, using NN simulation in our methodology allows for avoiding DEA-related problems associated with the possible presence of economies and diseconomies of scale; consequently, we suggest adopting the basic constant returns to scale (CRS) model.

The proposed methodology consists of five major steps that are summarized in Table 11.1; the description of steps 3, 4, and 5 follows. As previously mentioned, the proposed methodology is an extension of the three-step methodology of Samoilenko and Osei-Bryson (2008), which utilizes the CA and DEA as, correspondingly, the first and second steps, respectively. Consequently, in this section we focus our discussion on the remaining steps of the methodology proposed in this paper.

Table 11.1   Proposed Methodology

Step	Step 1	Step 2	Step 3	Step 4	Step 5
Purpose	Evaluate the scale heterogeneity status of the dataset	Determine the relative efficiency status of each DMU	Generate a black box model of transformative capacity of each cluster	Obtain simulated sets of the outputs for each DMU in each cluster	Determine the sources of the relative efficiencies of the DMUs in the sample
Dataset	Complete sample	Complete sample	Clusters generated in step 1	Clusters generated in step 1	Complete sample
Technique	CA	DEA	NNs	NNs	DEA
Outcome	One or more clusters	Scores of averaged relative efficiency for each cluster	Black box model of transformative capacity for each cluster	Simulated outputs for each cluster based on black box models of other clusters	Scores of averaged relative efficiency for each cluster based on the original inputs and the simulated outputs

Description of Steps 3–5 of the Methodology

Step 3: Generate a Black Box Model of Transformative Capacity of Each Cluster

For each cluster k, NN induction is used to generate a black box model of the transformative capacity of DMUs in the given cluster. Let the model for cluster "k" be labeled $BBTM_k$. This involves using the set of input variables for each cluster as input nodes and the set of output variables as output nodes of the NN. Then we train the NN in order to obtain the specific *nonexplanatory black box model of the transformative capacity*, by which the set of inputs is converted into the set of outputs; we call this *transformation model* of a given cluster.

Step 4: Obtain Simulated Sets of the Outputs for Each DMU in Each Cluster

For each cluster k_1, apply the black box transformative model $BBTM_{k1}$ to every other cluster k_2. The result is that for each $DMU_{i(k2)}$ in a given cluster k_2, simulated outputs are generated based on the application of $BBTM_{k1}$ to the inputs of $DMU_{i(k2)}$.

Step 5: Determine the Sources of the Relative Inefficiency of the DMUs in the Sample

For each pair of clusters (k_1, k_2),

1. Apply DEA to the original inputs of DMUs of cluster k_2 and the corresponding simulated outputs that resulted from $BBTM_{k1}$.
2. Calculate the average relative efficiency of cluster k_2 based on its original inputs and simulated outputs.
3. Compare this simulated average relative efficiency of cluster k_2 to that of its actual average relative efficiency in order to determine if there is any difference in the transformative capacities of clusters k_1 and k_2.
4. Compare this simulated average relative efficiency of cluster k_2 to the actual average relative efficiency of cluster k_1 in order to determine if any difference in the average performances of clusters k_1 and k_2 is due, in part, to scale heterogeneity.

Motivation for Steps 3 and 5 of the Methodology

Motivation for Step 3

The third step of out methodology utilizes NN to create a model of the transformative capacity for each of the k clusters identified in step 1. We propose that modeling of DEA scores can be used for the purposes of inquiring into the factors affecting relative efficiency, albeit indirectly. Despite the fact that the modeling of DEA scores is an often encountered approach (Hoff 2006), it comes with the penalty of inevitable misspecification of the model according to which inputs are converted into outputs. It is reasonable to suggest that the correct "white box" modeling of the DEA scores must have at least two prerequisites. First, the investigator must know the model of transformation of inputs into outputs utilized by DEA. Second, it must be possible to respecify correctly this known model within the data analytic technique, which is going to be used for the purposes of modeling of DEA scores. The nonparametric nature of DEA is another point to consider, because the use of parametric techniques, such as commonly used for this purpose Tobit regression, not only results in misspecification (Hoff 2006) but also requires a compliance with the data normality assumption that often used in DEA sample of convenience may not satisfy.

As a result, a misspecification of the model is inevitable; for the black box approach of DEA to the process of transformation of inputs into outputs leaves investigator no chance of knowing, let alone specifying, the correct model. Keeping the above-mentioned difficulties in mind, we decided instead to model a *new dataset*, and then use DEA to obtain a new set of scores. The black box approach of NN to modeling complex unknown relationship in the dataset fits well for this purpose, for we do not need to know and specify the relationship between the data ourselves.

We use the set of input variables for each cluster as input nodes and the set of output variables as output nodes of the NN. Then we train the NN and obtain the specific to each cluster *transformation function* according to which the set of inputs is converted into the set of outputs; we call this transformation function a *nonexplanatory black box model of the transformative capacity* of a given cluster. Thus, in step 3 we generate k *black box models* corresponding to each of the k clusters identified in step 1.

Motivation for Step 5

The purposes of this step are to determine if the DMUs in a given cluster k_2 would have improved performance if they had utilized the transformative model of another cluster k_1 and (2) to determine if any difference is due to scale heterogeneity. For a given cluster, this exploration is conducted using the transformative capacity model $BBTM_{k1}$ of every other cluster k_1, where $k_1 \neq k_2$.

Thus, if step 1 had resulted in two clusters, *Followers* and *Leaders*, during step 5, we would subject the original inputs and the simulated outputs of the Followers that were generated in step 4, as well as the original inputs and the simulated outputs of the Leaders, to DEA. Then we again calculate the averaged scores of the relative efficiency for every cluster and determine whether the averages of the Followers have improved. If this is the case, and the average relative efficiencies of the Followers have gone up, we have a reason to suggest that the disparity between the relative efficiencies of the Leaders and the Followers is due, in part, to the differences in their transformative capacities.

At this point, we need to determine a role of *scale heterogeneity* in the disparity of the levels of the relative efficiencies of the Leaders and the Followers. In order to do so, we conduct DEA again, this time using the dataset consisting of the original inputs and the outputs of the Followers, and the original inputs and the simulated outputs of the Leaders. Once the scores of the relative efficiency have been obtained, we group them according to the cluster membership (i.e., Followers and Leaders) and average the relative efficiency scores for each group. If, after the comparison of the averaged relative efficiencies, the Leaders still have a higher averaged relative efficiency score, then we have a reason to suggest that the disparity between the relative efficiencies of the Leaders and the Followers is due, in part, to scale heterogeneity. Meaning, even with the less efficient process of the transformative capacity, the Leaders are still capable of being more relatively efficient than the Followers.

Illustrative Example

Description of the Illustrative Dataset

We test the proposed methodology in the context of the set of countries classified by IMF (2000) as *transition economies in Europe* and *the former Soviet Union.* Using archival data drawn from the *Database of World Development Indicators*, which is the World Bank's comprehensive database on development data, and the *Yearbook of Statistics*, published yearly by the International Telecommunication Union, we aggregated the data on 18 economies for the period from 1993 to 2002. These 18 countries are Albania, Armenia, Azerbaijan, Belarus, Bulgaria, Czech Republic, Estonia, Hungary, Kazakhstan, Kyrgyz Republic, Latvia, Lithuania, Moldova, Poland, Romania, Slovak Republic, Slovenia, and Ukraine. As a result, we constructed the sample consisting of 180 data points, where each data point reflected a given transition economy (TE) per given year. Although these economies do share a common classification, they also display some important differences in terms of their levels of economic development, state of infrastructure, business environment, and so on. The research on the subject of the effect of investments in the Information and Communication Technologies (ICT), such as telecommunications, on economic development in the context of TEs suggested that small number of countries (e.g., Poland, Hungary, Slovenia, and Czech Republic) were able to benefit from investments in ICT. The much larger number of TEs, however, falls short of demonstrating the positive impact of such investments on their economic development. Multiple research studies identified the level of investments in ICT (Murakami 1997; Piatkowski 2002) as one of the variables that impact the level of returns on investments.

Consequently, while keeping all the possible differences between 18 TEs in our sample in mind, it is reasonable to suggest that two factors could be responsible for the discrepancy of the effects of the investments in telecommunications on the level of returns on investment. The first factor is a level of investments in telecommunications and the second factor is a level of the efficiency of the transformation of investments in telecommunications into revenues.

To demonstrate our methodology in action, we formulate the following broad research problem: *How to determine the appropriate, empirically justifiable route by which TEs could improve their level of relative efficiency of the production of revenues from investments in telecommunications?*

In the context of the illustrative example and our methodology, the answer to this research problem involves answering the following questions:

1. Whether the 18 TEs display significant differences in terms of the levels of investments in telecommunications and revenues from telecommunications (step 1)
2. Whether the subsets of the sample, which differ in terms of the levels of investments and revenues, also differ in terms of the relative efficiency of the production of revenues (step 2)
3. Whether the subsets of the sample differ in terms of the processes of transformation on investments into revenues (steps 3 and 4)
4. Whether the relative inefficiency of poor performers is associated with the insufficient levels of investments or whether it is a result of inefficient processes of the transformation of investments into revenues (step 5)

Application of the Methodology to the Illustrative Dataset

For the DEA part of the methodology, we have identified a model consisting of six input and four output variables, presented in Table 11.2. A theoretical justification of the chosen model and the discussion regarding the choice of the variables can be found in the works of Samoilenko (2008) and Samoilenko and Osei-Bryson (2008).

Table 11.2 Variables Selected for the DEA Model

Input Variables	Output Variables
GDP per capita (in current US $)	Total telecommunications services revenue per telecommunications worker
Full-time telecommunication staff (% of total labor force)	
Annual telecommunications investment per telecommunications worker	Total telecommunications services revenue (% of GDP in current US $)
Annual telecommunications investment (% of GDP in current US $)	
Annual telecommunications investment per capita	Total telecommunications services revenue per worker
Annual telecommunications investment per worker	Total telecommunications services revenue per capita

Results of Step 1: Evaluate the Scale Heterogeneity Status of the Dataset

To perform CA, we employed a partitional approach to generate the maximum possible number of clusters (i.e., k_{Max}), followed by the application of an agglomerative clustering method to combine pairs of clusters until the specified minimum number of clusters (i.e., k_{Min}) is obtained. Given our interest in determining whether a set of DMUs (i.e., 18 TEs) is a *scale heterogeneous*, we will use a user-specified threshold on outlier size to assess whether a given partition contains outlier clusters, and also use expert knowledge to further assess whether the partition is meaningful. A cluster will be considered an outlier if the percentage of the objects that it includes is less than $\tau_{Outlier}$ of the objects in the entire dataset. We are not claiming that this is the only or always best approach, particularly as for a given dataset it is never clear which approach is the most appropriate. The benefit of our approach, however, is that it allows for augmenting a context-independent solution with the context-dependent knowledge of a domain expert.

We used SAS Enterprise Miner to perform CA of the dataset and we were able to come up with a solution that partitions our dataset into two clusters (see Table 11.3). Based on the compiled information, we can see that although some of the TEs are "permanent residents" of one cluster, other TEs are "migrants," that is, they change the cluster membership depending on a year. Additional details of the results of CA are provided in the appendix.

Table 11.3 Membership of the Two-Cluster Solution

The Followers	The Leaders
Albania (1993–2002)	Bulgaria (2002)
Armenia (1993–2002)	Czech Rep (1993–2002)
Azerbaijan (1993–2002)	Estonia (1994–2002)
Belarus (1993–2002)	Hungary (1993–2002)
Bulgaria (1993–2001)	Latvia (1994, 1995, 1997–2002)
Estonia (1993)	Lithuania (1999–2002)
Kazakhstan (1993–2002)	Poland (1993–2002)
Kyrgyzstan (1993–2002)	Slovakia (1995–1998, 2000–2002)
Latvia (1993, 1996)	Slovenia (1993–2002)
Lithuania (1993–1998)	
Moldova (1993–2002)	
Romania (1993–2002)	
Slovakia (1993, 1994, 1999)	
Ukraine (1993–2002)	

Results of Step 2: Determine the Relative Efficiency Status of Each DMU

To perform DEA, we have chosen an output-oriented model and used it under the conditions of CRS, variable returns to scale, and nonincreasing returns to scale. Unlike in the case of the input-oriented model, the output orientation does not concern itself with the efficient utilization of the inputs, but rather with the maximization of the outputs. Thus, it is probably reflective of the perspective of the investor, especially in the case when the primary goal is to obtain the maximum revenue.

We present the summarized results in Table 11.4. This approach of using average countries inefficiencies over the period of time, as well as averaged inefficiencies of a group of countries, is consistent with the approach of Arcelus and Arocena (2005). It turned out that the averaged relative efficiency of the second cluster is greater than that of the first cluster; consequently, we labeled the first cluster as the Followers and the second cluster as the Leaders.

Results of Steps 3 and 4: Generate Simulated Sets of the Outputs for Each Cluster Based on Black Box Models of Transformative Capacity Processes

To conduct NN simulation of the outputs of our DEA model, we used SAS Enterprise Miner. For the purposes of this research, we used supervised mode of learning because the dataset that we are going to use contains not only the inputs but also the outputs. First, we used NN to simulate the outputs of the Followers based on the transformative capacity of the Leaders. We used the setting that allowed us to use "Samples of datasets" for preliminary training. We also used "Average error" as our model selection criterion; this setting chooses the model with the smallest average error for the validation dataset. Other settings were "None" as the number of preliminary runs and "Standard back propagation" as a training technique. After the running of the model, the convergence criterion was satisfied.

The process model diagram depicting stages involved into the simulation of the outputs is represented in Figure 11.1. Once the simulated outputs of the Followers were obtained, we used the same process to obtain the simulated outputs of the Leaders based on the transformative capacity of the Followers.

Table 11.4 DEA: Comparison of the Clusters Based on the Output-Oriented DEA Model

Relative Efficiency Score	Leaders	Followers	Difference	Difference%
CRS, average	1.94	2.54	−0.60	23.67%

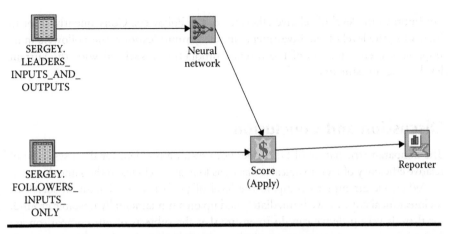

Figure 11.1   The process model diagram of NN simulation.

Results of Step 5

Once the simulated outputs were obtained, they were substituted instead of the real outputs. After that, we have conducted the DEA again and obtained the new values of relative efficiencies for the Followers and the Leaders. We adapted the approach used by Arcelus and Arocena (2000) and used averaged values of relative efficiency scores. The results are summarized in Table 11.5.

Based on the results of the DEA, we are able to establish that the Followers are capable of becoming more efficient than the Leaders, in the case if they improve the level of the transformative capacity. Thus, at this point, we can state that the lower level of the averaged relative efficiency of the Followers is, at least partially, a result of the inefficient processes of the revenue production. The results summarized in Table 11.5 also indicate that the increase in the level of the inputs does

Table 11.5   Summary of Step 5

Comparison of the DEA Scores Based on	Leaders, CRS Averaged (Actual)	Followers, CRS Averaged (Simulated)	Difference	Difference%
The simulated data of the Followers and the actual of the Leaders	2.04	1.62	0.42	25.62%
The simulated data of the Leaders and the actual of the Followers	2.09	2.30	−0.21	9.20%

not improve the level of relative efficiency of the Followers. Consequently, prior to increasing the level of the investments in telecommunications, the Followers must improve the effectiveness of the revenue production associated with the current level of the investments.

Discussion and Conclusion

The nonparametric nature of DEA does not present a problem for the assessment of relative efficiency of technological artifacts, as long as it belongs to the same domain.

When we attempt to compare the level of performance of natural, social, or sociotechnical entities, we immediately end up on a fundamentally unstable ground, for there is very little we can do to ensure that the subjects of our comparison are "alike." Let us consider some purely hypothetical examples. First, we compare a performance of two basketball players, Star and NotStar, in terms of their efficiency of converting minutes on the court into the points. Star, whose relative efficiency is higher, averages 35 minutes and 30 points per game, whereas NotStar, whose relative efficiency is lower, averages 5 minutes and 3 points per game. There are two possible explanations regarding the difference in the level of performance: First, Star is a better player than NotStar, and second, Star is spending more time on the court. Now, how do we go about increasing relative efficiency of NotStar? Do we proceed by allowing him to play more minutes, or by trying to make him a better player first?

Similarly, how do investors should go about increasing the level of performance of the less successful baseball teams in Major League Baseball? Should investors provide incentives for a better performance, or should they start from investing more in the team's roster, hoping that the results will follow? Essentially, this is a type of a problem that our methodology allows us to address.

Let us consider an example of possible application of the proposed methodology, which is closer in spirit and relevance to the illustrative example that we used in this chapter. On November 20, 2001, the UN Secretary General established, per request from the United Nations Economic and Social Council, an Information and Communication Technologies Task Force (ICTF). The purpose of this initiative was to provide a global dimension to the efforts in bridging the "digital divide," to encourage digital opportunity, and to place the ICT at the service of the development for all countries (Martinez-Frias 2003). At this point, we know that in terms of the bridging digital divide, the level of success from the investments in the ICT varies greatly from country to country. However, we do not know whether the variation in the results is due to differences in the levels of the investments of ICT, or whether it is due to the capability of a given economy to transform the investments into the outcomes, that is, bridging the digital divide. The answer to this question is very important, for it serves as one of the determinants of the investment strategy directed at the accomplishment of the goals of the ICTF. We hope that we were able to demonstrate the possible contribution of the proposed methodology from practical standpoint.

We suggest that the proposed approach makes methodological contributions as well. First, our methodology allows for increasing the discriminatory power of DEA in the samples in the presence of heterogeneity. Although traditional DEA alone categorizes DMUs in the sample as being relatively efficient or relatively inefficient, our approach allows for placing each DMU in one of the three categories: (1) relatively efficient, (2) relatively inefficient due to scale heterogeneity of the sample, and (3) relatively inefficient due to transformative capacity. Second, our methodology allows for explicit acknowledgment of the heterogeneity of the sample of DMUs, thus greatly expanding the domain of eligible for DEA DMUs. Finally, our approach allows for increasing prescriptive capabilities of DEA, providing a decision maker with distinct strategies regarding the increase of relative performance for each DMU in a nonhomogenous sample.

We must acknowledge, however, that our research is not without its limitations. First, despite applying CA to evaluate a sample of DMUs for heterogeneity, our approach does not provide any strict criteria with regard to what constitutes heterogeneity of the sample. Consequently, because heterogeneity is a relative concept, and because the determination of heterogeneity often requires intimate knowledge of the problem domain, we declare this issue as being beyond the scope of our methodology and delegate it to reside under the purview of an investigator. The second limitation of our study is associated with the assumption regarding the sources of relative inefficiency in the nonhomogenous sample. We assume that heterogeneity of the sample *or* a transformative capacity of DMUs can cause relative inefficiency. However, it is possible that there is interplay between the two factors, where heterogeneity of the sample affects transformative capacity or, conversely, heterogeneity arises due to the differences in transformative capacity. Nevertheless, we hope that contributions of our study outweigh its limitations.

References

Angelidis, D., Lyroudi, K., 2006. Efficiency in the Italian banking industry: Data envelopment analysis and neural networks. *International Research Journal of Finance and Economics* 1(5), 155–165.

Arcelus, F.J., Arocena, P., 2000. Convergence and productive efficiency in fourteen OECD countries: A non-parametric frontier approach. *International Journal of Production Economics* 66, 105–117.

Arcelus, F.J., Arocena, P., 2005. Productivity differences across OECD countries in the presence of environmental constraints. *Journal of the Operational Research Society* 56, 1352–1362.

Asmild, M., Paradi, J.C., Reese, D.N., Tam, F., 2007. Measuring overall efficiency and effectiveness using DEA. *European Journal of Operational Research* 178(1), 305–321.

Athanassopoulos, A.D., Thanassoulis, E., 1995. Separating market efficiency from profitability and its implications for planning. *Journal of the Operational Research Society* 46(1), 20–34.

Athanassopoulos, A.D., Curram, S., 1996. A comparison of data envelopment analysis and artificial neural networks as tools for assessing the efficiency of decision making units. *Journal of Operational Research Society* 47(8), 1000–1017.

Azadeh, A., Ghaderi, S.F., Tarverdian, S., Saberi, M., 2007. Forecasting electrical consumption by integration of neural network, time series and ANOVA. *Applied Mathematics and Computation* 186(2), 1753–1761.

Banfield, J., Raftery, A., 1992. Identifying ice floes in satellite images. *Naval Research Reviews* 43, 2–18.

Banker, R.D., Datar, S.M., Kemerer, C.F., Zweig, D., 1993. Software complexity and maintenance costs. *Communications of ACM* 36(11), 81–94.

Beasley, J.E., 1990. Comparing university departments. *Omega, International Journal of Management Science* 18(2), 171–183.

Ben-Dor, A., Yakhini, Z., 1999. Clustering gene expression patterns. In: *Proceedings of the 3rd Annual International Conference on Computational Molecular Biology*. Lyon, France, pp. 11–14.

Bessent, A., Bessent, W., 1980. Determining the comparative efficiency of schools through data envelopment analysis. *Educational Administration Quarterly* 16(2), 57–75.

Bishop, C.M., 1995. *Neural for Pattern Recognition*. Oxford University Press, Oxford.

Bojnec, S., Latruffe, L., 2007. Measures of farm business efficiency. *Industrial Management & Data Systems* 108(2), 258–270.

Bu, N., Fukuda, O., Tsuji, T., 2003. EMG-based motion discrimination using a novel recurrent neural network. *Journal of Intelligent Information Systems* 21(2), 113–126.

Çelebi, D., Bayraktar, D., 2008. An integrated neural network and data envelopment analysis for supplier evaluation under incomplete information. *Expert Systems with Applications* 35(4), 1698–1710.

Charnes, A., Clark, C.T., Cooper, W.W., Golany, B., 1985. A developmental study of data envelopment analysis in measuring the efficiency of maintenance units in the US air forces. *Annals of Operations Research* 2, 95–112.

Chen, C., van Dalen, J., 2010. Measuring dynamic efficiency: Theories and an integrated methodology. *European Journal of Operational Research* 203(3), 749–760.

Choi, Y.S., Yoo, S.I., 2001. Text database discovery on the web: Neural net based approach. *Journal of Intelligent Information Systems* 16(1), 5–20.

Costa, A., Markellos, R.N., 1997. Evaluating public transport efficiency with neural network models. *Transportation Research* 5(5), 301–312.

Crestani, F., van Rijsbergen, C.J., 1997. A model for adaptive information retrieval. *Journal of Intelligent Information Systems* 8(1), 29–56.

Cristofor, D., Simovici, D., 2002. An information-theoretical approach to clustering categorical databases using genetic algorithms. In: *Proceedings of the SIAM DM Workshop on Clustering High Dimensional Data*, Arlington, VA, pp. 37–46.

Demirbag, M., Tatoglu, E., Glaister, K.W., Zaim, S., 2010. Measuring strategic decision making efficiency in different country contexts: A comparison of British and Turkish firms. *Omega, International Journal of Management Science* 38(1/2), 95–104.

Dhillon, I., 2001. Co-clustering documents and words using bipartite spectral graph partitioning. In: *Proceedings of the 7th ACM SIGKDD*. San Francisco, CA, pp. 269–274.

Doyle, J.R., Green, R.H., 1991. Comparing products using data envelopment analysis. *Omega, International Journal of Management Science* 19(6), 631–638.

Doyle, J.R., Green, R.H., 1994. Strategic choice and data envelopment analysis: Comparing computers across many attributes. *Journal of Information Technology* 9(1), 61–69.

Dyson, R.G., Allen, R., Camanho, A.S., Podinovski, V.V., Sarrico, C.S., Shale, E.A., 2001. Pitfalls and protocols in DEA. *European Journal of Operational Research* 132, 245–259.

Emrouznejad, A., Shale, E.A., 2009. A combined neural network and DEA for measuring efficiency of large scale data sets. *Computers and Industrial Engineering* 56, 249–254.

Fisher, M.R., 1997. Segmentation of angler population by catch preference, participation, and experience: A management-oriented application of recreation specialization. *North American Journal of Fisheries Management* 17, 1–10.

Gillen, D., Lall, A., 1997. Developing measures of airport productivity and performance: An application of data envelopment analysis. *Transportation Research (Part E)* 33(4), 261–273.

Gronli, H., 2001. A comparison of Scandinavian regulatory models: Issues and experience. *The Electricity Journal* 14(7), 57–64.

Grosskopf, S., Margaritis, D., Valdmanis, V., 2001. The effects of teaching on hospital productivity. *Socio-Economic Planning Sciences* 35(3), 189–204.

Grosskopf, S., Moutray, C., 2001. Evaluating performance in Chicago public high schools in the wake of decentralization. *Economics of Education Review* 20(1), 1–14.

Gruca, T., Nath, D., 2001. The technical efficiency of hospitals under a single payer system: The case of Ontario community hospitals. *Health Care Management Science* 4(2), 91–101.

Harb, H., Chen, L., 2005. Voice-based gender identification in multimedia applications. *Journal of Intelligent Information Systems* 24(2/3), 179–198.

Hartman, T., Storbeck. J., Byrnes, P., 2001. Allocative efficiency in branch banking. *European Journal of Operational Research* 134(2), 232–242.

Hauser, J., Tellis, J., Griffin, A., 2006. Research on innovation: A review and agenda for marketing science. *Marketing Science* 25(6), 687–717.

Hirschberg, J.G., Lye, J.N., 2001. Clustering in a data envelopment analysis using bootstrapped efficiency scores. Department of Economics—Working Papers Series 800, The University of Melbourne, Melbourne, Australia.

Hoff, A., 2006. Second stage DEA: Comparison of approaches for modeling the DEA score. *European Journal of Operational Research* 181(3), 425–435.

Hollingsworth, B., Parkin, D., 2001. The efficiency of the delivery of neonatal care in the UK. *Journal of Public Health Medicine* 23(1), 47–50.

Huang, Z., 1997. Clustering large data sets with mixed numeric and categorical values. In: *Proceedings of the First Pacific Asia Knowledge Discovery and Data Mining Conference.* World Scientific, Singapore, pp. 21–34.

IMF, 2000. *International Financial Statistics Yearbook*, International Monetary Fund, Statistics Department, vol. 53, September 13.

Johnston, K., Gerard, K., 2001. Assessing efficiency in the UK breast screening programme: Does size of screening unit make a difference? *Health Policy* 56(1), 21–32.

Khalili, M., Camanho, A.S., Portela, M.C.A.S., Alirezaee, M.R., 2010. The measurement of relative efficiency using data envelopment analysis with assurance regions that link inputs and outputs. *European Journal of Operational Research* 203(3), 761–770.

Khouja, M., 1995. The use of data envelopment analysis for technology selection. *Computers and Industrial Engineering* 28(1), 123–132.

Kirigia, J., Sambo, L., Scheel, H., 2001. Technical efficiency of public clinics in Kwazulu–Natal province of South Africa. *East African Medical Journal* 78(2), S1–S13.

Kuosmanen, T., Post, T., 2001. Measuring economic efficiency with incomplete price information: With an application to European commercial banks. *European Journal of Operational Research* 134(1), 43–58.

Lemos, C.A.A., Lima, M.P., Ebecken, N.F.F., 2005. DEA implementation and clustering analysis using the k-means algorithm. In: *Data Mining VI—Data Mining, Text Mining and Their Business Applications*, A. Zanasi, C.A. Brebbia, and N. Ebecken, eds. Skiathos, Greece. vol. 1, pp. 321–329.

Lin, T.T., Lee, C., Chiu, T., 2009. Application of DEA in analyzing a bank's operating performance. *Expert Systems with Applications* 36(5), 8883–8891.

Lu, H., Setiono, R., Liu, H., 1996. Effective data mining using neural networks. *IEEE Transactions on Knowledge and Data Engineering* 8(6), 957–961.

Mahajan, V., Muller, E., Bass, F., 1995. Diffusion of new products: Empirical generalizations and managerial uses. *Marketing Science* 14(3), 79–88.

Marroquin, M., Pena, M., Castro, C., Castro, J., Cabrera-Rios, M., 2008. Use of data envelopment analysis and clustering in multiple criteria optimization. *Intelligent Data Analysis* 12, 89–101.

Martin, J., Roman, C., 2001. An application of DEA to measure the efficiency of Spanish airports prior to privatization. *Journal of Air Transport Management* 7(3), 149–157.

Martinez-Frias, J., 2003. The importance of ICTs for developing countries. *Interdisciplinary Science Reviews* 28(1), 10–14.

Mathijs, E., Swinnen, J., 2001. Production organization and efficiency during transition: An empirical analysis of East German agriculture. *The Review of Economics and Statistics* 83, 100–107.

Meimand, M., Cavana, R.Y., Laking, R., 2002. Using DEA and survival analysis for measuring performance of branches in New Zealand's accident compensation corporation. *Journal of the Operational Research Society* 53(3), 303–313.

Mostafa, M., 2009. A probabilistic neural network approach for modeling and classifying efficiency of GCC banks. *International Journal of Business Performance Management* 11(3), 236–258.

Mukherjee, K., Ray, S., Miller, S., 2001. Productivity growth in large US commercial banks: The initial post-deregulation experience. *Journal of Banking and Finance* 25(5), 913–939.

Murakami, T., 1997. *The Impact of ICT on Economic Growth and the Productivity Paradox*. Retrieved January 02, 2010. Available from http://www.tcf.or.jp/data/19971011_Takeshi_Murakami_2.pdf.

Murillo-Zamorano, L., Vega-Cervera, J., 2001. The use of parametric and non-parametric frontier methods to measure the productive efficiency in the industrial sector: A comparative study. *International Journal of Production Economics* 69(3), 265–275.

Navarro, J., Camacho, J., 2001. Productivity of the service sector: A regional perspective. *Service Industries Journal* 21(1), 123–148.

Okazaki, S., 2006. What do we know about mobile internet adopters? A cluster analysis. *Information and Management* 43, 127–141.

Pao, Y.-H., Sobajic, D.J., 1991. Neural networks and knowledge engineering. *IEEE Transactions on Knowledge and Data Engineering* 3, 185–192.

Pare, G., Sicotte, C., 2001. Information technology sophistication in health care: An instrument validation study among Canadian hospitals. *International Journal of Medical Informatics* 63(3), 205–223.

Pels, E., Nijkamp, P., Rietveld, P., 2001. Relative efficiency of European airports. *Transport Policy* 8(3), 183–192.

Pendharkar, P., Rodger, J., 2003. Technical efficiency-based selection of learning cases to improve forecasting accuracy of neural networks under monotonicity assumption. *Decision Support Systems* 36(1), 117–136.

Piatkowski, M., 2002. *The New Economy and Economic Growth in Transition Economies.* WIDER Discussion Paper No. 2002/63, Helsinki, Finland: WIDER.

Piot-Lepetit, I., Brummer, B., Kleinhanss, W., 2001. Impacts of environmental regulations on the efficiency of arable farms in France and Germany. *Agrarwirtschaft* 50(3), 184–188.

Portela, M., Thanassoulis, E., 2001. Decomposing school and school-type efficiency. *European Journal of Operational Research* 132(2), 357–373.

Raab, R., Lichty, R., 1997. An efficiency analysis of Minnesota counties: A data envelopment analysis using 1993 IMPLAN input-output analysis. *The Journal of Regional Analysis and Policy* 27(1), 75–93.

Rai, A., Tang, X., Brown, P., Keil, M., 2005. Assimilation patterns in the use of electronic procurement innovations: A cluster analysis. *Information and Management* 43(3), 336–349.

Ramanathan, R., 2001. Comparative risk assessment of energy supply technologies: A data envelopment analysis approach. *Energy* 26(2), 197–203.

Rogers, E.M., 2003. *Diffusion of Innovations.* Simon & Schuster, New York.

Samoilenko, S., 2008. Contributing factors to information technology investment utilization in transition economies: An empirical investigation. *Information Technology for Development* 14(1), 52–75.

Samoilenko, S., Osei-Bryson, K.-M., 2008. Increasing the discriminatory power of DEA in the presence of the sample heterogeneity with cluster analysis and decision trees. *Expert Systems with Applications* 34(2), 1568–1581.

Santin, D., Valino, A., 2000. *Artificial Neural Networks for Measuring Technical Efficiency in Schools with a Two-Level Model: An Alternative Approach*, II Oviedo Workshop on Efficiency and Productivity. Universidad de Oviedo, Oviedo, Spain.

Santín, D., Delgado, F.J., Valiño, A., 2004. The measurement of technical efficiency: A neural network approach. *Applied Economics* 36(6), 627–635.

Santos, J., Themido, I., 2001. An application of recent developments of data envelopment analysis to the evaluation of secondary schools in Portugal. *International Journal of Services Technology and Management* 2(1/2), 142–160.

Sarrico, C.S., Dyson, R.G., 2000. Performance measurement in UK universities—The institutional perspective. *Journal of Operational Research Society* 51(7), 789–800.

Sathye, M., 2001. X-Efficiency in Australian banking: An empirical investigation. *Journal of Banking and Finance* 25(3), 613–630.

Schaffnit, C., Rosen, D., Paradi, J.C., 1997. Best practice analysis of bank branches: An application of DEA in a large Canadian bank. *European Journal of Operational Research* 98(2), 269–289.

Schreyögg, J., von Reitzenstein, C., 2008. Strategic groups and performance differences among academic medical centers. *Health Care Management Review* 33(3), 225–233.

Shao, B., Lin, W., 2001. Measuring the value of information technology in technical efficiency with stochastic production frontiers. *Information and Software Technology* 43(7), 447–456.

Sharma, M.J., Yu, S.J., 2009. Performance based stratification and clustering for benchmarking of container terminals. *Expert Systems with Applications* 36(3), 5016–5022.

Shin, H.W., Sohn, S.Y., 2004. Multi-attribute scoring method for mobile telecommunication subscribers. *Expert Systems with Applications* 26(3), 363–368.

Sola, M., Prior, D., 2001. Measuring productivity and quality changes using data envelopment analysis: An application to Catalan hospitals. *Financial Accountability and Management* 17(3), 219–245.

Sueyoshi, T., Goto, M., 2001. Slack-adjusted DEA for time series analysis: Performance measurement of Japanese electric power generation industry in 1984–1993. *European Journal of Operational Research* 133(2), 232–259.

Sultan, F., Farley, J.U., Lehmann, D.R., 1990. A meta-analysis of applications of diffusion models. *Journal of Marketing Research* 27(1), 70–77.

Van den Bulte, C., Stremersch, S., 2004. Social contagion and income heterogeneity in new product diffusion: A meta-analysis test. *Marketing Science* 23(4), 530–544.

Vai, M., Xu, Z., 1995. Representing knowledge by neural networks for qualitative analysis and reasoning. *IEEE Transactions on Knowledge and Data Engineering* 7(5), 683–690.

Wallace, L., Keil, M., Rai, A., 2004. Understanding software project risk: A cluster analysis. *Information and Management* 42, 115–125.

Wang, S., 2003. Adaptive non-parametric efficiency frontier analysis: A neural network-based model. *Computers and Operations Research* 30(2), 279–295.

Wu, D., 2009. Supplier selection: A hybrid model using DEA, decision tree and neural network. *Expert Systems with Applications* 36(5), 9105–9112.

Wu, M.-C., Lin, S.-Y., Lin, C.-H., 2006. An effective application of decision tree to stock trading. *Expert Systems with Applications* 31(2), 270–274.

Appendix: Results of Cluster Analysis

Distance between two clusters

Cluster	Cluster 1	Cluster 2
1	0	1232316620.9
2	1232316620.9	0

Variables used in partitioning of the dataset

Name	Importance	Measurement	Type	Label
TOTAL_TELECOMMUNICATIONS_SERVICES_REVENUE_C	0	Interval	num	Total telecommunications services revenue (current US $)
TOTAL_TELECOMMUNICATIONS_SERVICES_REVENUE_0	0	Interval	num	Total telecommunications services revenue (current US $ per person)
TOTAL_TELECOMMUNICATIONS_SERVICES_REVENUE_1	0	Interval	num	Total telecommunications services revenue (current US $ per worker)
ANNUAL_TELECOMMUNICATIONS_INVESTMENT_CURREN	0	Interval	num	Annual telecommunications investment (current US $)
ANNUAL_TELECOMMUNICATIONS_INVESTMENT_CURRE0	0	Interval	num	Annual telecommunications investment (current US $ per person)
ANNUAL_TELECOMMUNICATIONS_INVESTMENT_OF_	0	Interval	num	Annual telecommunications investment (% of GDP)
ANNUAL_TELECOMMUNICATIONS_INVESTMENT_CURRE1	0	Interval	num	Annual telecommunications investment (current US $ per worker)
ANNUAL_TELECOMMUNICATIONS_INVESTMENT_CURRE2	1	Interval	num	Annual telecommunications investment (current US $ per telecommunications worker)
TOTAL_TELECOMMUNICATIONS_SERVICES_REVENUE_2	0	Interval	num	Total telecommunications services revenue (current US $ per telecommunications)
PRODUCTIVITY_RATIO_PER_TELECOMMUNICATIONS_W	0	Interval	num	Productivity ratio per telecommunications worker (revenue/investment)
FULL_TIME_TELECOMMUNICATIONS_STAF	0	Interval	num	Full-time telecommunications staff (% of total labor force)

Cluster's membership

Cluster	Frequency of Cluster	Root-Mean-Square Standard Deviation	Maximum Distance from Cluster Seed	Nearest Cluster	Distance to Nearest Cluster	Total Telecommunications Services Revenue (Current US $)
1	72	1.046794019	8.0433260935 2	2	4.0488755304	1410033116.9
2	108	0.5865984355	9.8373259377 1	1	4.0488755304	242498908.25

Decision tree of CA

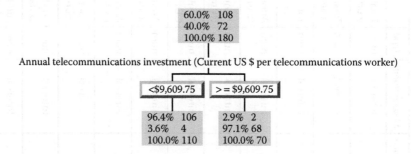

Decision rules of CA

> IF Annual telecommunications investment (Current US $ per telecommunications worker) < $9,610
>
> THEN
>
> NODE : 2
>
> N : 110
>
> 2 : 96.4%
>
> 1 : 3.6%
>
> IF $9,610 <= Annual telecommunications investment (Current US $ per telecommunications worker)
>
> THEN
>
> NODE : 3
>
> N : 70
>
> 2 : 2.9%
>
> 1 : 97.1%

Chapter 12

Applications of Data Mining in Organizational Behavior

Arash Shahin and Reza Salehzadeh

Contents

Introduction

Data mining has already been successfully applied in many domains. Research has shown that data mining techniques have the most applications in the field of marketing (e.g., Chang and Wand 2006; Lu et al. 2012; Sahi et al. 2012). In addition, many studies have been conducted in accounting and financial management (e.g., Lam 2003; Laitinen 2005; Gregoriou and Pascalau 2012); human resource management activities (see the literature review performed by Strohmeier and Piazza 2013); operations research (Meisel and Mattfeld 2010; Corne et al. 2012); industrial management (Braha 2001; Ni et al. 2007); and so on. However, one domain in which data mining has rarely been applied is organizational behavior. Organizational behavior is a field of study that investigates the impact that individuals, groups, and structure have on behavior within an organization, for the purpose of applying such knowledge toward improving an organization's effectiveness (Robbins and Judge 2012).

Data used in data mining is usually from a previously prepared database but data employed in the field of organizational behavior is obtained from questionnaires. Therefore, questionnaire data will have to be prepared for use in data mining. Now the question is "Can we use the data obtained from questionnaire and through self-reported for data mining too?" It seems that the application of data mining in this field can be effective for achieving better results. Questionnaires are usually analyzed statistically using hypothesis testing, which are either confirmed or rejected. Data mining techniques have the ability to seek knowledge (which is previously unknown) from data, and thus gives the analyst insights for future decision making. On the other hand, organizational studies seek to explain, predict, and control employees' behaviors and for such purposes, data mining techniques can be very helpful.

The objective of this chapter is to investigate the four different data mining techniques utilizing data from questionnaires in the field of organizational behavior. The examples shown in each part will reveal the effective role of data mining in organizational behavior studies.

Association Rules Mining

Association rules mining (ARM) was first introduced by Agrawal et al. (1993) and had received a great attention. Association analysis is a type of undirected data mining that finds data patterns. Using association rules, dependencies and relationships can be discovered among existing data in a database.

Association rules (AR) can be utilized in two ways for mining data from a questionnaire. The first method involves investigating all possible relationships between questions under the variables of interest. For instance, consider a questionnaire for assessing a variable of interest, "self leadership." Using the association rules, the relationship among self-leadership strategies can be investigated. Possible questions under this variable will ask respondents about self-goal setting and self-cueing. AR will then be used to assess relationships between the two questions (Shahin and Salehzadeh 2013).

The second method of utilizing AR in questionnaire data is to investigate relationships between demographic features and the variable of interest. For instance, the relationship among demographics such as age, education, and gender and the self-leadership strategies can be investigated, in order to find if the ratio of age, education, and gender type influence the ratio of self-leadership strategies. For a better understanding of the subject, consider the following example:

207 questionnaires including questions about the self-leadership strategies (behavior-focused strategies, natural reward strategies, and constructive thought

pattern strategies) and the demographic variables (age, education, and gender) are distributed among the students. Having collected the questionnaires, the data preparation process is performed. Then the relationship between the demographic features and the self-leadership strategies was mined using the association rules, and afterward the discovered rules are analyzed and compiled. In other words, the relationship between age and the behavior-focused strategies, age and the natural reward strategies, and age and constructive thought pattern strategies are investigated, and in this way the relationship between gender and education and three mentioned strategies are also mined, and thus this relationship is investigated in nine conditions. In order to discover the association rules, the Apriori algorithm can be used.

The answers to questions on self-leadership are redefined as very little = A; a little = B; moderately = C; very much = D; and extremely = E.

The answers to questions on demographic are redefined as age: 18–22 = A, 22–26 = B, 26–30 = C, higher than 30 = D; gender: female = A, male = B; educational level: undergraduate = A, postgraduate = B, PhD = C.

Then, the data is entered into the Excel software and is saved as a comma-separated value file format, in order to be useable in the Waikato Environment for Knowledge Analysis (Weka) software—Weka is a collection of machine-learning algorithms for data mining tasks. Weka contains tools for data preprocessing, classification, regression, clustering, association rules, and visualization. In Table 12.1, some of the entered data in Excel is illustrated.

As an example, consider the stages of investigating the relationship between age and behavior-focused strategies. First, the data file is opened by the Weka software. Then, as illustrated in Figure 12.1, alternatives 2, 3, 5, and 6 are selected and the *Remove* option is clicked.

Table 12.1 A Data Sample in Excel

Behavior-Focused	Constructive Thought Pattern	Natural Reward	Age	Gender	Educational Level
d	a	c	d	a	a
a	c	d	c	a	a
d	d	d	a	b	b
d	e	c	d	b	b
3	a	c	a	b	b
b	d	c	d	a	a
c	b	d	b	a	a
d	d	c	d	b	b

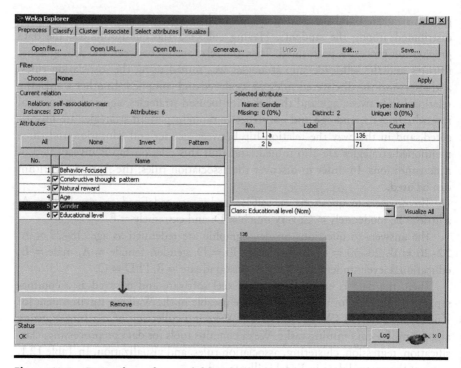

Figure 12.1 Removing other variables.

Therefore, as depicted in Figure 12.2, two alternatives 1 and 4 still remain unchecked.

In the following, the *Associate* tab is clicked, an Apriori algorithm is selected, and the necessary adjustments are made (Figure 12.3).

The software output is illustrated in Figure 12.4. As it is observed, three rules are discovered. Because our aim is to investigate the relationship between demographic characteristics and self-leadership strategies (in fact, the influence of demographic characteristics on self-leadership strategies), the first and third rules are used.

Similarly, other relationships between demographic characteristics and self-leadership strategies are investigated. The obtained results are summarized in Table 12.2.

The ARM results in Table 12.2 show that 11 rules are obtained: rules 1 and 2 represent the relationship between age and the behavior-focused strategies; rules 3, 4, and 5 represent the relationship between age and the natural reward strategies; rules 6 and 7 represent the relationship between age and the constructive thought pattern strategies; rule 8 represents the relationship between gender and the natural reward strategies; rule 9 represents the relationship between education and the behavior-focused strategies; and rules 10 and 11 represent the relationship between education and the natural reward strategies.

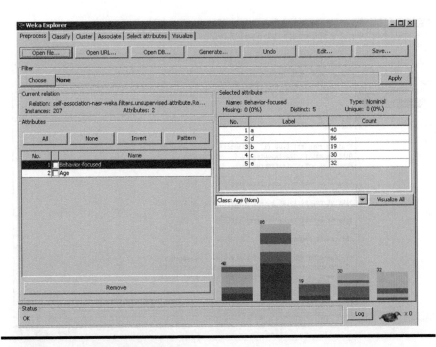

Figure 12.2 Two desired variables.

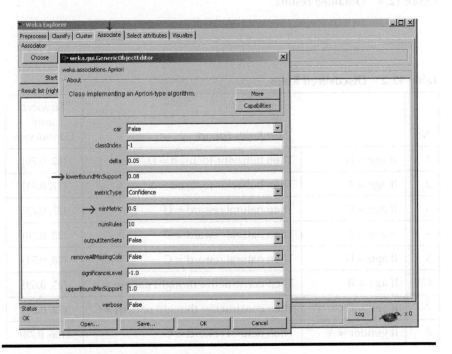

Figure 12.3 Selecting the Apriori algorithm.

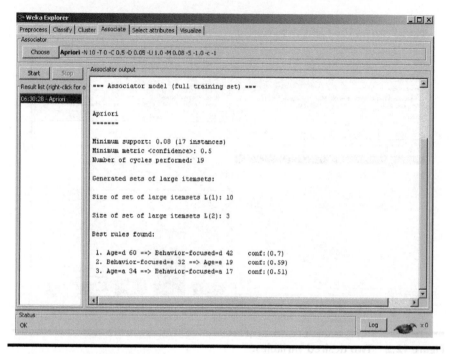

Figure 12.4   Obtained results.

Table 12.2   Discovered Rules

No	Best Rules Found		Support and Confidence
1	If age = D	Then behavior-focused = D	(42, 0.70)
2	If age = A	Then behavior-focused = A	(17, 0.51)
3	If age = C	Then natural reward = D	(27, 0.73)
4	If age = A	Then natural reward = D	(28, 0.70)
5	If age = D	Then natural reward = C	(18, 0.53)
6	If age = B	Then constructive thought pattern = B	(25, 0.69)
7	If age = C	Then constructive thought pattern = C	(22, 0.59)
8	If gender = A	Then natural reward = C	(106, 0.78)

Table 12.2 (*Continued*) Discovered Rules

No	Best Rules Found		Support and Confidence
9	If education = B	Then behavior-focused = D	(73, 0.69)
10	If education = A	Then natural reward = C	(48, 0.69)
11	If education = B	Then natural reward = C	(60, 0.57)

Rule 1: If the age of people is D (higher than 30), then by the chance of 70%, the behavior-focused strategies level would be D (very much); and this rule is obtained with 42 frequency in questionnaires. In other words, in 42 cases those who are higher than 30 years old have also high levels of behavior-focused strategies.

Rule 2: If the age of people is A (18–22 years), then by the chance of 51%, the behavior-focused level would be A (very little).

It can be concluded from these two rules that there is a direct relationship between age and behavior-focused strategies. Those who have lower age would have lower behavior-focused strategies level, and on the contrary, those who have higher age would have levels of higher behavior-focused strategies.

Rule 3: If the age of people is C (26–30), then by the chance of 73%, the natural reward strategies level would be D (very much).

Rule 4: If the age of people is A (18–22), then by the chance of 70%, the natural reward strategies level would be D (very much).

Rule 5: If the age of people is D (higher than 30), then by the chance of 53%, the natural reward strategies level would be C (moderately).

The three obtained rules indicate that there is no specific relationship between age and natural reward strategies.

Rule 6: If the age of people is B (22–26), then by the chance of 69%, the constructive thought pattern strategies level in people would be B (a little).

Rule 7: If the age of people is C (26–30), then by the chance of 59%, the constructive thought pattern strategies level would be C (moderately).

It can be concluded from these two obtained rules that there is a relationship between age and the constructive thought pattern strategies. By the increase of people's age, their constructive thought pattern strategies level would also increase.

Rule 8: If the gender is A (female), then by the chance of 78%, the natural reward strategies level would be C (moderately). Moreover, no relationship is found between the male gender and the self-leadership strategies.

Rule 9: If the education is B (postgraduate), then by the chance of 69%, the behavior-focused strategies level would be D (very much). In other words, people with postgraduate education have a good behavior-focused strategies level.

Rule 10: If the education is A (undergraduate), then by the chance of 69%, the natural reward strategies level would be C (moderately).

Rule 11: If the education is B (postgraduate), then by the chance of 57%, the natural reward strategies level would be C (moderately).

In other words, these two indicate that people with undergraduate and postgraduate educations have a medium natural reward strategies level. No relationship is found between education and the self-leadership strategies in other conditions.

The obtained results in Table 12.2 can be summarized as follows: (1) there is a direct relationship between age and the behavior-focused strategies. Those who have lower age have lower behavior-focused strategies level, and on the contrary, those who have higher age have higher behavior-focused strategies level; (2) there is no specific relationship between age and natural reward strategies, and the natural reward strategies level is medium and very high for most of the age groups; (3) there is a relationship between age and the constructive thought pattern strategies. With increasing students' age, their constructive thought pattern strategies level is increased; (4) there is a relationship between female gender and natural reward strategies; and (5) those with undergraduate and postgraduate educations have medium natural reward strategies level.

According to the findings, there is a relationship between some of the demographic characteristics of people and their self-leadership strategies; also, there is no relationship between some other characteristics and self-leadership strategies. By now, no similar research has been performed in which, the relationships are studied using association rules and therefore, more investigations are needed to be done in order to validate the findings. In addition to the explained example, this approach can be used in other questionnaires.

Artificial Neural Networks

Artificial neural network (ANN) is another technique for data mining inspired by the way the nervous system of a human body functions. Similar to the nervous system, ANN uses a network of computing units called "neurons," having an input layer, multiple hidden layers, and an output layer (Punniyamoorthy and Thoppan 2013). ANNs are used for investigating cause-and-effect relationships, predicting models, and prioritizing predictors. For this purpose, a research goal is identified and an independent variable, which is the input to the ANN, is defined. The output of the ANN is also defined as the dependent variable.

As an example, we want to know which of the factors influencing the employees' satisfaction has higher priority. At first, the factors influencing employees' satisfaction should be identified. By reviewing the literature, many factors can be found, some of which include the following: organizational culture (Lund 2003; Bellou 2010); personality characteristics (Chen and Silverthorne 2008); workplace

(Origo and Pagani 2008); ethical climate (Okpara and Wynn 2008); work motivation (Eskildsen et al. 2004); emotional intelligence (Chiva and Alegre 2008); person–organization fit (Silverthorne 2004); human resource management practices (Petrescu and Simmons 2008); empowerment (Savery and Luks 2001); and so on.

It is expected that the designed neural network has the ability to predict dependent variables (as output of network) by taking independent (as input) variables. For this purpose, a questionnaire is designed and distributed to assess the ratio of employees' satisfaction and also the factors influencing employees' satisfaction. The completed questionnaires are randomly divided into two categories. The first category is used for *training* the network, and the second category is used for *testing* the network. If the designed neural network shows a high efficiency, it means that the neural networks algorithm can be utilized as an empowered tool for predicting the dependent variable. If the efficiency of network is confirmed, the most important independent variables, that is, the factors that have the highest impact on the dependent variable can be identified. The neural network architecture is a determinant factor in increasing its efficiency and predictability. The number of neural layers, the weights of network, and the combination and transfer functions can be known as the "structural elements" of a neural network. Determination of the number of layers of a neural network (number of hidden layers) and the number of hidden neurons are performed by trial and error. In fact, by testing various scenarios, the best arrangement of the layers that produce the best response should be identified. Other factors that impact on the quality of network include momentum parameter (this parameter is used for preventing the convergence of network to a local optimization point) and learning speed (this parameter impacts on the speed that the network reaches a primary solution).

As it was stated, the data extracted from the questionnaires is divided into two categories for training and testing the efficiency of network. The network is trained using the data of the first category; the data of the second category, as new data, is used for testing the ability of generalizing the trained network. The *generalization capability* is the most important expected capability of a neural network. It means that when the network is adequately trained by the real data and achieved an appropriate predictability, it should have the ability of generalizing this capability, and in case of receiving new input data, predict the output of this data with similar accuracy. In other words, in order to achieve networks with high efficiency, their generalization capability should be upgraded. The generalization capability of a network depends on the number of neurons of the hidden layer, and the number of times the learning process of the network is performed. As an example, if the number of hidden neurons of the network is lower than the necessary limit, the processing power of network is reduced and the network will not be able to understand the relationship between the input and output variables of the problem. Because there is no standard formula for determining the number of neurons and the times of repeating the training process, it is tried to determine the values of these two factors in a best way by trial and error.

By applying the model after proving its high efficiency in exact prediction, it seems that a reliable analysis of the priority of factors influencing employees' satisfaction can be achieved. For this purpose, the factors influencing the employees' satisfaction are ranked by sensitivity analysis of neural network. The sensitivity analysis is a tool that assesses the extent to which a unit change in one or more input variables affects the output and in this way the factors determining the employees' satisfaction can be ranked based on their importance. For this purpose, each time one of the input variables of the network is changed ±1 rank ratio, and other variables are remained fixed, the neural network calculates the ratio of new output based on this change in a specific input. If the sensitivity ratio of output variable regarding the changes of a factor is higher, it can be concluded that the impact of the ratio of that factor on employees' satisfaction is higher, and in this way, the factors influencing employees' satisfaction can be prioritized.

For a better understanding of the concept, consider the following example: six factors are assumed as to influence on employees' satisfaction, including organizational culture, ethical climate, work motivation, person–organization fit, human resource management practices, and empowerment. For measuring satisfaction and also the factors influencing satisfaction, 608 questionnaires are used with Likert's five-point scale of response. It is assumed that after trial and error, the neural network includes an input layer (with six neurons), a hidden layer (with five neurons), and an output layer (with one neuron). After entering data into the NeuroSolutions 6 software, 400 questionnaires are used for training data and 208 questionnaires for testing data. The output of training neural network is illustrated in Figure 12.5.

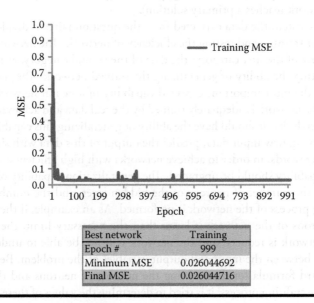

Best network	Training
Epoch #	999
Minimum MSE	0.026044692
Final MSE	0.026044716

Figure 12.5 MSE versus epoch.

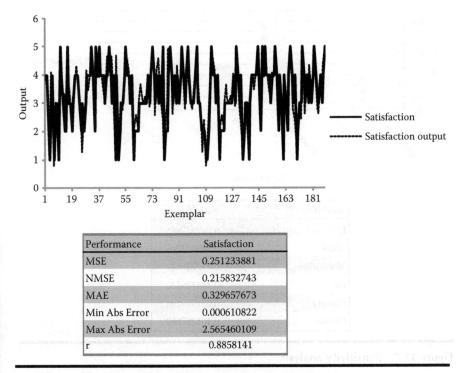

Figure 12.6 Desired output and actual network output.

The output of testing neural network is depicted in Figure 12.6. At this stage, Mean Square Error (MSE), Mean Absolute Error (MAE), ... indicators are computed by software and the real values are compared with the predicted values. As it is observed, these two values are relatively similar, which in turn implies the accuracy of the model in prediction.

Finally, sensitivity analysis is used for investigating the influence of input factors on the satisfaction computed by neural network. As illustrated in Figure 12.7, employees' satisfaction has the highest and lowest sensitivity to work motivation and ethical climate, respectively.

The results of sensitivity analysis can be utilized by managers. Based on the results, managers can increase employees' satisfaction by focusing on factors that have higher influence.

It is essential to mention that in addition to the subject of employees' satisfaction using this method for other variables (e.g., employees' motivation, employees' commitment, etc.), the factors influencing the dependent variable can also be prioritized.

Another important issue is that those factors that have higher impact on employees' satisfaction can be identified by solving regression model in statistical software such as statistical package for the social sciences (SPSS), but the literature review

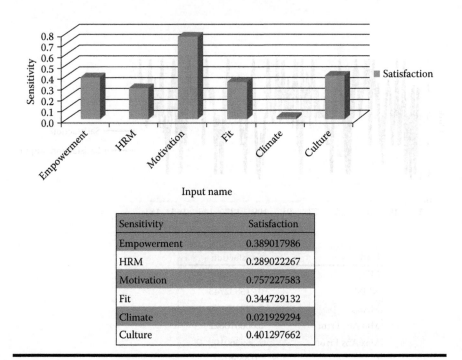

Figure 12.7 Sensitivity analysis.

shows that neural networks provide better results than regression (Ottenbacher et al. 2004; Pao 2008). However, although the capability of neural networks should not be exaggerated, such networks can develop the capability of statistical analysis as a complementary subject.

Clustering

The process of partitioning a large set of patterns into disjoint and homogeneous clusters is fundamental in knowledge acquisition. It is called "clustering" in most studies and is applied in various fields, including data mining, statistical data analysis, compression, and vector quantization (Liao et al. 2011). Clustering is an unsupervised learning technique of data mining. In unsupervised learning, feature selection aims to find a good subset of features that forms high-quality clusters for a given number of clusters (Corne et al. 2012).

Clustering is the task of grouping a set of objects in such a way that objects in the same group are more similar to each other than to those in other groups. In other words, the aim of cluster analysis is to maximize between-group variances and minimize within-group variances (Berson et al. 2001). Clustering is used when we are seeking to find groups of similar data without having a prediction about existing similarities.

In order to cluster data, the algorithms of clustering are required; these algorithms are used for finding data structure with high diversity. One proper clustering method creates clusters with good quality based on two criteria of high similarity of internal points and low similarity of external points. The methods of clustering are mostly used in marketing applications.

For a variety of marketing purposes, many companies find that segmenting their customers into groups that are expected to behave similarly is useful. These customer segments may be used for targeting cross-sell offers, for focusing retention efforts, for customizing messaging, or for a myriad of other purposes. The expectation is that by focusing on groups of similar customers, these efforts will be more effective than a "one-size-fits-all" approach (Linoff and Berry 2011).

Clustering can also be used in the organizational behavior topics. Whenever people interact in organizations, many factors come into play. Modern organizational studies attempt to understand and model these factors. Organizational studies seek to explain, predict, and control employees' behaviors. In order to achieve these goals, the ideal condition is that the managers of organization know each of their employees well, and according to this recognition, behave every person in a specific way, which is practically impossible (in particular in the large organizations). In addition, if everybody is behaved in the same way, this would not have adequate effectiveness either, because people have different features and are different with respect to organizational behavior variables such as satisfaction, motivation, commitment, performance, organizational citizenship behavior, organizational indifference, and so on. Thus, the use of clustering people will be a very appropriate approach.

For instance, the level of employees' organizational indifference can be measured using questionnaire. Then the data obtained from the questionnaire is clustered and in this way, the employees are put into several clusters regarding organizational indifference. In such cases, managers can perform appropriate planning based on the features of each cluster. Using a method for all employees who have different ratio of organizational indifference is not effective, and clustering the employees seems to be a more appropriate solution.

For a better understanding of the concept, consider the following example. Suppose that 195 employees of an organization are clustered based on their organizational indifference. Five criteria are considered for organizational indifference, including indifference to managers, organization, customers, colleagues, and job. The measurement scale of people's indifference is Likert's nine-point scales from 1: very low to 9: very high. The results of clustering based on the simple *K*-means algorithm with four clusters are addressed in Table 12.3.

As it is apparent in Table 12.3, the first, second, third, and the fourth clusters include 26, 53, 47, and 69 members, respectively.

The people of cluster 1 have low indifference to managers, medium indifference to the organization and customers, very low indifference to colleagues, and high indifference to the job. In this cluster, indifference to job and the organization

Table 12.3   Results of Clustering

		Cluster			
Attribute	Full Data (195)	1 (26)	2 (53)	3 (47)	4 (69)
Managers	5.0103	3.1154	7.9057	7.0851	2.087
Organization	3.4359	5.9615	3.0755	5.9149	1.0725
Customers	2.8615	5.0769	5.717	1.1064	1.029
Colleagues	3.0564	2.0769	6.9245	2.0851	1.1159
Job	2.6359	7.9231	2.0943	1.0851	2.1159

can be decreased by job enrichment, job's motivational theories, and improving organizational commitment. In special cases, the job of the people can be changed. Job motivation and decrease of indifference to job and organization will decrease indifference to customers, considerably.

The people of cluster 2 have high indifference to managers, low indifference to the organization, medium indifference to customers, high indifference to colleagues, and very low indifference to the job. Although the people of this cluster have low indifference to their organization and job, they are indifferent to managers, customers, and their colleagues. Therefore, it seems that the people of this cluster have difficulty in their relations with others and having good social relations with managers, customers, and colleagues is not important to them. In order to decrease indifference in this cluster, it is better to apply psychology and relations principles and techniques in addition to other approaches.

The people of cluster 3 have high indifference to managers; medium indifference to the organization; and very low indifference to customers, colleagues, and the job. It seems such people have been dissatisfied with organizational procedures and managers' actions for a long time, which resulted in their indifference to the organization and managers. In order to decrease the indifference of people in this cluster, it is necessary to pay more attention to the two criteria of managers and organization.

Finally, the people of cluster 4 have very low indifference in all criteria and therefore, there is no need to decrease the indifference of these people.

This approach can be utilized in the same way about other organizational behavior variables. As another example, the employees can be put in different clusters in respect of the ratio of motivation, so that the people of each cluster have almost similar features in respect of motivation and are different from other clusters. In such case, different managerial and leadership methods can be used with regard to the motivation ratio of the people of each cluster.

Decision Tree

A decision tree is a hierarchical collection of rules that describes how to divide a large collection of records into smaller groups of records, successively. With each successive division, the members of the resulting segments become more and more similar to one another with respect to the target (Linoff and Berry 2011). In decision tree, the goal is to create a model that predicts the value of a target variable based on several input variables. Decision tree is one of the most successful techniques for supervised classification learning. The main goal of feature selection in supervised learning is to find a feature subset that produces higher classification accuracy (Corne et al. 2012). Among other data mining methods, the decision tree is simple to understand and interpret.

Decision tree has already had many applications in different domains (Cervone 2010; Moore and Carpenter 2010). It is believed that the decision trees can effectively be used in the organizational behavior subjects.

The following example indicates one of the applications of the decision tree in organizational behavior. In this example, the decision tree is used in leader–member exchange (LMX) theory as one of the leadership theories.

The LMX theory is different from most traditional one-size-fits-all approach to leadership theories, in which it is assumed that a leader displays an *average leadership style* to all subordinates. LMX suggests that supervisors make distinctions among subordinates and develop different types of relationships in dealing with their subordinates (Graen and Uhl-Bien 1995; Truckenbrodt 2000; Beehr et al. 2006; Blau et al. 2010).

Based on this theory, leaders sort subordinates into two groups: in-group and out-group. The in-group (high LMX) members enjoy high-exchange quality relationship, which is characterized by liking, loyalty, professional respect, and contributory behavior. The out-group (low LMX) members, on the other hand, are deprived of all these behaviors (Bhal et al. 2009).

Many elements can contribute to the placement of employees in the in-group and out-group. As an example, four elements, such as employee conscientious, employee expertise, duration of knowing each other (leader and employee), and similarity or dissimilarity of the beliefs of leader and employee, are considered. Regarding the above-mentioned elements and using a questionnaire, 140 supervisors, managers, or leaders are asked to answer as to under which circumstances their employees would be placed in the in-group and out-group?

The answers to questions are redefined using the decision tree technique as follows: conscientious—low = 1, medium = 2, high = 3; expertise—low = 1, medium = 2, high = 3; duration—short = 1, medium = 2, long = 3; beliefs— similar = 1, dissimilar = 2; and LMX—in-group = 1, out-group = 2. The results of the classification using the random tree algorithm are presented in Figure 12.8.

According to Figure 12.8, if the employee conscientious is low (1), then the employee will be placed in the out-group (2). This rule is approved by 96 managers.

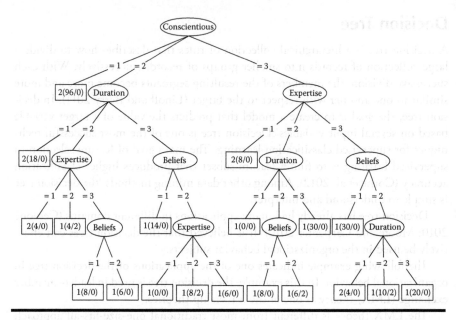

Figure 12.8   Results of classification.

If employee conscientious is medium (2), the duration of knowing the leader and employee is long (3), and the beliefs of employee and leader are similar (1), then the employee will be placed in the in-group (1). This rule is approved by 14 managers.

If employee conscientious is high (3), employee expertise is high (3), and beliefs of the leader and employee are similar (1), then the employee will be placed in the in-group (1). This rule is approved by 30 managers. Now, if employee conscientious is high (3), employee expertise is high (3), and the beliefs of the leader and employee are dissimilar (2), then if the duration of knowing the leader and employee becomes short (1), the employee will be replaced in the out-group (2); however, if the duration is medium (2) and high (3), the employee will be placed in the in-group (1). Other paths are analyzed, similarly.

By this decision tree, it is predicted that with which characteristics the employees can be placed in the in-group and with which characteristics they can be placed in the out-group. This subject has many applications in organizational behavior.

As mentioned in the ANN, here the amount of data should be applied as a training set and the rest should be applied in the form of the test set; that is, at first the model is specified using the training set and then its accuracy is tested using the test set. The reason of using two sets of data in the classification is to prevent overfitting. A classification algorithm is said to overfit to the training data if it generates a decision tree that depends too much on irrelevant features of the training instance, with the result that it performs well on the training data but relatively poorly on unseen instances (Bramer 2007). The size of classification trees is also important. If a tree becomes too large, the overfitting risk occurs in the training dataset. On the other hand, a small tree might ignore some important factors. In order to gain appropriate size of a tree, a method called "pruning" is used. Pruning entails eliminating the nodes with no extra information. Pruning makes a balance between the accuracy of tree and its simplicity. Finally, it is worth mentioning that the results obtained from these models should be used to support the decisions and should not be regarded as operation criterion, exclusively.

Conclusions

This chapter attempted to investigate data mining techniques applied in the field of organizational behavior. As it was demonstrated, the association rules can be used for mining the data of questionnaire in two ways. First, the relationship among the questions related to the research variables can be investigated, and second, the relationship between demographic features and the research variables can be investigated. The ANN can be used in the organizational behavior subjects to investigate the cause-and-effect relationship, making predicting model, and prioritizing predictor variables. Clustering can be used to cluster the employees with regard to the ratio of their organizational behavior variables such as organizational indifference, satisfaction, motivation, and so on. Based on the results of clustering, we can behave differently with regard to the employees' characteristics. Finally, prediction models can be designed using the decision tree.

The ideas offered in this chapter can also be used in other research studies performed by questionnaire. Another area in which data mining has had very few applications is psychology, in which data mining can be used regarding the topics explained in this chapter.

References

Agrawal, R., Imielinski, T., and Swami, A. (1993), "Mining association rules between sets of items in large databases," *Proceedings of the ACM SIGMOD Conference on Management of Data*, pp. 207–216, June 1, ACM, New York.
Beehr, T. A., Beehr, M. J., Wallwey, D. A., Glaser, K. M., Beehr, D. E., Erofeev, D., and Canali, K. G. (2006), "The nature of satisfaction with subordinates: Its predictors and importance to supervisors," *Journal of Applied Social Psychology*, Vol. 36, No. 6, pp. 1523–1547.
Bellou, V. (2010), "Organizational culture as a predictor of job satisfaction: The role of gender and age," *Career Development International*, Vol. 15, No. 1, pp. 4–19.
Berson, A., Smith, S., and Thearling, K. (2001), *Building Data Mining Applications for CRM*, McGraw-Hill, New York.
Bhal, K. T., Bhaskar, A. U., and Ratnam, C. S. V. (2009), "Employee reactions to M&A: Role of LMX and leader communication," *Leadership & Organization Development Journal*, Vol. 30, No. 7, pp. 604–624.

Blau, G., Oideenkutty, U., and Ingham, K. (2010), "Leader-member exchange as a significant correlate of organizational and occupational sportsmanship behaviors in a health services setting," *Leadership in Health Services*, Vol. 23, No. 3, pp. 219–232.

Braha, D. (2001), *Data Mining for Design and Manufacturing: Methods and Applications*, Kluwer Academic, Dordrecht, the Netherlands.

Bramer, M. (2007), *Principles of Data Mining*, Springer, London.

Cervone, H. F. (2010), "Applied digital library project management: Using decision tree analysis to clarify multipath problems," *OCLC Systems & Services*, Vol. 26, No. 1, pp. 14–17.

Chang, P. C. and Wang, Y. W. (2006), "Fuzzy Delphi and back-propagation model for sales forecasting in PCB industry," *Expert Systems with Applications*, Vol. 30, No. 4, pp. 715–726.

Chen, J. C. and Silverthorne, C. (2008), "The impact of locus of control on job stress, job performance and job satisfaction in Taiwan," *Leadership & Organization Development Journal*, Vol. 29, No. 7, pp. 572–582.

Chiva, R. and Alegre, J. (2008), "Emotional intelligence and job satisfaction: The role of organizational learning capability," *Personnel Review*, Vol. 37, No. 6, pp. 680–701.

Corne, D., Dhaenens, C., and Jourdan, L. (2012), "Synergies between operations research and data mining: The emerging use of multi-objective approaches," *European Journal of Operational Research*, Vol. 221, No. 3, pp. 469–479.

Eskildsen, J. K., Kristensen, K., and Westlund, A. H. (2004), "Work motivation and job satisfaction in the Nordic countries," *Employee Relations*, Vol. 26, No. 2, pp. 122–136.

Graen, G. B. and Uhl-Bien, M. (1995), "Relationship-based approach to leadership: Development of leader-member exchange (LMX) theory of leadership over 25 years: Applying a multi-level multi-domain perspective," *Leadership Quarterly*, Vol. 6, No. 2, pp. 219–47.

Gregoriou, G. N. and Pascalau, R. (2012), "A joint survival analysis of hedge funds and funds of funds using copulas," *Managerial Finance*, Vol. 38, No. 1, pp. 82–100.

Laitinen, E. K. (2005), "Survival analysis and financial distress prediction: Finnish evidence," *Review of Accounting and Finance*, Vol. 4, No. 4, pp. 76–90.

Lam, M. (2003), "Neural network techniques for financial performance prediction: Integrating fundamental and technical analysis," *Decision Support Systems*, Vol. 37, No. 4, pp. 567–581.

Liao, S. H., Chen, Y. J., and Hsieh, H. H. (2011), "Mining customer knowledge for direct selling and marketing," *Expert Systems with Applications*, Vol. 38, No. 5, pp. 6059–6069.

Linoff, G. S. and Berry, M. J. (2011), *Data Mining Techniques for Marketing, Sales, and Customer Relationship Management*, 3rd edition, Wiley, New York.

Lu, C. J., Lee, T. S., and Lian, C. M. (2012), "Sales forecasting for computer wholesalers: A comparison of multivariate adaptive, regression splines and artificial neural networks," *Decision Support Systems*, Vol. 54, No. 1, pp. 584–596.

Lund, D. B. (2003), "Organizational culture and job satisfaction," *Journal of Business & Industrial Marketing*, Vol. 18, No. 3, pp. 219–236.

Meisel, S. and Mattfeld, D. (2010), "Synergies of operations research and data mining," *European Journal of Operational Research*, Vol. 206, No. 1, pp. 1–10.

Moore, M. and Carpenter, J. M. (2010), "A decision tree approach to modelling the private label apparel consumer," *Marketing Intelligence & Planning*, Vol. 28, No. 1, pp. 59–69.

Ni, M., Xu, X., and Deng, S. (2007), "Extended QFD and data-mining-based methods for supplier selection in mass customization," *International Journal of Computer Integrated Manufacturing*, Vol. 20, No. 2/3, pp. 280–291.

Okpara, J. O. and Wynn, P. (2008), "The impact of ethical climate on job satisfaction, and commitment in Nigeria: Implications for management development," *Journal of Management Development*, Vol. 27, No. 9, pp. 935–950.

Origo, F. and Pagani, L. (2008), "Workplace flexibility and job satisfaction: Some evidence from Europe," *International Journal of Manpower*, Vol. 29, No. 6, pp. 539–566.

Ottenbacher, K. J., Linn, R. T., Smith, P. M., Illig, S. B., Mancuso, M., and Granger, C. V. (2004), "Comparison of logistic regression and neural network analysis applied to predicting living setting after hip fracture," *Annals of Epidemiology*, Vol. 14, No. 8, pp. 551–559.

Pao, H. T. (2008), "A comparison of neural network and multiple regression analysis in modeling capital structure," *Expert Systems with Applications*, Vol. 35, No. 3, pp. 720–727.

Petrescu, A. I. and Simmons, R. (2008), "Human resource management practices and workers' job satisfaction," *International Journal of Manpower*, Vol. 29, No. 7, pp. 651–667.

Punniyamoorthy, M. and Thoppan, J. J. (2013), "ANN-GA based model for stock market surveillance," *Journal of Financial Crime*, Vol. 20, No. 1, pp. 52–66.

Robbins, S. P. and Judge, T. A. (2012), *Organizational Behavior*, 15th edition, Prentice Hall, Englewood Cliffs, NJ.

Sahi, S. K., Dhameja, N., and Arora, A. P. (2012), "Predictors of preference for financial investment products using CART analysis," *Journal of Indian Business Research*, Vol. 4, No. 1, pp. 61–86.

Savery, L. K. and Luks, J. A. (2001), "The relationship between empowerment, job satisfaction and reported stress levels: Some Australian evidence," *Leadership & Organization Development Journal*, Vol. 22, No. 3, pp. 97–104.

Shahin, A. and Salehzadeh, R. (2013), "Investigating the relationship among self leadership strategies by association rules mining," *International Journal of Business Information Systems*, Vol. 14, No. 1, pp. 41–55.

Silverthorne, C. (2004), "The impact of organizational culture and person-organization fit on organizational commitment and job satisfaction in Taiwan," *Leadership & Organization Development Journal*, Vol. 25, No. 7, pp. 592–599.

Strohmeier, S. and Piazza, F. (2013), "Domain driven data mining in human resource management: A review of current research," *Expert Systems with Applications*, Vol. 40, No. 7, pp. 2410–2420.

Truckenbrodt, Y. B. (2000). "The relationship between leader-member exchange and commitment and organizational citizenship behavior," *Acquisition Review Quarterly*, Vol. 7, No. 3, pp. 233–244.

Chapter 13

Decision Making and Decision Styles of Project Managers: A Preliminary Exploration Using Data Mining Techniques

Kweku-Muata Osei-Bryson and Corlane Barclay

Contents

Abstract: Projects typically involve multiple participants, each with his or her own decision style. Given that projects involve group work, in which it is important that group members cooperate in a manner that avoids the *group think* and other value-depreciating phenomena. It is important that groups be carefully constituted and one factor to consider is the set of decision styles of potential group members. In this chapter, we present a preliminary exploration of relationships between a set of demographic variables and the dominant decision style. Our preliminary data analysis involves the use of a data mining-based approach to generate some relationships that could be worthy of future exploration.

Keywords: Decision style inventory, decision styles, project management, decision tree

Introduction

Projects are typically seen as temporary organizations used to deliver beneficial value to its client within a specified context, budget, and timeline (PMI 2008), and involve substantial knowledge processing (Reich 2005). These projects are typically delivered on a daily basis to meet the strategic and tactical needs of businesses. In almost all the instances, projects are initiated to create change—to develop new products, establish new processes, and/or create a new organization (Shenhar et al. 2002). Within this dynamic environment, a complex set of skills and resources have to be coordinated to help deliver business value. It has been further suggested that the manner in which a project manager makes decisions can significantly influence his or her effectiveness and ultimately the design of systems under his or her direction (Fox and Spence 1999) and thereby the organization's ability to deliver value to its client. It, therefore, stands to reason that the success of a project depends on the right mix of knowledge experiences and thus the dissemination and usage of knowledge is vital (Disterer 2002). However, there are many reasons that may prevent organizations and projects from effectively applying knowledge management (KM). Knowledge is difficult to manage because it originates and is applied in the mind of humans (Grover and Davenport 2001), and can even be more difficult with the transient nature of the project teams. Additionally, Reich (2007) found that there was a lack of common understanding on the meaning of KM within the context of projects, as some focused solely on explicit knowledge and lessons learned, whereas others incorporated more complex tacit considerations and the need to actively plan the knowledge needs of the project teams. This may pose a challenge for the effective formal applications of KM as team members having different views of knowledge may have different views of what is important to manage.

Rowe and Boulgarides (1992) argued that once the decision style of an individual is known, then one is more likely to predict outcomes in terms of the individual's decision behavior. This is especially relevant in today's fast-paced environment, where organizations are dependent on the successful management of multiple projects for economic and competitive sustainability. An appreciation of the project managers' characteristics, which are most desirable for specific projects and situations, can enable aid in minimizing risks.

Description of the Research Problem

The objective of the research is to examine the decision styles of project managers across various industries through the utilization of data mining techniques. We use an exploratory data analysis approach that is based on Osei-Bryson and Ngwenyama (2011), which is itself based on Pierce's perspective (cf 1867) that abduction is an approach to "studying the facts and devising a theory to explain them." The data mining techniques used in this study are the decision tree (DT) induction and cluster analysis, two common algorithms used to establish predictive attributes and to discover segments in the population.

Project activities range in complexities and time and are commonplace in organizations. Project managers are used to execute these projects and are generally not always given the designated title. The success or competitiveness of the organization is dependent on the success of these project activities. Despite this significance, empirical studies to examine the nature of the persons who manage these activities are rare. There have been multiple studies that examine the characteristics of managers and executives in different environments (e.g., Martinsons and Davison 2007; Nutt 1993), however there are few studies that analyzed the nature or characteristics of project managers, or other persons who manage are involved in projects in the organizations (e.g., Fox and Spence 1999). Furthermore, there is no known study that examines the relationship of demographic variables to the decision styles of project managers to find interesting or previously undetected relationships.

Importance of the Research Problem

Managerial decision style is an important hidden attribute that contributes to the success of those managers and, therefore, to the success of their organizations (Alqarni 2003). It has been suggested that the manner in which a project manager makes decisions can significantly influence his or her effectiveness (Fox and Spence 1999).

Therefore, the investigations into their decision styles can provide further insights into approaches to making decisions and obtaining beneficial results from the project activities. Rowe and Boulgarides (1992) argued that once we know the decision style, we may be able to predict outcomes in terms of decision behavior. They further clarified that the manner in which each style reacts to stress, motivation, problem solving, and thinking provides another basis for understanding decision makers' response behavior. Therefore, an assessment of a manager's decision style could be a reliable predictor of that manager's response (Rowe and Boulgarides 1992). Profiling the characteristics of decision makers using data mining techniques to aid in better informing on the nature of the project managers is undertaken in this study. This phase of the study is situated in the Jamaican context.

Overview of the Decision Styles Model

The decision style inventory (DSI) devised by Rowe (1981) and further elaborated by Rowe and Boulgarides (1983) and Rowe and Mason (1987) is a cognitive management tool to understand the type of decisions an individual is likely to make under certain situations. Each individual has a characteristic method or approach for making decisions, which will have its own strengths and weaknesses (DSI 2013). Understanding more about one's likely behavior or decisions can help not only the individuals, but the organizations in more strategic decision making.

Description of Decision Styles

Within the context of the decision styles model there are four decision styles: *directive, analytical, conceptual,* and *behavioral*. Each of these styles has its own characteristics with regard to level of tolerance for ambiguity, need for structure, people or task orientation, and so on (Tables 13.1 and 13.2). The decision style captures three varying factors as concepts (Rowe and Mason 1987):

1. How the individual thinks about the problems;
2. How the individual communicates with others;
3. How the individual's expectations of others pertinently affect his or her performance;

Martinsons and Davison (2007) observed that in different cultures, different individual decision styles are dominant, and that these differences determine the types of decision support system that are most appropriate. For example, they noted that in several non-Western societies, decision makers "focus on collective interests, emphasize relationships and intuition (at the expense of factual analysis), and discourage conflicting views that would threaten group harmony or the

Table 13.1 Decision Styles' Characteristics

	High Tolerance for Ambiguity (Low Need for Structure)	*Low Tolerance for Ambiguity (High Need for Structure)*
Task Oriented/ Technical Concerns	**Analytical** Solves problems by analysis, planning, and forecasting	**Directive** Solves problems by applying operational objectives in a systematic and efficient way
People Oriented/ Social Concerns	**Conceptual** Solves problems by exploring new options, forming new strategies, being creative, and taking risks	**Behavioral** Solves problems through people

Source: Rowe, A. and Mason, R. O., *Managing with Style: A Guide to Understanding, Assessing, and Improving Decision Making,* Jossey-Bass, San Francisco, CA, 1987.

Table 13.2 Decision Styles

Style	*Description*
Analytical	Achievement oriented without the need for external rewards; make decisions slowly because orientation to examine the situation thoroughly and consider many alternatives systematically
Behavioral	Strong people orientation, driven primarily by a need for affiliation; typically receptive to suggestions, willing to compromise, and prefer loose controls
Conceptual	Achievement and people oriented with the need for external rewards; make decisions slowly because orientation to examine the situation thoroughly and consider many alternatives systematically
Directive	Results and power oriented but have a low tolerance for ambiguity and cognitive complexity. They prefer to consider a small number of alternatives based on limited information

Source: Rowe, A. J. and Boulgarides, J. D., *Leadership & Organization Development Journal, 4*(4), 3–9, 1994.

face of the individual," with some having "greater acceptance of tacit knowledge management." To paraphrase Martinsons and Davison (2007), for such non-Western societies, KM systems (KMSs) that support interpersonal communications and encourage tacit knowledge sharing and individual discretion would be more helpful than KMSs that mainly involve codified knowledge.

Measurement of Decision Styles

Elicitation of decision styles information is done using the standard questionnaire that consists of 20 multiresponse questions (Rowe 1981). For each question, there is a set of four response statements, one for each of the four decision styles, and the respondent is required to rank the set of response statements: *most preferred* (8 points), *second most preferred* (4 points), *third most preferred* (2 points), and *least preferred* (1 point). This implies that for each question, 15 points have to be distributed across the four response statements. Therefore, the overall maximum number of points is 300; and overall maximum possible number of points for each decision style is 160 (= 20*8), with the corresponding minimum being 20 (= 20*1).

$$Score_{Analytical} + Score_{Behavioral} + Score_{Conceptual} + Score_{Directive} = 300$$

Application of DSI

DSI has been applied in multiple contexts. Nutt (1993) applied the method to measure attitude toward ambiguity and uncertainty and to determine the style of the participating top executives. The participants were asked to evaluate eight capital expansion projects in terms of adoptability and risk. Inferences about decision making were drawn from these evaluations. The tolerance for ambiguity and uncertainty scores and the adoptability and risk ratings were associated with the participant's style. Top executives with a flexible style who have access to each of the modes of understanding were found to be aggressive decision makers with a high tolerance for ambiguity and uncertainty. Fox and Spence (1999) surveyed a group of over 200 project managers from across the United States, attempting to measure their decision-making styles, especially as they relate to project management activity. Durkin (2004) reports on a study into Internet banking that focuses on the extent to which 480 retail bank customers can be clustered according to an adapted decision-making framework. How such clusters can help influence the adoption of the Internet-banking interface is explored. Findings show an encouraging match between the four sample clusters identified from the case bank and the a priori classification of decision styles. Martinsons and Davison (2007) examined the information systems (IS) issues that arise from the discovery of the distinctively American, Japanese, and Chinese styles of strategic decision making. The existence of international differences in analyzing and conceptualizing strategic decisions raises doubts about the global applicability of IS such as decision support systems and executive information systems.

Related Literature

Influences on Decision Making

Decision making is the core of organizational strategic and tactical activities. The decision-making process involves multiple endogenous and exogenous factors. According to Rowe and Boulgarides (1983), decision making is impacted by "the context in which a decision is made, the decision maker's way of perceiving and understanding cues, and what the decision maker values or judges as important." From the rational perspective, there are six steps that are generally taken in the decision-making process, which include defining the problem, identifying the criteria, weighing the criteria, generating alternatives, rating each alternative, and computing the optimal decision (Bazerman and Moore 2012). They further reasoned that cognitive styles may be classified into an intuitive system, which is typically fast, automatic, effortless, implicit, and emotional, and logical systematic process where reasoning is slower, conscious, effortful, explicit, and logical, that is, system 1 and system 2 thinking (Kahneman 2003). Depending on several factors decision makers may adopt the logical or intuitive approach. This view is extended where it is believed that not only cognitive perceptions are significant but values of the decision maker will influence the decision making (Martinsons and Davison 2007). The values and cognitive perceptions of the decision maker will in turn impact how the decision maker will interpret and respond to sets of decision contexts.

Decision-Making Behavior of Project Managers

The project managers' decision-making behavior is generally considered with the context of leadership style based on the literature. Müller and Turner (2010) examined the leadership competency profiles of successful project managers in different types of projects, where the results indicated high expressions of one intelligent quotient (IQ) subdimension (i.e., critical thinking) and three emotional quotient (EQ) subdimensions (i.e., influence, motivation, and conscientiousness) in successful managers in all types of projects. They, therefore, suggested that training in the soft factors of leadership, particularly for their types of projects would be ideal.

Turner and Muller (2005) in their study on leadership styles of project managers found that the literature on project success factors largely ignores the important dimension of leadership style and competence. Based on literature review, they concluded that project manager's emotional intelligence had an impaction on his or her perception of success of the particular project. It can also be considered that specific performance criteria generally reflect the values of the project stakeholders, including the project managers, as to how they will be able to view the project and its performance (Barclay and Osei-Bryson 2010). Consequently, the identification or vision of success influenced by the manager's emotional intelligence influences behaviors and perceptions.

Research Methodology

The study employed a survey research methodology. Survey research is a quantitative method, requiring standardized information from and/or about the subjects being studied (Pinsonneault and Kraemer 1993). A survey instrument was developed and used as the basis for data collection and analysis. The questionnaire included two parts: the demographic details and the DSI 20×4 matrix questions (Rowe and Mason 1997).

A survey is a means of "gathering information about the characteristics, actions, or opinions of a large group of people, referred to as a population" (Tanur 1982). This approach was most applicable based on our research objectives, and the content of the DSI instrument as it seeks to gather important characteristics on project managers' decision styles. A survey also has multiple advantages and has been successfully applied in multiple studies in IS research. Some of its advantages (Newsted et al. 1998) are as follows:

- Surveys determine the values and relations of variables and constructs.
- Responses can be generalized to other members of the population studied and often to other similar populations.
- Surveys can help confirm and quantify the findings of qualitative research.

Dillman (2000) shared that there are three essential elements of survey research quality, namely, research design, sampling procedures, and data collection methods. We integrated these principles in our methodology and followed a six-step process as part of our research strategy: survey design and data definition; data collection; data preparation; data analysis; interpretation of results; and the reporting of results (see Figure 13.1). The survey is primarily readymade with the content of the DSI instrument (see appendix); however, careful attention to the demographic details that would be likely to have a significant impact on decision styles was evaluated. Items such as age, gender, management levels, and educational levels, for example, were identified as important data elements.

Selection of Demographic Variables

Previous research (e.g., Ali 1989; Yousef 1998) suggested that decision styles vary based on the values of demographic variables such as management level, education level, field of education, age, industry sector, country, type of organization, and

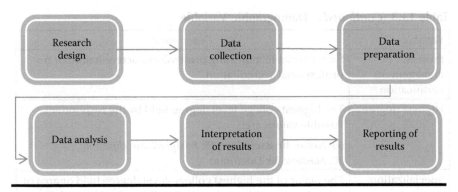

Figure 13.1 Research strategy.

culture. The variables for the demographical understanding were carefully chosen, and they formed part of the common set of items used to categorize respondents. More importantly, these variables are appropriate in helping to formulate an understanding of the characteristics of individuals and their decision choices. The set of variables are shown in Table 13.3.

Table 13.3 Demographic Variable

Variable	Description
Gender	Binary variable indicating *male* or *female*
Age group	Ordinal variable that indicates the age range category of the respondent. Possible values are: *18–24; 25–29; 30–39; 40–49; 50–59; 60 and over*
Industry work	Nominal variable indicating major classification of industry (or sectors) where the respondent is employed. Possible values are as follows: *banking and financial services; education; government; power/energy;* *information technology services; law and legal services; other*
Management level	Ordinal variable indicating hierarchical management levels in the organization. Possible values are as follows: 60TE: *top executive;* 50MM: *middle manager;* 40JM: *junior manager;* 30AS: *academic staff;* 20SS: *senior staff;* 10JS: *junior staff*
Year on the job (YOJ)	Experience (in current position and generally): number of years in current position and number of years of project work experience. Possible values are as follows: 0–5; 6–10; 11–15; 16–20; over 20

(Continued)

Table 13.3 (*Continued*)   Demographic Variable

Variable	Description
Project management certification	Binary variable indicating professional accreditation or no professional accreditation
Highest degree	The highest college level degree held by the respondent. Possible values are: 00: *None*; 10: *Bachelors*; 15: *Postgraduate diploma*; 20: *Masters*; 30: *Doctorate*
Specialization degree	The major of the highest college-level degree held or area of specialization without degree. Possible values are as follows: no degree; bachelors degree; postgraduate diploma; master's degree; terminal degree

Data Collection

The online survey was developed and distributed to the target population, that is, persons who have worked in projects in Jamaica. The survey consisted of 14 questions pertaining to demographic details as described in Table 13.3 and the 20 questions based on the framework of DSI and were derived from the work of Rowe (1981). The survey was reviewed for content validity and was pilot tested. Preliminary evidence found that instrument and scales were reliable and valid. The online survey link was distributed to the local project management chapter, business executives, and university lecturers who were deemed to have had major responsibilities in various types of projects. The survey remained active for approximately three months and during that time the targeted individuals and group were sent reminders to complete. Valid email addresses were used as a basis to prevent any duplication. Sixty-five responses were received and data was prepared to determine the summary descriptive statistics and the scores from the DSI tool. This information was analyzed and interpreted using DTs and cluster analysis, and information reported via this research artifact.

Our target population was experienced individuals that have worked in projects or managed projects of varying size and complexities including industry and educational/academic projects. The study was conducted in Jamaica and targeted organizations based in Jamaica. Projects are considered key business drivers in the delivery of strategic results (Barclay 2008). Project managers lead these activities to completion and enable the achievement of the organizational objectives. Based on the local statistical institute, the broad industrial classification of industries (Statin 2005) includes financial intermediaries, education, public administration, transport, electrical gas, and water supply, among others. These key categories were represented in our respondents. The respondents included a mix of certified and noncertified project managers, varying range of experience and across a wide cross section of industries, including financial services, academia, technology services, legal services, government, and other areas.

Data Exploration

Distributions of the Demographic Variables

Figures 13.2 through 13.7 displays the frequency charts for the demographic variables. The gender distribution was almost equal with males accounting for around 56%. Banking and financial services sector accounted for the largest percentage followed by education and other category. Most of the respondents were middle managers and top-level executives. Certified project managers accounted for a smaller percentage than noncertified project managers. Postgraduate training, that is, master's level accounted for the largest percentage relating to highest education level received.

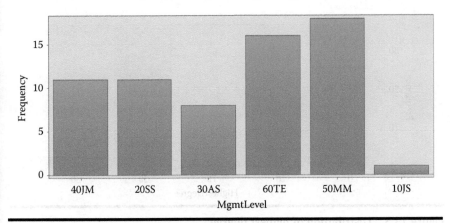

Figure 13.2   Distribution of management level.

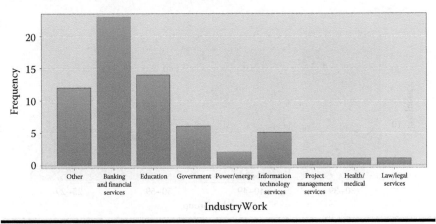

Figure 13.3   Distribution of industry.

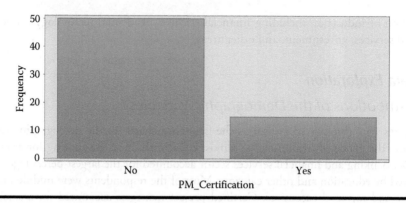

Figure 13.4 Distribution of project manager certification.

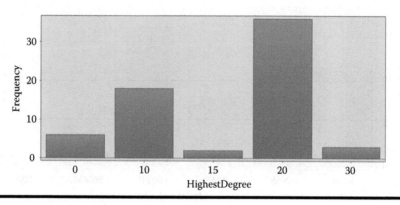

Figure 13.5 Distribution of highest degree.

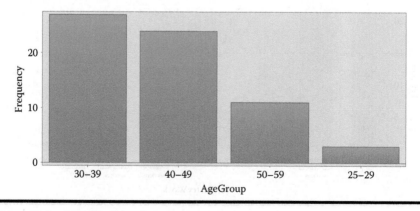

Figure 13.6 Distribution of age group.

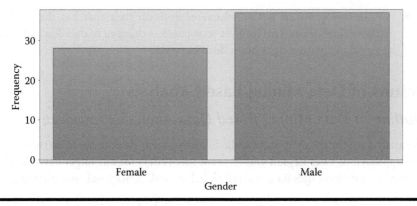

Figure 13.7   Distribution of gender.

Correlations between Scores of the Four Decision Styles

We calculated the correlations between the sets of scores for our four decision styles. Given that for each respondent the summed scores of the four decision styles equal a fixed value, then an increased larger score for one decision style would have to result in a lower score for at least one other decision style. It is, therefore, not surprising that the correlation between the sets of scores for a pair of decision styles would be negative. We are interested in finding the pairs of decision styles that have the statistically significant correlations (Table 13.4).

The results of our correlation analyses indicate for this dataset:

- For the *analytical* decision style, it is the *behavioral* decision style that is most diametrically opposed and vice versa. This is consistent with the relative positions of these decision styles in Table 13.1.
- For the *directive* decision style, it is the *conceptual* decision style that is most diametrically opposed and vice versa. This is consistent with the relative positions of these decision styles in Table 13.1.
- For the *analytical*, it is the *Directive* decision style that has the smallest negative correlation. This result is reasonable as this pair of decision styles can be associated with a left-brain decision style.

Table 13.4   Correlations between Decision Styles Scores

	Behavioral	*Conceptual*	*Directive*
Analytical	−0.484[a]	−0.201	−0.107
Behavioral	−	−0.125	−0.358[a]
Conceptual	−	−	−0.521[a]

[a] Statistically significant correlations.

■ For the *conceptual*, it is the *behavioral* decision style that has the smallest negative correlation. This result is reasonable as this pair of decision styles can be associated with a right-brain decision style.

Results of Data Mining-Based Analysis

Outline of Data Mining-Based Data Analysis Procedure

The analysis of the data will involve the following steps that are based on the abduction approach of Osei-Bryson and Ngwenyama (2011) for our target variable, that is, *dominant decision style* (i.e., analytical, behavioral, conceptual, and directive).

1. Compute the dominant decision style for each observation.
2. Use DT induction technology to do recursive partitioning of the given dataset resulting in sets (i.e., pairs) of sibling rules (e.g., Osei-Bryson and Ngwenyama 2011).
3. For each set of sibling rules, determine if the difference(s) in the relative frequencies is (are) statistically significant.

Results of Data Mining-Based Data Analysis Procedure

We calculated the dominant decision style (*dominant DS*) for each respondent by identifying the decision style that had the maximum score for the given respondent. It should be noted that although the maximum possible score for each decision style is 160, it is not unusual for none of the decision styles to achieve this maximum. We then generated several DTs in order to explore various relationships between the demographic variables and the dominant decision style.

Several interesting, tentative inferences can be made from an analysis of the ruleset of DTa displayed in Figure 13.8:

1. An examination of the distribution of the decision styles in the root of this DT indicated that dominant decision style of the majority of the respondents is the *analytical (A)* decision style (66.2%). Statistical analysis of the hypotheses H_0 ($p_{Analytical} = 0.50$) and H_A ($p_{Analytical} > 0.50$) results in the acceptance (i.e., nonrejection) of the alternate hypothesis H_A ($p_{Analytical} > 0.50$). Thus, if this sample is indeed representative of the population then this result would be very significant.
2. Respondents who work in the *banking and financial services* industry category may be more likely to have an *analytical (A)* decision style than respondents who work in the *government or other* industry categories as the difference in the relevant relative frequencies for the *analytical* decision style (i.e., 85.7% vs. 38.9%) is statistically significant. This tentative observation is even more interesting; as for the analytical decision style the relative frequency for the *banking and financial services* industry category is so much greater than that for the entire sample (i.e., 85.7% vs. 66.2%).

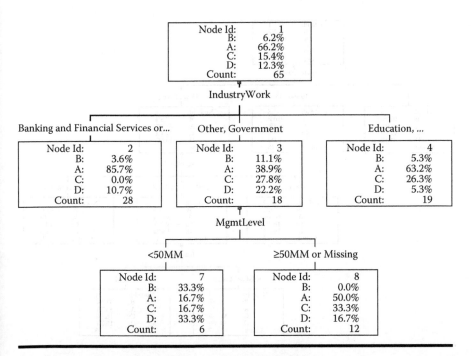

Figure 13.8   DTa—All candidate predictors included

3. It is also interesting that for the *analytical* decision style the relative frequency for the *government or other* industry categories is so much smaller than that for the entire sample (i.e., 33.89% vs. 66.2%).

4. *Middle managers* and *top executives* who work in the government or other industry categories may be more likely to have an *analytical (A)* decision style than respondents at other management levels since the difference in the relevant relative frequencies for the *analytical* decision style (i.e., 50.0% vs. 16.7%) is statistically significant.

Several interesting, tentative inferences can be made from analysis of the ruleset of DTb displayed in Figure 13.9:

1. Respondents whose highest degree is a *bachelor's degree* are likely to have an *analytical (A)* decision style (i.e., 83.3%). This tentative observation is even more interesting because for the *analytical* decision style, the relative frequency for respondents whose highest degree is a *bachelor's degree* is so much greater than that for the entire sample (i.e., 83.3% vs. 66.2%).

2. Respondents whose highest degree is a *bachelor's degree* and who are *middle managers (50MM)* or *top executives* (60TE) may be more likely to have an *analytical (A)* decision style than respondents whose highest degree is a *bachelor's degree* and who are *academic staff (30AS)* or *junior managers (40JM)* because

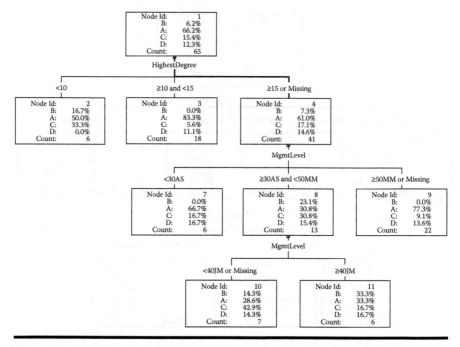

Figure 13.9   DTb—Candidate predictor *IndustryWork* suppressed.

the difference in the relevant relative frequencies for the *analytical* decision style (i.e., 77.3% vs. 30.8%) is statistically significant. This tentative observation is even more interesting because for the analytical decision style, these conditional relative frequencies are so much different than that for the entire sample (i.e., 77.7% vs. 66.2%; 30.8% vs. 66.2%).

Several interesting, tentative inferences can be made from analysis of the ruleset of the DTc displayed in Figure 13.10:

1. Respondents who are either *junior staff* or *senior staff* (MgmtLevel < 30AS ⇒ MgmtLevel = 10JS or 20SS) may be more likely to have an *analytical* decision style than respondents who are either an *academic staff* or a *junior manager* (MgmtLevel ≥ 30AS & MgmtLevel < 50MM ⇒ MgmtLevel = 30AS or 40JM) because the relevant relative frequencies for the *analytical* decision style are 66.7% versus 52.6%.

2. Respondents who are either *middle managers* or *top executives* (MgmtLevel ≥ 50MM ⇒ MgmtLevel = 50MM or 60TE) may be more likely to have an *analytical decision* style than respondents who are either an *academic staff* or a *junior manager* because the relevant relative frequencies for the *analytical* decision style are 73.5% versus 52.6%.

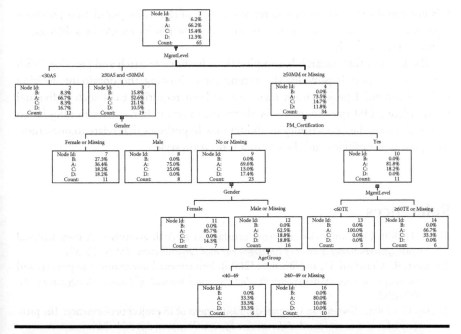

Figure 13.10 DTc—Candidate predictors IndustryWork and HighestDegree suppressed.

3. Respondents who are either *middle managers* or *top executives* may be more likely to have an *analytical* decision style if they are certified project management professionals (PMPs) because the relevant relative frequencies for the *analytical* decision style are 81.8% versus 69.6%.

4. *Male* respondents who are either *academic staff* or *junior managers* may be more likely to have an *analytical* decision style than corresponding *females* because the relevant relative frequencies for the *analytical* decision style are 75.0% versus 36.4%.

5. *Female* respondents who are either *middle managers* or *top executives* but are not certified PMPs may be more likely to have an *analytical* decision style than corresponding *males* because the relevant relative frequencies for the *analytical* decision style are 85.7% versus 62.5%.

6. *Male* respondents who are either *middle managers* or *top executives* but are not certified PMPs may be more likely to have an *analytical* decision style if they are *40 and older* because the relevant relative frequencies for the *analytical* decision style are 80.0% versus 33.3%.

Conclusion

In this chapter, we used a data mining-based data analysis approach to identify some of the relationships between a set of demographic variables and the individual's dominant decision style. We consider our results to be preliminary because it is not certain that our sample is representative of the entire population potential organizational project team members, and so these results should be subjected to future empirical analysis.

The focus of this research has implications for both research and practice. With regard to practice, it provides the means for estimating the dominant decision styles of potential project team members without requiring each such individual to complete a DSI questionnaire. With regard to research, our data mining-based approach offers the opportunity to abduct new hypotheses that relate to our candidate predictor variables and the dominant decision style.

References

Ali, A. (1989). Decision styles and work satisfaction of Arab executives: A cross-national study, *International Studies of Management and Organization, 19*(2), 22–37.

Atkinson, R., Crawford, L., and Ward, S. (2006). Fundamental uncertainties in projects and the scope of project management. *International Journal of Project Management, 24,* 687–698.

Barclay, C. (2008). Towards an integrated measurement of IS project performance: The project performance scorecard. *Information Systems Frontiers, 10,* 331–345.

Barclay, C. and Osei-Bryson, K. M. (2010). Project performance development framework: An approach for developing performance criteria and measures for information systems (IS) projects. *International Journal of Production Economics, 124*(1), 272–292.

Bazerman, M. and Moore, D. A. (2012). *Judgment in Managerial Decision Making.* 7th Edition. New York: Wiley.

Benbasat, I., Goldstein, D. K., and Mead, M. (1987). The case research strategy in studies of information systems. *Management Information Systems Quarterly, 11*(3), 368.

Boulgarides, J. D. and Oh, M. D. (1985). A comparison of Japanese, Korean and American managerial decision styles: An exploratory study. *Leadership & Organization Development Journal, 6*(1), 9–11. http://dx.doi.org/10.1108/eb053565.

Bredillet, C. N. (2007). Projects: Learning at the edge of organization. In P. Morris and J. K. Pinto (eds.) *The Wiley Guide to Project Organization and Project Management Competencies,* New York: Wiley.

Bresnen, M., Edelman, L., Newell, S., Scarbrough, H., and Swan, J. (2003). Social practices and the management of knowledge in project environments. *International Journal of Project Management, 21*(3), 157–166.

Chan, R. and Rosemann, M. (2001). Managing knowledge temporary organization. *Journal of Systems and Information Technology, 5*(2), 37–53.

Conroy, G. and Soltan, H. (1998). ConSERV, as a continual audit concept to provide traceability and accountability over the project life cycle. *International Journal of Project Management, 16*(3), 185–197.

Crawford, L., Morris, P., Thomas, J., and Winter, M. (2006). Practitioner development: From trained technicians to reflective practitioners, *International Journal of Project Management, 24,* 722–733.

Creswell, M. and Miller, D. (2008). Determining the validity in qualitative inquiry. *Theory in Practice, 39*(3), 124–130.

Darke, P., Shanks, G., and Broadbent, M. (1998). Successfully completing case study research: Combining rigor, relevance and pragmatism. *Information Systems Journal, 8*, 273–289.

Decision Style Inventory. Retrieved on September 3, 2013, at http://www.dsitest.com/.

Dillman, D. A. (2000). *Mail and Internet Surveys: The Tailored Design Method* (Vol. 2). New York: Wiley.

Disterer, G. (2002). Management of project knowledge and experiences. *Journal of Knowledge Management, 6*(5), 512–520.

Drucker, P. F. (1993). *Post-Capitalist Society*. New York: Butterworth-Heinemann.

Durkin, M. (2004). In search of the internet-banking customer: Exploring the use of decision styles. *International Journal of Bank Marketing, 22*(7), 484–503.

Fox, T. L. and Spence, J. W. (1999). An examination of the decision styles of project managers: Evidence of significant diversity. *Information & Management, 36*(6), 313–320.

Fox, T. L. and Spence, J. W. (2005). The effect of decision style on the use of a project management tool: An empirical laboratory study. *ACM SIGMIS Database, 36*(2): 28–42.

Gibbert, M., Guigrok, W., and Wicki, B. (2008). What passes as a rigorous case study? *Strategic Management Journal, 29*, 1465–1475.

Grover, V. and Davenport, T. H. (2001). General perspectives on knowledge management: Fostering a research agenda, *Journal of Management Information Systems, 18*(1), 5–21.

Gurteen, D. (1998). Knowledge, creativity and innovation. *Journal of Knowledge Management, 2*(1), 5–13.

Hansen, M. T., Nohria, N., and Tierney, T. (1999). What's your strategy for managing knowledge? *Harvard Business Review, 77*(2), 106–116.

Kasvi, J. J. J., Vartiainen, M., and Hailikari, M. (2003). Managing knowledge and knowledge competences in projects and project organisations. *International Journal of Project Management, 21*(8), 571–582.

Kock, N. and McQueen, R. (1998). Knowledge and information communication in organizations: An analysis of core, support and improvement processes. *Knowledge and Process Management, 5*(1), 29–40.

Leonard-Barton, D. (1990). A dual methodology for case studies: Synergistic use of a longitudinal single site with replicated multiple sites, *Organization Science, 1*(3), 248–266.

Love, P. E. D. (2005). *Management of Knowledge in Project Environments*. Amsterdam, the Netherlands: Elsevier.

Martinsons, M. G. and Davison, R. M. (2007). Strategic decision making and support systems: Comparing American, Japanese and Chinese management. *Decision Support Systems, 43*(1), 284–300.

Morris, P. W. G., Crawford, L., Hodgson, D., Shepherd, M. M., and Thomas, J. (2006). Exploring the role of formal bodies of knowledge in defining a profession—The case of project management, *International Journal of Project Management, 24*, 710–721.

Müller, R. and Turner, R. (2010). Leadership competency profiles of successful project managers. *International Journal of Project Management, 28*(5), 437–448.

Newell, S., Scarbrough, H., Swan, J., Robertson, M., and Galliers, R. D. (2002). The importance of process knowledge for cross project learning: Evidence from a UK hospital. *Proceedings of the 35th Annual Hawaii International Conference on System Sciences*, Hawaii, January.

Nonaka, I. (1994). A dynamic theory of organizational knowledge creation. *Organization Science, 5*(1), 4–37.

Nonaka, I. and Takeuchi, H. (1995). *The Knowledge-Creating Company: How Japanese Companies Create the Dynamics of Innovation*. New York: Oxford University Press.

Nutt, P. C. (1993). Flexible decision styles and the choices of top executives. *Journal of Management Studies, 30*(5), 695–721.

Pinsonneault, A. and Kraemer, K. L. (1993). Survey research methodology in management information systems: An assessment. Working Paper #URB-022. http://escholarship .org/uc/item/6cs4s5f0.

Project Management Institute (PMI). (2008). *A Guide to the Project Management Body of Knowledge (PMBOK® guide)*. 4th edn. Newtown Square, PA: Project Management Institute.

Reich, B. H. (2007). Managing knowledge and learning in IT projects: A conceptual framework and guidelines for practice, *Project Management Journal, 38*(2), 5–17.

Rowe, A. (1981). *The Decision Style Inventory*. June 6.

Rowe, A. J. and Boulgarides, J. D. (1983). Decision styles—A perspective. *Leadership & Organization Development Journal, 4*(4), 3–9.

Rowe, A. and Mason, R. O. (1987). *Managing with Style: A Guide to Understanding, Assessing, and Improving Decision Making*. San Francisco, CA: Jossey-Bass.

Scarbrough, H., Bresnen, M., Edelman, L. F., and Laurent, S. (2004). The processes of project-based learning: An exploratory study. *Management Learning, 35*, 491–506.

Scheepers, R., Venkitachalam, K., and Gibbs, M. R. (2004). Knowledge strategy in organizations: Refining the model of Hansen, Nohria and Tierney. *Journal of Strategic Information Systems, 13*(3), 201–222.

Shenhar, A. J., Dvir, D., Levy, O., and Maltz, A. C. (2001). Project success: A multidimensional strategic concept. *Long Range Planning, 34*, 699–725.

The Standish Group. (2007). CHAOS 2007 REX: A standish group research exchange.

Stanleigh, M. (2006). From crisis to control: New standards for project management. Ivey *Business Journal Online*. Retrieved July 23, 2008, from http://www.iveybusinessjournal .com/article.asp?intArticle_ID = 624.

Statistical Institute of Jamaica (Statin). (2005). Jamaica Industrial Classification. Retrieved July 12, 2014, http://statinja.gov.jm/Jamaica%20Industrial%20Classification%20 Structure%20Revised%20-%202005.pdf.

Straub, D. W. (1989). Validating instruments in MIS Research. *Management Information Systems Quarterly, 13*(2), 147–169.

Tanur, J. M. (1982). Advances in methods for large-scale surveys and experiments. In R. Mcadams, N. J. Smelser, and D. J. Treiman (eds.), *Behavioral and Social Science Research: A National Resource, Part II*. Washington, DC: National Academy Press.

Turner, J. R. and Müller, R. (2005). The project manager's leadership style as a success factor on projects: A literature review. *Project Management Institute, 36*(1), 59–61.

Weiser, M. and Morrison, J. (1998). Project memory: Information management for project teams. *Journal of Management Information Systems, 14*(4), 149–166.

Yousef, D. A. (1998). Predictors of decision-making styles in a non-western country, *Leadership & Organization Development Journal, 19*(7), 366–373.

Zmud, R. W. (1979). Individual differences and MIS success: A review of the empirical literature, *Management Science, 25*(10), 966–979.

Chapter 14

Application of the CRISP-DM Model in Predicting High School Students' Examination (CSEC/CXC) Performance

Corlane Barclay, Andrew Dennis,
and Jerome Shepherd

Contents

Abstract: This chapter reports on the application of the CRISP-DM methodology to manage the data mining (DM) project on education in Jamaica. The RapidMiner open-source software was used to extract knowledge from data on high school students' examination performance, particularly in the English language and mathematics, and the results from the use of the decision tree technique are shown. The findings revealed interesting associated conditions between subjects, including where students who fail English and information technology (IT) are also likely to fail mathematics, and where they pass chemistry, IT, and principles of business (POB), they are likely to also pass mathematics; if they pass mathematics, they are likely to pass English, and if they fail mathematics, chemistry, and IT, then they are likely to also fail the English language. Although these results are preliminary, insights into the possible relationships between certain subjects can help inform curriculum planning and examination preparation. The research also hopes to engage future discussions of the use of DM techniques in the education sector in Jamaica and the rest of the Caribbean.

Keywords: Data mining, education, CRISP-DM, decision tree technique, CSEC/CXC, Jamaica

Introduction

For more than a decade, there have been inconsistent and poor performances by many Jamaican students in the Caribbean Secondary Education Certificate (CSEC) examinations, particularly in the English language and mathematics. Experts have put forward possible solutions but nothing has adequately addressed the issues. In this chapter, we applied a knowledge discovery and data mining (KDDM) process model, the Cross Industry Standard Process for Data Mining (CRISP-DM), to gather insights or interesting patterns on secondary high school students' performance. The project seeks to find any associated conditions that can help predict performance and thereby better understand the conditions of student's examination performance, particularly in the core subjects, namely, English and mathematics. CRISP-DM is a comprehensive data mining (DM) methodology and process model that provides practitioners with a blueprint for conducting a DM project.

DM is a discipline that allows for the analysis of one or more datasets with a view of discovering any unknown or interesting patterns. Fayyad et al. (1996) describes it as a nontrivial process of identifying valid, novel, potentially useful, and understandable patterns in data. Hand et al. (2001) further describes DM as "the analysis of (often large) observational data sets to find unsuspected relationships and to summarize the data in novel ways that are both understandable and useful to the data owner" (p. 1). The importance of DM and knowledge discovery has been underlined in many studies through the exploration in multiple domains, including education.

Importance of Research

English language and mathematics are generally accepted as the core subject areas for students who hope to matriculate to higher learning. These subjects also serve as key prerequisites for most entry-level jobs. The Jamaica's Draft Mathematics and Numeracy Policy of the Ministry of Education (2003) states that the learning of mathematics is important to every child because of its significance to so many aspects of life. In Jamaica, the government outlined in its *Vision 2030* plan of its intention to gain "first world status" by 2030 (Vision 2030). The document further underlined that a skilled and motivated workforce was critical in achieving this goal. This suggests that education is the path to the achievement of this mission. One way of contributing is through the identification of sustainable strategies for high success rate in English and mathematics.

Implications from the Study

The successful completion of this research will create new opportunities and benefits for educators in the education arena, as it will aid in the continued reform of the Jamaican educational system. It should resonate with governments and policy makers who may use results as the basis to develop more relevant policies on students' education. It will also bolster and increase the knowledge that exists on DM and its potential in Jamaica; as well as to solidify the use and application of the CRISP-DM methodology in tackling DM problems more specifically in education. This research is not presented as the last word on using the CRISP-DM methodology as a DM approach for research. Rather, it should serve as springboard for initiating dialogue and adding to the knowledge base in pedagogy about using the CRISP-DM methodology in education and other domains as a standard to allay DM problems in Jamaica.

There is currently no study in Jamaica that satisfactorily tackles the poor performance of Jamaica's students in the English and mathematics examinations. Hence this research primarily attempts to provide opportunities for the educational sector, including the Ministry of Education to use this study to identify solutions. Similarly this research will afford the motivation to parents and communities alike in providing watchful eyes of the factors that affects performance and will, therefore, enable them to increase their respective roles to provide an atmosphere where schools, families, and communities join hands together to benefit students.

Review of Literature/Research Background

Factors Affecting Student Performance

Several studies have put forward perspectives on the factors impacting students' performance. Harb and El-Shaarawi (2006) pointed out that factors that may affect students' performance include family size, which may differ significantly among different ethnic and economic subgroups. Kennedy and Tay (1994) stated that the study effort, age, and an alignment between students' learning style and instructors' teaching style have positive effect on student's performance. Anderson and Benjamin (1994) identified students' effort, previous schooling, and parents' education as contributing factors. Self-motivation, age of student and learning preferences, family income (Devadoss and Foltz 1996), class attendance (Romer 1993), and basic entry level qualifications also serve as factors that have a significant effect on the students' academic performance in various settings.

Garvey-Clarke (2011) suggested that Jamaican teachers are ineffective in teaching English language and mathematics and proffered a number of factors that may affect learning and achievement at the secondary level in Jamaica. The factors identified are similar to those identified in other regions, and include curriculum and pedagogy, the school and home environment, socioeconomic factors, and student characteristics. Interestingly, curriculum and pedagogy was put forward as the main reason that students from working families do not do well (Evans 2001). This view is supported by Garvey-Clarke (2011), who noted that socioeconomic status is positively related to student academic achievement. Tremis (2009) further opined that students come to school with various deficiencies; consequently, it is critical for school systems to ameliorate these deficiencies so as to ensure maximum performance of these students.

Educational DM

Research has shown that DM can be used to discover at-risk students and help institutions become much more proactive in identifying and responding to said students (Luan 2002). Luan (2002) applied classification and regression trees to the educational data to predict the type of student that would be likely to drop out of school.

Countries such as Portugal also experience high rates of failure by their students in mathematics and their official first language, Portuguese, at the secondary level. DM research has been conducted there to find the problem. According to Cortez and Silva (2008), "… lack of success in the core classes of Mathematics and the Portuguese language is extremely serious. On the other hand, the fields of Business Intelligence (BI)/Data Mining (DM), which aim at extracting high-level knowledge from raw data, offer interesting automated tools that can aid the education domain." The study undertaken by Cortez and Silva (2008) revealed that the students' performance in mathematics and Portuguese were largely affected by previous performance in evaluation tests. However, it was also found that in some cases, other relevant features such as school-related characteristics (e.g., frequency of absenteeism, reason to choose school, and extra educational school support), demographic details (e.g., student's age, parent's job, and education), and social connections (e.g., going out with friends and alcohol consumption) played a significant role in performance.

Hijazi and Naqvi (2006) conducted a study of 300 students (225 males and 75 females) across Pakistan. Using a regression technique, it was discovered that factors such as the mother's education and the family income of the student were highly linked with the student's performance. Baradwaj and Pal (2011) used the Bayesian classification technique on a sample of 300 tertiary students in India with a 17-attribute dataset and found that factors such as living location, mother's qualification, family annual income, family status, previous exam grades, and the medium of teaching had an impact on the performance. Sembiring et al. (2011) found a relationship between mental condition of student and their final academic performance. This result was obtained by mining data collected by questionnaires responded to by students to obtain psychometric factors and the possible relationship with the students' academic performance.

Research Methodology

This study adopts the principles of a KDDM process model that specifies the phases for producing, deploying, and using DM models (Sharma and Osei-Bryson 2010) and provides a structure for organizing the DM effort by describing the tasks involved in DM. The KDDM process model being used for this research is the CRISP-DM. CRISP-DM separates the DM project into several phases. The phases of the CRISP-DM approach include understanding the business problem, capturing and understanding data, applying DM techniques, interpreting results, and deploying the knowledge gained in operations (www.crisp-dm.org), see Figure 14.1. Establishing standards for DM is essential especially as it becomes an integral decision-making tool (Kurgan and Musilek 2006). Using these standards will help to ensure that the process of DM is reliable and

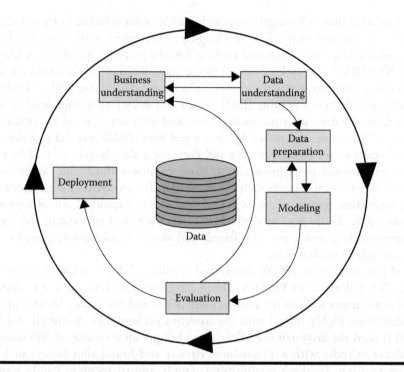

Figure 14.1 CRISP-DM. (Data from Chapman, P. et al. 2000. *CRISP-DM 1.0: Step-by-Step Data Mining Guide.*)

repeatable, especially for those persons who are not experts in the field (Mansingh et al. 2013).

CRISP-DM was chosen as the preferred KDDM model because it is (Leventhal, 2010):

- Nonproprietary
- Application/industry neutral
- Tool neutral
- Focuses on business issues as well as technical analysis
- Seminal in its nature with multiple successful applications across many domains

CRISP-DM has been used in several DM research projects and industries. For example, Mansingh et al. (2013) utilized the framework in their study of profiling Internet-banking users, and Rocha and de Sousa Junior (2010) applied it in their study on identifying bank fraud. Moro et al. (2011) in their study on bank direct marketing also used CRISP-DM to conduct the DM process.

The application of the methodology is described in Table 14.1. CRISP-DM breaks down the life cycle of a DM project into six phases: business understanding (BU),

Table 14.1   Application of CRISP-DM in Project

CRISP-DM	Application
Data	Datasets that include students' demographic background, academic performance, and financial information will be used. These will be collected from one university.
Business understanding	The objective of this research project is to better understand the performance of high school students, especially in key subjects such as mathematics and English. The records show consistently poor performance by our students in the aforementioned subjects, which, if not solved, will have a deleterious effect on the country's drive to attain first world status by 2030, as outlined in the government's strategic plan.
	For this project to be successful, the following criteria will have to be realized:
	1. Identification of the causative factors that negatively impact performance in mathematics and English.
	2. Useful insights or associations between factors or subjects that contribute to student performance.
	In addition, to carry out this study the following resources will be utilized:
	1. Three computers with Windows OS
	2. Microsoft Office Suite
	3. MS Visual Basic
	4. RapidMiner Data Mining Application
	In Jamaica, most of the data in the schools are paper based. This will serve as a constraint; significant time will have to be spent keying in data into a spreadsheet to make it available to RapidMiner.
	The overall goal of this data mining process is to extract information from the educational dataset and transform it into useful solutions for the business problem.
Data understanding	High schools across the Kingston metropolitan area were initially targeted for the collection of the necessary student data. Of the 11 secondary schools targeted, two responded in the affirmative to our request for student data. This student data does not contain sought-after attributes related to the students' financial and social data. Data collected thus far is exclusively academic in nature.

(Continued)

Table 14.1 (*Continued*) Application of CRISP-DM in Project

CRISP-DM	Application
	For those schools that did not respond positively to our request for data, they cited privacy issues, decentralization of the data, and lack of time as reasons why they could not assist with this study.
	Consequently data was requested from tertiary institutions who accept electronic applications from students leaving the secondary education system. The data received was used for knowledge extraction.
	An initial look at the data suggests that poor performance in mock exams leading up to the CXC exam manifests itself in poor performance in the CXC examinations. Conversely, good performance in the mock exams usually transfers into good performance in the CXC examinations.
Data preparation	The data was prepared in a spreadsheet application to fit with the data mining software being used, RapidMiner. Data validity will be managed through multiple persons conducting checks and reviews for completeness and accuracy. Unnecessary attributes will be removed from the overall dataset, leaving only those attributes relevant to the problem being analyzed.
Modeling	Multiple data mining techniques were used to classify and predict the data. Multiple data mining techniques can be applicable to a given dataset to fulfill a particular data mining goal, for example, for goals that require prediction both decision trees and logistic regression can be used (Osei-Bryson and Giles 2006).
Evaluation	Based on the results the top models were used as a basis for evaluation.
Deployment	The results of this project will largely be presented in academic venues and in the longer time shared with government and school officials to help improve their knowledge of the factors that may impact students' performance in mathematics and English.

data understanding, data preparation, modeling, evaluation, and deployment. These steps are reported in this chapter including the application of the decision tree technique to model and extract knowledge from the student data. Student data was requested spanning several high schools across Jamaica. This data was standardized (in spreadsheet format) and then mined using the software RapidMiner.

Application of CRISP-DM

In this section, we outline the description of activities based on the phases and steps described in CRISP-DM.

Business Understanding

In an effort to grasp the full extent of the problem, extensive examination of the literature surrounding education in Jamaica was done. This included various research papers done on the topic, transcripts of interviews done with the current and former education ministers, articles done by various stakeholders within the education sector, and whitepapers. We also relied on anecdotal evidence and our own experiences to inform our understanding of the research problem.

Industry and media reports showed that over the last decade, that is, between 2002 and 2012, the average percentage of students who successfully sat the mathematics exam was approximately 34.5% and 50% for the English language, respectively.

A major constraint faced by the research team was the unwillingness of most school authorities to facilitate the data collection due to schedule conflicts and privacy concerns. Another was the predominance of paper records that hindered the collection and preparation effort due to attempts to convert to digital data. This experience influenced the decision to use application data from tertiary institutions.

The key success criteria identified were organized based on descriptive and predictive analysis including the ability to predicting of students based on their performance in the English language and mathematics, and the ability to predict with at least 80% level of accuracy the performance of certain students in subjects such as mathematics and/or the English language.

Data Understanding

Data from a local university was due to help mitigate against data quality issues. The tertiary institution collects applications electronically via online application forms from prospective students who in most cases would have attended high school. A database with over 350,000 was received and Table 14.2 shows the attributes and description of the data received. Data for the 2008–2013 were received. The initial dataset contained 16 attributes. Of these 16 attributes, six were removed due to lack of relevancy to this DM project. There was also the addition of a derived attribute to the final dataset, see Tables 14.3 and 14.4.

The descriptive statistics of the dataset including the categorization of subjects used for analysis are summarized in Table 14.3. After data cleaning and preparation,

Table 14.2   List of Attributes Contained in the Dataset Provided by the University

Attributes	Description
PID	Personal identification (number)
DOB	Date of birth
Stu-gend	Student gender (i.e., male or female)
Marital_status	Marital status (i.e., single, married, or divorced)
Mcr-titl	Name of school/course being applied to by the applicant
Parish	Parish that the applicant student is from
Country	Country where the applicant lives
Nationality	Country of the applicant's birth
Religion	The faith to which the applicant belongs or practices
Disability	That is, physical or mental disability
Source of funding	This attribute represents the source of funding for their University degree/course. (i.e., Student Loan Bureau, parent, self, other family, private, overseas, Jamaican government)
Sqe_seqn	Separates each record
Exam	This represents the examination body that administered the examination taken by the student (e.g., GCE, CXC/CSEC, and so on). 30 exam bodies were identified.
Subject	Name of the subject that was taken. 154 unique subject areas were identified.
Grade	The grade achieved in the exam subject. For CXC/CSEC, grades 1–3 = pass, grades 4 and 5 = fail. An entry of *pending* means the applicant has previously failed the subject, re-did the subject and the university is now awaiting the result, or the student has sat the exam but had not received the grade at the time of applying to the university.
Year	The year the exam subject was taken.

Table 14.3 Descriptive Summary of CXC/CSEC Subjects

Subject	Pass	Fail	DNS[a]	Pending
Mathematics	11,799	330	0	10,992
English	18,815	208	770	3,328
Geography	3,389	77	19,176	479
History	1,771	41	20,953	356
Information technology	8,485	127	12,901	1,608
Physics	5,118	110	16,841	1,052
Principles of accounts	5,328	88	16,452	1,253
Principles of business	7,021	83	14,703	1,314
Biology	6,791	92	15,173	1,065
Chemistry	6,175	123	15,607	1,216
Total	75,971	133,855	155,239	253,873

[a] Did not sit.

Table 14.4 Excluded Attributes

Attribute	Rationale for Exclusion
Mcr-titl	This attribute represents the program to which the student is applying for acceptance at the university.
	We did not consider this attribute germane to the project because the desire to be in a particular program would have no bearing on if a student passed mathematics and/or the English language. We are interested in data that exists prior to the sitting of the exam; not data that speaks to the future aspiration of the student.
Nationality	The nationality attribute represents the country of which the student/applicant is a citizen of. Due to the fact that this study focuses exclusively on Jamaican nationals, and records where students are not Jamaicans will be removed, the nationality column becomes redundant and was removed from the dataset.
Marital_status	This attribute stores data on if an applicant is married, single, separated, or divorced. Our research focused on the 14- to 19-year-old constituents, which is based on perusal of the data containing almost exclusively unmarried.

(Continued)

Table 14.4 (*Continued*) Excluded Attributes

Attribute	Rationale for Exclusion
Exam	This study is dealing with CXC and as such records representing Cape and GCE will not be needed. Once these records were deleted, the exam field became redundant.
Sqe_seqn	This attribute is used to separate the results. This will not be necessary after the results are merged.

the total records were over 23,000. Students had an average age of 19, with 65% female and 71% from the rural areas.

1. Total number of records = 23,121
2. Average age = 19
3. Gender = female (14,998), male (7,921)
4. Parish = urban (6,750), rural (16,366)

Data Quality

Some instances of missing data and null value were identified in the data, along with other data quality concerns such as data inconsistency. For example:

- The *Parish* attribute had "NULL" as its value. This was attributed primarily to students who may have provided a non-Jamaican address.
- There were also some instances where the *Date of Birth* (*DOB*) attribute had incorrect values, that is, values greater than the present. This caused the (derived) age attribute in these cases to record a "#NUM!" value.
- NULL values also appeared in many instances for the *Religion* attribute and *Country* attribute.
- The *Grades* column was inconsistent with some records being represented by roman numerals (I, IV, V), others with integers (1, 4, 5), and then some with words/letter (Credit, Pass, Fail, DISTIN, A, B, C, UNG, and Pending). Instances of missing values were also found.
- There were many instances where the age of applicants at the time of sitting the exam exceeded 19. We consider the age 19 to be the limit after which a student would no longer be in high school (see Table 14.5).

Table 14.5   Included Attributes

Attribute	Rationale for Inclusion
PID	This attribute was used to identify records belonging to the same student as a consequence of how the initial data was stored in the Excel workbook. Each subject done by the student was stored in a separate row. For example, if a student did five subjects, that particular student's information would occupy five rows. All five rows would be identified by the same *PID*. Once cells are merged, the PID will be used to identify each record.
Age	This attributed is a derived attribute calculated from the date of birth (DOB) attribute, which was present in the initial dataset. Age represents a more precise attribute than its predecessor and will allow for the possibility of classification by age.
Stu-gend	This attribute represents the sex of the student and allows for the possibility of association and classification by way of gender.
Parish	Represents the parish the student is from and allows for classification (among other techniques) by parish.
Country	Represents the country where the student was born. Though the student's country of birth may not be Jamaica, the student could become a naturalized Jamaican citizen (i.e., a Jamaican national), hence making them eligible for the final dataset. This attribute is included because of the possibility of clustering by country.
Religion	This attribute speaks to the religious views that the student subscribes to and is important because linkages with religion and educational performance may be a factor.

(Continued)

Table 14.5 (Continued)   Included Attributes

Attribute	Rationale for Inclusion
Disability	This attribute represents a disability a student may have. The options of this attribute are *no disability* or the name of the disability, which could be physical or mental. This could also provide possible association or linkage between itself and educational performance.
SourceofFunding	We used the *sourceoffunding* attribute as an indicator of the applicants' socioeconomic status as we were unable to get more precise financial data on each applicant/student (as was requested). In particular, we view those applicants who have "Student Loan Bureau" as their source of funding as belonging to a lower income or poor household relative to the cost of education in Jamaica. Inversely, we view those students whose source of funding is self, parents as belonging to higher income households.
Subject = mathematics/ English language, etc.	This attribute/column was broken down and converted into individual subject areas. The result of this is the addition of a significant amount of columns, each column representing a unique subject.

One derived attribute that was added to the dataset was *Age*. This attribute is calculated from the *DOB* attribute, which was present in the initial dataset. *Age* represents a more precise attribute than its predecessor and will allow for the possibility of classification by age. The *DateIf* function in Microsoft Excel was used to calculate this field. All records (or rows) that share the same PID number were merged into one row using Visual Basic (VB) macros. This resulted in the addition of several new columns and the deletion of a few existing columns.

To address the data quality problems, the following general steps were taken with the assistance of VB macros that were written by the research team:

1. Instances where the *Religion* attribute is represented by "NULL" were replaced with "No Religion."
2. Instances where the *Exam* attribute is represented by "NULL" and the subject was verified as a CXC/CSEC subject, that NULL was changed to CXC.
3. Instances where the grades were represented by roman numerals or words were converted to the integer counterpart using the *find and replace* function of Microsoft Excel.

4. In instances where the word appearing for a grade does not indicate a specific grade (e.g., Pass/Fail/Credit), these entries were changed to a value that indicated a pass or a fail. For example, "1" for *Pass* and "4" for *Fail.*
5. In instances where the grade value is blank, it is replaced with an average of the entire grades column.
6. Records (or rows) where the values of the age attribute are greater than 19 or less than 14 were removed.
7. Records where nationality is not Jamaican were removed.
8. Records where exam is not CXC/CSEC were removed.
9. Records where the age attribute was "#NUM!" were removed.
10. Several columns were removed from the dataset, namely, Nationality, Sqe_sqn, Mcr_titl, Exam, and Marital_status.
11. In situations where a student attempted the same exam subject in different years, records representing attempts after the initial attempt were removed.

Modeling—Decision Tree Classifier

RapidMiner 5.3.005 was the mining/modeling software of choice primarily due to it being an open-source application and the availability of reference guide to support the learning process. This chapter will report the decision tree modeling results. The choice of using the decision tree model was that it is an inductive learning tool and possesses the ability to classify data and build predictive models (Osei-Bryson and Giles 2006) which are in line with the business objectives of this DM research.

Multiple rounds of modeling were performed to attain an optimal level without sacrificing any interestingness. The settings adjusted the decision tree panel to facilitate the iteration where

■ Criterion was changed from "gain_ratio" to "information_gain."
■ Minimal size for split was changed to 5.
■ Confidence was changed from 0.25 to 0.5.

Additionally, five "replace" operators were added to the model, which changed the values 1.0, 2.0, and 3.0 in the *subject* attributes to PASS, and 4.0, 5.0, and 6.0 to FAIL. 0.0 was also changed to PENDING. To bring the test dataset and the training dataset together in order for the decision tree model to predict, the "Apply Model" operator was used it had to be verified that both the *mod* and *lab* ports were connected to the *res* ports in order to generate the desired results.

Predicting Performance in Mathematics

Figure 14.2 shows the prediction for each student's mathematics (label) result, along with confidence percentages for each prediction. Table 14.6 reveals the English rules for the model.

Row No	pid	confidence(PASS)	confidence(0.0)	confidence(DNS)	confidence(FAIL)	prediction(English (A))	Disability	stu_gend	Biology	Chemistry	Geography	History	Information	Mathematics	Physics
23090	1362230	0.857	0.090	0.052	0.001	PASS	NO DISABILI	M	DNS	DNS	PASS	PASS	PASS	0.0	DNS
23091	1362235	0.962	0.021	0.016	0.001	PASS	NO DISABILI	F	PASS	DNS	DNS	PASS	PASS	PASS	DNS
23092	1362240	0.962	0.021	0.016	0.001	PASS	NO DISABILI	F	DNS	DNS	DNS	DNS	DN9	PASS	DNS
23093	1362242	0.962	0.021	0.016	0.001	PASS	NO DISABILI	M	DNS	PASS	PASS	DNS	DNS	PASS	PASS
23094	1362244	0.027	0	0.054	0.919	FAIL	NO DISABILI	M	DNS	DNS	PASS	DNS	PASS	FAIL	PASS
23095	1362248	0.027	0	0.054	0.919	FAIL	NO DISABILI	F	PASS	DNS	DNS	DNS	PASS	FAIL	DNS
23096	1362250	0.962	0.021	0.016	0.001	PASS	NO DISABILI	F	DNS	DNS	DNS	DNS	DNS	PASS	DNS
23097	1362256	0.851	0.079	0.070	0	PASS	NO DISABILI	F	DNS	DNS	DNS	DNS	DNS	0.0	DNS
23098	1362263	0.962	0.021	0.016	0.001	PASS	NO DISABILI	M	PASS	PASS	PASS	DNS	DNS	PASS	PASS
23099	1362275	0.962	0.021	0.016	0.001	PASS	NO DISABILI	M	DNS	DNS	DNS	DNS	DNS	PASS	DNS
23100	1362280	0.962	0.021	0.016	0.001	PASS	NO DISABILI	F	DNS	DNS	DNS	DNS	DNS	PASS	DNS
23101	1362285	0.962	0.021	0.016	0.001	PASS	NO DISABILI	F	PASS	PASS	DNS	DNS	DNS	PASS	PASS
23102	1362287	0.962	0.021	0.016	0.001	PASS	NO DISABILI	F	DNS	DNS	DNS	DNS	PASS	PASS	DNS
23103	1362293	0.962	0.021	0.016	0.001	PASS	NO DISABILI	M	DNS	DNS	DNS	DNS	DNS	PASS	DNS
23104	1362294	0.851	0.079	0.070	0	PASS	NO DISABILI	M	DNS	DNS	DNS	DNS	DNS	0.0	DNS
23105	1362301	0.962	0.021	0.016	0.001	PASS	NO DISABILI	M	DNS	DNS	PASS	DNS	PASS	PASS	DNS
23106	1362308	0.857	0.090	0.052	0.001	PASS	NO DISABILI	M	DNS	DNS	DNS	DNS	PASS	0.0	DNS
23107	1362311	0.962	0.021	0.016	0.001	PASS	NO DISABILI	F	PASS	PASS	DNS	DNS	PASS	PASS	DNS
23108	1362316	0.857	0.090	0.052	0.001	PASS	NO DISABILI	M	DNS	DNS	DNS	DNS	PASS	0.0	DNS
23109	1362321	0.962	0.021	0.016	0.001	PASS	NO DISABILI	F	PASS	PASS	DNS	DNS	PASS	PASS	DNS
23110	1362324	0.667	0.238	0.092	0.003	PASS	NO DISABILI	F	DNS	DNS	PASS	DNS	DNS	0.0	DNS
23111	1362325	0.962	0.021	0.016	0.001	PASS	NO DISABILI	M	DNS	DNS	DNS	PASS	PASS	PASS	DNS

Figure 14.2 Predictions for mathematics and their associated confidence percentages extract.

Table 14.6 DT English Rules—Mathematics

Decision Tree English Rules—Mathematics
1. IF English (A) = Did Not Sit AND age >17 AND Principle of Business = Did Not Sit THEN Mathematics = {PASS: 100%, FAIL: 0%}
2. IF English (A) = Did Not Sit AND age >17 AND Principle of Business = PASS AND student gender = F THEN Mathematics = {PASS: 97%, FAIL: 3%}
3. IF English (A) = Did Not Sit AND age >17 AND Principle of Business = PASS AND student gender = M THEN Mathematics = {PASS: 100%, FAIL: 0%}
4. IF English (A) = Did Not Sit AND age >17 THEN Mathematics = {PASS: 50%, FAIL: 50%}
5. IF English (A) = Fail AND Information Technology = Did Not Sit AND Principle of Business = Did Not Sit AND Chemistry = Did Not Sit AND SourceofFunding = Other THEN Mathematics = {PASS: 25%, FAIL: 75%}
6. IF English (A) = Fail AND Information Technology = Did Not Sit AND Principle of Business = Did Not Sit AND Chemistry = Did Not Sit AND SourceofFunding = Parents THEN Mathematics = {PASS: 0%, FAIL: 100%}
7. IF English (A) = Fail AND Information Technology = Did Not Sit AND Principle of Business = Did Not Sit AND Chemistry = Did Not Sit AND SourceofFunding = Self THEN Mathematics = {PASS: 0%, FAIL: 100%}

Table 14.6 (*Continued*)   DT English Rules—Mathematics

Decision Tree English Rules—Mathematics
8. IF English (A) = Fail AND Information Technology = Did Not Sit AND Principle of Business = Did Not Sit AND Chemistry = Did Not Sit AND SourceofFunding = Student Loan Bureau THEN Mathematics = {PASS: 0%, FAIL: 100%)
9. IF English (A) = Fail AND Information Technology = Did Not Sit AND Principle of Business = Did Not Sit AND Chemistry = Fail THEN Mathematics = {PASS: 0%, FAIL: 100%)
10. IF English (A) = Fail AND Information Technology = Did Not Sit AND Principle of Business = Did Not Sit AND Chemistry = PASS THEN Mathematics = {PASS: 100%, FAIL: 0%)
11. IF English (A) = Fail AND Information Technology = Did Not Sit AND Principle of Business = FAIL THEN Mathematics = {PASS: 0%, FAIL: 100%)
12. IF English (A) = Fail AND Information Technology = Did Not Sit AND Principle of Business = Pass THEN Mathematics = {PASS: 75%, FAIL: 25%)
13. IF English (A) = Fail AND Information Technology = Fail THEN Mathematics = {PASS: 0%, FAIL: 100%)
14. IF English (A) = Fail AND Information Technology = Pass AND Principle of Business = Did Not Sit THEN Mathematics = {PASS: 60%, FAIL: 40%)
15. IF English (A) = Fail AND Information Technology = Pass AND Principle of Business = Pass THEN Mathematics = {PASS: 100%, FAIL: 0%)
16. IF English (A) = PASS THEN Mathematics = {PASS: 98.6%, FAIL: 1.4%)
17. IF English (A) = Pending AND Chemistry = Did Not Sit THEN Mathematics = {PASS: 92%, FAIL: 8%)
18. IF English (A) = Pending AND Chemistry = Pass THEN Mathematics = {PASS: 100%, FAIL: 0%)
19. IF English (A) = Pending AND Chemistry = Pending THEN Mathematics = {PASS: 100%, FAIL: 0%)

The results revealed some interesting results, particularly the associated conditions between mathematics, principles of business (POB), information technology (IT), and chemistry.

Predicting pass conditions:
- If student passes English, then there is a 98.6% chance of also passing mathematics.
- If student passes chemistry and the English result is unknown, there is 100% chance of passing mathematics.
- If student passes both IT and POB, then there is a 100% chance of passing mathematics.

Predicting failure conditions:

- If student fails English and IT, then he or she are 100% likely to fail mathematics.
- If student fails English and POB, and did not sit IT, then he or she is 100% likely to fail mathematics.
- If student fails English and chemistry (and did not sit IT and POB), then there is 100% chance of failing mathematics.

Predicting Performance in English Language

Similar to the aforementioned processes the decision tree for the English language performance was derived. Figure 14.3 shows the prediction for each student's English language (label) result, along with confidence percentages for each prediction. Table 14.7 reveals the English rules for the model. Some of the interesting results show close relationship between IT, chemistry, and the English language and show associated conditions of examination performance.

Predicting pass conditions:

- Where a student over 18 passes mathematics, they also tend to pass the English language (with 98% chance).
- Where a student is over 18 and fails mathematics (and did not sit chemistry and IT), or she is likely to also pass English (81% chance).

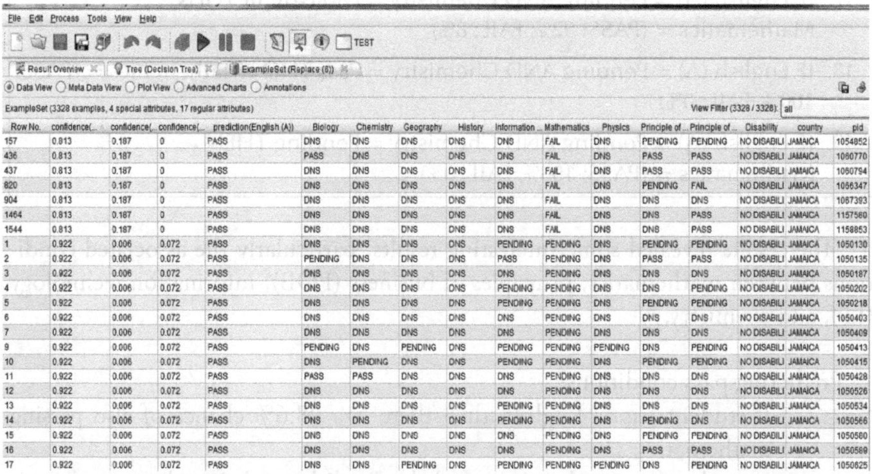

Row No.	confidence(...	confidence(...	confidence(...	prediction(English (A))	Biology	Chemistry	Geography	History	Information ...	Mathematics	Physics	Principle of ...	Principle of ...	Disability	country	pid
157	0.813	0.187	0	PASS	DNS	DNS	DNS	DNS	DNS	FAIL	DNS	PENDING	PENDING	NO DISABILI	JAMAICA	1054852
436	0.813	0.187	0	PASS	PASS	DNS	DNS	DNS	DNS	FAIL	DNS	PASS	PASS	NO DISABILI	JAMAICA	1060770
437	0.813	0.187	0	PASS	DNS	DNS	DNS	DNS	DNS	FAIL	DNS	PASS	PASS	NO DISABILI	JAMAICA	1060794
820	0.813	0.187	0	PASS	DNS	DNS	DNS	DNS	DNS	FAIL	DNS	PENDING	FAIL	NO DISABILI	JAMAICA	1066347
904	0.813	0.187	0	PASS	DNS	DNS	DNS	DNS	DNS	FAIL	DNS	DNS	DNS	NO DISABILI	JAMAICA	1067393
1464	0.813	0.187	0	PASS	DNS	DNS	DNS	DNS	DNS	FAIL	DNS	DNS	PASS	NO DISABILI	JAMAICA	1157560
1544	0.813	0.187	0	PASS	DNS	DNS	DNS	DNS	DNS	FAIL	DNS	DNS	PASS	NO DISABILI	JAMAICA	1158853
1	0.922	0.006	0.072	PASS	DNS	DNS	DNS	DNS	PENDING	PENDING	DNS	PENDING	PENDING	NO DISABILI	JAMAICA	1050130
2	0.922	0.006	0.072	PASS	PENDING	DNS	DNS	DNS	PASS	PENDING	DNS	PASS	PASS	NO DISABILI	JAMAICA	1050135
3	0.922	0.006	0.072	PASS	DNS	DNS	DNS	DNS	DNS	PENDING	DNS	DNS	DNS	NO DISABILI	JAMAICA	1050187
4	0.922	0.006	0.072	PASS	DNS	DNS	DNS	DNS	PENDING	PENDING	DNS	DNS	PENDING	NO DISABILI	JAMAICA	1050202
5	0.922	0.006	0.072	PASS	DNS	DNS	DNS	DNS	PENDING	PENDING	DNS	PENDING	PENDING	NO DISABILI	JAMAICA	1050218
6	0.922	0.006	0.072	PASS	DNS	DNS	DNS	DNS	DNS	PENDING	DNS	DNS	DNS	NO DISABILI	JAMAICA	1050403
7	0.922	0.006	0.072	PASS	DNS	DNS	DNS	DNS	DNS	PENDING	DNS	DNS	DNS	NO DISABILI	JAMAICA	1050409
9	0.922	0.006	0.072	PASS	PENDING	DNS	PENDING	DNS	PENDING	PENDING	PENDING	DNS	PENDING	NO DISABILI	JAMAICA	1050413
10	0.922	0.006	0.072	PASS	DNS	PENDING	DNS	DNS	PENDING	PENDING	DNS	PENDING	PENDING	NO DISABILI	JAMAICA	1050415
11	0.922	0.006	0.072	PASS	PASS	PASS	DNS	DNS	DNS	PENDING	DNS	DNS	DNS	NO DISABILI	JAMAICA	1050428
12	0.922	0.006	0.072	PASS	DNS	DNS	DNS	DNS	DNS	PENDING	DNS	DNS	DNS	NO DISABILI	JAMAICA	1050526
13	0.922	0.006	0.072	PASS	DNS	DNS	DNS	DNS	PENDING	PENDING	DNS	DNS	DNS	NO DISABILI	JAMAICA	1050534
14	0.922	0.006	0.072	PASS	DNS	DNS	DNS	DNS	PENDING	PENDING	DNS	PENDING	DNS	NO DISABILI	JAMAICA	1050566
15	0.922	0.006	0.072	PASS	DNS	DNS	DNS	DNS	DNS	PENDING	DNS	PENDING	PENDING	NO DISABILI	JAMAICA	1050580
16	0.922	0.006	0.072	PASS	DNS	DNS	DNS	DNS	DNS	PENDING	DNS	PASS	PASS	NO DISABILI	JAMAICA	1050589
17	0.922	0.006	0.072	PASS	DNS	DNS	PENDING	DNS	PENDING	PENDING	PENDING	DNS	PENDING	NO DISABILI	JAMAICA	1050625

Figure 14.3 Predictions for the English language label and their associated confidence percentages extract.

Table 14.7 English Rules—English

RapidMiner Tree Rules in English for English Language Decision Tree
Decision Tree English Rules—English
1. IF Mathematics = FAIL AND Age > 18 AND Information Technology = DNS AND Chemistry = DNS Then ENGLISH A = PASS (PASS = 81%, FAIL = 19%, DNS = 0%)
2. IF Mathematics = FAIL AND Age > 18 AND Information Technology = DNS AND Chemistry = FAIL Then ENGLISH A = FAIL (PASS = 20%, FAIL = 80%, DNS = 0%)
3. IF Mathematics = FAIL AND Age > 18 AND Information Technology = DNS AND Chemistry = PASS Then ENGLISH A = PASS (PASS = 100%, FAIL = 0%, DNS = 0%)
4. IF Mathematics = FAIL AND Age > 18 AND Information Technology = DNS AND Chemistry = PENDING Then ENGLISH A = PASS (PASS = 100%, FAIL = 0%, DNS = 0%)
5. IF Mathematics = FAIL AND Age > 18 AND Chemistry = FAIL AND Information Technology = FAIL Then ENGLISH A = FAIL (PASS = 10%, FAIL = 90%, DNS = 0%)
6. IF Mathematics = FAIL AND Age > 18 AND Chemistry = FAIL AND Information Technology = PASS Then ENGLISH A = PASS (PASS = 97%, FAIL = 1.5%, DNS = 1.5%)
7. IF Mathematics = FAIL AND Age > 18 AND Chemistry = FAIL AND Information Technology = PENDING Then ENGLISH A = PASS (PASS = 100%, FAIL = 0%, DNS = 0%)
8. IF Mathematics = PASS Then ENGLISH A = PASS (PASS = 98%, FAIL = 0.5%, DNS = 1.5%)
9. IF Mathematics = PENDING Then ENGLISH A = PASS (PASS = 92%, FAIL = 2%, DNS = 6%)

Predicting fail conditions:
- If a student is over 18 and fails mathematics and chemistry (and did not sit IT), there is a 80% likely chance of also failing the English language.
- If a student is over 18 and fails mathematics, chemistry, and IT, there is a 90% chance of also failing the English language.

Model Evaluation

The evaluation is done on the outputs of the various models from the modeling phase of CRISP-DM. This evaluation was based on the business and DM objectives as outlined in the BU phase. The key assessment applied was whether the models fit or met the measures defined in the BU phase.

Using the decision tree (and its rules), we were able to identify the subject profile of those students who fail mathematics and the English language. The profiles of existing students can be matched against the rules identified in the model. One stand out rule that the tree identified was that *100% of students who failed the English language and IT also failed mathematics*. Such a rule meets the stated business objectives and the statistical importance of this is that it informs the ability to predict performance of students. In other words, it provided an understanding of any associated conditions in failing mathematics.

Moreover, we can see where the model is able to predict which student will pass mathematics, this along with confidence percentage for each prediction. Figures 14.4 and 14.5 provide an extract of the results with the associated confidence levels.

Interestingly, results from the decision tree indicate that in terms of failures in mathematics, there was no discernible difference to be identified in relation to source of funding. Recall that in the data understanding and data preparation phases, it was indicated that the source of funding attribute would be used as a basis to determine the socioeconomic status of a student. To that end, it was noted that, according to the decision tree, *100% of those students who applied to the Student Loan Bureau AND did not sit chemistry AND did not sit POB AND did not sit IT AND failed the English language, also failed mathematics* and *100% of those students who got funding from parents AND did not sit chemistry AND did not sit POB AND did not sit IT AND failed the English language also failed mathematics*. As a result of this model meeting the business objectives and success criteria, it was approved for deployment.

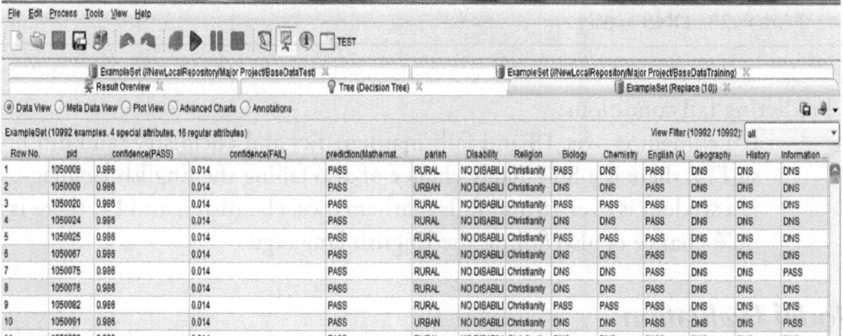

Row No.	pid	confidence(PASS)	confidence(FAIL)	prediction(Mathemat	parish	Disability	Religion	Biology	Chemistry	English (A)	Geography	History	Information…
1	1050008	0.986	0.014	PASS	RURAL	NO DISABILI	Christianity	PASS	DNS	PASS	DNS	DNS	DNS
2	1050009	0.986	0.014	PASS	URBAN	NO DISABILI	Christianity	DNS	DNS	PASS	DNS	DNS	DNS
3	1050020	0.986	0.014	PASS	RURAL	NO DISABILI	Christianity	PASS	PASS	PASS	DNS	DNS	DNS
4	1050024	0.986	0.014	PASS	RURAL	NO DISABILI	Christianity	DNS	DNS	PASS	DNS	DNS	DNS
5	1050025	0.986	0.014	PASS	RURAL	NO DISABILI	Christianity	PASS	PASS	PASS	DNS	DNS	DNS
6	1050067	0.986	0.014	PASS	RURAL	NO DISABILI	Christianity	DNS	DNS	PASS	DNS	DNS	DNS
7	1050075	0.986	0.014	PASS	RURAL	NO DISABILI	Christianity	DNS	DNS	PASS	DNS	DNS	PASS
8	1050076	0.986	0.014	PASS	RURAL	NO DISABILI	Christianity	DNS	DNS	PASS	DNS	DNS	DNS
9	1050082	0.986	0.014	PASS	RURAL	NO DISABILI	Christianity	PASS	PASS	PASS	DNS	DNS	DNS
10	1050091	0.986	0.014	PASS	URBAN	NO DISABILI	Christianity	DNS	DNS	PASS	DNS	DNS	PASS
11	1050093	0.986	0.014	PASS	RURAL	NO DISABILI	Christianity	DNS	DNS	PASS	DNS	DNS	DNS

Figure 14.4 "Pass" predictions and their associated confidence percentages (decision tree).

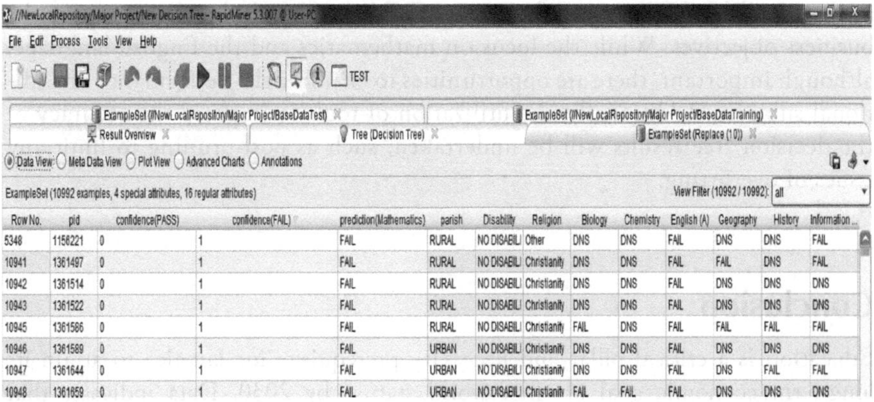

Figure 14.5 "Fail" predictions and their associated confidence percentages (decision tree).

Deployment

In this phase, the results gained from the modeling activities will be organized and presented in such a way as is to effectively communicate the newly discovered knowledge to the customer. Best practice indicates that it is useful to have knowledge gained from the modeling organized and presented in a way that the customer can understand and use. This ranges from the simplicity of a report to the more complex nature of implementing a repeatable DM process. Other aspects of this phase include setting out an actual plan for implementation (if necessary), monitoring that plan, and reviewing the previous phases of the CRISP-DM.

Deployment in the short term includes reporting on the findings of the DM project. Additionally in the long term, the following will be undertaken: share the findings with education policy makers on the likelihood of performance in the English language and mathematics given certain conditions and the development of relevant curriculum to match the new knowledge about the domain.

Limitations of Study and Future Work

The current study is still at the preliminary stages and, therefore, has some limitations that may affect its generalizability and help inform future work. The data used for analysis was from a tertiary institution and, therefore, may not have all the relevant attributes that could better inform an understanding of the domain. However, resources will be required to collect the data from the secondary schools as it is generally not available in a digital format. The use of only one modeling technique, decision tree, was undertaken in this study. It is envisioned that richer analysis will be forthcoming from use of additional techniques to support the business objectives. While the focus on mathematics and the English language, although important, there are opportunities to examine the performance of additional subjects. Additionally, the utilization of tools to improve the accuracy of the decision tree results will be undertaken, such as post-pruning to limit any issues of overfitting.

Conclusion

Education is a critical pillar and necessary prerequisite for Jamaica to attain its long-term economic goal of "first world status" by 2030. Data indicates that Jamaican students consistently perform poorly, which threatens to derail the *Vision 2030* plan. This study utilized several DM techniques to extract knowledge from data within the educational domain. To be more specific, this chapter focused on the core subjects of mathematics and the English language at the CXC level. CXC data was modeled using decision tree. The DM process was carried out within the framework of CRISP-DM.

The findings from the analysis indicate that a large majority of students who fail the English language also fail mathematics. However, outside of that knowledge, it was also revealed that students who fail the English language but pass POB, IT, or chemistry also pass mathematics. Conversely, students who fail the English language, POB, IT, and/or chemistry are likely to fail mathematics. The associated connection between chemistry, POB, IT, English, and mathematics presents new knowledge where generally these subjects are siloed into science versus business versus language subjects and requires future investigation. Implications for practice include policy changes in terms of the type of foundation subjects students should consider and the continued evolvement of the curriculum based on findings in knowledge discovery type of projects. Implications for research involved continued exploration of the advantages of improved decisions from KDDM projects can offer not only in education at levels, but other key sectors, especially for small developing countries such as Jamaica.

References

Anderson, G. and Benjamin, D. (1994). The determinants of success in university introductory economics courses. *Journal of Economic Education, 25*(2), 99–119.

Aripin, R., Mahmood, Z., Rohaizad, R., Yeop, U., and Anuar, M. (2003). Students' learning styles and academic performance. *22nd Annual SAS Malaysia Forum*, July 15, Kuala Lumpur Convention Center, Kuala Lumpur, Malaysia.

Baradwaj, B. and Pal, S. (2011). Mining educational data to analyze students' performance. *International Journal of Advanced Computer Science and Applications, 2*(6), 63–69.

Chapman, P., Clinton, J., Kerber, R., Khabaza, T., Reinartz, T., Shearer, C., and Wirth, R. (2000). *CRISP-DM 1.0: Step-by-Step Data Mining Guide*, SPSS Inc.

Cortez, P. and Silva, A. M. G. (2008). Using data mining to predict secondary school student performance. Retrieved from http://repositorium.sdum.uminho.pt/bitstream/1822/8024/1/student.pdf.

Devadoss, S. and Foltz, J. (1996). Evaluation of factors influencing student class attendance and performance. *American Journal of Agricultural Economics, 78*(3), 499–507.

Evans, H. (2001). *Inside Jamaican Schools*. Kingston, Jamaica: University of the West Indies Press.

Fayyad, U., Piatetsky-Shapiro, G., and Smyth, P. (1996). The KDD process for extracting useful knowledge from volumes of data. *Communications of the ACM, 39*(11), 27–34.

Gavey-Clarke, M. (2011). An Exploration of the Critical influences on the academic outcomes of students in an upgraded high school in Kingston, Jamaica. Northern Caribbean University.

Hand, D. J., Mannila, H., and Smyth, P. (2001). *Principles of Data Mining*. Cambridge, MA: MIT Press.

Harb, N. and El-Shaarawi, A. (2006). Factors Affecting Students' Performance. MPRA Paper No. 13621.

Hijazi, S.T. and Naqvi, S. M. M. R. (2006). Factors Affecting Students' Performance. A case of Private Colleges, *Bangladesh eJournal of Sociology, 3*(1).

International Educational Data Mining Society (IEDMS). (2013). Educational data mining. Retrieved January 4, 2014, from www.educationaldatamining.org.

Kennedy, P. and Tay, R. (1994). Students' performance in economics: Does the norm hold across cultural and institutional settings? *Journal of Economic Education, 25*(4): 291–301.

Kurgan, L. A. and Musilek, P. (2006). A survey of knowledge discovery and data mining process models. *Knowledge Engineering Review, 21*(1), 1–24.

Leventhal, B. (2010). An introduction to data mining and other techniques for advanced analytics. *Journal of Direct, Data and Digital Marketing Practice, 12*(2), 137–153. doi:10.1057/dddmp.2010.35.

Luan, J. (2002). Data mining and knowledge management in higher education applications. *Paper presented at the Annual Forum for the Association for Institutional Research*, Toronto, Ontario, Canada. Retrieved June 30, 2014, from http://eric.ed.gov/ERICWebPortal/detail?accno=ED474143.

Mansingh, G., Rao, L., Osei-Bryson, K.-M., and Mills, A. (2013). Profiling internet banking users: A knowledge discovery in data mining process model based approach. *Information Systems Frontiers*, 1–23.

Ministry of Education, Youth and Culture. (2003). Mathematics and Numeracy Policy. Retrieved from http://expanding-educational-horizons.com/Numeracy/NumeracyPolicy.pdf.

Moro, S., Laureano, R., and Cortez, P. (2011). Using Data Mining for Bank Direct Marketing: An Application of the CRISP-DM Methodology. Retrieved June 15, 2014, from http://repositorium.sdum.uminho.pt/handle/1822/14838.

Osei-Bryson, K.-M. and Giles, K. (2006). Splitting methods for decision tree induction: An exploration of the relative performance of two entropy-based families. *Information Systems Frontiers, 8*(3), 195–209.

Rocha, B. and De Sousa Junior, R. T. (2010). Identifying bank frauds using CRISP-DM and decision trees. *International Journal of computer science & Information Technology, 2*(5), 162–169.

Romer, D. (1993). Do students go to class? Should they? *Journal of Economic Perspectives*, 7(3),167–174.

Sembiring, S. et al. (2011). Prediction of student academic performance by an application of data mining techniques. *International Conference on Management and Artificial Intelligence*, 6.

Sharma, S. and Osei-Bryson, K. M. (2010). Toward an integrated knowledge discovery and data mining process model. *The Knowledge Engineering Review*, 25(1), 49–67.

Tremis, E. (2009). Closing the achievement gap: Breakthrough in the urban high school. University of Southern California. Retrieved June 20, 2013, from http://digitallibrary.usc.edu/cdm/ref/collection/p15799coll127/id/214963.

Vision 2030. (2009). Vision 2030 Jamaica National Development Plan. Retrieved June 30, 2014, from http://planipolis.iiep.unesco.org/upload/Jamaica/Jamaica_Vision_2030_Education_sector_plan.pdf.

DATA MINING ALGORITHMS

V

Chapter 15

Post-Pruning in Decision Tree Induction Using Multiple Performance Measures

Kweku-Muata Osei-Bryson

Contents

Abstract: The decision tree (DT) induction process has two major phases: the *growth phase* and the *pruning phase*. The *pruning phase* aims to generalize the DT that was generated in the *growth phase* by generating a sub-tree that avoids overfitting to the training data. Most post-pruning methods essentially address post-pruning as if it were a single-objective problem (i.e., maximize validation accuracy), and address the issue of simplicity (in terms of the number of leaves) only in the case of a tie. However, it is well known that apart from accuracy there are other performance measures (e.g., stability, simplicity, and interpretability) that are important for evaluating the DT quality. In this chapter, we propose that multiobjective evaluation be done during the *post-pruning phase* in order to select the best sub-tree, and propose a procedure for obtaining the optimal sub-tree based on user provided preferences and values.

Keywords: Decision Tree, post-pruning, performance measures, multi-criteria decision analysis, mixed integer programming, analytic hierarchy process

Introduction

The decision tree (DT) induction is one of the most popular data mining (DM) technique (e.g., Witten and Frank 2000), with applications in various fields. A DT is a tree structure representation of the given decision problem such that each nonleaf node is associated with one of the decision variables, each branch from a nonleaf node is associated with a subset of the values of the corresponding decision variable, and each leaf node is associated with a value of the target (or dependent) variable. There are two main types of DTs: (1) classification trees and (2) regression trees (RTs). For a classification tree, the target variable takes its values from a discrete domain, and for each leaf node, the DT associates a probability or each class (i.e., value of the target variable). The class that is assigned to a given leaf node of the classification tree results from a form of majority voting in which the winning class is the one that provides the largest class probability. On the other hand, the target variable of an RT takes its values from a continuous domain (numeric), and for each leaf, the RT associates the mean value of the target variable. In this chapter, we will focus on the classification tree, which is the most commonly used type of DT, and henceforth, in this chapter, whenever we use the term "decision tree" we will be referring to a classification tree.

There are two major phases of the DT induction process: the *growth phase* and the *pruning phase* (e.g., Kim and Koehler 1995). The *growth phase* involves a recursive partitioning of the training data resulting in a DT such that either each leaf node is associated with a single class or further partitioning of the given leaf would result in at least its child nodes being below some specified threshold. The *pruning phase* aims to generalize the DT that was generated in the *growth phase* by generating a sub-tree that avoids overfitting to the training data. The actions of the *pruning phase* is often referred to as "post-pruning" in contrast to *pre-pruning* that occurs during the *growth phase*, which aims to prevent splits that do not meet certain specified threshold (e.g., minimum number of observations for a split search and minimum number of observations for a leaf). In this chapter, we focus on the *post-pruning* activities that occur during the *pruning phase*.

Various approaches have been proposed for performing post-pruning (e.g., Almuallim 1996; Bohanec and Bratko 1994; Fournier and Cremilleux 2002; Li et al. 2001; Mingers 1987; Niblet and Bratko 1986; Quinlan 1987, 1993). Although some of these post-pruning approaches attempt to identify a sub-tree that gives the smallest error on the validation dataset (e.g., reduced error pruning method of Quinlan [1987]), others use an error estimate that is derived from training dataset only (e.g., minimum error pruning method of Niblet and Bratko [1986]). Some use a top-down approach (e.g., pessimistic error method of Quinlan [1987]), whereas others take a bottom-up approach (e.g., error-based pruning method of Quinlan [1993]). Some methods are suboptimal heuristics (e.g., Mingers 1987), whereas other methods produce optimal solutions (e.g., Almuallim 1996; Bohanec and Bratko 1994). It should be noted that several reviews on post-pruning methods (e.g., Esposito et al. 1997; Frank 2000) are available to the interested reader.

Overall, most of these methods attempt to generate the sub-tree that appears to have the best validation accuracy, and if multiple sub-trees appear to provide this value, then the sub-tree with the smallest number of leaves is selected. Thus, a sub-tree with a validation dataset accuracy rate of 0.959 and 29 leaves would be selected over a sub-tree with validation dataset accuracy rate of 0.958 and five leaves. Although some methods (e.g., Fournier and Cremilleux 2002) have attempted to address both simplicity and accuracy, most of these methods essentially address post-pruning as if it were a single objective problem (i.e., maximize validation accuracy), and address the issue of tree size (i.e., number of leaves) only in the case of a tie. However, it is well known that apart from accuracy there are other performance measures (e.g., stability, interpretability, and simplicity) that are important for evaluating the DT quality (e.g., Bradley 1997; Garofalakis et al. 2000; Han and Kamber 2001; Lim et. al. 2000; Provost and Fawcett 1998). It is also useful to note that even though traditional post-pruning methods focus on accuracy only, many may not even select the optimal sub-tree with regard to this measure. Kothari and Dong (2000) commented that the

> more popular pruning methods are based on removing a node (subtree) after the tree has been constructed. Of course, sequentially removing nodes is not without its drawbacks. In particular, there is considerable computational difficulty in evaluating high order removals (i.e. at each step the "least useful" node is removed, this corresponds to a greedy strategy, which may not be most optimal).

The approach that will be presented in this chapter can find the optimal sub-tree in the case where accuracy is the only performance measure or where several performance measures are to be simultaneously considered.

In a recent work (Osei-Bryson 2004), we presented a multicriteria approach for evaluating DTs that focused on the selection of the *best* DT in a set of generated DTs. In that work, the multicriteria evaluation was done after the *post-pruning phase* of the generation of each DT. A possible limitation of that approach is that the DTs that are selected for evaluation are those that were generated using traditional post-pruning approaches that did not consider all relevant performance measures. Thus, some strong candidate DTs might only be included in the set of those DTs that are to be compared if the DM project team retrieves them from the set of sub-trees that are generated in the traditional post-pruning phase. In this chapter, we propose that multiobjective evaluation be done during the *post-pruning phase* of the generation of each DT, in order to select the best sub-tree and propose a procedure for doing this. We, therefore, present a multiobjective mixed integer programming (MIP) formulation of the post-pruning problem that can be solved to obtain the optimal sub-tree based on user-provided preference and value function information.

Overview of Performance Measures for DTs

Various measures have been proposed for evaluating the performance of DTs, and some of these measures (e.g., accuracy, stability, and simplicity) are also relevant to the post-pruning process. It appears to us that the set of performance measures that are relevant for post-pruning are of two types: (1) those in which the value of the performance measure (e.g., accuracy rate) can be obtained simply using a weighted sum of the corresponding leaf level values and (2) those in which the value of the performance measure (e.g., simplicity) requires the use of a value function to transform the weighted sum of the corresponding leaf level values. In this chapter, we will be using the set of performance measures recently used by Osei-Bryson (2004). The reader should note that we do not claim that this set of performance measures is exhaustive or that each performance measure of this set is relevant in every situation, but rather that it does include both types of performance measures.

Accuracy

The most commonly used performance criterion for a DT is the predictive *accuracy rate*, ACC_V, based on the validation dataset. Let acc_{Tt} and acc_{Vt} be the accuracy rates of leaf t based on the training and validation datasets, respectively, and ρ_{Vt} be the proportion of validation cases associated with leaf t. The reader may observe that the validation accuracy rate $ACC_V = \sum_{t \in ILeaves} \rho_{Vt} acc_{Vt}$, the weighted sum of the validation accuracy rates of the leaves.

Stability

The *stability* performance criterion concerns our interest that there should not be much variation in this *predictive accuracy rate* when a DT is applied to different datasets. Thus, at a minimum, one might expect that there should not be much variation in predictive accuracy of the DT on the validation dataset when compared to that for the training dataset. Typically, there is no numeric performance measure for the stability property, but Osei-Bryson (2004) proposed a numeric measure of stability. The stability of leaf t based on the training and validation datasets can be defined as $stab_t = Min \{acc_{T_t}/acc_{V_t}, acc_{V_t}/acc_{T_t}\}$, where $stab_t \in (0, 1]$, with higher values indicates higher stability. Given this measure, the stability of the DT with regards to its performance on the training and validation datasets can be defined as $STAB_A = \sum_{t \in Leaves} \rho_{V_t} stab_t$, where $STAB_A \in (0, 1]$, with higher values of $STAB_A$ indicating higher stability. The reader may note $STAB_A$ is just the weighted sum of the stability of the individual leaves.

We could also assess whether the degree of stability of a given leaf is acceptable. Let τ_s be a threshold such that leaf t is considered to be sufficiently stable if $stab_t \geq \tau_s$, and unstable otherwise. We define the binary measure $stabbin_t(\tau_s)$, where $stabbin_t(\tau_s) = 1$, if $stab_t \geq \tau_s$, and 0 otherwise. $STAB_B(\tau_s)$, our second tree level stability measure, which is defined as $STAB_B(\tau_s) = \sum_{t \in Leaves} \rho_{V_t} stabbin_t(\tau_s)$. It is thus the weighted proportion of leaves that are considered to have an acceptable level of stability based on threshold τ_s.

Simplicity

Tree simplicity has also been considered by many researchers. For some, a measure of tree simplicity has been limited to the number of leaves in the DT (e.g., Shafer et al. 1996), whereas others have suggested that the sizes of the corresponding rules (i.e., number of predictor variables) are also relevant, particularly when the rules are to be applied by human beings rather than computers (e.g., Han and Kamber 2001).

Simplicity Based on Number of Leaves (SIMPL$_{Leaf}$)

Although it is often stated that with all else being approximately equal, the fewer the leaves the better, one should include a caveat with that statement as we are often not interested in a DT with only a single leaf and for other situations even a DT with two leaves might not be useful. For example, if two DTs have the same validation accuracy rate but one DT consists of a single node whereas the other consists of three leaves, then the second DT could be more useful than the first, but the post-pruning approach would select the first DT, which is essentially useless. This issue has also been recognized by other researchers such as Fournier and Cremilleux (2002), who believed that it is important to not "systematically discard a sub-tree whose classification error rate is equal to the rate of the root." It appears to us that for different end users and different DT problem instances, there may be different value functions that map the number of leaves to this simplicity measure. We assume that such a value function could have a continuous, concave piecewise linear representation. Let F be the set of leaves in the DT, we assume simplicity $SIMPL_{Leaf} = f_{Leaf}(|F|)$, where $f_{Leaf}(|F|)$ is a concave piecewise linear function (e.g., trapezoidal) such that $SIMPL_{Leaf} \in (0, 1]$, with higher values of $SIMPL_{Leaf}$ indicating higher simplicity.

Simplicity Based on Average Chain Length (SIMPL_Rule)

For a given rule, its length (i.e., number of predictor variables) provides a measure of the complexity of the rule. Therefore, another simplicity measure for the DT could be based on the average rule length of the rules in the DT. Some researchers (e.g., Fournier and Cremilleux 2002) have proposed post-pruning methods that include chain length (or node depth) as a performance measure, but typically these methods involve the assumption that smaller chain lengths are always better than larger chain lengths. However, in some situations, such an assumption may not be appropriate (e.g., end users may consider a DT that has multiple predictors for some or all rules to be superior to one that has a single predictor). We, therefore, take a more general approach.

Let Len_t be the rule length for rule $t \in I_{Leaves}$. The mean rule length of the DT could be defined as $Len_{Mean} = \sum_{t \in ILeaves} \rho_{Vt} len_t$, which is just the weighted sum of the length of each rule based on the validation dataset. The corresponding rule length-based simplicity measure is defined as $SIMPL_{Rule} = f_{Rule}(Len_{Mean})$, where $f_{Rule}(Len_{Mean})$ is a continuous, concave piecewise linear function such that $SIMPL_{Rule} \in (0, 1]$, with higher values of $SIMPL_{Rule}$ indicating higher simplicity.

Concave, Piecewise Linear Simplicity Value Functions

We assume each simplicity value function is continuous, piecewise linear, and concave. Because we assume that users will provide specification of each value function, we will be using the trapezoidal value function as it only requires the user to provide values for a small number of parameters. It should, however be noted that the solution approach that we are presenting in this chapter could, however, accommodate any continuous, piecewise linear value function.

We assume that our trapezoidal value function that has parameters CutOffBot, IdealBot, IdealTop, and CutOffTop with regard to the given simplicity measures (i.e., number of Leaves, average chain length):

- The DT would be considered to be ideal if $s \in$ [IdealBot, IdealTop].
- The DT would be considered to be unacceptable if $s \leq$ CutOffBot or $s \geq$ CutOffTop.
- The value of other acceptable DTs would be based on how well they compared with an ideal DT with regard to the s.

■ Given these assumptions, the value function SIMPL(s) can be defined as follows:

- $f(s) = 0$ if $s \leq$ CutOffBot or $s \geq$ CutOffTop
- $f(s) = (s\text{-CutOffBot})/(\text{IdealBot-CutOffBot})$ if CutOffBot $< s <$ IdealBot
- $f(s) = 1$ if IdealBot $\leq s \leq$ IdealTop
- $f(s) = (\text{CutOffTop-}s)/(\text{CutOffTop-IdealTop})$ if IdealTop $< s <$ CutOffTop

It is known that if $f(s)$ is a continuous, concave piecewise linear value function defined on the interval $[a_1, a_{Last}]$ with specified points $(a_r, f[a_r])$, where $a_1 < a_2 < \cdots < a_{Last}$, then for a given value "s" of our measure, using the convex combination formulation (e.g., Dantzig 1960; Keha et al. 2004) the corresponding value $f(s)$ can be obtained by solving the following MIP problem:

$$f(s) = \text{Max} \sum_{r \in [1,\text{Last}]} \lambda_r f(a_r)$$

s.t.

$$\sum_{r \in [1,\text{Last}]} \lambda_r a_r = s$$
$$\sum_{r \in [1,\text{Last}]} \lambda_r = 1$$
$$\lambda_1 \leq y_1$$
$$\lambda_r \leq y_{r-1} + y_r \qquad \forall \, r = 2, \ldots, (\text{Last} - 1)$$
$$\lambda_{\text{Last}} \leq y_{(\text{Last}-1)}$$
$$\sum_{r \in [1,(\text{Last}-1)]} y_r = 1$$
$$y_r \in \{0,1\} \qquad \forall \, r = 1, \ldots, (\text{Last} - 1)$$
$$\lambda_r \geq 0 \qquad \forall \, r = 1, \ldots, \text{Last}$$

The appendix presents an example of this MIP problem.

Discriminatory Power

Another measure that could affect the interpretability of the DT is the degree of discriminating power of the leaves. Ideally one would like to have leaves that are totally pure (i.e., for each leaf, all classes except one have zero probability) but in many cases, this does not occur and so, as was previously mentioned, the class that is associated with the leaf is simply the class with the largest frequency for the given leaf based on the training dataset. However, for a human being, a given rule might not be considered to be particularly useful if the probability of the assigned class is less than 50%. In general, for many users of a DT, the rule that is associated with a given leaf is only useful if the probability of the majority class is at least some specified cutoff value τ_d (>0.50). Thus, for some situations, a *discriminatory power* performance measure might also be appropriate for evaluating the performance of the DT. For a given predictive modeling problem, let τ be the cutoff value for the posterior probability such that the user would be comfortable with the decision associated with that leaf only if the posterior probability of the decision event (i.e., target event with the largest posterior probability based on the training data) was greater than or equal to τ_d. For leaf f, let $\text{dscpwr}_t(\tau_d) = 1$ if $\text{acc}_{Tt} \geq \tau_d$; and $\text{dscpwr}_t(\tau_d) = 0$ if $\text{acc}_{Tf} < \tau_d$. A fine measure of accuracy could be defined as: $\text{DSCPWR}(\tau_d) = \sum_{t \in \text{lLeaves}} \rho_{Vt} \text{dscpwr}_f(\tau_d)$, where $\text{DSCPWR}(\tau_d) \in [0, 1]$, with higher values of $\text{DSCPWR}(\tau_d)$ indicating higher discriminatory power.

Multiobjective Approach to Ranking the Sub-Trees

Post-pruning will result in the generation of a set of sub-trees, each with a performance vector $\boldsymbol{v_k} = (v_{k1}, v_{k2}, \ldots, v_{k|J|})$, where v_{kj} is Sub_DT$_k$'s score with regard to performance measure j, and J is the index set of the performance measures. Because each sub-tree has multiple performance measures then the problem of selecting the most appropriate sub-tree is in fact a multiple criteria decision-making (MCDM) problem.

Overview of MCDM Problems

In formal terms, MCDM problems are said to involve the prioritization of a set of alternatives in situations that involve multiple, sometimes conflicting criteria. MCDM problems may be addressed informally or formally. In the informal approaches, while there might be acknowledgment that multiple criteria are involved, there is either no formal identification of the relevant criteria, no formal approach to evaluation, or no formal approach to synthesis of each alternative's criteria ratings. Thus, unarticulated, implicit decision-making procedures are used to determine the ranking of the alternatives. In some cases, the use of these informal approaches amounts to pretending that a multiple criteria decision is in fact a single-criteria decision. It is, therefore, advisable to use formal approaches for addressing MCDM problems.

Although any formal model will suffer from the disadvantage of screening out some aspects of the decision-making problem, all alternatives can be treated consistently, evaluations can be reviewed, and the basis for the ranking of the alternatives can be articulated and justified within the context of the model. Various formal techniques have been proposed, including the weighing model, which is a popular formulation for MCDM and other problems (e.g., Hodgkin et al. 2004; Ngai 2003; Park and Han 2002) that have relative simplicity and intuitive appeal. In this chapter, we will focus on the weighing model formulation.

MCDM problems often have no single alternative that provides the best value for each criterion. Rather for each problem there is a set of alternatives that are said to be *nondominated*. An alternative is *nondominated* if there is no other alternative that outscores it with regard to each criterion. Given that MCDM problems do not in general have an objectively unique *best* alternative, then procedures for addressing these problems cannot *solve* them. Rather, such procedures aid the decision maker(s) in analyzing the given decision-making problem, and facilitate the identification of a ranking of the alternatives that is consistent with the decision maker's beliefs in the importance of the various criteria. Such a procedure is thus

often referred to as being a "multiple criteria decision aid." Multiple criteria decision aids that are based on the weighing model formulation to MCDA follow the
general procedure outlined as follows:

1. Identifying the relevant criteria and structuring the relationships between
   these criteria.
2. Determining the importance ratings (or weights) for the relevant criteria.
3. Specifying feasibility threshold values for the criteria.
4. Determining the score for each criterion for each alternative.
5. Eliminating alternatives that do not satisfy the criteria feasibility threshold values.
6. Computing the composite score for each alternative as the weighted sum of
   the alternative's scores with regard to the criteria.
7. Ranking the alternatives based on their composite scores.

Weighting Model

The weighting model formulation will involve implicitly computing each sub-tree's
composite score as the weighted sum of its performance with regard to the individual measures. Thus, for sub-tree "k," the composite score would be $s_k = \sum_{j \in J}$
$v_{kj} w_j$, where w_j is the weight of performance "j" for the given evaluation problem.
Given a pair of sub-trees and our set of weights, Sub_DT_h would be preferable to
Sub_DT_k if $s_h > s_k$.

An important assumption in weighting models is that the performance measures are independent, or at a minimum that they are not highly correlated. We
would expect this assumption to hold in our case. For example, while, in general,
the training accuracy rate is a nondecreasing function of the number of leaves, the
validation accuracy rate is not necessarily a nondecreasing function of the number
of leaves. It should be noted that our simplicity function for the leaf-based measure
is not a strictly decreasing function of the number of leaves but rather a trapezoidal
function. Further, it is possible to have multiple sub-trees with the same number
of leaves but different validation accuracy rates. In the same manner, it is possible
to have multiple sub-trees with the same number of leaves and the same validation
accuracy rates but different values for the stability measure.

Estimation of Weights

The weighing model obviously requires the specification of a set of nonnegative
weights for our performance measures. Various approaches are available for generating weights w_j from the subjective inputs of evaluators, both for individual and
group decision-making contexts, and for situations where the inputs are precise or
imprecise, including those that involve the use of pairwise comparison matrices
(e.g., Bryson 1995; Bryson and Joseph 1999, 2000; Bryson et al. 1995; Choo and
Wedley 2004; Fichtner 1986; Saaty 1980; Saaty and Vargas 1984). Some of these

techniques have been previously used to address various other problems in computer science and information systems (e.g., Monti and Carenini 2000; Ngai 2003; Osei-Bryson 2004; Park and Han 2002).

The use of these weight vector generation techniques requires estimates of the relative importance of pairs of performance measures, and result in a weight vector that is a synthesis of the input pairwise comparison information. A pairwise comparison matrix is $N \times N$ matrix $A = \{a_{ij}\}$, where a_{ij} is a positive rational number that is the numerical equivalent of the relative importance of object "i" compared to object "j." The pairwise comparison matrix A is said to be consistent if for each triple of objects (i, j, k) the equality $a_{ij} = a_{ik}a_{kj}$ holds; otherwise it is said to be inconsistent. Now because the matrix A is sometimes inconsistent, it is necessary to measure its level of inconsistency in order to determine if the resulting weight vector w will be meaningful. Consistency measures have been proposed by various researchers (e.g., Aguaron and Moreno-Jimenez 2003; Bryson 1995; Saaty 1980; Salo and Hämäläinen 1997). Some commercial MCDM software (e.g., Expert Choice) provides tools for elicitation of pairwise comparison data from evaluator(s), after which the associated consistency measure and weight vectors are automatically generated.

MIP for Post-Pruning with Multiple Measures

Multiobjective MIP Formulation

Let I be the index set of nodes in the *unpruned* DT, and $I_{Leaves} \subseteq I$ be the set of leaf nodes in this DT. For a given leaf node $t \in I_{Leaves}$, let $I_t \subset I$ be the set of all internal nodes plus node t that are on the path from the root node of the *unpruned* DT to leaf node t. Let x_i be a binary variable such that $x_i = 1$ if node i is included as a leaf node in the optimal sub-tree and $x_i = 0$ otherwise.

Given that our rule simplicity value function $f_{Leaf}(\sum_{i \in I} x_i)$ is a piecewise continuous linear function, we assume that

- $f_{Leaf}(\sum_{i \in I} x_i)$ is defined on the interval $[a_1, a_{LLast}]$ with "LLast" specified points $(a_\ell, f_{Leaf}[a_\ell])$, such that $a_1 < a_2 < \ldots < a_{LLast}$
- If $a_\ell \leq (\sum_{i \in I} x_i) \leq a_{\ell+1}$, then $\sum_{i \in I} x_i = \lambda_\ell a_\ell + \lambda_{\ell+1} a_{\ell+1}$, and $\lambda_\ell + \lambda_{\ell+1} = 1$, where both λ_ℓ and $\lambda_{\ell+1}$ are nonnegative.

Similarly, as our leaf simplicity value function $f_{Rule}(\sum_{i \in I} len_i x_i)$ is a piecewise continuous linear function, we assume that

- $f_{Rule}(\sum_{i \in I} len_i x_i)$ is defined on the interval $[b_1, b_{RLast}]$ with RLast specified points $(b_r, f_{Rule}[b_r])$, such that $b_1 < b_2 < \ldots < b_{RLast}$.
- If $b_r \leq (\sum_{i \in I} len_i x_i) \leq b_{r+1}$, then $\sum_{i \in I} len_i x_i = \gamma_\ell b_\ell + \gamma_{\ell+1} b_{\ell+1}$, and $\gamma_\ell + \gamma_{\ell+1} = 1$ where both γ_ℓ and $\gamma_{\ell+1}$ are nonnegative.

Also, let w_{ACC}, w_{STAB}, w_{DSCPWR}, w_{Leaf}, and w_{Rule} be the specified nonnegative weights associated with the accuracy, stability, discriminatory power, leaf simplicity, and rule simplicity measures, where $w_{ACC} + w_{STAB} + w_{DSCPWR} + w_{Leaf} + w_{Rule} = 1$.

Our multiobjective, MIP formulation of the DT post-pruning problem with multiple performance measures can be expressed as follows:

$P_{SubTree}$: Max $w_{ACC}ACC + w_{STAB}STAB_A + w_{DSCPWR}DSCPWR + w_{Leaf}SIMP_{Leaf} + w_{Rule}SIMP_{Rule}$ subject to

1: $\sum_{i \in It} x_i$ $= 1$ $\forall t \in I_{Leaves}$

2a: $\sum_{i \in I} x_i - \sum_{\ell \in [1, LLast]} \lambda_\ell a_\ell$ $= 0$

2b: $\sum_{\ell \in [1, LLast]} \lambda_\ell$ $= 1$

2c: $\lambda_1 \leq y_1$

2d: $\lambda_\ell \leq y_{\ell-1} + y_\ell$ $\forall \ell = 2, \ldots, (LLast - 1)$

2e: $\lambda_{Last} \leq y_{(LLast-1)}$

2f: $\sum_{\ell \in [1,(LLast-1)]} y_\ell = 1$

2g: $y_\ell \in \{0,1\}$ $\forall \ell = 1, \ldots, (LLast - 1)$

2h: $\sum_{\ell \in [1, RLast]} \lambda_r f_{Leaf}(a_r)$ $- SIMP_{Leaf}$ $= 0$

3a: $\sum_{i \in I} \rho_{Vi} len_i x_i - \sum_{r \in [1, RLast]} \gamma_r b_r$ $= 0$

3b: $\sum_{r \in [1, RLast]} \gamma_r$ $= 1$

3c: $\gamma_1 \leq z_1$

3d: $\gamma_r \leq z_{r-1} + z_r$ $\forall r = 2, \ldots, (RLast - 1)$

3e: $\gamma_{Last} \leq z_{(RLast-1)}$

3f: $\sum_{r \in [1,(RLast-1)]} z_r = 1$

3g: $z_r \in \{0,1\}$ $\forall r = 1, \ldots, (RLast - 1)$

3h: $\sum_{r \in [1,RLast]} \gamma_r f_{Rule}(b_r)$ $- SIMP_{Rule}$ $= 0$

4: $\sum_{i \in I} \rho_{Vi} acc_i x_i$ $- ACC$ $= 0$

5: $\sum_{i \in I} \rho_{Vi} stab_i x_i$ $- STAB_A$ $= 0$

6: $\sum_{i \in I} \rho_{Vi} dscpwr_i(\tau_d) x_i$ $- DSCPWR$ $= 0$

7: $x_i \in \{0, 1\}$ $\forall i \in I$

This problem has $(|I| + [LLast-1] + [RLast-1])$ binary variables, and $(|I_{Leaves}| + 2*7)$ constraints excluding those that are used to simplify the representation of the objective function (i.e., 2h, 3h, and 4–6) and to define the binary variables (i.e., 2g, 3g, and 7).

■ Constraint 1 ensures that for each path from the root to a leaf of the unpruned DT, exactly one node is selected as a leaf node for the optimal sub-tree. It should be noted that if node "i" is an internal node then $x_i = 1$ implies that sub-tree T_i has been pruned and replaced with node "i" as a leaf. Almuallim (1996) notes that "Pruning can be viewed as deciding for each node t_i in the initial decision tree whether or not that node is to be included in the final tree." Given our objective function, constraint 1 indicates that

- If $x_i = 1$ then node i is included as a leaf node in the optimal sub-tree.
- If $x_i = 0$, then either node i is an internal node of the optimal sub-tree, or it is not included in the optimal sub-tree. This follows from the fact that for each path from the root to a leaf node in the unpruned DT, a single node (say t) is selected to be a leaf in the optimal sub-tree (see constraint 1) and so $x_t = 1$. For other nodes "i" on this path $x_i = 0$. The ancestor nodes to the node "t" will be internal nodes in the optimal sub-tree while the corresponding descendant nodes are pruned and will not appear in the optimal sub-tree.

■ Constraints 2a–2h are used to determine the value (i.e., $SIMP_{Leaf}$) that corresponds to the number of leaves (i.e., $\sum_{i \in I} x_i$) in the optimal sub-tree. Similarly constraints 3a–3h are used to determine the value (i.e., $SIMP_{Rule}$) that corresponds to the average chain length (i.e., $\sum_{i \in I} len_i x_i$) in the optimal sub-tree. It should be noted that use of constraints similar to 2a–2h (and also 3a–3h) are well known in integer programming (IP) approaches for dealing with piecewise linear functions (e.g., $SIMP_{Leaf} = \{Max \sum_{\ell \in [1, RLast]} \lambda_r f_{Leaf}(a_r) \mid 2a–2h\}$).

■ Constraints 2h, 3h, and 4–6 are used to express the values of the accuracy, stability, discriminatory power, leaf simplicity, and rule simplicity performance measures, and as such could have been expressed directly in the objective function than as constraints. With regard to these constraints, we have taken this approach for comprehension purposes only.

Procedure for Generating the Optimal Sub-Tree

Step 1: Preparation
a. Specify the set of performance measures J.
b. Specify the values of the pre-pruning parameters (e.g., minimum number of cases per leaf, minimum number of cases for a split, maximum number of branches from a node, and maximum depth of tree).
c. If the stability measure $STAB_B$ is selected as a performance measure, specify the cutoff value τ_S for leaf stability.
d. If discriminatory power is selected as a performance measure, specify the cutoff value τ_D for leaf ambiguity.
e. Specify the value function for simplicity based on the number of leaves, and the value function for simplicity based on the chain lengths of the rules.
f. Specify relevant threshold values for the performance measures (e.g., sub-tree accuracy: ξ_{ACC}; sub-tree stability: ξ_{STAB}; sub-tree discriminatory power: ξ_{DSCPWR}; sub-tree leaf simplicity: ξ_{Leaf}; rule simplicity: ξ_{Rule}).

Step 2: Generate weights for performance measures
a. The evaluator(s) from the DM project team specifies numeric pairwise comparison data on relevant importance of pairs of performance measures. It is not necessary that a pairwise comparison entry be made for each pair of performance measures, but each performance measure must be included in at least one pairwise comparison.

b. Generate the corresponding normalized weight vector and consistency indicator using a weight vector generation technique (e.g., Bryson 1995; Bryson and Joseph 1999).

c. If the consistency indicator value is acceptable, then go to step 3, otherwise repeat step 2.

Step 3: Generate the *best* sub-tree

a. In the growth phase, generate the full DT that is consistent with the set of pre-pruning parameter values.

b. For each internal and leaf node of the unpruned DT, compute the values of relevant node level measures (e.g., ρ_{Vi}, $stab_i$, $leaf_i$, and $dscpwr_i[\tau_d]$).

c. Let problem $P_{SubTree-Aug}$ be the same as problem $P_{SubTree}$ but which also includes any relevant threshold constraints (e.g., $ACC \geq \xi_{ACC}$). Formulate and solve problem $P_{SubTree-Aug}$, resulting in the identification of the "best" sub-tree.

Illustrative Example

Our example involves generating a DT that describes a set of clusters of the Abalone dataset of the UCI Irvine machine library (Murphy and Aha 1994).

Step 1: Preparation

a. **Specify parameters for the growth phase of DT induction**

In discussion with the end users, the DM analyst was able to determine that the minimum number of cases per leaf parameter should be set to 20, and the minimum number of cases for a split parameter should be set to 40.

b. **Specify the simplicity value functions**

For each simplicity measure, it was determined that it could be adequately represented by a trapezoidal value function that has parameters CutOffBot, IdealBot, IdealTop, and CutOffTop. We assume that the values presented in Table 15.1 have been specified for the relevant value functions.

c. **Specify the leaf-level cutoff values and the tree-level threshold values**

In discussion with the end users, the DM analyst was able to determine the cutoff value for leaf stability is $\tau_S = 0.90$; the cutoff value for leaf ambiguity is $\tau_D = 0.75$; the threshold value for the sub-tree validation accuracy was $\xi_{ACC} = 0.90$; the threshold value for the sub-tree discriminatory power is $\xi_{DSCPWR} = 0.75$; and the threshold value for the sub-tree stability $STAB_A$ is $\xi_{STAB} = 0.90$; if a sub-tree did not have positive values for $SIMPL_{Leaf}$ and

Table 15.1 Parameter Values for Simplicity Measures

Simplicity Measure	CutOffBot	IdealBot	IdealTop	CutOffTop
Number of leaves	2	3	6	9
Average chain length	1.50	1.75	2.50	3.50

$SIMPL_{Leaf}$, then it should be excluded no matter how well it performed with regard to the other measures (Figures 15.1a and 15.1b).

Step 2: Generation of weights for the performance measures

Elicitation of preference information on the relative importance of the performance measures resulted in the weight vector displayed in Table 15.2. The consistency indicator had a value of 0.964, indicating that the input pairwise comparison data is highly consistent.

Step 3: Generate the *best* sub-tree

The full DT was generated in the growth phase in a manner that was consistent with the set of parameter values, after which the values of relevant node level measures (e.g., ρ_{Vi}, $stab_i$, $leaf_i$, $dscpwr_i[\tau_d]$) were computed. Table 15.3 displays the values for each internal and leaf node of the DT that that was generated in the *growth phase*. The leaf nodes are highlighted (Figure 15.2).

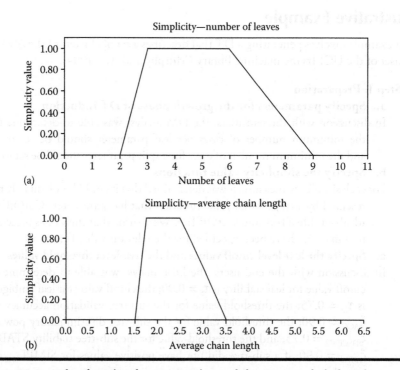

Figure 15.1 Value function for (a) tree size and (b) average chain length.

Table 15.2 Weight Vector

ACC	DSCPWR	STAB_A	SIMPL_Rule	SIMPL_Leaf
0.252763	0.203765	0.246988	0.150937	0.145547

Table 15.3   Values of Node Level Performance Measures

Node i	VN	acc_{Vi}	acc_{Ti}	len_i	$stab_i$	$stabbin_i(\tau_s)$	$dscpwr_i(\tau_d)$	ρ_{Vi}
1	449	0.961	0.969	1	0.992	1.000	1.000	0.430
11	413	0.998	0.988	2	0.990	1.000	1.000	0.396
111	399	1.000	0.995	3	0.995	1.000	1.000	0.383
112	14	0.923	0.786	3	0.852	0.000	1.000	0.013
12	17	0.872	1.000	2	0.872	0.000	1.000	0.016
13	19	0.349	0.526	2	0.663	0.000	0.000	0.018
131	6	0.571	1.000	3	0.571	0.000	1.000	0.006
132	13	0.864	0.692	3	0.801	0.000	0.000	0.012
2	78	0.628	0.731	1	0.859	0.000	0.000	0.075
21	13	0.842	0.615	2	0.730	0.000	0.000	0.012
22	16	0.586	0.566	2	0.966	1.000	0.000	0.015
23	49	0.900	0.878	2	0.976	1.000	1.000	0.047
231	13	0.714	0.692	3	0.969	1.000	0.000	0.012
232	25	1.000	0.920	3	0.920	1.000	1.000	0.024
233	11	0.955	1.000	3	0.955	1.000	1.000	0.011
3	526	0.985	0.986	1	0.999	1.000	1.000	0.504
31	4	0.524	0.750	2	0.699	0.000	1.000	0.004
32	27	0.942	0.852	2	0.904	1.000	1.000	0.026
321	10	0.864	0.700	3	0.810	0.000	0.000	0.010
322	17	1.000	0.941	3	0.941	1.000	1.000	0.016
33	485	0.998	1.000	2	0.998	1.000	1.000	0.465
331	20	0.976	1.000	3	0.976	1.000	1.000	0.019
3311	13	1.000	1.000	4	1.000	1.000	1.000	0.012
3312	7	0.950	1.000	4	0.950	1.000	1.000	0.007
332	13	0.963	1.000	3	0.963	1.000	1.000	0.012
333	452	1.000	1.000	3	1.000	1.000	1.000	0.433

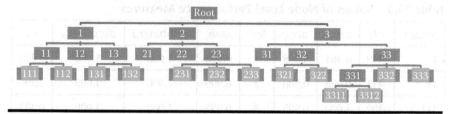

Figure 15.2 Unpruned DT.

Problem $P_{\text{SubTree-Aug}}$, which is the same as problem P_{SubTree} but which also includes any relevant threshold constraints (i.e., ACC $\geq$ 0.90; $STAB_A \geq$ 0.90; DSCPWR $\geq$ 0.75; $SIMPL_{\text{Leaf}} >$ 0.00; and $SIMPL_{\text{Rule}} >$ 0.00), was formulated and solved for two different weight vectors: (a) 1.00000, 0.00000, 0.00000, 0.00000, and 0.00000, which corresponds to the traditional approach to post-pruning that considers accuracy as the only objective and (b) 0.252763, 0.203765, 0.246988, 0.150937, and 0.145547, which is the weight vector that was generated in step 2. It should be noted that in generating the pruned DT1a and DT2a, we did not include the threshold constraints, as they are not used in the traditional approach to post-pruning, but in generating DT1b and DT2b we included the threshold constraints. The reader may note that DT2a and DT2b are the same, demonstrating that for some situations it is the weight vector and not the threshold constraints that determines which nodes are pruned (see Figures 15.3 through 15.5) (Tables 15.4 and 15.5).

Conclusion

In this chapter, we have proposed that approaches to post-pruning should explicitly factor in multiple performance measures that are relevant to evaluating the quality of a DT and which would be available at the time that post-pruning occurs. We have thus presented a multiobjective formulation of the post-pruning problem

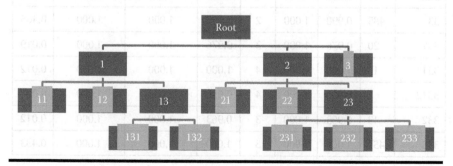

Figure 15.3 Pruned DT1a—traditional post-pruning.

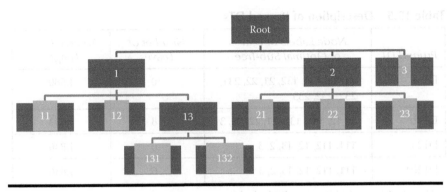

Figure 15.4 Pruned DT1b—traditional post-pruning + thresholds.

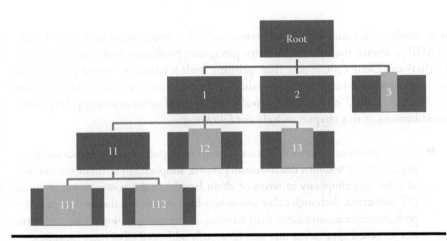

Figure 15.5 Pruned DT2a—post-pruning using multiple measures.

Table 15.4 Input Weight and Corresponding Output Performance Vectors

Pruned DT	Weight Vector (ACC, DSCPWR, STAB$_A$, SIMPL$_{Rule}$, SIMPL$_{Leaf}$)	Performance Vector of Optimal Pruned DT					
		ACC	STABa	STABb	SIMP$_{Leaf}$	SIMP$_{Rule}$	DSPWR
DT1a	(1.00000, 0.00000, 0.00000, 0.00000, 0.00000)	0.983	0.991	0.963	0.000	0.320	0.957
DT1b[a]		0.982	0.993	0.963	0.333	0.132	0.969
DT2a	(0.252763, 0.203765, 0.246988, 0.150937, 0.145547)	0.959	0.986	0.887	1.000	1.000	0.917
DT2b[a]		0.959	0.986	0.887	1.000	1.000	0.917

[a] Threshold constraints were included

Table 15.5 Description of Pruned DTs

Pruned DT	Node Labels of Leaves of Optimal Sub-Tree	Number of Leaves	Average Chain Length
DT1a	11, 12, 131, 132, 21, 22, 231, 232, 232, 233	10	1.580
DT1b[a]	11, 12, 131, 132, 21, 22, 23, 3	8	1.533
DT2a	111, 112, 12, 13, 2, 3	6	1.836
DT2b[a]	111, 112, 12, 13, 2, 3	6	1.836

[a] Threshold constraints were included.

that involves elicitation of the preference and value functions of user, and the use of MIP to obtain the optimal sub-tree given user preference and value functions. Kothari and Dong (2000) note that "pruning itself is based on a greed strategy and as such cannot guarantee the optimality of the solution or a vicinity of a solution to the optimal one," our approach involves an optimal solution strategy. Important contributions of this chapter include the following:

- Simultaneous consideration of a set of multiple important performance measures (e.g., accuracy, stability, discriminatory power, simplicity in terms of the number of rules, and simplicity in terms of chain length) in the post-pruning phase of DT induction. Although other researchers have established the need to consider performance measures other than accuracy in the post-pruning phase, they have not proposed approaches that simultaneously addressed all of these measures.
- Provision for the automatic generation of the values of these performance measures, stability and simplicity in particular, based on user-specified value functions.
- Allowing the user the opportunity to specify user-defined value functions for simplicity. It should be noted that none of the previously proposed approaches to post-pruning offers this opportunity. Although we have used trapezoidal value functions in our illustrative example, the algorithms allows for the use of any continuous, piecewise linear value function. It should be noted that many nonlinear continuous functions can be reasonably approximated by continuous, piecewise linear functions. Further, the proposed approach provides significantly more flexibility than the current approach of using an implicit linear function for simplicity.
- Allowing the user the opportunity to specify the preference structure that is used in the determination of the most appropriate sub-tree. Again, it should be noted that none of the previously proposed approaches to post-pruning offers this opportunity.

Some readers might wonder why we did not use one of the traditional post-pruning algorithms or some other recursive algorithm. If all the performance measures were decomposable on the leaves (i.e., what happens at one leaf does not affect the others), then it might be possible to adopt such an approach. However, two of the performance measures (i.e., simplicity in terms of the number of rules and simplicity in terms of chain length) are not decomposable on the leaves and so such approaches are not appropriate. It should also be noted that our post-pruning algorithm could take the output of any tree growing algorithm and do post-pruning based on multiple performance measures, value functions, and preference structure as specified by the given user.

We have established that our multiobjective MIP problem can be solved in polynomial time. Further, instances of this problem are expected to be relatively small in terms of the number of nodes of the unpruned DT by IP standards and can be efficiently solved by many IP solvers. Further various pre-pruning techniques (e.g., Garofalalis et al. 2000) are also available to ensure that the DT that results from the *growth phase* are relatively small. Thus, if necessary our multiobjective MIP approach can be applied in situations in which the *growth phase* involves aggressive approaches to pre-pruning (e.g., Garofalalis et al. 2000).

Acknowledgment

Material in this chapter previously appeared in: "Post-pruning in decision tree induction using multiple performance measures," *Computers & Operations Research* **34:11** (2007), 3331–3345.

References

Aguaron, J. and Moreno-Jiménez, J. M. (2003). The geometric consistency index: Approximated thresholds. *European Journal of Operational Research* **147:1**, 137–145.

Almuallim, H. (1996) "An Algorithm for the Optimal Pruning of Decision Trees," *Artificial Intelligence* **83:2**, 347–362.

Bohanec, M. and Bratko, I. (1994) "Trading Accuracy for Simplicity in Decision Trees," *Machine Learning* **15**, 223–250.

Bradley, A. (1997) "The Use of Area under ROC Curve in the Evaluation of Machine Learning Algorithms," *Pattern Recognition Letters* **30:7**, 1145–1159.

Bryson, N. (1995) "A Goal Programming for Generating Priority Vectors," *Journal of the Operational Research Society* **46**, 641–648.

Bryson, N., Mobolurin, A., and Ngwenyama, O. (1995) "Modelling Pairwise Comparisons on Ratio Scales," *European Journal of Operational Research* **83**, 639–654.

Bryson, N. (K.-M.) and Joseph, A. (1999) "Generating Consensus Priority Point Vectors," *Computers & Operations Research* **26**, 637–643.

Bryson, N. (K.-M.) and Joseph, A. (2000) "Generating Consensus Priority Interval Vectors for Group Decision Making in the AHP," *Journal of Multi-Criteria Decision Analysis* **9:4**, 127–137.

Choo, E. and Wedley, W. (2004) "A Common Framework for Deriving Preference Values from Pairwise Comparison Matrices," *Computers & Operations Research 31*, 893–908.

Dantzig, G. (1960) "On the Significance of Solving Linear Programming Problems with Some Integer Variables," *Econometrica 28*, 30–44.

Esposito, F., Malerba, D., and Semeraro, G. (1997) "A Comparative Analysis of Methods for Pruning Decision Trees," *IEEE Transactions on Pattern Analysis and Machine Intelligence 19:5*, 476–491.

Fichtner, J. (1986) "On Deriving Priority Vectors from Matrices of Pairwise Comparisons," *Socio-Economic Planning Sciences 20:6*, 399–405.

Fournier, D. and Cremilleux, B. (2002) "A Quality Index for Decision Tree Pruning" *Knowledge-Based Systems 15*, 37–43.

Frank, E. (2000) "Pruning Decision Trees and Lists," Ph.D. Dissertation, Department of Computer Science, University of Waikato, Hamilton, New Zealand.

Han, J. and Kamber, M. (2001) *Data Mining: Concepts and Techniques*, Morgan Kaufmann, New York.

Hodgkin, J., Pedro, J., and Burstein, F. (2004) "Quality of Data Model for Supporting Mobile Decision Making," *Proceedings of the 2004 IFIP TC8/WG8.3 International Conference: Decision Support in an Uncertain and Complex World*, 372–379.

Keha, A., de Farias, I., and Nemhauser, G. (2004) "Models for Representing Piecewise Linear Cost Functions," *Operations Research Letters 32*, 44–48.

Kim, H. and Koehler, G. (1995) "Theory and Practice of Decision Tree Induction," *Omega 23:6*, 637–652.

Kothari, R. and Dong, M. (2000) "Decision Trees for Classification: A Review and Some New Results," in S. Pal and A. Pal (editors), *Lecture Notes in Pattern Recognition*, World Scientific Publishing Company, Singapore.

Li, X.-B., Sweigart, J., Teng, J., Donohue, J., and Thombs, L. (2001) "A Dynamic Programming Based Pruning Method for Decision Trees," *INFORMS Journal on Computing 13:4*, 332–344.

Lim, T.-S., Loh, W.-Y., and Shih, Y.-S. (2000) "A Comparison of Prediction Accuracy, Complexity, and Training Time of Thirty-Three Old and New Classification Algorithms," *Machine Learning 40*, 203–228.

Mingers, J. (1987) "Expert Systems—Rule Induction with Statistical Data," *Journal of the Operational Research Society 38*, 39–47.

Monti, S. and Carenini, G. (2000) "Dealing with the Expert Inconsistency in Probability Elicitation," *IEEE Transactions on Knowledge and Data Engineering 12:4*, 499–508.

Murphy, P. M. and Aha, D. W. (1994). *UCI Repository of Machine Learning Databases*, University of California, Department of Information and Computer Science, Irvine, CA.

Ngai, E. (2003) "Selection of Web Sites for Online Advertising Using the AHP," *Information and Management 40*, 233–242.

Niblet, T. and Bratko, I. (1986) "Learning Decision Rules in Noisy Domains," *Proceedings of Expert Systems 86*, 25–34.

Osei-Bryson, K.-M. (2004) "Evaluation of Decision Trees: A Multi-Criteria Approach," *Computers & Operations Research 31:11*, 1933–1945.

Park, C.-S. and Han, I. (2002) "A Case-Based Reasoning with the Feature Weights Derived by Analytic Hierarchy Process for Bankruptcy Prediction," *Expert Systems with Applications 23:3*, 255–264.

Quinlan, J. (1987) "Simplifying Decision Trees," *International Journal of Man-Machine Studies 27*, 221–234.

Quinlan, J. (1993) *C4.5: Programs for Machine Learning*, Morgan Kaufmann, San Mateo, CA.

Saaty, T. (1980) *The Analytic Hierarchy Process: Planning, Priority Setting, Resource Allocation*, McGraw-Hill, New York.

Saaty, T. and L. Vargas (1984) "Comparison of Eigenvalue, Logarithmic Least Squares and Least Squares Methods in Estimating Ratios," *Mathematical Modelling* **5**, 309–324.

Salo, A. A. and Hämäläinen, R. P. (1997). On the measurement of preferences in the analytic hierarchy process. *Journal of Multi-Criteria Decision Analysis* **6:6**, 309–319.

Shafer, J., Agrawal, R., and Mehta, M. (1996) "SPRINT: A Scalable Parallel Classifier for Data Mining," *Proceedings of the 22nd International Conference on Very Large Data Bases*, Mumbai, India, September, 544–555.

Witten, I. and Frank, E. (2000) *Data Mining: Practical Machine Learning Tools and Techniques with Java Implementations*, Morgan Kaufmann, San Francisco, CA.

Appendix

Given the set of points specified in the following table, we provide the corresponding MIP representation that could be used to compute the value of s, based on the value function $f(\cdot)$.

R	a_r	$f(a_r)$
1	1.00	0.00
2	1.50	0.00
3	1.75	1.00
4	2.50	1.00
5	3.50	0.00
6	20.00	0.00

$f(s) = \text{Max } \lambda_3 + \lambda_4$

s.t.

$$\lambda_1 + 1.5\lambda_2 + 1.75\lambda_3 + 2.50\lambda_4 + 3.50\lambda_5 + 20.0\lambda_6 = s$$
$$\lambda_1 + \lambda_2 + \lambda_3 + \lambda_4 + \lambda_5 + \lambda_6 = 1$$
$$\lambda_1 - y_1 \leq 0$$
$$\lambda_2 - y_1 - y_2 \leq 0$$
$$\lambda_3 - y_2 - y_3 \leq 0$$
$$\lambda_4 - y_3 - y_4 \leq 0$$
$$\lambda_5 - y_4 - y_5 \leq 0$$
$$\lambda_6 - y_5 \leq 0$$
$$y_1 + y_2 + y_3 + y_4 + y_5 = 1$$
$$y_1 \in \{0,1\}; y_2 \in \{0,1\}; y_3 \in \{0,1\}; y_4 \in \{0,1\}; y_5 \in \{0,1\}$$
$$\lambda_r \geq 0 \qquad \forall\, r = 1, \ldots, 6$$

Chapter 16

Selecting Classifiers for an Ensemble—An Integrated Ensemble Generation Procedure

Kweku-Muata Osei-Bryson

Contents

Abstract: Classifiers are being increasingly used in many modern organizations. For some time, it has been well known that for some datasets, a combination of individually trained classifiers can give better performance than any of the individual classifiers. This realization has led to the development of various techniques for generating ensembles that typically involve using some form of weighted or unweighted voting to combine the given set of candidate classifiers. In this chapter, we are concerned with ensembles that may include multiple classifier types (e.g., decision tree, neural network, and regression), and in which not every candidate classifier is automatically included in the ensemble. We present an integrated ensemble generation procedure (IEGP) that allows for the generation and evaluation of multiple ensembles using multiple mathematical programming (MP) formulations as well as heuristic approaches.

Keywords: Data mining, classification, ensemble, decision tree, mathematical programming

Introduction

Data mining (DM) techniques are being increasingly used in many modern organizations to retrieve valuable knowledge structures from organizational databases, including data warehouses. DM predictive models either involve the use of a discrete target variable or a continuous target variable. If the target variable is discrete, then the predictive model is referred to as a "classifier." There are various types of predictive classifiers, including decision trees (DTs), artificial neural networks (ANNs), and logistic regression (e.g., Au et al. 2012; Cao et al. 2011). For a given dataset, it is possible to induce multiple classifiers of different types, some of which may have different overall accuracy rates as well as different results with regard to any given example. Many DM software packages (e.g., C5.0, SAS Enterprise Miner, and IBM Intelligent Miner) provide facilities that make the generation of classifiers a relatively easy task.

For some time (e.g., Bauer and Kohavi 1999; Breiman 1996; Freund and Schapire 1996), it has been well known that for some datasets, a combination (i.e., ensemble) of individually trained predictive classifiers (i.e., base classifiers) can give better accuracy than any of the base classifiers. This realization has led to the development of various techniques for generating ensembles, including bagging (e.g., Breiman 1996) and boosting (e.g., Freund and Schapire 1996). Typically, these ensemble techniques use some form of weighted or unweighted voting to combine base classifiers (Dietterich 2000). Some limitations of previous approaches are that they focus on a single type of base classifier (Opitz and Maclin 1997), and in some cases include each candidate base classifier in the ensemble, with only poorly performing base classifiers being excluded. In this chapter, we are concerned with ensembles that may include multiple base classifier types, and in which not every good base classifier is automatically included in the ensemble. Our research problem involves the identification of an appropriate subset of the base classifiers for inclusion in the ensemble. We address this in two parts, namely, (1) an approach for generating candidate ensembles and (2) an approach for selecting the strongest of the candidate ensembles. Similar to Adem and Gochet (2004) and Zhang et al. (2006), we allow for the use of mathematical programming (MP) to generate ensembles. We, however, present multiple MP formulations of the ensemble generation problem, and a procedure that allows for the generation and evaluation of multiple ensembles using multiple MP formulations as well as heuristic approaches (e.g., Ulas et al. 2009). Our approach also acknowledges the stochastic nature of the accuracy of a classifier.

Overview of Ensembles

It has been known for some time (e.g., Banfield et al. 2005; Breiman 1996) that the following two points are considered for an ensemble to give a strong performance: (1) each constituent base classifier should be competent and (2) the constituent base classifiers should be complementary to each other, so that there is a great likelihood that whenever some of the classifiers make an error, the other classifiers make the correct prediction.

The goal of ensemble construction is thus to identify a set of base classifiers that are competent but complementary (i.e., uncorrelated) classifiers. Within this context, several issues are relevant, including whether to use multiple types of classifiers, which subset of the classifiers to include, and the weights that should be applied to the base classifiers.

Type(s) of Classifiers

Research on the generation of ensembles has typically focused on using a single type of learning algorithm (e.g., DT or regression or ANN or naïve Bayes) to generate the candidate classifiers. A popular early approach for generating ensembles involves re-sampling the training data and fitting a separate base classifier for each sample using a single modeling technique. Two popular methods that fit into this approach are boosting and bagging.

1. Boosting (e.g., Freund and Schapire 1996) involves the creation of an ensemble of uncorrelated classifiers using the same induction algorithm (e.g., DT induction) on subsets of the data, each obtained by sampling with replacement from the full training dataset, where all observations are unequally weighted in the sampling process such that incorrectly classified observations are preferentially sampled in later iterations of the sampling process.
2. Bagging (e.g., Breiman 1996) is similar to boosting except that in the sampling process of the bagging method there is no preferential sampling and so all observations are equally weighted.

However, it is known that in some situations the use of multiple types of classifiers (e.g., DT, regression, ANN, and naïve Bayes) could result in an ensemble that outperforms an ensemble produced using a single type of classifier (i.e., DT only). For example, Ulas et al. (2009) reported that "In constructing ensembles, the most critical factor is to have classifiers that are accurate and diverse. Our experiments have shown that the best way for this is to use different algorithms."

Combination Method

Several methods (e.g., Banfield et al. 2005; Caruana et al. 2004; Hansen 1999; Kittler et al. 1998; Tax et al. 2000; Wood et al. 2000) have been proposed for combining the predictions of the base classifiers, including linear combination (e.g., majority vote [MV] and averaging) and fixed rules (e.g., median, minimum, and product). Previous research suggests that no combination method provides the best performance on all datasets. Thus, although in many situations, the majority voting method is robust to noise and works very well (e.g., Ulas et al. 2009), it has been reported that for classification problems involving more than two classes, the product rule outperforms the MV rules (e.g., Tax et al. 2000). Ulas et al. (2009) also reported that in their experiment: "We have also seen that it is better to combine classifiers with soft outputs (for example, posterior probabilities) rather than 0/1 decisions. ... soft outputs allow representing confidence and provide more information to the combiner." In this chapter, we present methods that are based on MV and averaging of soft outputs (in the form of posterior probabilities).

1. Majority vote
   For a given observation, the predicted class is the one that is predicted by the majority of the constituent base classifiers.
2. Averaging
   i. For a given observation, the predicted class is that, which has the largest average posterior probability based on the constituent classifiers.
   ii. Only classifiers that generate posterior probabilities can be used with this method.

Classifiers That Can Be Included in the Ensemble

Early approaches involved including all generated base classifiers, in some cases, with unequal weights. It is, however, known that in some situations, some classifiers are either redundant or perform poorly. As noted by Ulas et al. (2009), "Care should be taken that classifiers that are to be combined are both accurate and diverse and that they are combined appropriately; otherwise we will just pay without any significant gain." Zhou et al. (2002) demonstrated that in some situations, a subset of the classifiers might outperform the full set. Hence, it is important to determine whether a given classifier adds value to the ensemble.

An incremental approach (e.g., Caruana et al. 2004; Ulas et al. 2009) is sometimes used to generate the subset of classifiers. The bottom-up version of the incremental approach involves selecting the best performing classifier as the initial classifier. In the succeeding iterations, the classifier whose inclusion in the ensemble would lead to the best improvement in the performance of the ensemble is added to the ensemble. This is similar to an approach in bottom-up (i.e., agglomerative) hierarchical clustering where the pair of clusters that is merged is the one that is locally *best* in terms of its impact on the objective function. A top-down (i.e., divisive) version of the incremental approach involves at the first iteration including all candidate base classifiers, and in succeeding iterations removing the base classifier whose exclusion would lead to the best improvement in the performance of the ensemble. The incremental approach can be considered to be a greedy suboptimal approach. The mixed integer programming (IP) approaches that are presented in this chapter can be considered to be a generalization of both incremental approaches.

Determination of the Weights for the Classifiers

In combination approaches that involve weighting, the higher the weight for a base classifier, the more that base classifier is trusted to provide the correct answer. Several approaches have been proposed for assigning weights to the base classifiers including the following:

1. Having equal weights for all candidate classifiers, such as in bagging.
2. Using the relative performance of the base classifier on its training dataset to determine its weight. Thus, a classifier with lower error (e.g., minimum square error and error rate) would have a higher weight.
3. Applying data envelopment analysis (e.g., Sohn and Choi 2001).

Ueda (2000) noted that many of the proposed methods involve approach type (b), often involving the minimum square error, and that while this approach type might appear to be promising, it has some significant problems that were also noted earlier by Breiman (1996):

> this approach poses two serious problems in practice: 1) The data is used both in the training of each predictor and in the estimation of $a^{(k)}$, and 2) individual predictors are often strongly correlated since they try to predict the same task. Because of these problems, the generalizaton will be poor.

In the approach proposed in this chapter, the classifiers could be generated using different training datasets with the caveat that the training sets used to generate the base classifiers do not overlap with any ensemble training dataset and any ensemble assessment (EA) dataset.

Selection of Training Dataset

In developing any predictive model, it is important that the generated model should not be overfitted to the training dataset, and so the model dataset is at a minimum partitioned into training and validation datasets. Within this context, while it may appear advantageous to use large training datasets, as more information would be available to determine an appropriate model during the construction phase, several researchers (e.g., Hand 1998; Smyth 2001) have noted that such an approach could result in spurious nongeneralizable associations appearing to be significant. This observation has motivated some researchers (e.g., Fu et al. 2003; Lutu and Engelbrecht 2006, 2010) to use multiple relatively small training datasets, each of which was obtained by sampling from the original training dataset. It should be noted that the approach presented in this chapter also involves sampling to form multiple relatively small ensemble training datasets.

Scoring and Posterior Probabilities

Some types of classifier models (e.g., regression, DT, and ANNs) generate for each observation a posterior probability for each class, $\rho_{ijr(c)}$ is the posterior probability each class $c \in C$ for observation "i" based on classifier "r." The class $c_{(i)}$ that is assigned by base classifier "r" to observation "i" is the one that provides the largest class probability, $\rho_{ijr(c(i))} = \text{Max} \{\rho_{ijr(c)}, c \in C\}$, even if $\rho_{ijr(c(i))} \leq 0.50$.

Associated with each base classifier "r" is a scoring code that when applied to any dataset, say EL_j, that has the same set of input variables as the dataset that was used to build the classifier, will for observation "i" generate posterior probabilities $p_{ijr(c)}$, for each class $c \in C$. It should be noted that for each candidate base classifier "r," it is sufficient to apply its *scoring code* to each *ensemble learning (EL)* dataset (say EL_j) exactly once and to each *ensemble assessment* dataset (say EA_k) exactly once in order to generate the class posterior probabilities for the given dataset.

Proposed Solution Approach

Partitioning the Model Dataset

Typically, the DM process for developing a classifier involves partitioning the model dataset into two major components learning (which is broken down into training and validation datasets) and assessment (i.e., test datasets). In the case of DT induction, an overfitted DT is generated using the training dataset, and the validation (or pruning) dataset is used to prune this overfitted DT in order to reduce the chance of overfitting. The training and validation datasets play a similar role in the development of regression classifiers. Thus, for each of these techniques, the selection of the final base classifier is dependent on both the training and validation datasets, but is independent of the test (assessment) dataset that is used to evaluate the generalization accuracy of the classifier.

In this chapter, we take the position that the ensemble should have its own training and assessment (evaluation) datasets. We use multiple ensemble training datasets to generate multiple ensembles and multiple EA datasets to evaluate each of the ensembles. In our approach, the base classifiers could be generated using different training datasets with the caveat that the training sets that are used to generate the base classifiers do not overlap with any ensemble training dataset and any EA dataset.

We, therefore, partition the model dataset into three major nonoverlapping components: *individual learning (IL)*, *EL*, and *EA* (Figure 16.1). Although the generation of each base classifier will involve data from the IL component only, we allow for the situation in which the actual training and validation sets for any two such base classifiers may not be the same. In order to generate ensembles, sampling will be done on the *EL* component.

Fu et al. (2003) in an interesting work demonstrated that on very large datasets, their sampling-based approach could give superior performance than the traditional approach of using all the training data (i.e., *IL*) to construct a single DT. Other researchers (e.g., Lutu and Engelbrecht 2006, 2010) also adopted a similar approach of generating multiple small training datasets. We will adopt a similar approach and use a stratified sampling with replacement based on the target variable in order to generate several relatively small subsets (say EL_j) of the EL

Model dataset									
Individual learning (IL)		Ensemble learning (EL)				Ensemble assessment (EA)			
Training	Validation	EL_1	EL_2	...	$EL_{|J|}$	EA_1	EA_2	...	$EA_{|K|}$

Figure 16.1 Partitioning of model dataset.

component and several subsets (EA_k) of the EA component. Each EL_j will be used to generate an ensemble EM_j, and in some situations, identical ensembles may be generated for different EL_j. Such an outcome would be viewed as being desirable, but is not guaranteed, and for at least this reason, there is the need to have a process for selecting the ensemble EM_j that provides the *best* generalization accuracy rate. Given the fact that the generalization accuracy rate is known to be a random variable, similar to Fu et al. (2003), each EM_j will be evaluated against multiple assessment sets, in our cases against all EA_k.

It should be noted that our approach has some similarity to that of Ulas et al. (2009) who state that: " ... a trained combiner needs its own training data which should be distinct from the data used to train the classifiers. If a model selection is to be done for the combiner, it also needs its own validation data." It also has some similarity to the method of Adem and Gochet (2004) who state that "In data rich conditions, a methodological sound approach ... would be to divide the available data at random into three independent datasets: one to design the component classifiers, one to design the aggregated classifier and one data set to evaluate both the component and aggregated classifiers." Our approach differs from that of both Adem and Gochet (2004) and Ulas et al. (2009) in that we further partition ensemble training and EA (i.e., evaluation) components into multiple subsets, so that multiple ensembles can be generated and each ensemble evaluated on multiple datasets. It should be noted that a larger model set would offer the option of generating more EA datasets (EA_ks), thus allowing for more thorough statistical analysis.

New MP Models for Generating Ensembles

MP formulations for generating ensembles have been presented by other researchers including Adem and Gochet (2004) and Zhang et al. (2006). Adem and Gochet (2004) noted that: "Aggregating with mathematical programming guarantees that ... the aggregated classifier will be at least as good as the best predictor on the design data set for a given criterion function." In this section, we present some new MP models for generating candidate ensembles.

Adem and Gochet (2004) presented a mixed IP formulation that calculated the nonnegative weights of candidate base classifiers, such that any candidate base classifier whose weight was zero was not included in the ensemble. The objective function was to minimize the number of observations that were incorrectly predicted by the ensemble. This formulation is similar to the coarse weighted average (CWA) formulation, which is presented in section "CWA Model." Zhang et al. (2006) presented a quadratic IP formulation that selected a specified number of ensembles for inclusion in the ensemble. It should be noted that neither of these approaches directly used posterior probabilities to select the subset of candidate base classifiers for inclusion in the ensemble. However, as noted earlier, Ulas et al. (2009) report that in their experiment: "We have also seen that *it is better to combine classifiers with soft outputs (for example, posterior probabilities) rather than 0/1 decisions.*" In section "FWA Model," we present one such approach that uses the posterior probabilities generated by the candidate base classifiers.

Let

- EL_{All} ($= EL_1 \cup EL_2 \cup \ldots \cup EL_{|J|}$) be the entire EL dataset
- R be the set of base classifiers
- C be the set of classes
- J be the set of EL datasets EL_j
- K be the set of EA datasets EA_k
- I_j be the set of observations from the given EL_j
- $c_{(i)}$ be the actual class of observation "i"
- $a_{ijr(*)} = 1$ if classifier "r" correctly predicts the class of observation "i" of EL_j, and $a_{ijr(*)} = 0$ otherwise
- $a_{ijr(c)} = 1$ if classifier "r" incorrectly predicts "c" as the class of observation "i" of EL_j, and $a_{ijr(c)} = 0$ otherwise
- w_{rj} be the weight associated with base classifier r in ensemble EM_j
- x_{rj} be a binary variable such that $x_{rj} = 1$ if base classifier "r" is selected for the ensemble EM_j, and $x_{rj} = 0$ otherwise
- y_{ij} be a binary variable such that $y_{ij} = 1$ if the ensemble EM_j misclassifies observation "i" of EL_j, and $y_{ij} = 0$ otherwise

We will present three ensemble generation models, for each of which our objective is to maximize the EL accuracy rate, which is equivalent to minimizing the number of EL observations that are misclassified by the generated ensemble (i.e., Min $\Sigma_{i \in I_j} y_{ij}$).

MV Model

This model involves the generation of an ensemble in which the ensemble's prediction is based on the MV of the predictions of the selected constituent base classifiers. The relevant set of base classifiers to include in the MV ensemble EM_j can be obtained by solving the following 0–1 IP problem:

Min $\sum_{i \in I_j} y_{ij}$
such that
3.2.1a: $\sum_{r \in R} (a_{ijr(*)} - a_{ijr(c)}) x_{rj} + (1 + |R|) y_{ij} \geq 1$ $\forall i \in EL_j, \forall c \in (C - c_{(i)})$
3.2.1b: $x_{rj} \in \{0, 1\}$ $\forall r \in R$
3.2.1c: $y_{ij} \in \{0, 1\}$ $\forall i \in EL_j$

Constraint 3.2.1a requires that $y_{ij} = 1$ if the majority of base classifiers in the selected ensemble incorrectly predicts the class of observation "i." The reader may recall that since if for observation $i \in EL_j$ there is at least one class $c \in (C - c_{(i)})$ that has at least the same number of ensemble votes as the actual class $c_{(i)}$ of observation "I," then $\sum_{r \in R} (a_{ijr(*)} - a_{ijr(c)}) x_{rj} \leq 0$, which would require $y_{ij} = 1$ for constraint 3.2.1a to hold. Since the objective function Min $\sum_{i \in I_j} y_{ij}$ then $y_{ij} = 1$, if and only if ensemble EM_j incorrectly predicts observation "i."

It should be noted that the number of rows in this problem is $(|C| - 1)*|EL_j| + |R| + |EL_j| = |C|*(|EL_j| + |R|$. The number of binary integer variables is $|R| + |EL_j|$. It is expected that $|EL_j| > $ Max $\{|R|, |C|\}$, and so the dimensions of the problem would be most influenced by $|EL_j|$. It should be noted that $w_{rj} > 0$ if and only if base classifier "r" is included in ensemble EM_j. It should be noted that $x_{rj} = 1$ indicates that base classifier "r" is included in ensemble EM_j.

CWA Model

The CWA model involves the generation of an ensemble in which the ensemble's prediction is based on a weighted average of the predictions of the constituent base classifiers. Thus, the set of base classifiers to include in the EM_j would be determined by solving the following mixed IP problem:

Min $\sum_{i \in I_j} y_{ij}$
such that
3.2.2a: $\sum_{r \in R} (a_{ijr(*)} - a_{ijr(c)}) w_{rj} + y_{ij}$ ≥ 0 $\forall i \in EL_j, \forall c \in (C - c_{(i)})$
3.2.2b: $\sum_{r \in R} w_{rj}$ $= 1$
3.2.2c: w_{rj} ≥ 0 $\forall r \in R$
3.2.2d: $y_{ij} \in \{0, 1\}$ $\forall i \in EL_j$

Constraint 3.2.2a requires that $y_{ij} = 1$ if a weighted majority of the base classifiers in the selected ensemble incorrectly predicts the class of observation "i." Since if for observation $i \in EL_j$ there is at least one other class "$c \in (C - c_{(i)})$" that has at least the same weighted number of ensemble votes as the actual class $c_{(i)}$ of observation "i," then $\sum_{r \in R} (a_{ijr(*)} - a_{ijr(c)}) w_{rj} \leq 0$, which would require $y_{ij} = 1$ for constraint 3.2.2a to hold. Since the objective function Min $\sum_{i \in I_j} y_{ij}$ then $y_{ij} = 1$ if and only if ensemble

EM_j incorrectly predicts observation "i." It should be noted that $w_{rj} > 0$ indicates that base classifier "r" is included in ensemble EM_j.

FWA Model

The FWA model involves the averaging of the posterior probabilities of each constituent base classifier of the ensemble. Let ρ_{ijr} be the posterior probability that base classifier "r" assigns to the actual class of observation "i" of EL_j. Another approach to selecting the set of base classifiers to include in the EM_j involves solving the following mixed IP problem:

Min $\sum_{i \in I_j} y_{ij}$
such that
3.2.3a: $\sum_{r \in R} (\rho_{ijr(*)} - \rho_{ijr(c)}) w_{rj} + y_{ij} \geq 0 \qquad \forall\, i \in EL_j, \forall\, c \in (C - c_{(i)})$
3.2.3b: $\sum_{r \in R} w_{rj} \qquad\qquad\qquad = 1$
3.2.3c: $w_{rj} \qquad\qquad\qquad\qquad\quad \geq 0 \qquad \forall\, r \in R$
3.2.3d: $y_{ij} \in \{0, 1\} \qquad\qquad\qquad\qquad \forall\, i \in EL_j$

where $\rho_{ijr(*)}$ is the posterior probability of the actual class for observation "i" based on classifier r, and $\rho_{ijr(c)}$ is the posterior probability of the class "c" for observation "i" based on classifier r.

Since if for observation i $\in EL_j$ there is at least one other class "$c \in (C - c_{(i)})$" that has at least the same weighted average posterior probability as the actual class $c_{(i)}$ of observation "i," then $\sum_{r \in R} (a_{ijr(*)} - a_{ijr(c)}) w_{rj} \leq 0$, which would require $y_{ij} = 1$ for constraint 3.2.2a to hold. Since the objective function Min $\sum_{i \in I_j} y_{ij}$ then $y_{ij} = 1$ if and only if ensemble EM_j incorrectly predicts observation "i." It should be noted that $w_{rj} > 0$ indicates that base classifier "r" is included in ensemble EM_j. It should be also noted that commercial classifier software (e.g., SAS Enterprise Miner) generates the posterior probability $\rho_{ijr(c)}$ for each class for a given observation and classifier.

Heuristics and MP Ensemble Generation Methods

For a given ensemble $EM_{j(m)}$ that was generated by the heuristic ensemble generation method "m" using EL set EL_j, its solution describes, $R_{j(m)\_Incl}$, the subset of base classifiers "r" that are included in $EM_{j(m)}$, and $R_{j(m)\_Excl}$ ($= R - R_{j(m)\_Incl}$), the subset of base classifiers "r" that are not included in $EM_{j(m)}$. This solution could be used as an initial feasible solution for each of the MP formulations described earlier.

For the MV formulation, this initial starting solution would involve setting $x_{rj} = 1$ for each r $\in R_{j(m)\_Incl}$ and $x_{rj} = 0$ for each r $\in R_{j(m)\_Excl}$. Each y_{ij} would take the value 1 if and only if this was necessary to ensure that constraint 3.2.1a was satisfied.

For the CWA formulation, this initial starting solution would involve setting $w_{rj} = 1/|R_{j(m)\_Incl}|$ for each r $\in R_{j(m)\_Incl}$ and $w_{rj} = 0$ for each r $\in R_{j(m)\_Excl}$. This ensures that constraints 3.2.2b and 3.2.2c are satisfied. Each y_{ij} would take the value 1 if and only if this was necessary to ensure that constraint 3.2.2a was satisfied. The FWA formulation would be treated in a similar manner.

For a given EL_j, an attempt to solve a given MP formulation could thus take advantage of the results of any previously executed heuristic or MP ensemble generation method that was also applied to EL_j. If the solution of a previously executed ensemble generation method that provided the lowest error rate was used as the initial starting solution for the given MP method m_{MP}, then it seems reasonable to expect that the execution of m_{MP} should proceed faster. It should be noted that while the error rate of the given m_{MP} based on EL_j will be better than the corresponding best error rate for the previously executed ensemble generation methods, this situation may or may not hold when it is applied to the EA datasets as each of the methods would be overfitted to the given EL_j.

Description of the IEGP

Step 1: Initialization

1. Specify the partitioning distribution for the IL, EL, and EA components of the model dataset.
2. Specify the partitioning distribution for the training and validation subsets of the IL dataset.
3. Specify $|J|$, the number of EL subsets, and $|I_j|$ the number of observations in each EL subset.
4. Specify $|K|$ the number of EA subsets, and the number of observations in each EA subset.
5. Specify the set of induction algorithms (e.g., DT induction, regression, and ANN) and parameter settings to be used to generate the set of classifier models. Let this set be Ψ.
6. Specify M, the set of ensemble generation methods (e.g., the MPs and heuristics such that of Ulas et al. [2009] and Caruana et al. [2004]) that are to be used to generate the set of ensembles.

Step 2: Data Preparation

1. Based on the partitioning distribution for IL, use stratified sampling based on the target variable to generate the training dataset IL_{Trn} and validation dataset IL_{Val} from the IL dataset IL_{All} are to be used for the generation of the individual models (*IL*) dataset.
2. Use stratified sampling with replacement based on the target variable to generate $|J|$ EL datasets EL_j from EL_{All}, each of the same size $|I_j|$.
3. Use stratified sampling without replacement based on the target variable to generate $|K|$ EA datasets EA_k from EA_{All}, each of the same size.

Step 3: Generate Base Classifiers

Apply the relevant set of induction algorithms and parameter settings to the IL datasets to generate the set of base classifiers.

Step 4: Generate Ensembles

Sub-Step 4a: Generate Ensembles Using EL Subsets

For each $m \in M$ and for each EL dataset, formulate and solve the associated ensemble generation problem, resulting in the generation of the ensemble $EM_{j(m)}$. Let Ω_{Req} be the set of ensemble models that were generated in this sub-step.

Sub-Step 4b (Optional): Generate Ensembles Using EL Subsets

For each $m \in M$ and for the entire EL dataset EL_{All} formulate and solve the associated ensemble generation problem, resulting in the generation of the ensemble $EM_{All(m)}$. Let Ω_{Opt} be the set of ensemble models that were generated in this sub-step.

Step 5: Assess Ensemble Models

For each ensemble $EM_{j(m)} \in \Omega_{Req} \cup E_{Opt}$, score and record its performance with regard to each EA dataset EA_k.

Step 6: Compare Ensemble Models

For each pair of ensembles (EM_{j1}, EM_{j2}), do a statistical difference of means test for paired samples in order to determine whether there is a statistically significant difference in the performance of the given pair of ensembles with respect to accuracy.

Discussion on the IEGP

Step 1: Initialization

Sub-Steps 1a–1b:

In developing the base classifiers, the importance of partitioning the model dataset into training and validation datasets in order to avoid the resulting model being overfitted to the training dataset. A similar motivation is involved in our approach of developing separate partitions for EL and EA.

Sub-Step 1d:

Because accuracy is a random variable, the assessment of accuracy-based performance of the ensembles should involve statistical analysis. This is the motivation for having multiple assessment datasets.

Sub-Steps 1e–1f:

In sub-step 1f, we propose the use of multiple ensemble generation techniques, as it is never known which technique will give the best performance on a given dataset. This is similar to the approach for the generation of the base classifiers, where multiple induction algorithms are used as it is never known which induction algorithm will give the best performance on a given dataset.

Step 2: Data Preparation

Sub-Step 2b:
Because the EL datasets will be used to generate the candidate ensemble,

1. Each pair of EL datasets could be overlapping. The sampling with replacement approach is similar to what is used in bagging and boosting to generate candidate training datasets, which are used in each iteration of those methods.
2. For each EL dataset EL_j, the distribution of the records based on the target variable should be roughly similar to the distribution in the model dataset.

Sub-Step 2c:
Because the EA datasets will be used in statistical hypothesis testing, it is important that:

1. Each pair of EA datasets should not be overlapping.
2. For each EA dataset EA_k, the distribution of the records based on the target variable should be roughly similar to the distribution in the model dataset.

Step 3: Generate Base Classifiers

This is a fairly well-accepted approach for generating base classifiers as for a given dataset, it is never known which induction algorithm dataset will generate the classifier with the best accuracy.

Step 4: Generate Ensembles

Sub-Step 4a: Generate Ensembles Using EL Subsets
This step involves the generation of at most $|M|*|J|$ ensembles. Each of the MPs that would have to be solved would be relatively small as the corresponding EL_j would be relatively small. It should be noted that current commercial MP software can solve IP problems with even several hundreds of rows in a few seconds.

Sub-Step 4b (Optional): Generate Ensembles Using EL Subsets
This sub-step involves using each ensemble generation method (e.g., the MPs and heuristics such that of Ulas et al. [2009]) on the entire EL set as is typically done in approaches of Ulas et al. (2009) and Adem and W. Gochet (2004). Thus, any ensemble that would be generated by each of

these ensemble generation methods would also be generated in this sub-step of the integrated ensemble generation procedure (IEGP).

If adequate computing resources are available, then this sub-step could be done in parallel with sub-step 4a. It should be noted that at most $|M|$ ensembles would be generated in this sub-step.

Step 5: Assess Ensemble Models

It should be noted that the calculation of the *accuracy* of the candidate ensembles involves the following:

1. For each candidate base classifier, apply its *scoring code* to each assessment dataset exactly once. The result is that for each candidate base classifier, each row (i.e., observation) in a given assessment dataset now has a posterior probability for each class of the target variable in addition to an actual value of the target variable.
2. For each candidate ensemble $EM_{j(m)} \in \Omega_{Req} \cup E_{Opt}$ and each assessment dataset EA_k,
    a. The combination rule of the ensemble along with the posterior probability values of its constituent base classifiers can be used to generate the predicted class of the ensemble for each row in the given assessment dataset.
    b. Given that predictions of the ensemble are available, the relevant accuracy rate can be calculated.

It should be noted that all the operations of this sub-step could even be done quickly in a spreadsheet.

Step 6: Compare Ensemble Models

Because accuracy is a random variable, it seems reasonable that comparison of the relative performance of a pair of ensembles should involve statistical hypothesis testing, particularly using paired samples. The fact that each generated ensemble will be assessed against the same set of multiple EA datasets allows for such statistical analysis.

Summary

The typical approach to empirical evaluation of a proposed method involves comparing its relative performance against other methods with regard to a limited set of datasets from a test bank such as the UCI library. Based on such limited evaluation, the given researcher(s) typically proclaims that his or her proposed method offers superior performance when compared to that of the methods included in the evaluation. But the given researcher(s) is never able to state with absolute assurance that his or her proposed method will give a superior performance on all datasets, or even of a given dataset. It, therefore, seems somewhat naïve to generalize on the results of any limited empirical evaluation.

So what do DM practitioners do in practice? Experiment with multiple algorithms and parameter settings. This reality has been recognized by commercial DM software vendors. So, for example, Classification and Regression Trees (CART) software of both SAS Enterprise Miner and Salford Systems include multiple splitting methods and other options. Further CART provides the *battery* facility, which allows for the simultaneous selection of multiple settings for several parameters, followed by the automatic execution of multiple parameter combinations. Obviously, this approach would be more computationally costly than if a single classifier was built using a single combination of the parameters' options. The additional computational cost would be considered to be worth the effort if it was outweighed by the value that was added. This value may include not only, for example, an improved accuracy rate but also the increased confidence with regard to the results given the fact that multiple options were explicitly considered.

Thus, our approach to ensemble generation does not adopt the single-method approach. The IEGP allows for the execution of both the new MP-based formulations that were presented in this chapter as well as other methods including previously proposed heuristics (e.g., Caruana et al. 2004; Ulas et al. 2009) and previously proposed MP techniques (e.g., Adem and Gochet 2004; Zhang et al. 2006). Thus, for a given dataset, the IEGP should not give results that are inferior to these previously proposed techniques that are specified in sub-step 1f.

Further, unlike several other approaches, it does not generate a single ensemble but multiple ensembles that are subjected to statistical hypothesis testing in order to compare their relative performance in terms of accuracy. Thus, if it were to be the case that an ensemble generated by one of the previously proposed techniques turned out to be the top-ranked one, then the user could have had greater confidence in such a result, as it was not based on a single ensemble being generated but rigorous analysis.

Illustrative Example

The purpose of this illustrative example is to demonstrate how the IEGP would determine the strongest performing ensembles with respect to accuracy. It involves the use of the German credit dataset of the UCI test bed. The dataset was partitioned as follows:

- Individual learning
  - Training   450 (45% of Model Set)
  - Validation   200 (20% of Model Set)
- EL 174 ($\cong$17.5% of Model Set)
  - 10 EL subsets, each of size 25
- EA 176 ($\cong$17.5% of Model Set)
  - 10 EA subsets, each of size 25

We used SAS Enterprise Miner to generate eight (8) base classifiers: three DTs (i.e., DT_E, DT_C, and DT_G), three logistic regression classifiers (i.e., REG_S, REG_B, and REG_F), and two ANN classifiers (i.e., NN_HN and NN_GL). We manually generated an ensemble that consisted of all eight base classifiers (i.e., Ens_ALL). Given that the purpose of our illustration is not to demonstrate which of the MP formulations is best, but rather to demonstrate how the IEGP could be used to determine the most appropriate ensemble, we select three ensembles (Ens_GI1, Ens_GI2, and Ens_GI3) that were generated using the MP models (Table 16.1).

Using the performance data of the ensembles on the assessment datasets (see Table 16.2), we compared each pair of ensembles using statistical

Table 16.1 Description of the Ensembles

	Base Classifiers							
Ensembles	*DT_C*	*DT_E*	*DT_G*	*Reg_S*	*Reg_B*	*Reg_F*	*NN_HN*	*NN_GL*
Ens_ALL	√	√	√	√	√	√	√	√
ENS_GI1						√	√	√
ENS_GI2	√		√	√			√	√
ENS_GI3				√			√	√

Table 16.2 Performance of Ensembles on Assessment Datasets

Assessment Dataset	*ENS_ALL*	*ENS_GI1*	*ENS_GI2*	*ENS_GI3*
1	**0.7600**	0.6800	0.7200	0.7200
2	0.7600	0.7200	0.7600	0.7200
3	0.7200	0.7200	**0.7600**	0.7200
4	**0.8400**	0.8000	0.8000	0.8000
5	0.7600	0.7200	**0.8400**	0.7200
6	0.6000	0.7200	0.7200	0.7200
7	0.7600	0.6400	**0.8000**	0.6400
8	0.7600	0.7200	**0.8000**	0.7200
9	0.7200	**0.7600**	0.7200	**0.7600**
10	0.7600	0.8000	**0.8800**	0.8000

difference of means test for paired samples (i.e., t-test) at significance level $\alpha = 0.05$.

- Ens_GI2 outperforms the other ensembles: Ens_ALL, Ens_GI1, Ens_GI3
- It follows that Ens_GI2 is the most appropriate ensembles among this set of candidate ensembles.

Conclusion

In this chapter, we have investigated the problem of selecting the most appropriate ensemble of base classifiers, and have presented a procedure for addressing this problem. Our solution procedure involves the formulation and solution of one or more ensemble generation techniques (e.g., MP and heuristics such as incremental approaches) based on selections made by the end user. It should be noted that although we have presented three MP formulations of the ensemble generation problem, our procedure also allows for the utilization of other MP formulations (e.g., Adem and Gochet 2004, Zhang et al. 2006) and heuristic approaches, including the incremental approach of Ulas et al. (2009). It should be noted that instances of the associated MP problems are expected to be relatively small by IP standards in terms of the number of variables and number of rows and can be efficiently solved by current commercial IP solvers.

It should be noted that there is no restriction on the induction techniques that are used to generate candidate classifiers for inclusion in any ensemble as we allow for DT, logistic regression, neural networks, naïve Bayes, nearest neighbor classifiers, and so on. We also allow for candidate base classifiers to themselves be ensembles that may have been generated using bagging, boosting, or some other ensemble-generating technique.

Our procedure offers not only an approach to EL that is used to identify candidate ensembles but also to determine the strongest performing ensembles with respect to accuracy.

We do this in a manner that acknowledges the stochastic nature of the accuracy of a classifier, including ensemble classifiers. Given that it is known that none of the previously proposed methods for generating ensembles gives the best performance on all datasets, our solution procedure is not aimed at identifying the *best* MP model. For, in fact, it is a well known in DM and machine learning that there is no technique that is guaranteed to give superior performance on all datasets. Therefore, we allow for the application of multiple MP and heuristic models on multiple EL datasets to generate multiple candidate ensembles. The relatively low costs of processors that could be used to solve the relatively small MP problems makes it feasible to solve these multiple MP problems in parallel.

References

Adem, J. and Gochet, W. "Aggregating classifiers with mathematical programming." *Computational Statistics and Data Analysis 47:4* (2004) 791–807.

Au, S.-T., Duan, R., and Jiang, W. "A data mining framework for product and service migration analysis." *Annals of Operations Research 192* (2012) 105–121.

Banfield, R.E., Hall, L.O., Bowyer, K.W., and Kegelmeyer, W.P. "Ensemble diversity measures and their application to thinning." *Information Fusion 6:1* (2005) 49–62.

Bauer, E. and Kohavi, R. "An empirical comparison of voting classification algorithms: bagging, boosting, and variants." *Machine Learning 36* (1999) 105–139.

Breiman, L. "Bagging predictors." *Machine Learning 24* (1996) 123–140.

Cao, Q., Parry, M., and Leggio, K. "The three-factor model and artificial neural networks: Predicting stock price movement in China." *Annals of Operations Research 185* (2011) 25–44.

Caruana, R., Niculescu-Mizil, A., Crew, G., and Ksikes, A. "Ensemble selection from libraries of models." *Proceedings of the 21st International Conference on Machine Learning* (2004) (p.18), July, ACM.

Dietterich, T. "Ensemble methods in machine learning." In Kittler, J. and Roli, F. (Eds.) *Proceedings of the 1st International Workshop on Multiple Classifier Systems*, Lecture Notes in Computer Science, Vol. 1857 (2000) Springer-Verlag, Germany.

Domingos, P. "When and how to subsample: Report on the KDD-2001 Panel." *SIGKDD Explorations 3:2* (2001) 74–75.

Freund, Y. and Schapire, R. "Experiments with a new boosting algorithm." In *Proceedings of the 13th International Conference on Machine Learning* (1996) 148–156. Bari, Italy.

Fu, Z., Golden, B., Lele, S., Raghavan, S., and Wasil, E. "A genetic algorithm-based approach for building accurate decision trees." *INFORMS Journal on Computing 15:1* (2003) 3–22.

Hand, D. "Data mining: Statistics and more?" *The American Statistician 52:2* (1998) 112–118.

Hansen, J. "Combining predictors: Comparison of five meta machine learning methods." *Information Sciences 119* (1999) 91–105.

Kittler, J., Hatef, M., Duin, R., and Matas, J. "On combining classifiers." *IEEE Transactions on Pattern Analysis and Machine Intelligence 20:3* (1998) 226–239.

Lutu, P. and Engelbrecht, A. "A comparative study of sample selection methods for classification." *South African Computer Journal 36* (2006) 69–85.

Lutu, P. and Engelbrecht, A. "A decision rule-based method for feature selection in predictive data mining." *Expert Systems with Applications 37* (2010) 602–609.

Opitz, D. and Maclin, R. "An empirical evaluation of bagging and boosting for artificial neural networks." *Proceedings of the International Conference on Neural Networks 3* (1997) 1401–1405.

Ruta, D. and Gabrys, B. "Classifier selection for majority voting." *Information Fusion 6:1* (2005) 63–81.

Smyth, P. "Data mining at the interface of computer science and statistics." In Grossman, R., Kamath, C., Kegelmeyer, P., Kumar, V., and Namburu, R. (Eds.) *Data Mining for Scientific and Engineering Applications* (2001) Dordrecht, the Netherlands, Kluwer Academic Publishers.

Sohn, S. and Choi, H. "Ensemble based on data envelopment analysis." *ECML Meta Learning Workshop* (2001), vol. 53, September.

Tax, D., van Breukelen, M., Duin, R., and Kittler, J. "Combining multiple classifiers by averaging or multiplying?" *Pattern Recognition 33:9* (2000) 1475–1485.

Ueda, N. "Optimal linear combination of neural networks for improving classification performance." *IEEE Transactions on Pattern Analysis and Machine Intelligence 22:2* (2000) 207–215.

Ulas, A., Semerci, M., Yıldız, O., and Alpaydın, E. "Incremental construction of classifier and discriminant ensembles." *Information Sciences 179* (2009) 1298–1318.

Woods, K., Kegelmeyer, W., and Bowyer, K. "Combination of multiple classifiers using local accuracy estimates." *IEEE Transaction on Pattern Analysis and Machine Intelligence 19* (1997) 405–410.

Zhou, Z.-H., Wu, J., and Tang, W. "Ensembling neural networks: Many could be better than all." *Artificial Intelligence 137* (2002) 239–263.

Zhang, Y., Burer, S., and Street, W. "Ensemble pruning via semi-definite programming." *Journal of Machine Learning Research 7* (2006) 1315–1338.

Chapter 17

A New Feature Selection Technique Applied to Credit Scoring Data Using a Rank Aggregation Approach Based on Optimization, Genetic Algorithm, and Similarity

---

Waad Bouaguel, Ghazi Bel Mufti,
and Mohamed Limam

Contents

Abstract: Credit scoring has been developed as an essential tool, especially in the credit departments of banks that have to deal with a huge sum of credit data. A credit scoring model makes loaning process faster. However, it is nearly unfeasible to analyze this large amount of data; the feature selection techniques have been used to address this issue. Feature selection is the process of selecting a subset of relevant features for use in model construction. Unlike the existing feature selection techniques that cause bias using distinct statistical properties of data for feature evaluation, the feature selection based on rank aggregation is more robust, thus reducing this bias. Over the past years, rank aggregation has emerged as an important tool. Despite its numerous advantages, rank aggregation may be a deep problem. In fact, rankings provided by the different filters may be in many cases incomplete and similar features may be given disjoint ranking. We first consider the rank aggregation problem as an optimization problem, in which we aim to find an optimal list that approximates all the aggregated lists. Then we concentrate on the problem of disjoint ranking; subsequently, we perform a new algorithm that eliminate disjoint ranking for similar features and remove the features that bring less information to the target concept. The performance of our approach was tested using four credit datasets and compared to three individual filters and four well-known aggregation techniques. The result indicates that the proposed technique is more robust across a wide range of classifiers and has higher accuracy than other traditional feature selection techniques.

Keywords: Filter, aggregation, feature selection, genetic algorithm.

Introduction

"Credit scoring" is the term used to describe a statistically derived numeric expression of an applicant's creditworthiness that is used by credit institutions to access the possibility that this applicant will refund his credit. For years, creditors have been using credit scoring systems to determine if a credit applicant will be at a good risk for credit (Zhang et al. 2010). Information about the credit applicant and his or her credit experiences, such as the number and type of accounts he or she has, whether he or she pays his or her debts by the due date, the age of his or her accounts, and so on, is collected from the applicant in a credit report, generally, using a statistical program, and then lenders compare this information to the loan repayment history of consumers with similar profiles (Tsai and Wu 2008).

The on-hand collection of booked loans is used to build a credit scoring model that would be used to identify the associations between the applicant's characteristics and how good or bad is the creditworthiness of the applicant. In order to have parsimonious credit models, we should only consider a limited number of features (Thomas 2009). Using only a few features to decide on the credit approval, the scorecard builder will gain more insight into the model and better understand its working (Rodriguez et al. 2010).

Choosing the appropriate set of features is one of the most interesting and difficult tasks that have a key effect on the performance of credit scoring models. Typically, a feature selection technique looks for a suitable subset of features from the original features set. Feature selection algorithm can be divided into two categories: filter and wrapper. Filter methods use general characteristics of the data independently from the classifier for the evaluation process (Forman 2008). The obtained results are generally a ranked list of features, where the top-ranked features are the most relevant and features at the bottom are not so relevant or totally unwanted. Wrappers, on the other hand, search for an optimal feature subset by exploiting the resulting classification performance of a specific classifier. Therefore, a wrapper's result is a subset of the most relevant features rather than an ordered list of all the features as given by a filter. Although effective, the exponential number of possible subsets places computational limits on wrapper algorithm, which make filter methods more suitable to our study (Wu et al. 2009).

Because finding the best filtering method is usually intractable in real application, an alternative path is to fuse the results obtained by different filtering methods. Combining preference lists from those individual rankers into a single better ranking is known as "rank aggregation." Rank aggregation methods have emerged as an important tool for combining information in credit scoring case. The problem of combining the ranked preferences of many filters is a deep problem. The rankings provided by the different filters may be in many cases incomplete, or even disjoint. In fact, the majority of rankings involve a set of similar feature, but despite the similarity between these features, they are not ranked similarly that, additionally to the problem of incomplete rankings, may lead to noisy ranking.

In this chapter, we propose to deal with the rank aggregation problem as an optimization problem, in which we aim to find the best list, which would be the closest as possible to all individual ordered lists all together. We use genetic algorithms (GAs) as a powerful tool for solving the proposed optimization problem. Once an aggregated list is obtained from the GAs, we perform a simple approach that extend GA results to consider similarity between items in the various ranked lists, in addition to their rankings. The intuition is that similar items should receive similar rankings, given an appropriate measure of similarity.

The reminder of the chapter is organized as follows. The sections "The Business Challenge of Credit Scoring" and "Filter Framework" present an overview of the credit scoring and the financial data proprieties, and an overview of filter feature selection framework and rank aggregation and their issues, respectively. In section "New Approach," we develop a method to combine a set of ordered lists of feature based on an optimization function and GA and then we present a framework to extend previous methods of rank aggregation based on a similarity study applied to credit scoring. The section "Empirical Study" gives experimental investigations on four credit datasets. The last section concludes this chapter.

Business Challenge of Credit Scoring

According to Volk (2012), credit risk is one of the major issues in financial researches. Over the past few years, many companies fell apart and were forced into bankruptcy or to a significantly constrained business activity, because of deteriorated financial and economic situation. When banks are unprepared to a variation in the economic activity, they will probably suffer from huge credit losses. In fact, it is very obvious that credit risk increases in economic depression. However, this effect might be augmented when bank experts underestimate or overestimate the creditworthiness of credit applicants. Expressing why some companies or individuals do default while others do not, what are the main factors that drive credit risk, and how to build robust credit model are very important for financial stability.

Background of Credit Scoring

Credit scoring consists of the evaluation of the risk related to lending money to an organization or a person. In the past few years, the business of credit products increased enormously. Approximately every day, individual's and company's records of past lending and repaying transactions are collected and then evaluated (Hand and Henley 1997). This information is used by lenders such as banks to evaluate an individual's or a company's means and willingness to repay a loan. The set of collected information makes the managers' task simple because it helps to determine whether to extend credit duration or to modify a previously approved credit limit, to quantify the probability of default (PD), and bankruptcy or fraud associated to a company or a person. When assessing the risk related to credit products, different problems arise, depending on the context and the different types of credit applicants. Sadatrasoul et al. (2013) summarize the different kind of scoring as follows:

- Application scoring—it refers to the assessment of the creditworthiness for new applicants.
- It quantifies the risks, associated with credit requests, by evaluating the social, demographic, financial, and other data collected at the time of the application.
- Behavioral scoring—it involves principles that are similar to application scoring, with the difference that it refers to existing customers. As a consequence, the analyst already has evidence of the borrower's behavior with the lender. Behavioral scoring models analyze the consumer's behavioral patterns to support dynamic portfolio management processes.
- Collection scoring—collection scoring is used to divide customers with different levels of insolvency into groups, separating those who require more decisive actions from those who do not need to be attended to immediately. These models are distinguished according to the degree of delinquency (early, middle, late recovery) and allow a better management of delinquent customers, from the first signs of delinquency (30–60 days) to subsequent phases and debt write-off.
- Fraud detection—fraud scoring models rank the applicants according to the relative likelihood that an application may be fraudulent no matter what kind of credit is used, data is at the heart of everything in any credit organization does and, over past years, many techniques and expertise in the interpretation and use of credit bureau and clients' customer data have been implemented for every aspect of the client relationship. In fact, analytics turn the collected data into information, which enables organizations to predict how applicants and customers will behave in the future. The business processes in the market of leading industry should be composed of four major parts: the origination of a credit application, customer management, collections and recoveries, and the estimation the default probability.
- Origination—application scoring in the beginning process. With the applicants' information, decisions can be made about whether to accept or decline an applicant. This view of each individual can help develop a picture of the potential value of an accepted applicant, to inform decisions about the product and terms offered.
- Customer management—behavioral scoring is used throughout the life of a customer relationship to inform management strategies for each customer, whether managing bad customers or extending the relationship with good customers. For organizations that have many relationships with their customers, customer-level scoring brings together the different aspects of the relationship into one complete picture.

- Collections and recoveries—behavioral scoring is also used to prioritize collection activities to maximize recoveries and reduce collection costs.
- Estimating the default probability—estimating the borrower's risk level, namely, the PD, by assigning a different PD to each borrower is now widely employed in many banks. PD indicates that a given counterparty will not be able or willing to meet its obligations. The false estimation of PD leads to unreasonable rating, incorrect pricing of financial instruments, and thereby it was one of the causes of the recent global financial crisis.

In this chapter, we will address the application scoring problem also known as "consumer credit scoring." In this context, the term "credit" will be used to refer to an amount of money that is borrowed to a credit applicant by a financial institution and that must be repaid, with interest, in a regular interval of time. The probability that an applicant will default must be estimated from the information about the applicant provided at the time of the credit application, and the estimate will serve as the basis for accepting or rejecting a decision. According to Hand and Henley (1997), accurate classification is of benefit both to the creditor in terms of increased profit or reduced loss and to the applicant in terms of avoiding overcommitment. This activity deciding whether or not to grant credit is generally carried out by banks and various other organizations. It is an economic activity that has seen rapid growth over the last 30 years.

Traditional methods of deciding whether to grant credit to a particular individual use human judgment of the risk of default, based on experience of previous decisions. Nevertheless, economic demands resulting from the arising number of credit requests joined with the emergence of new machine learning technology and have led to the development of sophisticated models to help the credit granting decision.

The statistical credit scoring models, called "scorecards" or "classifiers," use predictor from application forms and other sources to estimate the probabilities of defaulting. A credit granting decision is taken by comparing the estimated probability of defaulting with a suitable threshold. Standard statistical methods used in the industry for developing scorecards are discriminant analysis, linear regression, and logistic regression (LR). Despite their simplicity, Tuff'ery (2007) and Thomas (2009) show that both discriminant analysis and LR prediction accuracy is in some particular cases erroneous. Hence, other models based on data mining methods are proposed. These models do not lead to scorecards but they indicate directly the class of the credit applicant (Jiang 2009). Artificial intelligence methods such as decision trees (DTs), artificial neural networks, K-nearest-neighbor, and support vector machines (SVMs) (Bellotti and Crook 2009) can be used as alternative methods for credit scoring. These methods extract knowledge from training datasets without any assumption on the data distributions. In the industry, the predictor variables are typically called "features," a terminology which we shall retain here.

Proprieties of Financial Data

Credit scoring portfolios are frequently voluminous and they are in the range of several thousand, well over 100,000 applicants measured on more than 100 variables are quite common (Hand and Henley 1997). These portfolios are characterized by noise, missing values, complexity of distributions, and by redundant or irrelevant features (Piramuthu 2006). Clearly, the applicants characteristics will vary from situation to situation: an applicant looking for a small loan will be asked for different information from another who is asking for a big loan. Furthermore, the data that may be used in a credit model is always subject to changing legislation.

The initial application form filed by the credit applicants are accepted or rejected immediately based on some obvious characteristics such as the salary. Further information is then collected on the remaining credit applicants using additional forms. This process of collection of the borrower's information allows banks to avoid losing time on obvious nonworthy applicants as well as permitting a quick decision.

The used data in credit scoring are often categorical. Classically, continuous variables are categorized in order to accelerate the credit models. As any classification problem, choosing the number of appropriate features to be included in the credit model is an important task. One might try to use as many features as possible. However, the more the number of features grows, the more computation is required and model accuracy and scoring interpretation are reduced (Liu and Schumann 2005; Howley et al. 2006). There are also other practical issues, in fact with too many questions or a lengthy vetting procedure, the applicants will deter and will go elsewhere. Based on a standard (Hand and Henley 1997), the statistical and pattern recognition strategy here is to explore a large number of features and to identify an effective subset (of say 10 ± 12) of those features for application in practice and for building the credit model.

Filter Framework

The basic idea of filter methods is to select the best features according to some prior knowledge. Filter feature selection methods can be grouped into two categories, that is, feature weighting methods and subset search methods. This categorization is based on whether they evaluate the relevance of features separately or through feature subsets. In feature weighting methods, weights are assigned to each feature independently and then the features are ranked based on their relevance to the target variable. Relief is a famous algorithm that studies features relevance (Kira and Rendell 1992). This method uses the Euclidean distance to select a sample composed of a random instance and the two nearest instances of the same and opposite classes. Then a routine is used to update the feature weight vector for every sample triplet and determines the average feature weight vector relevance. Then, features with average weights over a given threshold are selected.

Subset search methods explore all possible feature subsets using a particular evaluation measure. The best possible subset is selected when the search stops. According to Yu and Liu (2003), two existing evaluation measures that efficiently decrease irrelevance and redundancy are consistency measure and correlation measure (Arauzo-Azofra et al. 2008; Bouaguel et al. 2013b). Yu and Liu (2003) recommended two main approaches to measure correlation; the first one is based on classical linear correlation of two random variables and the second one is based on information theory.

Numerous correlation coefficients can be used under the first approach, but the most common is the Pearson correlation coefficient (PCC). PCC is a simple measure that has been shown to be effective in a wide variety of feature selection methods (Rodriguez et al. 2010). Formally, the PCC is defined as

$$PCC = \frac{\text{cov}(X_i, X_j)}{\sqrt{\text{var}(X_i)\text{var}(X_j)}} \tag{17.1}$$

where:
cov is the covariance of variables
var is the variance of each variable

Simple correlation measure in general measures the linear relationship between two random variables, which may be not suitable in some cases. The second approach based on information theory measures how much knowledge two variables carry about each other. Mutual information (MI) is a well-known information theory measure that captures nonlinear dependencies between variables. Formally, the MI of two continuous random variables X_i and X_j is defined as:

$$I(x_i, x_j) = \sum_{x_i \in S} \sum_{x_j \in S} p(x_i, x_j) \log \frac{p(x_i, x_j)}{p(x_i) p(x_j)} dx_i dx_j \tag{17.2}$$

where:
$p(x_i, x_j)$ is the joint probability density function
$p(x_i)$ and $p(x_j)$ are the marginal probability density functions

In the case of discrete random variables, the double integral become a summation, where $p(x_i, x_j)$ is the joint probability mass function, and $p(x_i)$ and $p(x_j)$ are the marginal probability mass functions.

Feature ranking consists on ranking the features with respect to their relevance; one selects the top-ranked features, where the number of features to select is specified by the user or analytically determined.

Many feature selection algorithms include feature ranking as a principal selection mechanism because of its simplicity, scalability, and good empirical success (Caruana et al. 2003).

Let X be a matrix containing m instances $x_i = (x_{i1}, ..., x_{id}) \in R^d$, $i = 1, ..., m$. We denote the vector of class labels for the m instances by $y_i = (y_1, ..., y_m)$. F is the set of features $f_j = (f_1, ..., f_d)$.

Feature ranking makes use of a scoring function $H(j)$ computed from the values x_{ij} and y_i using one of the criteria discussed above (i.e., weighting, consistency, and correlation). By convention, we assume that a high score is indicative of a valuable variable and that we sort variables in decreasing order of $H(j)$.

Even when feature ranking is not optimal, it may be preferable to use other feature subset selection methods because of its computational and statistical scalability: computationally, it is efficient as it requires only the computation of d scores and sorting the scores; Statistically, it is robust against overfitting because it introduces bias but it may have considerably less variance (Hastie et al. 2001).

Selection Trouble and Rank Aggregation

Given the variety of filter-based techniques, it is difficult to identify which of the filter criteria would provide the best output for the experiments. The question is then, how to choose the best criterion for a specific feature selection task. In Wu et al. (2009), we call this problem a selection trouble. There exists no universal solution for this problem unless to evaluate all existing methods and then establish a general conclusion, which is an impossible solution. The best approach is to independently apply a mixture of the available methods and see what results it will yield. Combining preference lists from those individual rankers into a single better ranking is known as "rank aggregation." Rank aggregation methods have emerged as an important tool for combining information in credit scoring case (Bouaguel et al. 2013a, 2013c). Ensemble feature selection techniques (i.e., rank aggregation) use an idea similar to ensemble learning for classification (Dietterich 2000). In the first step, a number of different feature selectors (i.e., rankers) are used, and in the final phase, the output of these separate selectors is aggregated and returned as the final ensemble result.

Ensemble methods have been the most applied to bring together a set of classifiers for building robust predictive models. It has been shown that these ensemble classifiers are competitive with other individual classifiers and in some cases are superior. Recently, there have been studies applying the ensemble concept to the process of feature selection (Dittman et al. 2013). Rank aggregation might be used to improve the robustness of the individual feature selection techniques. Different rankers may yield to different ranking lists that can be considered as local optima in the space of feature subsets, and ensemble feature selection might give a better approximation to the optimal ranking of features. Also, the representational power of a particular feature selector might constrain its search space such that optimal subsets cannot be reached. Ensemble feature selection could help in alleviating this problem by aggregating the outputs of several feature selectors (Saeys et al. 2008).

As discussed earlier, rank aggregation has many merits. However, with ensemble feature selection, the question is how to aggregate the results of individual rankers. A number of different rank aggregation methods have been proposed in the literature: some are easy to set up such as the mean, median, highest rank, or lowest rank aggregation, and some are more complicated to set up.

All rank aggregation methods assume that the ranked lists being combined assign a value to each feature, from 1 to d, where rank 1 is assigned to the most relevant feature, the second-best feature is 2, and so on until the least relevant feature is assigned d. Simple rank aggregation technique use straightforward way to find the final aggregated list, in all cases, once each feature has been given a single value based on the mean, median, highest, or lowest value, all features are ranked based on these new values (Dittman et al. 2013). For example, mean aggregation simply finds the mean value of the feature's rank across all the lists and uses this as that feature's value. Likewise, median finds the median rank value across all the lists being combined, using the mean of the middle two values if there are an even number of lists. Highest rank and lowest rank use related strategies: either the highest (best, smallest) or lowest (worst, largest) rank value across all the lists is assigned as the value for the feature in question.

Simple ranking methods are easy to set up. However, in many cases, it is possible for two features to end up tied, even if this was not the case in any of the lists being combined and even when these features does not have any tie of similarity. Recent work in the area of rank aggregation techniques has centered on developing unique and innovative approaches. These new techniques can focus on different aspects of the ranking process, including comparing results to randomly generated results. Kolde et al. (2012) proposed an approach that detects features that are ranked consistently better than expected under null hypothesis of uncorrelated inputs and assigns a significance score for each feature. The underlying probabilistic model makes the algorithm parameter free and robust to outliers, noise, and errors. Other researches focus on giving more weight to top-ranking features or combining well-known aggregation techniques in order to enhance each other. In this chapter, we approach rank aggregation from another perspective. In fact, we aim to find the best list, which would be the closest as possible to all individual ordered lists all together, and this can be seen as an optimization problem. More details will be given in section "New Approach."

Incomplete Ranking and Disjoint Ranking for Similar Features

According to Sculley (2007), the rankings provided by the different filters may be in many cases incomplete, or even disjoint. In fact, Sculley pointed out that the incomplete rankings may come in two forms. In the first form, the different filters or some of them may each provide rankings for only the k best features and ignore the remaining features provided in the beginning. In the second form, the used filters may provide complete rankings over a limited subset of available features, due to incomplete knowledge.

Incomplete rankings are common in many financial applications, but still not the only problem with rank aggregation. In fact, the majority of rankings involve a set of similar feature, but despite the similarity between this features they are not ranked similarly which additionally to the problem of incomplete rankings may lead to noisy ranking. Let us give an illustrative example.

Assume we have seven features $\{f_1, f_2, f_3, f_4, f_5, f_6,$ and $f_7\}$, were f_2 and f_5 are highly similar, but not identical. We consider the two following rank lists from two different filters: list one is given by $\{f_3, f_2, f_7, f_5\}$ and list 2 is given by $\{f_2, f_7, f_3, f_4, f_1\}$.

If we have no preference of one filter over the other, then standard methods of rank aggregation may interrupt the rankings in the following ways: $\{f_2, f_3, f_7, f_5, f_4, f_1\}$. In this standard aggregation the features f_2 and f_5 are given divergent rankings, in spite of their high similarity, which make this kind of aggregation unacceptable. A more acceptable ranking that verify our vision and give a closer ranking to similar features will be $\{f_3, f_2, f_5, f_7, f_4, f_1\}$. The last aggregation agrees with our intuition that f_5 should be ranked behind f_2 because they are highly similar so they should have a close ranking. To avoid disjoint ranking for similar features, we present in section "Rank Aggregation Based on Similarity," a simple approach that extend any standard aggregation technique in order to take similarity into account.

New Approach

In this section, we propose a novel approach for filter feature selection. We consider building a two-stage filter feature selection model. In the first step, an optimization function and GA are used to resolve the selection trouble and the rank aggregation problem and to sort the features according to their relevance. In the second step, a standard algorithm is proposed in order to resolve the problem of disjoint ranking for similar features and to eliminate the redundant ones.

Optimization Problem

Rank aggregation provides a mean of combining information from different ordered lists and at the same time, to set their weak points. The aim of rank aggregation when dealing with feature selection is to find the best list, which would be the closest as possible to all individual ordered lists together.

This can be seen as an optimization problem, when we look at argmin(D, σ), where argmin gives a list σ at which the distance D with a randomly selected ordered list is minimized. In this optimization framework, the objective function is given by:

$$F(\sigma) = \sum_{i=1}^{m} w_i \times D(\sigma, L_i) \qquad (17.3)$$

where:

w_i represent the weights associated with the lists L_i

D is a distance function measuring the distance between a pair of ordered lists

L_i is the ith ordered list of cardinality k (i.e., number of features in each list L_i).

The best solution is then to look for σ^*, which would minimize the total distance between σ^* and L_i given by

$$\sigma^* = \arg\min \sum_{i=1}^{m} w_i \times D(\sigma, L_i) \qquad (17.4)$$

Measuring the distance between two ranking lists is classical and several well-studied metrics are known (Carterette 2009; Kumar and Vassilvitskii 2010), including the Kendall's tau distance and the Spearman footrule distance. Before defining this two distance measures, let us introduce some necessary notation.

Let $S_i(1),\ldots, S_i(k)$ be the scores coupled with the elements of the ordered list L_i, where $S_i(1)$ is associated with the feature on top of L_i that is most important, and $S_i(k)$ is associated with the feature, which is at the bottom that is least important with regard to the target concept. All the other scores correspond to the features that would be in between, ordered by decreasing importance. For each item $j \in L_i$, $r(j)$ shows the ranking of this item. Note that the optimal ranking of any item is 1; rankings are always positive, and higher rank shows lower preference in the list.

Spearman Footrule Distance

Spearman footrule distance, between two given rankings lists L and σ, is defined as the sum of the overall absolute differences between the ranks of all unique elements from both ordered lists combined. Formally, the Spearman footrule distance between L and σ, is given by

$$\text{Spearman}(L,\sigma) = \sum_{f \in (L \cup \sigma)} |r_L(f) - r_\sigma(f)| \qquad (17.5)$$

Spearman footrule distance is a very simple way for comparing two ordered lists. The smaller the value of this distance, the more similar the lists. When the two lists to be compared have no elements in common, the metric is $k(k + 1)$.

Kendall's Tau Distance

The Kendall's tau distance between two ordered rank list L and σ, is given by the number of pairwise adjacent transpositions needed to transform one list into another (Dinu and Manea 2006). This distance can be seen as the number of pairwise disagreements between the two rankings. Hence, the formal definition for the Kendall's tau distance is:

$$\text{Kendall}(L,\sigma) = \sum_{i,j \in (L \cup \sigma)} K \qquad (17.6)$$

where:

$$K = \begin{cases} 0 \text{ if } r_L(i) < r_L(j), r_\sigma(i) < r_\sigma(j) \text{ or} \\ \quad r_L(i) < r_L(j), r_\sigma(i) > r_\sigma(j) \\ 1 \text{ if } r_L(i) < r_L(j), r_\sigma(i) < r_\sigma(j) \text{ or} \\ \quad r_L(i) < r_L(j), r_\sigma(i) > r_\sigma(j) \\ p \text{ if } r_L(i) = r_L(j) = k+1 \\ r_\sigma(i) = r_\sigma(j) = k+1 \end{cases} \quad (17.7)$$

That is, if we have no knowledge of the relative position of i and j in one of the lists, we have several choices in the matter. We can either impose no penalty (0), full penalty (1), or a partial penalty ($0 < p < 1$).

Weighted Distance

In case, the only information available about the individual list is the rank order, the Spearman footrule distance and the Kendall's tau distance are adequate measures. However, the presence of any additional information about the individual list may improve the final aggregation. Typically, with filter methods, weights are assigned to each feature independently and then the features are ranked based on their relevance to the target variable. It would be beneficial to integrate these weights into our aggregation scheme. Hence, the weight associated to each feature consists of taking the average score across all of the ranked feature lists. We find the average for each feature by adding all the normalized scores associated to each lists and dividing the sum by the number of lists. Thus, the weighted Spearman's footrule distance between two list L and σ is given by

$$\sum_{f \in (L \cup \sigma)} \left| W[r_L(f)] \times r_L(f) - W[r_\sigma(f)] \times r_\sigma(f) \right|$$

$$= \sum_{f \in (L \cup r)} \left| W[r_L(f)] - W[r_\sigma(f)] \right| \times \left| r_L(f) - r_\sigma(f) \right| \quad (17.8)$$

Analogously to the weighted Spearman's footrule distance, the weighted Kendall's tau distance is given by

$$WK(L, \sigma) = \left| W[r_L(i)] - W[r_L(j)] \right| K \quad (17.9)$$

Solution to Optimization Problem Using GA

The introduced optimization problem in section "Optimization Problem" is a typical integer programming problem. As far as we know, there is no efficient solution to such kind of problem. One possible approach would be to perform complete search. However, it is too time demanding to make it applicable in real applications. We need to look for more practical solutions.

The presented method uses a GA for rank aggregation. GAs were introduced by Holland (1992) to imitate the mechanism of genetic models of natural evolution and selection. GAs are powerful tools for solving complex combinatorial problems, where a combinatorial problem involves choosing the best subset of components from a pool of possible components in order that the mixture has some desired quality (Clegg et al. 2009). GAs are computational models of evolution. They work on the basis of a set of candidate solutions. Each candidate solution is called a "chromosome," and the whole set of solutions is called a "population." The algorithm allows movement from one population of chromosomes to a new population in an iterative fashion. Each iteration is called a "generation." GAs in our case proceeds in the following manner as explained through the below sections.

Initialization

Once a set of aggregation rank lists are generated by several filtering techniques, it is necessary to create an initial population of features to be used as starting point for the GA, where each feature in the population represents a possible solution. This starting population is then obtained by randomly selecting a set of ordered rank lists.

Despite the success of GA on a wide collection of problems, the choice of the population size is still an issue. Gotshall and Rylander (2000) proved that the larger the population size, the better chance of it containing the optimal solution. However, increasing population size also causes the number of generations to converge. In order to have great results, the population size should depend on the length of the ordered lists and on the number of unique elements in these lists. From empirical studies, over a wide range of problems, a population size between 30 and 100 is usually recommended by Gotshall and Rylander (2000).

Selection

Once the initial population is fixed, we need to select new members for the next generation. In fact, each element in the current population is evaluated on the basis of its overall fitness (the objective function score given in Equation 17.3. Depending on which distance is used, new members (rank lists) are produced by selecting high-performing elements.

Crossover

The selected members are then crossed over with the crossover probability CP. Crossover randomly select a point in two selected lists and exchange the remaining segments of these lists to create a new ones. Therefore, crossover combines the features of two lists to create two similar ranked lists.

Mutation

In case only the crossover operator is used to produce the new generation, one possible problem that may arise is that if all the ranked lists in the initial population have the same value at a particular rank, then all future lists will have this same value at this particular rank. To come over this unwanted situation, a mutation operator is used. Mutation operates by randomly changing one or more elements of any list. It acts as a population perturbation operator. Typically mutation does not occur frequently so mutation is of the order of 0.001 (Gotshall and Rylander 2000).

Rank Aggregation Based on Similarity

Once an initial ranking Initial$_R$ is obtained from the proposed rank aggregation algorithm (Figure 17.1), as discussed in section "Solution to Optimization Problem Using GA," we move to solving the problem of disjoint ranking for similar features. Therefore, we first propose to perform a simple algorithm that give a new ranking that incorporate similarity knowledge. Then we move to the elimination of redundant feature and then the final feature set is obtained by comparing the relevance of each pair of redundant feature using the relevance to the target class (see Figure 17.2).

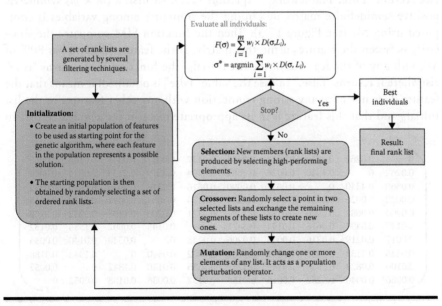

Figure 17.1   Genetic algorithms for rank aggregation.

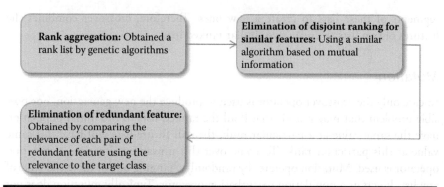

Figure 17.2   A rank aggregation based on similarity.

Solution to Disjoint Ranking for Similar Features

We take as staring point the ranked list $Initial_R$, where each item r_{f_i} of this list, presents the rank of a feature f_i. Remind that we always give 1 as optimal ranking to the most significant feature, rankings are always positive, and lower rank shows higher preference in the list.

In each iteration, we study the similarity between the first feature (i.e., the feature with the most relevance to the target concept and where $r_{f_1} = 1$) and the remaining features in the aggregated list, and for that, we use the similarity function (SIM). This function use MI as a similarity measure given its efficiency (see section "Filter Framework," Equation 17.2). At first, a $(m \times m)$ symmetric positive semidefinite matrix describing the similarity among variables is computed using MI (see Figure 17.3). Then the function SIM compares the similarity between the features using this matrix. If the feature in hand has 80% of MI with any of the features in the list $Initial_R$, the function SIM returns "true" elsewhere it returns "false." In case the value "false" is obtained, it means that the feature does not have any strong connection with any other features in the list $Initial_R$ and that this feature is in its appropriate place in the aggregated list. In

$$
\begin{pmatrix}
0 & 0.0262 & 0.0360 & 0.0022 & 0.0204 & 0.0127 & 0.0017 & 0.0345 & 0.0106 & 0.0060 \\
0.0262 & 0 & 0.4340 & 0.0026 & 0.0682 & 0.0494 & 0.0219 & 0.2133 & 0.0824 & 0.0040 \\
0.0360 & 0.4340 & 0 & 0.0037 & 0.0990 & 0.0616 & 0.0316 & 0.3035 & 0.0930 & 0.0252 \\
0.0022 & 0.0026 & 0.0037 & 0 & 0.0283 & 0.0194 & 0.0004 & 0.0091 & 0.0149 & 0.0015 \\
0.0204 & 0.0682 & 0.0990 & 0.0283 & 0 & 0.6471 & 0.0206 & 0.1102 & 0.2252 & 0.0158 \\
0.0127 & 0.0494 & 0.0616 & 0.0194 & 0.6471 & 0 & 0.0143 & 0.0802 & 0.1535 & 0.0132 \\
0.0017 & 0.0219 & 0.0316 & 0.0004 & 0.0206 & 0.0143 & 0 & 0.0540 & 0.0140 & 0.0036 \\
0.0345 & 0.2133 & 0.3035 & 0.0091 & 0.1102 & 0.0802 & 0.0540 & 0 & 0.1342 & 0.0188 \\
0.0106 & 0.0824 & 0.0930 & 0.0149 & 0.2252 & 0.1535 & 0.0140 & 0.1342 & 0 & 0.0052 \\
0.0060 & 0.0040 & 0.0252 & 0.0015 & 0.0158 & 0.0132 & 0.0036 & 0.0188 & 0.0052 & 0
\end{pmatrix}
$$

Figure 17.3   Example of the matrix of similarity produced by the SIM function.

this case, this feature is removed from the initial aggregated list and automatically added to the final list. In case the returned value is "true," we proceed by a set of steps in order to move the similar features closer and resolve the problem of divergent rankings.

In order to make the rank of similar features closer in the aggregated list, we take the feature in the top of the list and we study the distance in terms of rank between this feature and the feature with the next rank. We also use the function PLUS-SIM to study the distance between the feature with the next rank and the feature with the highest similarity with the first feature. More details are given in Algorithm 1, given below with a detailed description of the different functions used in this approach.

Algorithm 1

Require: $Initial_R$: Initial rank aggregation.
Ensure: $Final_R$: Final Rank List.
1: while $Initial_R = \emptyset$ do
2: Var = $Initial_R[1]$.
3: Var_{list} = SUBLIST ($Initial_R$, 2).
4: if SIM(Var, Var_{list}) = =FALSE then
5: $Final_R$ = CONCAT ($Final_R$, Var).
6: $Initial_R$ = Varlist.
7: else
8: Var_{next} = Var_{list} [1].
9: if Var_{next} = = PLUS-SIM (Var, Var_{list}) then
10: $Final_R$ = CONCAT ($Final_R$, Var).
11: $Final_R$ = CONCAT ($Final_R$, Var_{next}).
12: REMOVE(Var_{next}, Var_{list}).
13: $Initial_R$ = Var_{list}.
14: else
15: while Var_{next} = = PLUS-SIM (Var, Var_{list}) do
16: if DIST-POS(Var-next,PLUS-SIM (Var, Var_{list}), Var_{list}) > 1 then
17: PERMUTE(Var-next, Var,$Initial_R$).
18: else
19: PERMUTE(PLUS-SIM(Var, $Initial_R$),Var-next,$Initial_R$)).
20: end if
21: end while
22: end if
23: end if
24: end while
25: Return $Final_R$.

- SIM(E, L): return: false, true
  Takes a parameter list L and a feature E and verify if the feature E has a similarity with one of the elements of the list L. If the similarity with one of the elements of the list is superior to 80%, the function returns true else false.
- CONCAT(L, E): return: list
  Takes a parameter list L to be concatenated and appends the second argument E into the end of the list L.
- POS(E, L): return: number
  Searches for the feature E in the List L, and returns its position in the list L, or zero if the feature E was not found in L.
- PLUS-SIM(E, L): return: feature
  Searches for a feature in the list L with the biggest similarity to the feature E.
- SUBLIST(L, P): return: list
  Returns a list of the elements in the list L, starting at the specified position P in this list.
- REMOVE(E, L)
  Remove the element E given as argument from the list L.
- DIST-POS(E1, E2, L): return: number
  Count the number of positions between the two given elements E1 and E2 in the list L.
- PERMUT(E1, E2, L)
  Swap the positions of the two features E1 and E2 in the list L.

Removing Unwanted Features

Once the selection trouble is resolved and a consensus list of mutual features is obtained, we come across the issue of choosing the appropriate number of features to retain. In fact, a list of sorted features does not provide us with the optimal features subset. In general, a predefined set of small number of features is retained from the consensus list in order to build the final model. If the number of used features is relatively small or big, then the final classification results may be degraded.

Despite the fact that most of the features that had a disjoint ranking in section "Solution to Disjoint Ranking for Similar Features" are relevant (see Algorithm 1), the underlying concepts can be concisely captured using only a few features, while keeping all of them has substantially detrimental effect on the credit model accuracy. Therefore, while we solve the problem of disjoint ranking, we use a marker to mark each pair of treated feature as similar items. A matrix S is then created in order to stock each pairs of similar item, were each row of S contains a feature and their similar items. Then we study each row of S by looking into the computed MI in order to identify the feature that supplies the most information about the target class. As a result the feature with the highest MI is kept and the others similar features are removed from the aggregated list. Let us take the illustrative example that we used in section "Incomplete Ranking and Disjoint Ranking for Similar Features."

We suppose that after dealing with the problem of disjoint ranking, we obtain this list $\{f_3, f_2, f_5, f_7, f_4, f_1\}$, as we introduced before the features f_2 and f_5 are highly similar, looking into the results of MI, we observe that f_5 obtained the highest MI, consequently f_2 is removed from the list.

Empirical Study

Datasets

The adopted herein datasets are four real-world datasets: two datasets from the University of California, Irvine (UCI) repository of machine-learning databases: Australian and German credit datasets, a dataset from a Tunisian bank, and the home equity loans (HMEQ) dataset. Table 17.1 displays the characteristics of the datasets that have been used for evaluation.

- Australian credit dataset presents an interesting mixture of attributes: six continuous, eight nominal, and a target attribute with few missing values. This dataset is composed of 690 instances where 306 are creditworthy and 383 are not. All attribute names and values have been changed to meaningless symbols for confidentiality.
- German credit dataset covers a sample of 1000 of credit consumers, where 700 instances are creditworthy and 300 are not. For each applicant, 21 numeric input variables are available, that is, seven numerical, 13 categorical, and a target attribute.
- HMEQ is composed of 5960 instances describing recent home equity loans, where 4771 instances are creditworthy and 1189 are not. The target is a binary variable that indicates if an applicant is eventually defaulted. For each applicant, 12 input variables were recorded where 10 are continuous features, one is binary, and one is nominal.
- Tunisian bank covers a sample of 2970 instances of credit consumers, where 2523 instances are creditworthy and 446 are not. Each credit applicant is described by a binary target variable and a set of 22 input variables, where 11 features are numerical and 11 are categorical.

Table 17.1   Datasets Summary

Names	Australian	German	HMEQ	Tunisian
Total	690	1000	5960	2970
Nominal features	6	13	2	11
Numeric features	8	7	10	11
Total features	14	20	12	22
Number of classes	2	2	2	2

Experimental Setting

As discussed in section "Filter Framework," in general, MI computation requires estimating density functions for continuous variables. For simplicity, each variable is discretized, knowing that discretization of continuous features depends of the context. In this study, we are in the supervised learning context. The discretization step should be performed prior to the learning process. Several tools can be used for that, and we selected Weka 3.7.0 for its simplicity (Bouckaert et al. 2009).

Our feature selection ensemble is composed of three different filter-selection algorithms: relief algorithm, PCC, and MI (see section "Filter Framework"). These algorithms are available in Weka 3.7.0 machine-learning package (Bouckaert et al. 2009).

The aggregation of these filters is first performed by our GA approach with Kendall and Spearman distances (i.e., GA-K and GA-S) and then compared to the mean, median, highest rank, or lowest rank aggregation (see section "Selection Trouble and Rank Aggregation"), these aggregation techniques were tested using a MATLAB® implementation of the R package "RobustRankAggreg" written by Kolde et al. (2012), and also to the results given by the individual approaches. We use in this study three different classifiers, namely, DTs, SVM, and the LR. These three classifiers are available in Weka 3.7.0 machine-learning package (Bouckaert et al. 2009).

The classification models were created and tested using a 10-fold cross validation, where the different models were trained using nine of the folds. Then the resulting models were validated on the remaining part of the data (i.e., it is used as a test set to compute a performance measure). The performance measure reported by 10-fold cross validation is then the average of the values computed in the loop. The experiment was performed 30 times.

Performance Metrics

The performance of our system is evaluated using the standard information retrieval performance measures: precision, recall, and *F*-measure metrics. Precision, also known as "specificity," measures how often the system is correct. It is calculated as the ratio of the number of credit applicants correctly identified by the model as positives (TP) to the total number of credit applicants. The total number of credit applicants is the number of applicants correctly identified as positives plus the number of incorrectly classified applicants (FP). Precision is given by

$$\text{Precision} = \frac{|\text{TP}|}{|\text{TP}| + |\text{FP}|} \tag{17.10}$$

Recall, also known as "true positive rate" or "sensitivity," measures how often the system correctly finds the right class to a credit applicant. It is defined as the proportion of true positives against potential correct examples. The total number of potential correct examples is the number of correct examples (TP) plus the count of applicants that should have been output but not (FN).

Recall is given by

$$\text{Recall} = \frac{|TP|}{|TP| + |FN|} \qquad (17.11)$$

F-measure combines both recall and precision into a global measure and it is given by

$$F\text{-measure} = 2\frac{\text{Precision} \cdot \text{Recall}}{\text{Precision} + \text{Recall}} \qquad (17.12)$$

Results

This section contains the results from our experiment regarding the classification performance given in section "Performance Metrics" of four classifiers.

Tables 17.2 and 17.3 summarize the results obtained using four datasets, where the best results are shown in bold. Columns 2, 3, and 4 in Tables 17.2 and 17.3 present the precision, recall, and *F*-measure achieved by the different feature selection techniques using the Australian and the HMEQ datasets, respectively. Columns 5, 6, and 7 present the precision, recall, and *F*-measure achieved by the different feature selection techniques using the German and the Tunisian datasets, respectively.

Table 17.2 Results Summary for the Australian and German Datasets

	Precision	Recall	F-measure	Precision	Recall	F-measure
LR						
Relief	0.885	0.926	0.905	0.556	0.511	0.533
MI	0.929	0.873	0.902	0.612	0.534	0.572
PCC	0.926	0.924	0.926	0.721	0.500	0.591
Mean	0.927	0.934	0.931	0.781	0.586	0.656
Median	0.925	0.937	0.931	0.778	0.591	0.671
Highest rank	0.929	0.940	0.934	0.770	0.600	0.674
Lowest rank	0.896	0.975	0.933	0.765	0.602	0.673
GA-K	0.931	0.953	0.941	0.821	0.706	0.759
GA-S	0.929	0.883	0.905	0.819	0.708	0.759

(Continued)

Table 17.2 (*Continued*)   Results Summary for the Australian and German Datasets

	Precision	Recall	F-measure	Precision	Recall	F-measure
SVM						
Relief	0.795	0.898	0.843	0.517	0.511	0.514
MI	0.931	0.870	0.900	0.603	0.534	0.566
PCC	0.918	0.935	0.927	0.705	0.489	0.577
Mean	0.923	0.943	0.928	0.766	0.552	0.627
Median	0.921	0.945	0.932	0.756	0.560	0.643
Highest rank	0.933	0.940	0.936	0.762	0.623	0.685
Lowest rank	0.894	0.980	0.935	0.708	0.602	0.650
GA-K	0.945	0.921	0.933	0.823	0.812	0.817
GA-S	0.943	0.942	0.943	0.812	0.799	0.805
DT						
Relief	0.786	0.917	0.846	0.682	0.555	0.669
MI	0.930	0.870	0.900	0.516	0.534	0.525
PCC	0.932	0.86	0.905	0.737	0.477	0.579
Mean	0.931	0.890	0.910	0.750	0.542	0.612
Median	0.931	0.888	0.909	0.750	0.545	0.613
Highest rank	0.920	0.943	0.931	0.788	0.605	0.684
Lowest rank	0.900	0.902	0.901	0.700	0.642	0.669
GA-K	0.946	0.923	0.934	0.792	0.701	0.743
GA-S	0.952	0.950	0.951	0.756	0.697	0.725

Overall, we remark that when we train the different algorithms over the feature subset obtained by the proposed approach, we obtain in the majority of cases, the highest precision rates. In general, if we have an algorithm with high precision, we can trust the classification judgments made by it, and we can conclude that the selected features are worthy to be investigated.

Table 17.3 Results Summary for the HMEQ and Tunisian Datasets

	Precision	Recall	F-measure	Precision	Recall	F-measure
LR						
Relief	0.663	0.715	0.688	0.827	0.847	0.830
MI	0.681	0.788	0.730	0.822	0.852	0.826
PCC	0.838	0.974	0.901	0.833	0.850	0.832
Mean	0.850	0.966	0.904	0.875	0.964	0.917
Median	0.848	0.971	0.905	0.881	0.951	0.914
Highest rank	0.842	0.980	0.905	0.901	0.894	0.897
Lowest rank	0.870	0.880	0.875	0.878	0.888	0.887
GA-K	0.902	0.972	0.935	0.924	0.902	0.912
GA-S	0.896	0.955	0.924	0.916	0.943	0.929
SVM						
Relief	0.845	0.807	0.728	0.845	0.807	0.728
MI	0.822	0.828	0.784	0.822	0.828	0.784
PCC	0.822	0.828	0.784	0.822	0.828	0.784
Mean	0.830	0.987	0.902	0.830	0.987	0.902
Median	0.823	0.906	0.862	0.889	0.975	0.930
Highest rank	0.905	0.945	0.924	0.922	0.907	0.914
Lowest rank	0.900	0.891	0.895	0.881	0.880	0.880
GA-K	0.966	0.933	0.949	0.967	0.952	0.959
GA-S	0.942	0.940	0.941	0.966	0.923	0.944
DT						
Relief	0.747	0.8	0.736	0.876	0.888	0.882
MI	0.814	0.831	0.801	0.885	0.883	0.884

(Continued)

Table 17.3 (*Continued*)   Results Summary for the HMEQ and Tunisian Datasets

	Precision	Recall	F-measure	Precision	Recall	F-measure
PCC	0.818	0.832	0.798	0.876	0.880	0.879
Mean	0.821	0.981	0.887	0.860	0.962	0.913
Median	0.808	0.926	0.863	0.871	0.899	0.884
Highest rank	0.906	0.921	0.913	0.901	0.907	0.904
Lowest rank	0.842	0.922	0.880	0.889	0.902	0.895
GA-K	0.920	0.921	0.921	0.922	0.912	0.917
GA-S	0.923	0.912	0.917	0.917	0.908	0.912

Clearly, from both Tables 17.2 and 17.3, the feature subset obtained using the GA-K achieved the highest precision value when trained with the SVM classifier, that is, lowest number of false positive errors committed by this classifier. This was also the case for the other classifiers, where GA-K achieved 0.931 of precision with LR classifier for the Australian dataset and 0.821 for the German dataset, respectively. GA-K also reached the highest precision with LR classifier for the HMEQ and the Tunisian datasets. The DT classifier was not an exception where GA-K was in lead with by 0.792 precision for the German dataset and 0.922 for the Tunisian dataset, respectively. The results for the GA-S came in the second place in term of precision except for DT classifier, where the subset of feature that was generated by GA-S achieved the best precision with the Australian and HMEQ datasets.

The mean, median, and highest rank aggregation almost perform the same with equal number of minimum false positives. The lowest rank aggregation gives less precision but is still better than the results given by the individual filters. Looking now on the recall results, we remark that the proposed approach also achieves high rate both for Kendall and Spearman distances, which justify the high value for the *F*-measure.

As we examine closely the results, we observe that the mean aggregation method achieve four times the best recall (i.e., with LR, SVM, and DT for the Tunisian dataset and DT for the HMEQ dataset) followed by lowest rank aggregation (i.e., with LR and SVM for the Australian dataset), GA-K (i.e., SVM and DT for the German dataset), and GA-S (i.e., LR for German dataset and DT for the Australian dataset). In the final place comes the median and highest rank aggregation that achieve just for one time the highest rate of recall (with SVM for the Tunisian dataset and LR for HMEQ dataset, respectively).

The computed values or scores of recall, precision, and the *F*-measures are used to measure the performance of the feature selection techniques. The differences between any two features selection techniques may be due to chance or may be due to a significant difference between the two feature selection algorithms. To rule out the possibility that the difference is due to chance and to confirm our conclusions, statistical hypothesis testing is used.

A key element in hypothesis testing is obviously the hypothesis. Statistics can be used to reject a hypothesis. In statistical hypothesis testing, it is important to compose the hypothesis in such a way as to be able to use statistics to reject it and to thereby be able to conclude that something of interest is true. The hypothesis formulated to be rejected is called the "null hypothesis."

We are interested in determining whether two feature selection techniques are significantly different in their performance. To conclude that a set of feature selection techniques are significantly different, we would formulate null hypotheses of the following form: The absolute value of the difference between a feature selection technique A's overall precision, recall, and *F*-measure score for the features filtering task and a feature selection technique B's overall precision, recall, and *F*-measure score for the same features filtering task is approximately equal to zero. If this null hypothesis can be rejected, then we can conclude that the results obtained by the different feature selection techniques are significantly different.

The ANOVA test is used here in order to evaluate the null hypothesis. The *P* values are calculated from the ANOVA table. If the computed *P* value between the two feature selection techniques is large, the data do not give any reason to conclude that the means differ and then that the proposed results are ineffective. When the *P* value turns out to be less than 0.05, such a result indicates that the observed result would be highly unlikely under the null hypothesis. Table 17.4c summarize the mean of the dependent variable differs significantly among the levels of precision, recall, and *F*-measure.

Conclusion

Feature selection is a fundamental step in building robust and simple models for credit scoring. However, choosing the appropriate feature selection technique is not an easy task. We investigate in this study the effect of the fusion of a set of ranking techniques. Our work was conducted on two parts. First, we conducted a preliminary study in which, the issue of rank aggregation was first presented as an optimization problem that we resolved using GA and distance measures. Second, we investigated on resolving the problem of disjoint ranking for similar features and choosing the right number of features from the final ranked list, for that we relate the similarity of the feature to their ranking. We evaluated the proposed approach on four credit datasets; results show that there is a generally beneficial effect of aggregating feature rankings as compared to the ones produced by single methods and four other well-known aggregation methods.

Table 17.4 The P Values between the Proposed Rank Aggregation Approach and a Set of Others Feature Selection Techniques

Relief	MI	PCC	Mean	Median	Highest	Lowest	GA-K	GA-S
(a) P Value for Precision								
LR								
GA-K 0.022722917	0.020182	0.007056333	0.003680917	0.003839333	0.004955	0.003501583		
GA-S 0.017023816	0.009612013	0.0032657	0.005461467	0.002424667	0.002553667	0.011539571	0.042563310	
SVM								
GA-K 0.021602667	0.02132425	0.00771825	0.004181583	0.005117667	0.006336917	0.00763625		
GA-S 0.004034917	0.004630917	5E-05	0.004332917	0.019224025	0.0311406964	0.000253125	0.02789775	
DT								
GA-K 0.00657825	0.03474025	0.00695025	0.005713667	0.006122	0.003724917	0.008464917		
GA-S 0.004854667	0.007860667	0.028150875	0.0345845	0.0336275	0.01729225	0.0067255	0.0067255	
(b) P Value for Recall								
LR								
GA-K 0.027019333	0.027275	0.036550917	0.04200425	0.032535	0.025606667	0.017866667		
GA-S 0.011867583	0.013164917	0.046369	0.022896113	0.040682987	0.031192744	0.025650421	0.018225338	

SVM								
GA-K	0.021602667	0.02132425	0.00771825	0.004181583	0.005117667	0.006336917	0.00763625	
GA-S	0.004034917	0.004630917	5E-05	0.004332917	0.019224025	0.0311406964	0.000253125	0.02789775
DT								
GA-K	0.003965667	0.004696667	0.013053736	0.025723444	0.01298225	0.007036545	0.025861488	
GA-S	0.03291025	0.02436025	0.045858667	0.034193	0.032955667	0.029795667	0.026238917	0.014836917
(c) P Value for F-measure								
LR								
GA-K	0.007409583	0.020246333	0.008911125	0.001485125	0.0019845	0.010473625	0.020246333	
GA-S	0.006533583	0.029646125	0.014959625	0.04118675	0.01520425	0.023471125	0.023385667	0.0418295
SVM								
GA-K	0.014440917	0.03224932	0.02222875	0.016583333	0.004739583	0.004339667	0.018614917	
GA-S	0.004633722	0.011598292	0.133370875	0.010661458	0.020266917	0.03773648	0.01654153	0.02222875
DT								
GA-K	0.0478675	0.010467583	0.016347907	0.003160125	0.019938625	6.6125E-05	0.005983437	
GA-S	0.00965825	0.030219	0.02191025	0.021646	0.018894917	0.013582	0.01251025	0.008242917

References

Arauzo-Azofra, A., J. M. Benitez, and J. L. Castro (2008). Consistency measures for feature selection. *J. Intell. Inf. Syst.* 30(3), 273–292.

Bellotti, T. and J. Crook (2009). Support vector machines for credit scoring and discovery of significant features. *Expert Syst. Appl.* 36, 3302–3308.

Bouaguel, W., A. Ben Brahim, and M. Limam (2013a). Feature selection by rank aggregation and genetic algorithms. In *International Conference on Knowledge Discovery and Information Retrieval.*

Bouaguel, W., G. Bel Mufti, and M. Limam (2013b). A fusion approach based on wrapper and filter feature selection methods using majority vote and feature weighting. In *International Conference on Computer Applications Technology.*

Bouaguel, W., G. Bel Mufti, and M. Limam (2013c). A three-stage feature selection using quadratic programming for credit scoring. *Applied Artificial Intelligence: An International Journal* 27, 721–742.

Bouckaert, R. R., E. Frank, M. Hall, R. Kirkby, P. Reutemann, A. Seewald, and D. Scuse (2009). Weka manual (3.7.1), June 4.

Carterette, B. (2009). On rank correlation and the distance between rankings. In *Proceedings of the 32nd International ACM SIGIR Conference on Research and Development in Information Retrieval*, New York, pp. 436–443. ACM, July 19–23.

Caruana, R., V. R. D. Sa, I. Guyon, and A. Elisseeff (2003). Benefitting from the variables that variable selection discards. *J. Mach. Learn. Res.* 3: 1245–1264.

Clegg, J., J. F. Dawson, S. J. Porter, and M. H. Barley (2009). A genetic algorithm for solving combinatorial problems and the effects of experimental error—Applied to optimizing catalytic materials. *QSAR Comb. Sci.* 28(9), 1010–1020.

Dietterich, T. G. (2000). Ensemble methods in machine learning. In *Proceedings of the 1st International Workshop on Multiple Classifier Systems*, London, pp. 1–15. Springer-Verlag, June 21–23.

Dinu, L. P. and F. Manea (2006). An efficient approach for the rank aggregation problem. *Theor. Comput. Sci.* 359(1), 455–461.

Dittman, D. J., T. M. Khoshgoftaar, R. Wald, and A. Napolitano (2013). Classification performance of rank aggregation techniques for ensemble gene selection. In C. Boonthum-Denecke and G. M. Youngblood (Eds.), *The 26th International FLAIRS Conference.* St. Pete Beach, FL, May 22–24, AAAI Press.

Forman, G. (2008). BNS feature scaling: An improved representation over tf-idf for svm text classification. In *Proceedings of the 17th ACM Conference on Information and Knowledge Mining*, New York, pp. 263–270. ACM, October 26–30.

Gotshall, S. and B. Rylander (2000). Optimal population size and the genetic algorithm. *Genetic and Evolutionary Computation Conference*, Las Vegas, NV, July 8–12.

Hand, D. J. and W. E. Henley (1997). Statistical classification methods in consumer credit scoring: A review. *Journal of the Royal Statistical Society Series A* 160, 523–541.

Hastie, T., R. Tibshirani, and J. Friedman (2001). *The Elements of Statistical Learning.* Springer series in statistics. Springer, New York.

Holland, J. H. (1992). *Adaptation in Natural and Artificial Systems.* Cambridge, MA: MIT Press.

Howley, T., M. G. Madden, M. L. O'Connell, and A. G. Ryder (2006). The effect of principal component analysis on machine learning accuracy with high-dimensional spectral data. *Knowl. Based Syst.* 19, 363–370.

Jiang, Y. (2009). Credit scoring model based on the decision tree and the simulated annealing algorithm. In *Proceedings of the 2009 WRI World Congress on Computer Science and Information Engineering*, Vol. 04, Washington, DC, pp. 18–22. IEEE Computer Society, March 31.

Kira, K. and L. A. Rendell (1992). A practical approach to feature selection. In *Proceedings of the 9th International Workshop on Machine Learning*, San Francisco, CA, pp. 249–256. Morgan Kaufmann Publishers Inc, July 12–16.

Kolde, R., S. Laur, P. Adler, and J. Vilo (2012). Robust rank aggregation for gene list integration and meta-analysis. *Bioinformatics* 28(4), 573–580.

Kumar, R. and S. Vassilvitskii (2010). Generalized distances between rankings. In *Proceedings of the 19th International Conference on World Wide Web*, New York, pp. 571–580. ACM, April 26–30.

Liu, Y. and M. Schumann (2005). Data mining feature selection for credit scoring models. *J. Oper. Res. Soc.* 56, 1099–1108.

Piramuthu, S. (2006). On preprocessing data for financial credit risk evaluation. *Expert Syst. Appl.* 30, 489–497.

Rodriguez, I., R. Huerta, C. Elkan, and C. S. Cruz (2010). Quadratic Programming Feature Selection. *J. Mach. Learn.* 11, 1491–1516.

Sadatrasoul, S. M., M. R. Gholamian, M. Siami, and Z. Hajimohammadi (2013). Credit scoring in banks and financial institutions via data mining techniques: A literature review. *J. AI Data Min.* 1(2), 119–129.

Saeys, Y., T. Abeel, and Y. Peer (2008). Robust feature selection using ensemble feature selection techniques. In *Proceedings of the European Conference on Machine Learning and Knowledge Discovery in Databases—Part II*, Berlin, Germany, pp. 313–325. Springer-Verlag.

Sculley, D. (2007). Rank aggregation for similar items. In *Proceedings of the 7th SIAM International Conference on Data Mining*, pp. 587–592, April 26–28.

Thomas, L. (2009). Consumer credit models: Pricing, profit, and portfolios. Oxford University Press, Oxford.

Tsai, C. F. and J. W. Wu (2008). Using neural network ensembles for bankruptcy prediction and credit scoring. *Expert Syst. Appl.* 34, 2639–2649.

Tuff'ery, S. (2007). Data mining et statistique d'ecisionnelle: l'intelligence des donn'ees. Editions Ophrys, Paris, France.

Volk, M. (2012). Estimating probability of default and comparing it to credit rating classification by banks. *Econ. Bus. Rev.* 14(4), 299–320.

Wu, O., H. Zuo, M. Zhu, W. Hu, J. Gao, and H. Wang (2009). Rank aggregation based text feature selection. In *Web Intelligence*, pp. 165–172, September 15–18.

Yu, L. and H. Liu (2003). Feature selection for high-dimensional data: A fast correlation-based filter solution. In *ICML*, pp. 856–863, August 21–24.

Zhang, D., X. Zhou, S. C. H. Leung, and J. Zheng (2010). Vertical bagging decision trees model for credit scoring. *Expert Syst. Appl.* 37, 7838–7843.

Index

For Product Safety Concerns and Information please contact our
EU representative GPSR@taylorandfrancis.com Taylor & Francis
Verlag GmbH, Kaufingerstraße 24, 80331 München, Germany